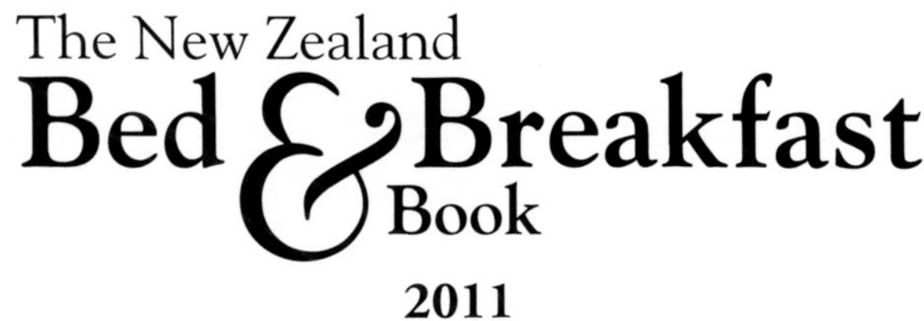

The New Zealand
Bed & Breakfast Book

2011

PUBLISHED BY:

Moonshine Press
P.O. Box 6843
Wellington
New Zealand
Tel: +64 4 385-2615
Fax: +64 4 385-2694
Web: www.bnb.co.nz
Email: info@bnb.co.nz

© Moonshine Press, 2010

ISBN 978-0-9582569-6-4

Every effort has been made to ensure that the information in this book is as up to date as possible at the time of going to press. All listing information has been supplied by the hosts. The publishers do not accept responsibility arising from reliance on any contents in the book.

Welcome to this edition of The Bed & Breakfast Book.

Bed & Breakfast in New Zealand means a warm welcome and a unique holiday experience. Most B&B accommodation is in private homes with a sprinkling of guesthouses and small hotels. Each listing in the guide has been written by the host themselves and you will discover their warmth and personality through their writing.

The New Zealand Bed & Breakfast Book is not just an accommodation guide – it is an introduction to a uniquely New Zealand holiday experience. The best holidays are often remembered by the friends one makes. How many of us have loved a country because of one or two memorable individuals we encountered? For the traveller who wants to experience the real New Zealand and get to know its people, bed and breakfast offers an opportunity to do just that.

We recommend you don't try to travel too far in one day. Take time to enjoy the company of your hosts and other local people. You will find New Zealand hosts friendly and generous, and eager to share their local knowledge with you.

Tidesong, Whangarei

Inspection & Standards

B&B Logo. All B&Bs in The New Zealand Bed & Breakfast Book have undertaken to conform to The Schedule of Standards which is on the next page. As important as the requirement of meeting a physical standard, we expect all our properties will offer excellent hospitality. Some hosts who are members of associations or marketing groups which undertake inspections have chosen to display the logos below..

The @home NEW ZEALAND logo represents the largest organisation of hosted accommodation providers in New Zealand. It assures you of a warm welcome from friendly, helpful hosts. Accommodations displaying this logo are regularly assessed every two years and have met the quality standards set by the Association.

Qualmark™ is New Zealand tourism's official mark of quality. All Qualmark™ licenced accommodation listed in this directory means they have been independently assessed as professional and trustworthy, so you can book and buy with confidence. They will meet your essential requirements of cleanliness, safety, security and comfort; and offer a range and quality of services appropriate to their star grade.

Heritage Inns; A collection of luxury historic hosted character bed and breakfast lodges across NZ, are superior and often recommended by tourists. Our B&Bs have knowledgeable and friendly hosts. Our luxury accommodation ranges from the quiet honeymoon lodge in boutique romantic locations to central city accommodation - rivaling superior apartments, hotels or motels. Alternatively, enjoy the genuine NZ experience of an idyllic farmstay, lodge or luxury country B&B.

Finding your way around

We travel from north to south listing the towns as we come to them. In addition, we've divided New Zealand into geographical regions, a map of which is included at the start of each chapter. In some regions, such as Southland, our listings take a detour off the north to south route, and follow their nose – it will soon become obvious.

GUARANTEE

Hosts in The New Zealand Bed & Breakfast Book are committed to offering quality hospitality. If you receive hospitality which is less than you expected please discuss your concerns with your hosts at the time. If you are not satisfied you should contact the publishers who will take up the matter with the hosts. If you are still not satisfied the publishers will refund their assessment of a fair proportion of the tariff you paid.

Your comments

We welcome your views on The Bed & Breakfast Book and the hosts you meet. Please visit our website **www.bnb.co.nz** or write to us at, PO Box 6843, Wellington, New Zealand.

COMMENT FORMS

Please help us to maintain our high standards by sending us comments about where you stayed. Guest Comments forms are available from your hosts.

- You may submit your comment on our website **www.bnb.co.nz**

- Or your hosts will give you a comment form.

- Or simply cut one from the back of the book.

- Each comment returned will be in our ongoing monthly draw for a free night's B&B.

- Each person staying can submit a comment for an increased chance of success.

- Guest comments are displayed on the hosts' pages at **www.bnb.co.nz**

About Bed & Breakfast

Our B&Bs range from homely to luxurious, but you can always be assured of generous hospitality.

TYPES OF ACCOMMODATION

Traditional B&B Generally small owner-occupied home accommodation usually with private guest living and dining areas.

Homestay A homestay is a B&B where you share the family's living area.

Farmstay Country accommodation, usually on a working farm.

Self-contained Separate self-contained accommodation, with kitchen and living/dining room. Breakfast provisions usually provided at least for the first night.

Separate/suite Similar to self-contained but without kitchen facilities. Living/dining facilities may be limited.

BATHROOMS

Ensuite and private bathrooms are for your use exclusively.

Guests share bathroom means you will be sharing with other guests.

Family share means you will be sharing with the family.

TARIFF

The prices listed are in New Zealand dollars and include GST. Prices listed are subject to change, and any change to listed prices will be stated at time of booking. Some hosts offer a discount for children - this applies to age 12 or under unless otherwise stated. Most of our B&Bs will accept credit cards.

RESERVATIONS

We recommend you contact your hosts well in advance to be sure of confirming your accommodation. Most hosts require a deposit so make sure you understand their cancellation policy. Please let your hosts know if you have to cancel, they will have spent time preparing for you. You may also book accommodation through some travel agents or via specialised B&B reservation services.

BREAKFAST & DINNER

Breakfast is included in the tariff, with each host offering their own menu. You'll be surprised at the range of delicious breakfasts available, many using local produce. If you would like dinner most hosts require 24 hours notice.

SMOKING

Most of our B&Bs are non-smoking, but smoking is permitted outside. Listings displaying the no smoking logo do not permit smoking anywhere on the property. B&Bs which have a smoking area inside mention this in their text.

ACCESSIBILITY

Certified as being wheelchair accessible.

Schedule of Standards

SCHEDULE OF STANDARDS

→ General

→ Friendly, warm greeting at door by host

→ Local tourism and transport information available to guests

→ Property appearance neat and tidy, internally and externally

→ Absolute cleanliness of the home in all areas used by the guests

→ Absolute cleanliness of kitchen, refrigerator and food storage areas

→ Gate or roadside identification of property

→ Protective clothing and footwear available for farmstay guests

→ Hosts accept responsibility to comply with local body bylaws

→ Host will be present to welcome and farewell guests

→ Hosts' pets and young children mentioned in listing

→ Smoke alarms in each guest bedroom and above each landing

→ Evacuation advice card displayed in each bedroom (recommended)

→ Working torch beside every bed

→ Suitable fire extinguisher in kitchen and on landing of each upper floor (recommended)

→ Fire blanket in kitchen (recommended)

HOSTS ACCEPT RESPONSIBILITY TO COMPLY WITH APPLICABLE LAWS AND REGULATIONS

→ Fire safety laws and requirements

→ Insurances

→ Swimming and spa pool regulations

→ Other laws impacting on operation of a B&B

BEDROOMS

Each bedroom solely dedicated to guests with...

→ Bed heating

→ Heating

→ Light controlled from the bed

→ Wardrobe space with variety of hangers

→ Drawers

→ Good quality floor covering

→ Mirror

→ Power point near a mirror

→ Waste paper basket

→ Drinking glasses

→ Clean pillows with additional available

→ No Host family items stored in the room

→ Night light for guidance to w.c. if not adjacent to bedroom

→ Blinds or curtains on all windows where appropriate
Good quality mattresses in sound condition on a sound base

→ Clean bedding appropriate to the climate, with extra available

BATHROOM & TOILET FACILITIES

At least one bathroom adequately ventilated and equipped with...

→ Bath or shower

→ Wash handbasin and mirror

→ Covered wastebasket in bathroom

→ Extra toilet roll

→ Lock on bathroom and toilet doors

→ Electric razor point if bedrooms are without a suitable power point

→ Soap, towels, bathmat, facecloths, fresh for each new guest

→ Towels changed or dried daily for guests staying more than one night

→ Sufficient bathroom and toilet facilities to serve family and guests

New Zealand & Regions

North Island   PAGE

South Island   PAGE

www.bnb.co.nz

Northland
Houhora
Cape Karikari
Coopers Beach
10
Kaitaia
Bay of Islands
Ahipara
1
Kerikeri
Okaihau
Paihia
Russell
Opua
Pakaraka
Opononi
12
Omapere
1
12
Whangarei
Taiharuru
14
Whangarei Heads
Ruakaka
Dargaville
Waipu
Waipu Cove
Paparoa
Matakohe
Kaiwaka
Te Hana
Wellsford
Warkworth
Sandspit
1
Snells Beach
Puhoi
Orewa
Kaukapakapa
Whangapa
Helensville
Silverdale
Albany
Auckland
0
Kilometres
45
0
Miles
27

Houhora *44 km N of Kaitaia*

Houhora Lodge & Homestay *B&B Homestay*

Jacqui & Bruce Malcolm
3994 Far North Road,
Houhora, RD 4,
Kaitaia

Tel (09) 409 7884
or 021 926 992
Fax (09) 409 7801
houhora.homestay@xtra.co.nz
www.topstay.co.nz

Double/Twin $140 - $200
Single $110 - $140
(Full breakfast)
Children $30
Dinner $45 by arrangement
Visa MC accepted
Children welcome
3 King/Twin 3 Single (3 bdrm)
Bathrooms: 2 Ensuite 1 Private

We have fled our largest city with Max our Hunterway cross dog to live on the shores of Houhora Harbour, and look forward to sharing this special part of New Zealand with you. Come and enjoy remote coastal walks, shell-collecting, Cape Reinga, 90 Mile Beach and other attractions. We can arrange 4x4 trips, sport or game fishing and provide relaxed and quality accommodation on your return. Home-made bread, home-grown fruit, home-pressed olive oil, vegetables and eggs. Wireless internet, fax and laundry facilities available.

Coopers Beach *4 km N of Mangonui*

Doubtless Bay Lodge *B&B*

Ian & Barbara Easterbrook
33 Cable Bay Block Road,
Coopers Beach, Mangonui

Tel (09) 406 1661
or 021 824 571
Fax (09) 406 1662
enquiries@doubtlessbaylodge.co.nz
www.doubtlessbaylodge.co.nz

Double/Twin $105 - $125
Single $75 - $85
(Full breakfast)
Children $25
Visa MC Eftpos accepted
Children welcome
3 Queen 1 Twin (4 bdrm)
Own kitchenettes - no cooking,
Queens with table and chairs
Bathrooms: 4 Ensuite

Friendly New Zealand hosts. Breakfast on the balcony or in the dining room with panoramic views over Doubtless Bay and surrounding countryside. Short walk to the golden sands of Coopers Beach and local shops. Each room has own ensuite, Sky TV, fridge, tea/coffee making facilities. Guest laundry and barbeque available. Cape Reinga tours, fishing trips and golf games can be arranged. Visit the many historic places, isolated beaches and local wineries in the area. Let us help you make this the perfect holiday destination.

Kaitaia *15 km S of Kaitaia*
Bush Walk B&B/Homestay *B&B Homestay*

Sandra
42 Te Rore Road,
RD 1,
Kaitaia, 0481

Tel (09) 408 4959
or 021 182 7553
Fax (09) 408 4009
sandra21madhousefarm@xtra.co.nz

Double/Twin $90
Single $70 (Full breakfast)
Children 3-12 half price,
Under 3 free
Visa MC Eftpos accepted
Pet free home
Children welcome
1 Queen 1 Single (2 bdrm)
Bathrooms: 1 Family share

Enjoy a relaxing sojourn in a peaceful bush setting and experience all Northland has to offer. A warm welcome awaits guests who come to stay at this unusual 'A' frame, timber interior home situated on 6 acres of garden and native bush. Wake up to birdsong and at the end of the day relax and watch the sun set behind the hills. BBQ facilities are available.

Ahipara *15 km SW of Kaitaia*
Ahipara Beachfront *2 self contained and serviced apartments*
Paul and Jenny Steele
14 Kotare Street, Ahipara,
90 Mile Beach, Northland, 0449

Tel 09 409 4007
or 021 227 3376
Fax 09 409 4007
pauljenny@beachfront.net.nz
www.beachfront.net.nz

Double/Twin $120 - $350
Single $120 - $350
(Breakfast by arrangement)
Children $20 per extra person
Dinner $60 pp by arrangement
Breakfast $15-$25
Visa MC Eftpos accepted
Children welcome Internet available
4 double bedrooms - super king beds
convert to singles - 1 sofa bed in living room of each apartment
Bathrooms: 4 Ensuite

With the sand of 90 Mile Beach at your doorstep and unsurpassed surf views from every pillow this is the ultimate in prime oceanfront accommodation. You'll love it! Choose between an upstairs two double bedroom apartment with sundecks or at ground level the Studio with an additional adjoining double bedroom option. WiFi. Cape Reinga Tour pickup from door - links golf course 5 minutes away. Torpedo fishing a specialty. Paul and Jenny are 5th generatiion New Zealanders with a cat called Sunshine who is not allowed in the apartments.

Bay of Islands - Kerikeri *10 km N of Kerikeri Central*
Kerikeri Inlet View *B&B Homestay Farmstay*

Trish & Ryan Daniells
99C Furness Road,
RD 3,
Kerikeri, 0293

Tel (09) 407 7477
or 027 567 4477
Fax (09) 407 7478
kerikeriinletview@gmail.com

Double/Twin $95
Single $50
(Full breakfast)
Children $15
Dinner $20 by arrangement
Visa MC accepted
Children and pets welcome
1 Queen 2 Double 2 Single (3 bdrm)
Bathrooms: 1 Ensuite
1 Private 1 Guest share

We welcome you to our spacious home on top of our 1100 acre beef and sheep farm. Enjoy the panoramic views from the Kerikeri Inlet to the Bay of Islands while you relax in our spa pool. Join us for breakfast consisting of seasonal fruit, homemade bread and butter, free-range chook eggs, and our own sausages, before exploring the many attractions around Kerikeri. We have avocado and olive orchards and free farm tours. Note: Please phone first for detailed directions. We can speak some Japanese.

Bay of Islands - Kerikeri *2 km SW of Kerikeri*
Palm View House *Luxury B&B*

Judy & Tony Pratt
8 Kotare Heights,
Kerikeri,
Bay of Islands

Tel (09) 407 6883
or 021 024 50615
palmview@xtra.co.nz
www.palmview.co.nz

Double/Twin $215 - $315
Single $195 - $295
(Full breakfast)
Children not suitable
Visa MC accepted
Not suitable for children
Internet available
1 King/Twin 2 King (3 bdrm)
Bathrooms: 3 Ensuite

If you are looking for luxury holiday accommodation, with stunning views, peace and tranquility, then you have found Palm View House, set in 1 acre of beautiful gardens, which was built in 2007, and was awarded bronze for House of the Year 2008. We have 3 luxury suites, with ensuites,bathrobes, fluffy towels and many toiletries.All suites have fridges,TV, DVD, CD electric blankets, iron and ironing board, coffee/tea making facilities,also spectacular inlet views. We are 2 ks from Kerikeri village.Judy and Tony offer you a warm welcome.

Bay of Islands - Kerikeri *20 km N of Paihia*
Glenfalloch *B&B Homestay*

Keith
48 Landing Road,
Kerikeri

Tel (09) 407 5471
Fax (09) 407 5473
glenfall@ihug.co.nz
www.kerikeri-accommodation.co.nz

Double/Twin $90 - $115
Single $80 - $90
(Full breakfast)
Children $25
Dinner $30pp by arrangement
Visa MC accepted
Children welcome
1 King 3 Queen 1 Single (4 bdrm)
Bathrooms: 3 Ensuite 1 Private

Venture down Glenfalloch's driveway to our secluded bed and breakfast, nestled in a garden paradise. Enjoy the hospitality of Keith. Relax in the spa and swimming pool and on teh decks, or for the energetic there is lawn tennis. Glenfalloch is just 500 metres from Kerikeri's Stone Store and Kemp Mission House, and adjacent to the lovely Rainbow Falls walking track. Kerikeri is unique and offers some good golf courses within short distances, lovely shops and excellent restaurants.

Kerikeri - Waipapa *5 km NE of Waipapa*
Ipipiri Lodge *Luxury B&B*

Elaine and Graham Belben
216 Ness Road,
Waipapa,
Kerikeri, 0295

Tel (09) 407 4159
or 0800 407 4159
or mob 0272 12 4159
info@ipipirilodge.co.nz
www.ipipirilodge.co.nz

Double/Twin $260 - $299
(Full breakfast)
Dinner by arrangement, extra cost
Seasonal local produce and goods
Visa MC accepted
Not suitable for children
Internet available
1 King Single Twin 2 King (3 bdrm)
Bathrooms: 3 Ensuite

Welcome to Ipipiri Lodge a great holiday destination set within rural farmland. Each suite has luxurious towels, hair dryer, bathrobe/slippers, and complimentary toiletries, fridge, tea/coffee making facilities, tv/stereo/alarm clock, iron and ironing board and own patio. Elaine has retired after 27 years in the Navy. She has a huge passion in wine, arts and crafts and local history. Graham has also retired after 30 years in the navy and his interests are wine, rugby, and gardening. We share our house with Reilly the cat.

Kerikeri - Opito Bay *13 km N of Kerikeri*
Waitui Lodge *Luxury B&B*

Jean and Ian Dunn
10 Yacht Drive,
RD 1,
Kerikeri, 0294

Tel (09) 407 9033
Fax (09) 407 7176
waituilodge@actrix.co.nz
www.waituilodge.co.nz

Double/Twin $180 - $180
Single $160 - $160
(Full breakfast)
10% discount for 2 or more nights
Visa MC accepted
Pet free home
2 Queen (2 bdrm)
Bathrooms: 2 Ensuite

The Lodge separate from the main house is set in one acre of tranquil sub-tropical gardens. Catering for four guests our priority is your comfort and relaxation. Two luxury rooms complete with large en-suites, queen beds, tv, cd players, complimentary beverages, delicious home baking. Easy reach of all activities the beautiful Bay of Islands and the Far North has to offer, or simply chill out by the pool or on one of the secluded decks. Ours is a stressfree enviroment...relax and enjoy.

Bay of Islands - Paihia *0.5 km SE of Wharf*
Craicor Accommodation *Luxury B&B Apartment with Kitchen*

Garth Craig & Anne Corbett
49 Kings Road Paihia,
PO Box 15 Paihia, 0247,
Paihia, Bay of Islands

Tel (09) 402 7882
Fax (09) 402 7883
craicor@actrix.gen.nz
www.craicor-accom.co.nz

Double/Twin $160
Single $120
(Continental breakfast optional
by arrangement $7.50pp)
Visa MC Amex accepted
Not suitable for children
2 King 2 Single (2 bdrm)
King size beds luxury
100% cotton linen, down comforters
Bathrooms: 2 Ensuite

The perfect spot for those seeking a quiet, sunny and central location. Discover the Garden Suite and Tree House. Self-contained modern apartments nestled in a garden setting with trees that almost hug you, native birds and sea views. Each apartment has ensuite bathroom, fully equipped kitchen for self-catering, super king bed, TV, insect screens and is tastefully decorated to reflect the natural colours of the surroundings. Safe off-street parking, all within a 5 minute stroll to the waterfront, restaurants and town centre.

Bay of Islands - Paihia *0.5 km NW of Paihia*
Windermere *B&B Apartment with Kitchen*

Richard & Jill Burrows
168 Marsden Road,
Paihia, Bay of Islands

Tel (09) 402 8696
or 021 115 7436
Fax (09) 402 5095
office@windermere.co.nz
www.windermere.co.nz

Double/Twin $120 - $220
Single $100 - $180
(Continental breakfast provisions)
Children $25
Extra adult $50
Visa MC accepted
2 Queen 2 Single (2 bdrm)
Very large studio units
Bathrooms: 2 Ensuite

If you want a holiday in a secluded bush-clad setting with sea views and be only across the road from Paihia's main swimming beach, then this is your ideal location. Windermere is a leisurely stroll along the waterfront to Paihia village, restaurants and shops. Superior ensuited accommodation is provided. For longer stays one suite has its own laundry, and full kitchen. The other suite has microwave and fridge. Each suite has its own decks where you can view the spectacular sunsets. Sky TV. Outdoor Spa.

Bay of Islands - Paihia *6 km SW of Paihia*
Appledore Lodge *B&B Separate Suite Cottage with Kitchen*

Janet & Jim Pugh
624, Puketona Road,
Paihia, Bay of Islands

Tel (09) 402 8007
or 021 165 0072
Fax (09) 402 8007
appledorelodge@xtra.co.nz
www.appledorelodge.co.nz

Double/Twin $175 - $275
Single $160 - $200
(Continental breakfast)
Minimum 2 nights occupancy
Visa MC accepted
Not suitable for children under 12
Pet free home   Internet available
2 King/Twin 1 Queen
1 Double (4 bdrm)
River views from every pillow
Bathrooms: 4 Large Ensuite

Miniature waterfalls and rapids await your discovery as the Waitangi River gently tumbles past your bedroom window. Tranquillity & peace is here to rediscover with our spellbinding riverside setting where. Fish for trout, stroll the riverbank or swim in our new solar heated pool. Set in two acres all our accommodation have magnificent views up & down the river, are self-contained with ensuite & private decks. Janet's special home made breakfast basket is provided to take at your leisure. We look forward to meeting you.

Bay of Islands - Paihia *0.2 km S of wharf*
Chalet Romantica *B&B Apartment with Kitchen*
Ed & Inge Amsler
Bedggood Close,
Paihia/Bay of Islands, 0200

Tel (09) 402 8270
or 027 226 6400
Fax (09) 402 8270
info-chalet@xtra.co.nz
www.chaletromantica.co.nz

Double/Twin $135 - $225
Single $125 - $210
(Full breakfast)
Children $25 when sharing room with parents
Apartments $ 155 -$ 27
Breakfast$ 15 pp
Visa MC Eftpos accepted
Children welcome
2 King/Twin 1 Queen (3 bdrm)
Bathrooms: 2 Ensuite 1 Private

Spoil yourself and experience the magic of Chalet Romantica.

Each upstairs room has its own balcony with superb seaviews, quality furnishings and fittings, wireless internet, crisp linen and extra comfy beds. Central town location within a stroll to shops, wharf and excellent restaurants.In house pool, spa, gym and laundry facilities.

For our B&B guests a gourmet breakfast is served in stunning conservatory overlooking the Bay.

We'd love to welcome you and to share our home and glorious location with you where 'haven has a new address'!

Bay of Islands - Paihia *0.2 km N of Paihia-Central*
Allegra House *B&B Apartment with Kitchen*

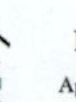

Heinz & Brita Marti
39 Bayview Road,
Paihia, Bay of Islands

Tel (09) 402 7932
or 027 470 1137
Fax (09) 402 7930
allegrahouse@xtra.co.nz
www.allegra.co.nz

Double/Twin $135 - $230
Single $135 - $230
(Continental breakfast)
Children negotiable
Apartment $175-$265
Visa MC Eftpos accepted
Internet Available
2 King/Twin 1 King 1 Queen (4 bdrm)
3 B&B rooms, 1 self contained apartment
Bathrooms: 4 Ensuite

Allegra House, our spacious, modern home is centrally located, just up the hill from central Paihia. You will enjoy the spectacular views from all rooms as well as the balcony where we usually serve breakfast. B&B rooms have tea/coffee making facilities, fridge, TV and balcony. Self catering apartment (breakfast extra charge) with separate bedroom, large bathroom, fully equipped kitchen and spacious lounge opening onto a large balcony. Air conditioning in each room. BBQ, laundry facilities, spa pool. Bush walk down to the village.

Bay of Islands - Paihia *0.5 km SW of Post Office*
Decks of Paihia *Luxury B&B*

Philip & Wendy Hopkinson
69 School Road,
Paihia, Bay of Islands

Tel (09) 402 6146
or 021 278 7558
Fax (09) 402 6147
info@decksofpaihia.com
www.decksofpaihia.com

Double/Twin $165 - $245
(Continental breakfast)
Visa MC accepted
Not suitable for children
Internet available
3 King/Twin (3 bdrm)
Stylishly furnished, ensuite,
aircon & heating, TV/DVD
Bathrooms: 3 Ensuite
Stylish tile & granite bathrooms

Recently constructed contemporary home incorporating 3 guest suites with private ensuite bathrooms. Quiet peaceful central Paihia location. Stylish modern furnishings provide a very comfortable interior with generous living spaces. All guest suites open onto secluded deck areas overlooking the swimming pool offering ample sun drenched outdoor living space. Philip and Wendy are experienced operators in the hospitality industry, and offer an extensive knowledge of Northland. Philip has strong links to the area - his great grandfather Patrick McGovern was Russell's police constable during the 1880s.

Bay of Islands - Paihia *7 km NW of Paihia*
Quilters Rest *B&B Separate Suite*

Sue & Andy Brown
41 Retreat Road,
Paihia,
Bay of Islands, 0204

Tel Landline (09)402 6047
or Mobile 021 164 7483
a.s.brown@xtra.co.nz
www.quiltersrest.co.nz

Double/Twin $120 - $180
Single $110 - $160
(Special breakfast)
Visa MC accepted
Pet free home
Not suitable for children
Internet available
1 Queen (1 bdrm)
Bathrooms: 1 Ensuite

Enjoy the peace and tranquility at our privately located home. Set in 3 acres of English style gardens. Minutes from Paihia waterfront and within easy reach of all the Bay of Islands offers. Relax by the pool and spa, for your exclusive use or sit above the valley and watch the sunset. A slice of paradise in your private suite with husband and wife hosts discretely on hand, devoted to making your stay completely memorable. Wireless internet connection available.

Bay of Islands - Paihia *1 km N of Paihia Central*
Admiral's View Lodge *B&B Separate Suite Apartment with Kitchen*

Deb & Mark Yarrall
2 MacMurray Road,
Paihia, 0200

Tel (09) 402 6236
or 0800 247 234
Fax (09) 402 6237
admiralsviewlodge@ihug.co.nz
www.admiralsviewlodge.co.nz

Double/Twin $95 - $195
(Breakfast by arrangement)
Children welcome in
apartments and twin studios
Apartments $175-$275
Visa MC Diners Amex
Eftpos accepted
4 King 6 Queen 2 Double
6 Twin 11 Single (11 bdrm)
Bathrooms: 11 Ensuite

Relax at our Qualmark rated 4+ star lodge in a quiet location. Sea views (many units), sunny terraces. 2 spacious Apartments, 7 Luxury studios, 2 with spa baths, plus our popular Garden studios. Meander along to the beach, restaurants/cafes & activities, take the ferry to romantic Russell or soak up historic Waitangi. Meet our children - Guy and Anna - and our friendly cat, Eva. Sky TV; airconditioning (most units); high speed internet; free internet kiosk, Dvd players, activity booking service; free bikes & tennis; guest BBQs & laundry; Filtered water.

Paihia *1 km S of Paihia Central*

All View Lodge *B&B*
Robyn & Peter Rhodes
30 H Sullivans Road, Paihia, 0200

Tel (09) 402 8606
Fax (09) 402 8607
allviewlodge@xtra.co.nz
www.allviewlodge.co.nz

Double/Twin $225 - $275 (Full breakfast)
2 day min stay may apply during peak season
Visa MC accepted
3 Queen 2 Single (3 bdrm)
Bathrooms: 1 Ensuite 1 Private
Island View Suite has large 2 person bath.

Showcasing Paihia's best private beachfront location, uninterrupted sea and island views. Architecturally designed for your pleasure and privacy. Stroll along the beach to restaurants, cafes and tourist pier, crusie 144 islands, hole in the rock tour or take a 10 min ferry ride to historic Russell. Our 1 bedroom suite has 2 queen beds, ensuite with a 2 person bath. Our 2 bedroom suite has 1 queen bed and 2 single beds, private bathroom. Both suites have large walk-in showers, toiletries, hairdriers, bathrobes. Spacious dining/lounge areas, TVs, garden and patio areas from which dolphins are often seen. Furnishings and fittings are to a high standard. Guests full laundry & kitchenette adjacent to both suites. Private access to both suites is by external stairway or internal lift. Comprehensive breakfast menu is included in tariff and served in our conservatory dining area. Local art and sculptures displayed throughour the Lodge. Friendly local hosts. Complimentary kayaks, start of the coastal walking track. Free Wi-Fi access. Tariff for single, extra person, longer stays or off-peak are available on application. We have 2 friendly toy poodles, Cleo and King Louis. Courtesy pickup from Kerikeri airport or bus depot.

Paihia *8 km NW of Paihia*
Morepork Riverside Lodge *B&B Homestay*

Paul & Barbara
846 Puketona Road,
Paihia, Bay of Islands

Tel 64 9 402 5577
or 021 986 687
Fax (09) 402 5575
enquiries@moreporklodge.co.nz
www.moreporklodge.co.nz

Double/Twin $125 - $195
Single $115 - $155
(Full breakfast)
May not suit younger children,
please enquire before booking
Gourmet evening meals b/a
Visa MC accepted
Internet available
1 King/Twin 1 King 1 Single (2 bdrm)
Single is comfortable folding slat bed
Bathrooms: 2 Ensuite

Welcome to our B&B/Homestay set in four acres on the Waitangi River. Stroll through native bush & gardens, home to many NZ birds including Moreporks. Feed our alpacas, sheep and goat. Meet our personable cat. We'll happily advise you on attractions and places to dine. We provide full breakfast and offer gourmet meals. Rain-water from our reservoir is UV sterilized/filtered. We are both 'Kiwi' born & bred. Rooms have: Private Deck, Ensuite (one with large bath), TV/DVDs, Sofa, Tea/Coffee, Refrigerator.

Bay of Islands - Paihia - Opua *5 km S of Paihia*
Rose Cottage *B&B Separate Suite*

Pat & Don Jansen
37A Oromahoe Road,
Opua, 0200,
Bay of Islands

Tel (09) 402 8099
or 027 605 9560
Fax (09) 402 8096
pdjansen@xtra.co.nz
www.bnb.co.nz/rosecottageopua.html

Double/Twin $100 - $130
Single $100
(Full breakfast)
Minimum bookings two nights
Pet free home
Not suitable for children
1 Queen 1 Double (2 bdrm)
Bathrooms: 1 Private

Welcome to our peaceful hilltop home.Sunny guest rooms open onto a private deck overlooking panoramic upper harbour,bush and rural views.Guest wing has private entrance,tea/coffee and fridge facilities,also T.V. Hosting one party at a time is ideal for 2,3 or 4 guests.Close to coastal and bush walks,also wineries.Pat is a retired nurse and Don a retired carpenter.Interests include hosting guests,local history,gardening,reading and fishing. We look forward to sharing this beautiful and historic area with you.

Bay of Islands - Paihia - Opua *5 km S of Paihia*
Seascape *B&B Homestay Self-contained Flat*

Vanessa & Frank Leadley
17 English Bay Road,
Opua,
Bay of Islands

Tel (09) 402 7650
or 027 475 6793
Fax (09) 402 7650
frankandvanessa@leadley.co.nz

Double/Twin $140 - $160
Single $100 - $120
(Special breakfast)
Self-contained flat $140-$160
Visa MC accepted
1 Queen (1 bdrm)
Bathrooms: 1 Ensuite

Seascape is on a tranquil bush-clad ridge. Enjoy spectacular views, stroll through bush to the coastal walk-way, enjoy our beautifully landscaped garden, experience the many activities in the Bay, or relax on your deck. We are keen NZ and international travellers. Other interests include music, art, gardening, boating, and Rotary. Our fully self-contained flat has queen bed, TV, laundry, kitchen, BBQ, own entrance and deck. You are welcome to join us for breakfast or to look after yourselves. 2 night minimum preferred.

Bay of Islands - Paihia - Opua *5 km S of Paihia*
Pt Veronica Lodge *B&B Homestay*

Audrey & John McKiernan
39 Point Veronica Drive,
Opua,
Bay of Islands

Tel (09) 402 5579
or 021 182 0697
Fax (09) 402 5579
stay@ptveronicalodge.co.nz
www.ptveronicalodge.co.nz

Double/Twin $160 - $220
Single $160 - $200
(Full breakfast)
Visa MC accepted
Not suitable for children
Internet available
1 King/Twin 1 Queen (2 bdrm)
Bathrooms: 2 Ensuite

On the coast between Paihia and Opua located above the coastal track with views towards Paihia and Russell. A special place, peaceful, romantic, restful, with bush and coastal walks. We invite you to soak in the spa or rest on the decks. Bedrooms are air conditioned with views over an inlet. Shops, Cafe's and restaurants are within 10 minutes drive. An ideal base to explore the Bay of Islands and Northland. Audrey, John and our friendly dog, Bonnie, welcome you.

Bay of Islands - Russell - Matauwhi Bay *1 km E of Russell*
Ounuwhao B&B *B&B Cottage with Kitchen Seperate Suite*

Marilyn Nicklin
16 Hope Avenue, Matauwhi Bay, Russell,
The Heart of the Bay of Islands

Tel (09) 403 7310 or 027 414 1310
Fax (09) 403 8310   thenicklins@xtra.co.nz
www.bedandbreakfastbayofislands.co.nz

Double/Twin $200 - $350
Single $160 - $200 (Full breakfast)
Children under 12 $45
Self-contained &; garden suite double $280-$350
Visa MC accepted
2 King 4 Queen 3 Twin 2 Single (7 bdrm)
4 in guestlodge, 1 in garden suite, 2 in cottage
Bathrooms: 5 Ensuite 2 Private

Welcome to historic Russell, the Heart of the Bay of Islands and the first settled area of NZ. Take a step back into a bygone era and spend some time with us in our delightful, nostalgic, immaculately restored Victorian villa (Circa 1894). Enjoy your own large guest lounge; tea/coffee and biscuits always available, with open fire in the cooler months, and wrap-around verandahs for you to relax and take in the warm sea breezes. Each of our 4 queen rooms have traditional wallpapers and paintwork, with hand-made patchwork quilts and fresh flowers to create a lovingly detailed, traditional romantic interior. Breakfast is served in our farmhouse kitchen around the large kauri dining table or alfresco on the verandah if you wish. It is an all home-made affair; from the freshly baked fruit and nut bread, to the yummy daily special and the jam conserves. Our self-contained cottage is set in park-like grounds for your privacy and enjoyment: with 2 double bedrooms, it is ideal for a family or 2 couples travelling together. It has a large lounge overlooking the reserve and out into the bay, a sunroom and fully self-contained kitchen. Wonderful for people looking for that special place for peace and time-out. Maximum 4 persons. Breakfast is available if required. Complimentary afternoon tea on arrival. Laundry service available. We look forward to meeting you soon. Our homes are SMOKE-FREE. We are closed June and July.
EXPERIENCE OUR HISTORIC B&B. ENJOY A WORLD OF DIFFERENCE.

Bay of Islands - Russell *Right in Russell*
Arapohue House *B&B*

Bradley & Vivienne Morrison
9 Wellington Street,
Russell, Bay of Islands

Tel 09 403 8109
or 027 272 8881
Fax (09) 403 8107
bookings@arapohue.co.nz
www.arapohuehouse.com

Double/Twin $160 - $220
Single $150 - $165
(Full breakfast)
Visa MC Eftpos accepted
Pet free home
Not suitable for children
Internet available
2 Queen (2 bdrm)
Comfortable beds, robes, tea & coffee
Bathrooms: 2 Ensuite all ensuite

This beautiful old bungalow has been rebuilt recently. Only 200 metres from Russell Beach, it is an easy leisurely, level walk to all the fine restaurants and coffee houses. Historic Russell, with it's museum and craft shops, offers natural history with nature walks, and beautiful beaches. We can organise any trips you wish, and you are welcome to spend time in our beautiful garden. All bedrooms have tea & coffee facilities, digital radio clocks, hair dryers & colour TV. Free wireless internet available.

Bay of Islands - Russell *1 km E of Russell*
Lesley's *B&B*
Lesley Coleman
1 Pomare Road, Russell,
Northland, 0202

Tel Landline (09) 403 7099
or Mobile 021 108 0369
three.gs@xtra.co.nz

Double/Twin $140 - $160
Single $110 - $135
(Special breakfast)
Children $30
Dinner by arrangement
2 nights minimum
Visa MC accepted
Children welcome
Internet available
1 Queen 2 Single (2 bdrm)
Main bedroom plus loft room for children
Bathrooms: 1 Private clawfoot bath, shower and toilet

Walk beside palms to our secluded home inspired by living in Greece. See Matauwhi Bay and boats from the deck. Enjoy breakfast (with organic emphasis) and eggs from our hens in the cosy guest conservatory. Our guest room has its own entrance and tea/coffee making facilities. Lesley's original artwork on the walls and the private bathroom features a clawfoot bath. Guestbook comments: ' We came exhausted and left refreshed!' 'Awesome waffles.' Billy the terrior lives here too. Ten minutes walk to Russell central. Welcome. Free internet connection.

Bay of Islands - Russell *0.5 km N of Russell*
La Veduta *B&B Homestay*

Danielle & Dino Fossi
11 Gould Street,
Russell,
Bay of Islands

Tel (09) 403 8299
Fax (09) 403 8299
laveduta@xtra.co.nz
www.laveduta.co.nz

Double/Twin $180
Single $150 - $180
(Full breakfast)
King-size rooms $220- $ 240
Visa MC accepted
Internet available
1 King/Twin 1 King
1 Queen 2 Double (5 bdrm)
Bathrooms: 3 Ensuite 2 Private

La Veduta. Enjoy our mix of traditional European culture in the midst of the beautiful Bay of Islands. Historic heartland of New Zealand. La Veduta is the perfect pied a terre for your Northland holiday. We offer our guests a warm welcome and personalised service. All our bedrooms are individually styled, offering full sea view. A delicious cooked breakfast is served on the balcony. We can arrange tours and activities. Restaurants, beach, ferries handy. French and Italian spoken. Complimentary afternoon tea.

Bay of Islands - Russell *0.4 km NE of Russell Central*
A Place in the Sun *B&B Separate Suite Apartment with Kitchen*

Pip & Oliver Campbell
57 Upper Wellington Street,
Russell 0202, Bay of Islands

Tel (09) 403 7615
Fax (09) 403 7610
BayView_Russell@paradise.net.nz
www.aplaceinthesun.co.nz

Double/Twin $135 - $185
Single $125 - $165
(Breakfast by arrangement)
Children by arrangement
Group of 4 $260-$295
(two en-suites plus studio)
Visa MC accepted
Pet free home
2 Queen 1 Double (3 bdrm)
2 queen bedrooms, a double sofa-bed in Bay View studio
Bathrooms: 2 Ensuite

Our special place, 'Romantic Russell', this retired Kiwi sailing couple's perfect anchorage. Two queen bedroom en-suite apartments, Fern or BayView, (separate entrances) ideally combined for two couples. B&B or self-catering options. Ranchsliders open to patio and garden (no stairs).T.Vs Barbecues. Great views overlooking Russell village and the Bay. Sunny, peaceful setting bordering bush reserve (kiwi habitat). Uncrowded beaches, heritage trails, brilliant night sky, cleaner air!. Perfect for relaxing holidays, honeymoons. All cruises depart Russell. Explore or simply unwind. A different world. It's Paradise.

Bay of Islands - Russell *0.2 km N of Russell Central*
Villa Russell *Luxury B&B*

Sue & Steve Western
2 Little Queen Street,
Russell,
Bay of Islands

Tel (09) 403 8845
or 027 492 8912
Fax (09) 403 8845
info@villarussell.co.nz
www.villarussell.co.nz

Double/Twin $185 - $320
(Full breakfast)
Suitable for children up to 6,
Rollaway bed available
Visa MC accepted
2 King/Twin 1 Queen (3 bdrm)
Spacious rooms with large
ensuites and awesome views
Bathrooms: 3 Ensuite

Enjoy a welcoming visit to Villa Russell, 2 minutes from the beach and Russell's restaurants. Relax with magnificent views of the bay and wharf from the deck of our beautifully restored 1910 Villa, or from one of two spacious suites in the new guest cottage. A short walk takes you to a surf beach or up the historic Flagstaff Hill. Off-street parking provided. Charters on our 11.6 metre yacht Kingfisher may also be arranged to sail the Bay of Islands. Friendly family dog.

Bay of Islands - Russell - Te Wahapu *7 km SW of Russell*
A Tranquil Place *B&B*

Susanne
14 Major Bridge Drive,
off Te Wahapu Road,
Russell, 0242

Tel (09) 403 7588
or 021 403 976
Fax (09) 403 7588
TranquilPlace@xtra.co.nz
www.atranquilplace.co.nz

Double/Twin $160 - $195
Single $130 - $160
(Special breakfast)
Dinner by arrangement
Visa MC accepted
Internet available
1 Queen (1 bdrm)
Guestroom with separate entrance
Bathrooms: 1 Ensuite

Our cosy home is nestled in native bush on Te Wahapu peninsula opposite historic Russell. You can access the secluded beach via a footpath next to the house. Otherwise just relax on our spacious deck, go for a walk, enjoy romantic Russell or join a coach or boat trip to explore the further environment. We speak German and we love sailing, golfing & travelling, have been living in Asia for more than 10 years.

Bay of Islands - Russell - Okiato *9 km SW of Russell*
Pipiroa Bay Homestay and Garden *B&B Apartment with Kitchen*

Paula & Gary Franklin
348 Aucks Road, Russell, 0272

Tel (09) 403 8856
or 027 2953640
Fax (09) 403 8856
gpfranklin@xtra.co.nz
www.bay-of-islands.co.nz/accomm/
pipiroa.html

Double/Twin $120 - $150
Single $80 - $120 (Full breakfast)
Children $20 for each child
Dinner $40 per person includes wine
Waterbased activities from $20 pp
Visa MC accepted
Children and pets welcome
Internet available
3 Queen 2 Single (4 bdrm)
Bathrooms: 2 Ensuite 1 Guest share

Nestled in the hillside, overlooking historically significant Pipiroa Bay, at Okiato Point, handy to Russell, Opua and Paihia, our warm north facing purpose built homestay bed and breakfast will delight you. As kiwis, with years of sailing experience in the Bay of Islands, we will ensure you enjoy the best the Bay can offer. Choose from our self contained apartment and bed and breakfast suite and savour our delicious breakfast using fresh produce from the garden.Other meals by arrangement. A shy silver persian cat also lives with us.

Bay of Islands - Russell *0.4 km N of Russell village centre*
Russell Bay Lodge *Luxury B&B*

Aom & Dave Metcalfe
71 Wellington Street,
Russell, 0202

Tel (09) 403 7376
or 027 417 3310
Fax (09) 403 7376
info@russellbay.co.nz
www.russellbay.co.nz

Double/Twin $175 - $295
(Continental breakfast provisions)
Visa MC accepted
Not suitable for children
Internet available
3 King (3 bdrm)
Bathrooms: 3 Ensuite

Romantic Russell, luxury accommodation, fabulous bay views. Contemporary Russell Bay Lodge has an idyllic location overlooking Russell and it's beautiful harbour. Just a short walk to waterfront cafes, shops and al fresco dining. The purpose designed accommodation offers king suites, two with mini kitchen, lounge area with TV/DVD/CD/Wifi, own entrance and own patio area. We provide a sumptuous breakfast basket each day. Select from a wide range of local activities, then later relax on the balcony soaking up possibly the best sea views in Russell !

Bay of Islands - Russell *0.1 km SE of Information Centre*
The White House *Luxury B&B Guest House*

Emma & Steve Jury
7 Church Street,
Russell, 0202

Tel (09) 403 7676
or 021 241 1010
Fax (09) 403 7676
info@thewhitehouserussell.com
www.thewhitehouserussell.com

Double/Twin $195 - $295
Single $175.50 - $267.50
(Full breakfast)
Visa MC Eftpos accepted
Not suitable for children under 12
Internet available
3 Super King (3 bdrm)
Bathrooms: 3 Ensuite

Come and have a truly unique stay with us in one of NZs oldest houses (circa 1840)ideally situated in the heart of Russell. A beautifully restored villa with plenty of character. She features 3 well appointed rooms with super-king size beds and fresh new ensuites along with guest lounge and full kitchen. Indulge in absolute luxury, with a dip in the spa pool, read a book on the shaded sundeck or wander to the waterfront. 12 midday check-out, free WiFi & SKY TV.

Please let others know how you enjoyed your
B&B experience.
Add a comment to the listing on the internet.
www.bnb.co.nz.

Bay of Islands - Pakaraka *Pahia/ Kerikeri/Kaikohe km N of*
Jarvis Family Farmstay & Equestrian Centre
B&B Farmstay Cottage with Kitchen

Frederika & Douglas Jarvis
State Highway 1, Pakaraka,
RD2 Ohaeawai, Bay of Islands

Tel (09) 405 9606
or 021 259 1120
baystay@igrin.co.nz
www.nzbaystay.com

Double/Twin $130 - $150
Single $75 (Continental breakfast)
Children half price up to 9 yrs
Dinner $35 by arrangement
Longer stay - discount
Visa MC accepted
Pets welcome   Internet Available
2 Queen 2 Double 1 Twin (4 bdrm)
Four poster suite
Bathrooms: 1 Ensuite 3 Private spa bathroom

The middle of everywhere en route SH 1. A gateway for touring North (Cape Reinga 90 mile beach) & West coast Giant Kauri tree. Opononi's Hokianga harbour, Rawene ferry and the Bay of Islands. Swim with the dolphins, sailing & fishing. Ngawha hot springs/ pools, golf. Kerikeri vineyards and Farmers market. Share the sunset at our homely, pet friendly Farmstay, with Winnie the Pooh B & B sign at our gate. Book a ride at Charlies Stables or stroll on the (30 aker) parkland to visit the horses and ponies with Winston (our Gt. Dane) and foxy pal Piglet, while the Patron can prepare a dinner party in his kitchen. Breakfast includes home made conserves, an orchard bowl of fruitfullness, (parsley scrambled eggs a 'specialty'). Al fresco dining on the deck with local wine and a crackling log chiminea. Queensize honeymoon 4 poster bed suite and Scottish room overlook our fabulous subtropical palm and water garden is a bird lovers 'Bay of Islands' haven. Also in the garden 'Treetops Cottage' a s/c studio for a quiet retreat (minimum stay 2 nights) . Dinner available on request. Free wireless broadband available click on www.nzbaystay.com for Northland weather reports and local links info.

Opononi *6 km SW of Opononi*
Koutu Lodge *B&B Homestay*

Tony and Sylvia Stockman
607 Koutu Loop Road,
Opononi,
RD 3,
Kaikohe

Tel (09) 405 8882
Fax (09) 405 8893
koutulodgebnb@xtra.co.nz
www.wairereboulders.co.nz/
koutulodge

Double/Twin $90 - $110
Single $70
(Full breakfast)
Visa MC accepted
1 King 1 Queen 1 Double (3 bdrm)
Our No1 room has extensive
views down the harbour
Bathrooms: 2 Ensuite 1 Private

Situated on Koutu Point overlooking the beautiful Hokianga Harbour, our home has views both rural and sea. Two rooms have private entrances, decks, and ensuites, and are very comfortable. We are a friendly, relaxed Kiwi couple, and our aim is to provide a memorable stay in the true B&B tradition. Stay a while and enjoy everything the historic Hokianga has to offer. Koutu Loop Rd is 4.3 kms north of Opononi then left 2.3 kms on tar seal to Lodge on right.

Opononi *57 km SW of Kaikohe*
Opononi Dolphin Lodge *B&B Separate Suite*

Sue & John Reynard
Corner of SH12 & Fairlie Crescent,
Opononi

Tel (09) 405 8451
or 021 064 4050
Fax (09) 405 8451
opononidolphinlodge@xtra.co.nz

Double/Twin $85 - $120
Single $65 - $95
(Continental breakfast)
1x Self Contained unit - Sleeps 6
Visa MC accepted
Internet available
1 Queen 1 Double 1 Twin
1 Single (3 bdrm)
Bathrooms: 2 Ensuite
1 Private 1 Guest share

Situated on the corner of Fairlie Crescent and SH12, opposite a beach reserve on the edge of the pristine Hokianga Harbour. Our sunsets are breathtaking. 20 minutes from 'Tane Mahuta' the largest kauri tree in the world. Step outside for picture postcard views of beautiful blue beconing waters and huge sand dunes. Visit the boulders, sand board, walking tracks, boating, great fishing, local crafts. Come, enjoy the friendly hospitality. The West Coast Diamond in the North awaits you.

Dargaville *1.5 km S of Dargaville*

Kauri House Lodge *Luxury B&B*

Doug Blaxall
PO Box 382, Dargaville
60 Bowen Street, Dargaville

Tel (09) 439 8082
or 027 454 7769
Fax (09) 439 8082
kaurihouselodge@orcon.net.nz
kaurihouselodge.co.nz

Double/Twin $225 - $300
Single $200
(Full breakfast)
Visa MC accepted
Internet Available
1 King/Twin 2 King (3 bdrm)
Bathrooms: 3 Ensuite

Kauri House Lodge sits high above Dargaville amongst mature trees. The 1880s villa retains all it's unique charm, style and grace with original kauri panelling and period antiques in all rooms. Start your day woken by native birds, walk through extensive landscaped grounds or read in our library. In summer enjoy a dip in the large swimming pool. In winter our billiard room log fire is a cosy spot to relax for the evening. Join Doug to explore beautiful mature native bush on the nearby farm overlooking the Wairoa

River and Kaipara Harbour. The area offers many activities including deserted white sand beaches, fresh water lakes, river tours, horse treks, bush walks and restaurants.

THE MOST COMMON COMMENT IN OUR VISITOR BOOK: 'SAVE THE BEST TO LAST'.

I have been hosting Bed & Breakfast for over 30 years, 'Perfect Accommodation, good host, these things make holidays worthwhile' - Frank & Annie, Holland 'Fantastic house and timber furniture, best we've seen' - Gary & Trish, Australia

Dargaville *2 km SW of Dargaville*
Awakino Point Boutique Motel *3 Separate suites & Apartment with kitchenette*

June & Mick
State Highway 14, Dargaville
PO Box 168 Dargaville

Tel (09) 439 7870
or 027 451 9474
awakinopoint@xtra.co.nz
www.awakinopoint.co.nz

Quad Rate from $175 2 Bdrm Unit
Double Rate From $115
Each extra person $25
(Special breakfast)
Visa MC accepted
3 X 1 & 2 bdrm
All have private bathrooms

Unique property set on its own acreage surrounded by attractive gardens. Just 2 mins drive from Dargaville on SH14 (The Whangarei Road) The best features of a NZ motel and a b&b have been amalgamated to give our guests the best of both worlds. You will enjoy your own 1 or 2 b/rm self-contained suite with own entrance and private bathroom.An attractive breakfast trolley delivered each morning. Guest laundry & BBQ available. Smoke-free Indoors. Wi Fi access available

Matakohe *9 km S of Matakohe*
Petite Provence *B&B Homestay*

Linda & Guy Bucchi
703C Tinopai Road,
RD 1,
Matakohe

Tel (09) 431 7552
petite-provence@clear.net.nz
www.petiteprovence.co.nz

Double/Twin $150
Single $110
(Continental breakfast)
Dinner $45 by arrangement
Visa MC accepted
Pet free home
2 King/Twin 1 King
2 Queen (3 bdrm)
Bathrooms: 2 Ensuite 1 Private

Ten minutes from Matakohe Kauri museum,eco friendly Petite Provence is set on 7 hectares of rolling farmland. All rooms (insect screens) open onto a covered deck with panoramic and distant water views. Relaxing and peaceful atmosphere. Evening meals, mediterranean, vegetarian, local cuisine. Guy is French, Linda a New Zealander. Our home in France was also a Bed & Breakfast. . Directions: From the beginning of Matakohe West or Matakohe East Road, drive 2 kms towards Tinopai, turn into Tinopai road, drive 7kms. Roadside sign on left.

Paparoa *1 km E of Paparoa*
The Old Post Office Guesthouse *B&B Guest House*

Janice Booth
Corner of State Highway 12
& Oakleigh Road,
PO Box 79, Paparoa

Tel (09) 431 6444
paparoa.jan@xtra.co.nz

Double/Twin $100 - $110
Single $55 - $55
(Continental breakfast)
Dinner $30 - 3 courses
2 bdrm suite from $200 (sleeps 5)
Visa MC accepted
Pet free home Children welcome
2 Queen 1 Double 2 Twin 4 Single
(6 bdrm)
Single, Twin, Double, Queen, 2 bdrm
(1 queen, 3 single)
Bathrooms: 1 Ensuite 4 Private

From the moment you step inside you will succumb to the character and charm of this lovely old historic building (circa 1903), with delightful cottage garden and rural backdrop. Enjoy our true Kiwi hospitality, cuisine and homely atmosphere with separate guests lounges and free tea/coffee. Dinner by prior arrangement. Local restaurants W/Th/F/Sat/Sun only. Spend a day at the world famous Matakohe Kauri Museum only 8km away or if, like us, you enjoy the outdoors, visit Pahi Beach or our local bush reserve.

Whangarei *12 km SW of Whangarei*
Owaitokamotu *B&B Homestay*

Minnie & George Whitehead
727 Otaika Valley Road,
Otaika,
Whangarei

Tel (09) 434 7554
Fax (09) 434 7554
minniegeorge@xtra.co.nz

Double/Twin $85 - $100
Single $65
(Full breakfast)
Dinner $25 by arrangement
Children and pets welcome
2 King/Twin 2 Queen (3 bdrm)
Bathrooms: 2 Guest share

Come, enjoy the tranquility of Owaitokamotu, place of water. Magnificent rocks of all shapes and sizes, pristine bush, rambling walks, set in 10 acres, easy contour. Created gardens, featuring ponds, bridges, archways, windmill, 1850s style shanty and more. Home wheelchair friendly. All bedrooms private access from exterior. TV, tea/coffee facilities. Join us for 3 course evening meal, $25 by arrangement. Restaurants nearby. Interests: travel, wood carving, our garden. Smoke-free indoors. Laundry facilities available. Warm welcome awaits you.

Whangarei - Onerahi *9 km E of Whangarei*
Channel Vista *B&B Apartment with Kitchen Cottage with Kitchen*

Braia & Paul Larsen
254 Beach Road,
Onerahi,
Whangarei

Tel (09) 436 5529
or 021 124 2800
Fax (09) 436 5529
channelvista@igrin.co.nz
www.bnbwhangarei.co.nz

Double/Twin $160
Single $120
(Full breakfast)
Visa MC accepted
Children welcome
Internet available
3 Queen (2 bdrm)
Bathrooms: 2 Ensuite 1 Guest share

Channel Vista is situated on the shores of Whangarei Harbour. We have 2 self-contained units each with their own private decks where you can relax and watch boats go by. Laundry, fax and wireless facilities available. Local shopping centre only 3 minutes away, 5 minute walk along waterfront to top restaurant. Sports facilities eg, golf, diving, game fishing, bowls etc nearby. We are 1 hour from the Bay of Islands, so it is a good place to base yourself for your Northland holiday.

Whangarei Heads - Taiharuru Estuary *25 km E of Whangarei*
Tidesong *B&B Homestay Apartment with Kitchen*

Ros & Hugh Cole-Baker
146 Beasley Road
(Taiharuru Estuary), RD 1,
Onerahi, Whangarei 0192

Tel (09) 436 1959
or 027 776 4991
stay@tidesong.co.nz
www.tidesong.co.nz

Double/Twin $110 - $140
Single $85 - $90 (Full breakfast)
Dinner $30-$35
Visa MC accepted
Pet free home   Children welcome
Internet available
3 Queen 1 Single (3 bdrm)
Comfortable, warm and private,
separate building from hosts
Bathrooms: 2 Ensuite

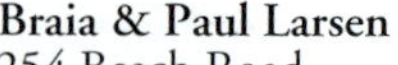

From Whangarei drive east for 25 minutes to Taiharuru Estuary. Comfortable secluded accommodation in a separate upstairs flat. Full breakfast with extra homecooked meals available. Safe kayaking and other boating from our jetty. Large garden with bush tracks and outdoor games. Close to fishing, shellfish, varied birdlife, and great walks on surf beaches, spectacular ridges and Te Araroa Walkway. Relax afterwards in the outdoor bath. Try tasting pizzas and bread baked in our woodfired oven. Warm, friendly hospitality. Members of Northland Sustainable Business Network.

Whangarei *7 km N of Whangarei City*
Lotus Lodge *B&B Farmstay Self Contained Studio (double)*

Keith & Jill Clarke
58 Great North Road,
Springs Flat,
Kamo,
Whangarei

Tel (09) 435 2294
Fax (09) 435 2294
lotuslodge@clear.net.nz

Double/Twin $100 - $140
Single $65 - $80
(Continental breakfast)
Dinner by arrangement
2 Double 1 Twin (3 bdrm)
Studio - 1 Double
Bathrooms: 1 Guest share

We invite you to share in our 200 acres of paradise. 2 minutes from Kamo, 5 minutes to golf course. Experience moving cattle/sheep with farm dog Del, view native bush, find amazing limestone rocks,laze in the quietness of the garden, or read in the lounge. Make this your stop for seeing the north - beaches, fishing, diving, kauri forests, shopping, all in a days outing. Our interests: gardening, classic cars, travel, art and people.

Whangarei - Parua Bay *18 km E of Whangarei*
Eden House *Luxury B&B Homestay*

Richard & Carole Harris
510 Owhiwa Road, Parua Bay,
RD 1 Onerahi, Whangarei

Tel (09) 436 1938 or 021 112 5532
edenhouse@orcon.net.nz
www.edenhomestay.co.nz

Double/Twin $120 - $140
Single $90 (Full breakfast)
No charge for baby sharing room
Families by arrangement
Dinner pp: $40 /35 /30 (3/ 2/1 course)
Wine and drinks list available
Complimentary beverages
Visa MC accepted Children and pets
welcome Internet available
1 King/Twin 2 Queen 1 Twin (3 bdrm)
Large, Unique character, personal deck and super views
Bathrooms: 1 Ensuite 1 Private 1 Guest share Luxury ensuite or private bathroom

Eden House lies in beautiful tranquil 11 acres of natural New Zealand forest, with spectacular views to the distant pacific. Enjoy warm, friendly hospitality in your luxury accommodation, comprising spacious character bedrooms - en suite or private bathrooms. Amenities include, swimming pool, twin lounges, DVD/Library and wifi. And cuisine best described as... delicious. Locally are walks, exotic coves and beaches, only minutes away. 20 minutes drive to charming Whangarei. And, with the Bay of Islands an easy 75 minutes, we are ideally located for touring

Whangarei - Kamo *4 km N of Kamo*
Little Bush *Homestay self contained unit*

Jean & Robert Pedersen
250 Pipiwai Road,
Kamo,
Whangarei, 0121

Tel (09) 435 5330
or 021 0272 1759
Fax (09) 435 5330
rjpedersen@xtra.co.nz

Double/Twin $110 - $150
Single $90 - $130
(Full breakfast)
Pet free home
Not suitable for children
2 Queen (2 bdrm)
Bathrooms: 1 Ensuite 1 Private
Private with spa bath

We welcome you to the beauty and tranquillity of 'Little Bush'. Native trees and birds and an awesome view of Northland Golf Course and beyond will be yours to enjoy as you relax by the pool. 30mins to Tutukaka and other east coast beaches. 45mins to Bay Of Islands. Close to Whangarei Falls and many walkways and other attractions. Laundry facilities available Our self-contained unit has full kitchen facilities including dish washer and fridge/freezer. Breakfast provisions supplied if preferred

One Tree Point - Ruakaka *25 km S of Whangarei*
Edgewater B&B *B&B Separate Suite*

Penny Britton
225 One Tree Point Road,
Ruakaka,
Northland

Tel (09) 432 7174
or 021 1150 918
penez@xtra.co.nz
www.edgewaterbnb.co.nz

Double/Twin $100 - $115
Single $85 - $85
(Continental breakfast provisions)
Pets on site
Not suitable for children
1 Double (1 bdrm)
Double sleeper sofa available
Bathrooms: 1 Ensuite

A warm and friendly welcome awaits you at my near new beachfront retreat. Enjoy beach walks and magnificent uninterrupted views of Whangarei harbour and Mt. Manaia. The unit is private and self contained with a double bed and ensuite. The living area consists of a sleeper/sofa with microwave oven, fridge and Sky TV, plus tea and coffee making facilities. A full continental breakfast is provided within the tariff. Surfing beaches, fishing, golf and restaurants are all within a few minutes drive. Pets on site.

Ruakaka - Bream Bay *30 km S of Whangarei*

Island View Lodge *Luxury B&B Homestay Farmstay Separate Suite Apartment with Kitchen*

Joyce & Vince Roberts
34 Doctors Hill Road, Ruakaka,
 Postal: 34 Doctors Hill Rd RD 2 Waipu 0582

Tel (09) 432 7842
or 027 441 9585
Fax (09) 432 7847
 robertsb.b@xtra.co.nz
www.breambayfarmstay.co.nz

Double/Twin $120 - $160
Single $90 - $100
(Full breakfast)
Children $30
Dinner $30
Visa MC accepted
Children and pets welcome
Internet Available
1 King 2 Queen 1 Double 1 Single (3 bdrm)
4 in main suite (dble bed setee
plus king single in lounge)
Bathrooms: 3 Ensuite 3 Private

"Come stressed, leave refreshed" Spectacular is the only words to describe the sea views from this 3 year old home built especially for the discerning travelers. The main suite has its own kitchen & laundry with large lounge area. We have air con/heat pumps plus under floor heating for your comfort. Have a swim in the heated lap pool or relax in the spa after having a game of pool in the games room. Beautiful beaches, golf course, racetrack where Vince trains our racehorses and good restaurants are a short drive from our home.

Meals include our home grown lamb. As ex dairy farmers with grown up family of four, we have enjoyed hosting B&B for 19 years, other interests include travel, golf & gardening. We look forward to meeting you and helping make your holiday enjoyable.

Waipu Cove *10 km S of Waipu*

labonte@xtra.co.nz *Homestay Farmstay Apartment with Kitchen*

Andre & Robin La Bonte
PO Box 60,
Waipu,
Northland

Tel (09) 432 0645
Fax (09) 432 0645
labonte@xtra.co.nz

Double/Twin $120
Single $75
(Continental breakfast)
Dinner $25 by arrangement
Visa MC accepted
1 King 1 Queen
2 Double 2 Single (3 bdrm)
Bathrooms: 2 Private

Sleep to the sound of the ocean in a separate studio apartment or in guest bedrooms on our 36 acre seaside property. Explore our limestone rock formations or just sit and relax under the mature trees that grace our shoreline. The beach at Waipu Cove is a 10 minute walk along the sea. We are a licensed fish farm, graze cattle, have flea-free cats and an outside dog. We are ocean and coastal engineers who enjoy hosting guests from around the world. American spoken.

Waipu Cove *9 km SE of Waipu*

Melody Lodge *B&B Homestay*

Melody Gard
996 Cove Road,
Waipu,
Northland, 0582

Tel (09) 432 0939
melody@melodylodge.co.nz
www.melodylodge.co.nz

Double/Twin $90 - $120
Single $70 - $100
(Continental breakfast)
Not suitable for children
1 King/Twin 1 Queen
2 Single (3 bdrm)
Bathrooms: 1 Ensuite 1 Guest share

Offering panoramic sea views from all rooms, Melody Lodge overlooks the whole of Bream Bay. We extend a warm welcome to our BnB with it's quiet ambience, peaceful garden and spectacular location. Enjoy refreshments on the patio watching weather moods over Bream Head and experience the ethereal magic of our natural forest track. Attached Gallery features works of six local artists plus exclusive souvenirs, cards etc. Resident artist and cat. Beach 1km. Magnificent sandy beaches, great walks, golf, birdllife, restaurants, glowworm caves, museums.

Auckland
Waipu
Waipu Cove
Langs Beach
Paparoa
Kaiwaka
Mangawhai
Te Hana
Wellsford
Omaha Beach
Warkworth
Puhoi
Waiwera
Orewa
Great Barrier Island
See
Auckland City
next page
Hobsonville
Kumeu
Devonport
Waitakere
Auckland
central
Bethells Beach
Maratai
Swanson
Mangere
Papakura
Drury
Ramarama
Miranda
Kilometres
0 20
Miles
0 12

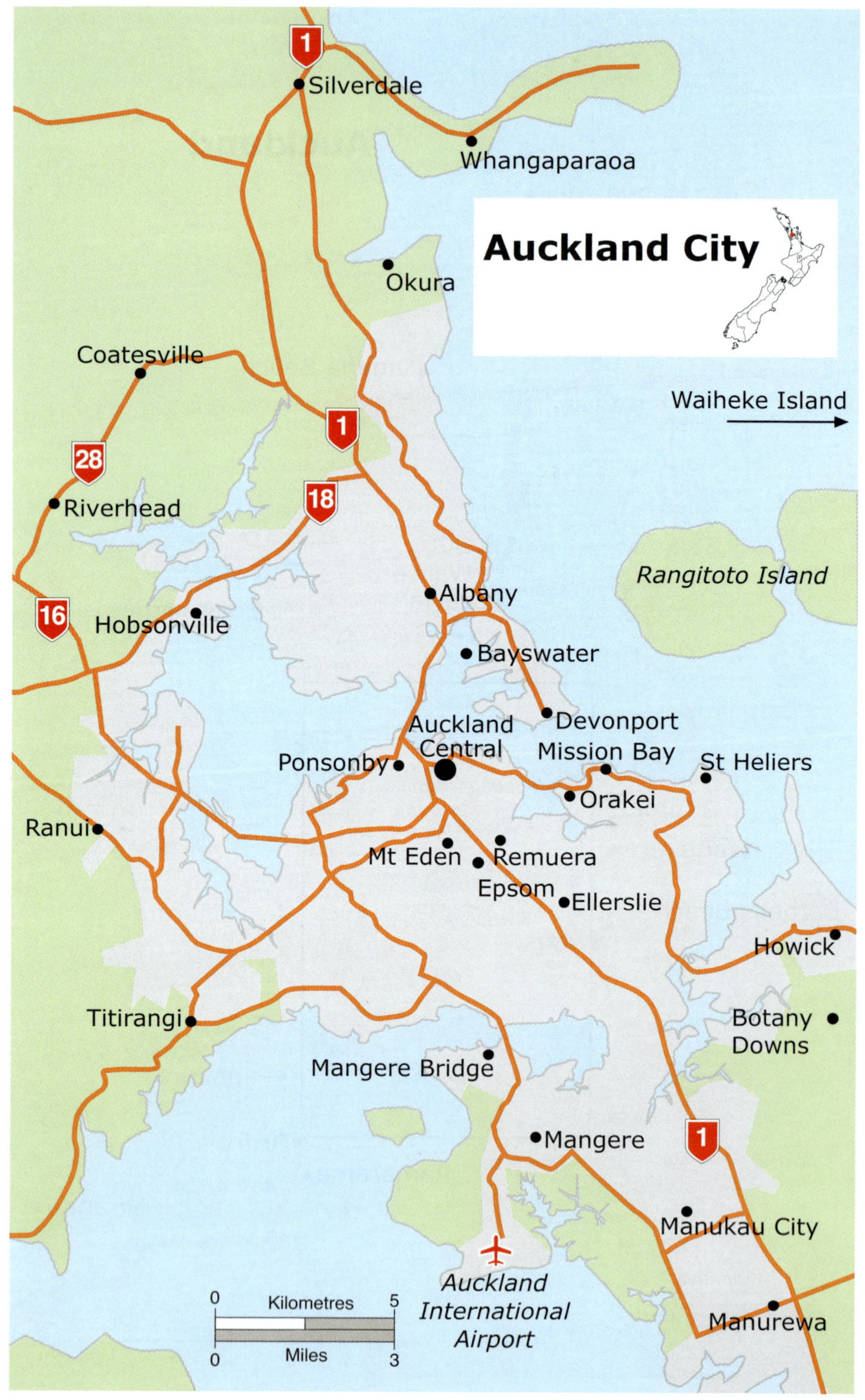

1
Silverdale
Whangaparaoa
Okura
Auckland City
Waiheke Island
Coatesville
28
Riverhead
1
18
Rangitoto Island
16
Hobsonville
Albany
Bayswater
Auckland Central
Devonport
Mission Bay
St Heliers
Ponsonby
Orakei
Ranui
Mt Eden
Remuera
Epsom
Ellerslie
Howick
Titirangi
Botany Downs
Mangere Bridge
Mangere
1
Manukau City
Auckland International Airport
Manurewa
0 Kilometres 5
0 Miles 3

Mangawhai Heads *0 km E of Mangawhai Heads*
Mangawhai Lodge - a room with a view Boutique B&B Inn
B&B S/catering apartment

Jeannette Forde
4 Heather Street,
Mangawhai Heads, 0505

Tel (09) 431 5311
info@seaviewlodge.co.nz
www.seaviewlodge.co.nz

Double/Twin $175 - $250
Single $160 - $185
(Special breakfast)
Suit children over 10
Mid winter Xmas Dinner for groups
Visa MC Eftpos accepted
Pet free home   Internet available
3 King/Twin 2 Queen
8 Single (5 bdrm)
Stylish rooms, all with bathrooms open to verandahs
Bathrooms: 3 Ensuite 2 Private 3 ensuite, 1 s/catering apartment, 1 guest suite

Midway between Auckland & Whangarei, Mangawhai Lodge offers the perfect beach destination for couples, groups, golfers & singles. Three stylish guest rooms, 1 luxury suite and 1 s/catering apartment(short and long stays) open to verandahs, seating and views of sea or garden. Two guests lounges offer a stylish, relaxing atmosphere with spectacular sea, and island views. Golf course adjacent. Enjoy beaches, walkways, bird sanctuary. Walk to cafes and shops. A sumptuous cooked/continental breakfast served. Complimentary internet access. secure parking. For winter specials visit www.seaviewlodge.co.nz

Wellsford - Te Hana *6 km N of Wellsford*
The Retreat Historic Farmhouse *Farmstay & Cottage with Kitchen*

Colleen & Tony Moore
Te Hana, RD 5, Wellsford 0975
Tel (09) 423 8547
enquiry@sheepfarmstay.com
www.sheepfarmstay.com
Double/Twin $120
Single $80 (Full breakfast)
Dinner $30pp by arrangement
Visa MC Diners accepted
Internet available
2 Queen 1 Double 1 Single (3 bdrm)
2 in B&B 1 in cottage
Bathrooms: 1 Ensuite 1 Private

Tony and Colleen welcome you to The Retreat, a spacious 1860s farmhouse built for a family with 12 children. Set well back from the road, the house is surrounded by an extensive landscaped garden, including a productive vegetable garden and orchard. Fresh produce from the garden is a feature in our home cooking.

Colleen is a spinner and weaver and our flock of sheep provides the raw material for the woollen goods that are hand-made and for sale from the studio. If you haven't got close up to a sheep this is your chance, as we always have friendly sheep to hand feed. We have hosted guests at The Retreat since 1988 and appreciate what you require.

We know New Zealand well, our families have lived in NZ for several generations and we have visited most places in our beautiful country, so if you have any questions on what to see or do, we are well equipped to provide the answers.

Also available is a self-contained cottage, close to the house, with the option of having meals with us, or self-catering.

The Retreat is very easy to find. Travelling North on SH1, we are 6km north of Wellsford, look for the Weaving Studio sign on your left. You will pass through Te Hana before arriving at The Retreat. Kaiwaka is 13km north of The Retreat.

Warkworth - Matakana *13 km E of Warkworth*
Self Contained B and B *B&B Self-contained unit*

Barbara & John Maltby
Omaha Orchards,
282 Point Wells Road,
RD 6, Warkworth 0986

Tel (09) 422 7415
or 027 659 1385
Fax (09) 422 7419
jmaltby@clear.net.nz

Double/Twin $85 - $95
Single $75
(Full breakfast provisions)
Extra guest $12
Dinner $20-$25 by arrangement
Check for seasonal specials
Children welcome
1 Queen 1 Double (1 bdrm)
Bathrooms: 1 Ensuite

Our home and self-contained unit is nestled beside the Whangateau Harbour. Relax in the extensive gardens and swim in the beautifully appointed pool.Only 5 minutes by car to the popular 'Boutique' village of Matakana with its movie theatres,shops, eateries etc. Nearby is Omaha Beach, golf,tennis, vineyards, restaurants, art and craft studios, pottery works, and Kawau Island. This is some of the prettiest coastline in New Zealand. John and Barbara look forward to sharing their little slice of paradise with you.

Warkworth *1.5 km SE of Warkworth, 10 mins from Matakana*
RibbonWood B&B Apartment *B&B Apartment with Kitchen*

Berris & Alan Spicer
7 Thompson Rd, Warkworth, 0981

Tel (09) 422 2685 or 027 241 9986
Fax (09) 422 2684
berris@ribbonwoodwarkworth.co.nz
www.ribbonwoodwarkworth.co.nz

Double/Twin $120 - $155
(Special breakfast)
Dinner by arrangement from $20pp
Extra person $20+
Special rates for self cater & longer stays
Visa MC accepted
Pet free home   Children welcome
1 Queen 1 Twin (2 bdrm)
1 Queen, Queen sofabed in lounge
Twin room available with apartment
Bathrooms: 1 Private
Luxury bathroom with separate bath & shower, heated floor

True NZ hospitality awaits you at RibbonWood, our stylish and modern, quality apartment. Private entrance and patio, super comfortable bedrooms, luxury bathroom, well equipped lounge dining kitchen. Complimentary WiFi internet, homebaking, fruit bowl, chocolates. Wonderful value! Evening meals ... self-cater, enjoy Berris' legendary home cooking or indulge at the nearby cafes. Our delightful 1 acre country setting is on the edge of Warkworth Village, close to wineries, minutes from Matakana. Peace, privacy, panoramic views; a night or a month; you won't regret choosing RibbonWood.

Warkworth - Sandspit *10 km E of Warkworth*
Kotare Lodge *Luxury B&B Apartment with Kitchen*

Judy & Graeme Maker
5 Kotare Place, RD 2,
Sandspit Heights,
Warkworth 0982

Tel (09) 425 7331 or 021 279 8116
Fax (09) 425 0311
makers@ihug.co.nz
www.sandspitkotarelodge.co.nz

Double/Twin $195
Single $195
(Continental breakfast)
2 Guest lounges
Visa MC accepted
Children welcome
1 Queen 1 Double
1 Twin 1 Single (3 bdrm)
Sofa Queen bed
Bathrooms: 2 Private

Kotare Lodge has arguably the best views at Sandspit from Kawau Bay, Hauraki Gulf, Great Barrier, Little Barrier, the rural areas of Matakana and the inner harbour of Sandspit. Relax in your luxury self-contained, air-conditioned apartment including swimming pool, Sky TV and spacious viewing decks. Enjoy bush walks to beaches, visit the many vineyards, galleries, cafes, restaurants, golf courses, Kawau Island ferry, all within a few minutes drive. Spend time cruising Kawau Bay and islands aboard our 54' Riviera launch

---

Warkworth - Snells Beach *7 km E of Warkworth*
Heaven's Haven *B&B*

Beulah Heaven
23 Ariki Drive,
Snells Beach,
Warkworth 0920

Tel 09 425 6545
or 021 289 5523
by.heaven@xtra.co.nz

Double/Twin $125
Single $0 - $100
(Full breakfast)
Dinner $50 by arrangement
Visa MC accepted
Not suitable for children
1 Queen 1 Double 1 Twin (2 bdrm)
Bathrooms: 1 Ensuite 1 Guest share

Share this slice of Heaven. Relax and enjoy the stunning sunrises and breath-taking crimson sunsets from this absolute beachfront property. You're on the beach already! Relax with a complimentary bottle of wine on arrival. Enjoy a delicious breakfast with seasonal produce from the pristine Matakana Valley. Relax and soak up the views with Sophie(the genteel dog) or visit the boutique vineyards, cafes, art galleries or many walkways that dot this sparkling area. Dinner by arrangement at $50 per head.

Warkworth - Sandspit *7 km SE of Warkworth*
EbbTide Homestay *Luxury B&B Homestay*

Shona & Julian Huxtable
36 Kanuka Road,
Sandspit, RD 2,
Warkworth 0982

Tel (09)425 8681
or 021 238 3850
stay@ebbtide.co.nz
www.ebbtide.co.nz

Double/Twin $150 - $180
Single $130
(Special breakfast)
Dinner $50 (by prior arrangement)
Not suitable for children
1 King/Twin 1 King
1 Queen (2 bdrm)
1 King or King Twin &
1 Queen, both en-suite
Bathrooms: 2 Ensuite

Overlooking the stunning Sandspit Harbour EbbTide commands magnificent views enhanced by the call of Skylarks and Tui. Situated within easy reach of Matakana, Warkworth and Kawau. This is an ideal resting place for travellers requiring comfort, tranqility and of course a great breakfast. The tastefully decorated bedrooms have their own en-suite, television, tea/coffee facilities and heating/air conditioning. Relax in the gardens with our pet Collies,a glass of wine and the expectation of a sumptuous dinner cooked by Shona with the use of home-grown produce.

Omaha Beach *12 km NE of Warkworth*
Omaha Beach Bed and Breakfast *B&B*

Shelley and Evan Kemp
174 Omaha Drive,
Omaha Beach,
RD 6, Warkworth

Tel (09) 422 9372
or 022 674 6022
or 022 674 0025
Fax (09) 422 9372
info@omahabandb.co.nz
www.omahabandb.co.nz

Double/Twin $150 - $200
(Continental breakfast)
Pet free home
Not suitable for children
3 Queen (3 bdrm)
Bathrooms: 3 Ensuite

Situated at the northern end of Omaha Beach between the ocean and the inlet, unwind at our place. We have 3 double size rooms all second level, opening onto their own deck. Boutique shopping, surrounding vineyards, cafes and restaurants are only 5 minutes away at Matakana village. Available for charter is our 14m sailing catamaran designed for comfortable performance cruising, weather permitting.

Puhoi *9 km N of Orewa*
Westwell Ho *B&B*
Fae & David England
34 Saleyards Road,
Puhoi, 0951

Tel (09) 422 0064
or 027 280 5795
Fax (09) 422 0064
dhengland@xtra.co.nz

Double/Twin $130
Single $95
(Full breakfast)
Children $35
Visa MC Amex accepted
Children welcome
1 Queen 1 Double 1 Single (2 bdrm)
Bathrooms: 1 Ensuite 1 Private

We welcome you to our sunny colonial-style home in the lovely Puhoi Valley. We are only 2 minutes by car west of Main North Highway up a small road behind the old pub in this historic Puhoi Village. The homestead has wide verandahs around 3 sides where you can relax as you view the gardens and beautiful trees. Nearby are the fantastic Waiwera Thermal Pools, or you could hire a canoe and paddle down the Puhoi River to Wenderholm Beach and Park. Sky TV available.

Waiwera *6 km N of Orewa*
Estuary Cottage *B&B*
Jenny & Bob Kelly
15 Weranui Road,
Waiwera, 0950
PO Box 92, Waiwera

Tel (09) 426 2621
or 021 426 262
Fax (09) 426 2614
rj.kelly@ihug.co.nz

Double/Twin $110 - $130
Single $80 - $100
(Full breakfast)
Visa MC accepted
Internet available
1 Queen 1 Single (1 bdrm)
Large triple, with ensuite
Bathrooms: 1 Ensuite

A comfortable, centrally located B&B in the village of Waiwera - the beautiful Hibiscus Coast thermal area, with a safe scenic ocean beach, native bush covered hills, and world famous hot pools. Estuary Cottage - 'Owaimaru', is located on the tidal waters' edge, and offers quality accommodation with a stunning bedroom view, satellite television, tea & coffee making facilities, refrigerator, hot Spa pool, kayaks, Wireless Internet, and a private en-suite. Our guests receive a generous discount to the nearby thermal pools.

Orewa *35 km N of Auckland Central*
Villa Orewa *Luxury B&B*

Sandra & Ian Burrow
264 Hibiscus Coast Highway,
Orewa,
Auckland

Tel (09) 426 3073
or 021 626 760 (Ian)
Fax (09) 426 3053
rooms@villaorewa.co.nz
www.villaorewa.co.nz

Double/Twin $175 - $250
(Full breakfast)
Visa MC accepted
1 King/Twin 2 Queen (3 bdrm)
Greek-style rooms with
white vaulted roofs
Bathrooms: 3 Ensuite

Welcome to our beautifully appointed Mediterranean style home, with white-washed walls and blue vaulted roofs. A taste of the Greek Isles on beautiful Orewa Beach. Stay in 1 of our self-contained rooms, each with private balcony, and enjoy the panoramic beach and sea views, or socialise with us in our spacious living areas. Orewa offers a great range of activities and amenities; with cafes, restaurants, and shopping all within a short level walk. We are sure your stay will be enjoyable and memorable.

Orewa - Red Beach *5 km S of Orewa*
Hibiscus House *B&B*

Judy & Brian Marsden
13A Marellen Drive, Red Beach,
Whangaparaoa - Hibiscus Coast, 0932

Tel (09) 427 6303 or 0274 492 025
Fax (09) 427 6303
jb.marsden@clear.net.nz

Double/Twin $110
Single $85
(Continental breakfast)
Only children 12 years or over
Dinner $30 by prior arrangement
Pet free home
2 Queen 2 Twin (3 bdrm)
Tastefully furnished
Have courtyard or balcony
Bathrooms: 2 Ensuite 1 Private
Modern tile and glass with exellent showers.

We offer quality bed & breakfast, opposite a beach for the relaxing break you deserve, on route to Northland. Judy and Brian give friendly, personal hospitality in a very convenient location. Handy to shops, markets, cinema, beaches, golf courses and a leisure centre complex with heated swimming pool. Easy walks to surf, tennis and squash clubs. RSA 5 minutes away. Gulf Harbour Marina for ferries, fishing and sailing. Restaurants/bars/cafes for all tastes and occasions 5-15 minutes away. Sorry no pets. Children over 12 welcome. We have an outdoor spa pool available all year round.

Orewa *35 km N of Auckland*
Art & The Sea B&B *Apartment with Kitchen*

Vicki & John Lambert
12 Chelverton Tce,
Red Beach,
Whangaparaoa,
Auckland 0932

Tel (09) 426 1060
or 021 426 107
vickilambert@actrix.co.nz
www.homeexchange.com ID#62402

Double/Twin $160
Single $140
(Full breakfast provisions)
Pet free home
Not suitable for children
1 Queen (1 bdrm)
Large bedroom with queen bed
Bathrooms: 1 Private Shower

Enjoy beautiful sea views and peace and quiet in this top-class cul-de-sac, where only a reserve separates you from beautiful Red Beach. Spread yourselves out in over 80sq.m. of exclusive use living area, with art, sky TV, stereo, books and games, well-equipped kitchen, washing machine, and patio with barbeque, table & chairs and sun-lounger. Double kayak also available. All this plus shops, golf courses, regional parks, restaurants and tourist attractions while only 30mins north of Auckland city. To view living areas, visit www. homeexchange.com ID#62402.

Whangaparaoa *4 km E of Orewa*
Duncansby by the Sea *B&B*

Kathy & Ken Grieve
72 Duncansby Road,
Whale Cove,
Stanmore Bay,
Whangaparaoa

Tel (09) 424 0025
or 027 200 9688
Fax (09 424 0025
duncansby@xtra.co.nz
www.duncansbybnb.co.nz

Double/Twin $125
Single $95
(Full breakfast)
Visa MC accepted
2 Queen (2 bdrm)
Bathrooms: 1 Ensuite 1 Private

Duncansby, our new home, offers relaxing panoramic sea views of the Hibiscus Coast. Located at Whale Cove between Red Beach and Stanmore Bay, our modern sunny well appointed rooms have own entrances, TV, decks, white linen, tea/coffee facilities. Paradise for golfers with 3 local courses including International Gulf Harbour Course with its boating marina. Bird watchers visit Tiritiri Island Bird Sanctuary, walk Shakespeare Park. Enjoy petanque, 9 superb beaches, excellent local restaurants and cafes. Only 35 minutes north of Auckland City, we welcome you.

Whangaparaoa *5 km E of Orewa*
Peone Place *B&B Homestay Apartment with Kitchen*

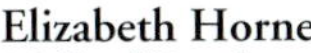

Elizabeth Horne
35 Surf Road,
Whangaparaoa, 0932

Tel (09) 424 1455
info@peone.co.nz
www.peone.co.nz

Double/Twin $150 - $175
Single $35 - $100
(Continental breakfast)
Children welcome
Dinner by arrangement
Seasonal rates apply
Visa MC accepted
Children welcome
2 King/Twin 1 Queen
3 Single (4 bdrm)
Bathrooms: 1 Private 1 Guest share

Welcome to our large, comfortable home. Enjoy genuine, warm hospitality, wide sea views, or relax in our peaceful private garden with resident tuis. We have 2 double bedrooms & a self-contained apartment.(Sleeps 5) Enquire about extended stay/group rates. Attractions: beaches, thermal pools, golf courses, walks & quality restaurants. Peone Place is an ideal base for trips to boutique wineries, colourful markets, distinctive galleries & potteries, or nearby beautiful islands including Tiritiri Matangi Bird sanctuary. Guest ferry discounts available +'Tiri' lunches & maps. Be at ease at Peones!

Silverdale - Waitoki *14.5 km SW of Silverdale*
Plover Lodge *B&B*
Michael & Pauline Tuckett
149 Ireland Road,
Waitoki,
RD 1,
Kaukapakapa, 0871

Tel (09) 420 5282
ploverlodge@slingshot.co.nz
www.travelbug.co.nz/visit/plover/
plover-lodge

Double/Twin $140
Single $100
(Full breakfast)
Visa MC accepted
Not suitable for children
1 Double (1 bdrm)
Bathrooms: 1 Ensuite

Magnificent sunsets can be seen from your own air-conditioned lounge overlooking a lush valley, only 12 minutes from the Silverdale motorway exit and 35 minutes from Auckland Harbour Bridge. Come and relax on your own patio on this 7 acre property, meet the animals, or go for a stroll to Riverhead Forest and enjoy the spectacular views. Enjoy a delicious wholesome breakfast made with fresh home baked bread served in the separate dining room. Michael, Pauline and their 2 cats welcome you to their home.

Kumeu *26 km NE of Auckland*
Calico Lodge B & B *Countrystay B&B*

Kay & Kerry Hamilton
250 Matua Road,
Kumeu,
Auckland 0891

Tel (09) 412 8167
or 0800 50 18 50
bed@calicolodge.co.nz
www.calicolodge.co.nz

Double/Twin $150 - $225
Single $140 - $190
(Full breakfast)
Visa MC accepted
Internet available
1 King 2 Queen 2 Twin (4 bdrm)
Warm, decorated with
quilts and artwork
Bathrooms: 2 Ensuite 2 Private
Bathroom amenities, heated, hairdryer, double spa bath

Calico Lodge is 25 minutes from Auckland City in the Wine country of Kumeu. Owned and operated by Kerry & Kay, New Zealanders, we love to share our peaceful gardens with our guests. Small dog, 3 cats, and tame sheep complete the setting. Patchwork quilts and Teddy Bears decorate the guest wing with its own entrance and lounge, TV, DVD, and fridge. Golf courses (6), black sand beaches, cafes, restaurants, function centres, Gannet Colony and Waitakere Rainforest walks are all nearby. Free wireless Internet.

Kumeu *29 km NW of Auckland*
Mockingbird Hill *B&B Homestay Apartment with Kitchen Cottage with Kitchen*

Bob & Sue Leech
25 School Road,
Waimauku, 0881

Tel (09) 411 9696
or 027 203 6897
info@mockingbirdhill.co.nz
www.mockingbirdhill.co.nz

Double/Twin $134 - $170
Single $107 - $116
(Full breakfast)
Dinner by arrangement
Equestrian Facilities
Children and Pets welcome
3 Queen 1 Double 1 Single (3 bdrm)
2 bedrooms in B&B,
1 bedroom in cottage
Bathrooms: 1 Private 1 Guest share

Bob and Sue warmly invite you to share their Lifestyle and Homestay, nestled in its own valley on the fringe of Waimauku village. The homestead surrounded by rambling relaxing gardens is also home to 'Shorty', our westie, cats 'Romney' and 'Mouse', native and exotic birds and a small flock of Wiltshire sheep and cattle. Close to wineries, restaurants, cafes, function centres, 6 golf courses, beaches and forests. Equestrian facilities are available to accommodate your horses. Pets welcome by arrangement.

Hobsonville *20 km NW of Auckland*
Eastview *B&B Homestay Separate Suite*

Joane & Don Clarke
2 Parkside Road,
Hobsonville, Auckland

Tel (09) 416 9254
or 027 437 3400
enquiries@eastview.co.nz
www.eastview.co.nz

Double/Twin $120 - $135
Single $85 - $100 (Full breakfast)
Children $30 (cot available)
Dinner by arrangement
Extra adult discount in Marina Suite
Visa MC accepted
Children welcome
2 Queen 2 Single (3 bdrm)
Marina Suite has 2 bedrooms,
Rosies Retreat has a queen-bed
Bathrooms: 2 Private
1 for Marina Suite 1 for Rosies Retreat

Situated at the western end of Auckland's beautiful harbour. Eastview is easy to find from the airport or travel routes north and south. Well located for exploring Auckland. Panoramic water/city views. Near to Kumeu wine country (popular for weddings), superb beaches, rainforest clad hills, gannet colony. We offer many personal homely touches. 2 sunny accommodation areas. A 2 bedroomed suite, and a queen bedroom with private bathroom. A great place to relax after your trip or a day's sightseeing. Friendly cat.

Waitakere Ranges - Swanson *4 km SW of Swanson*
Panorama Heights *B&B*

Allison & Paul Ingram
42 Kitewaho Road,
Swanson,
Waitakere City,
Auckland, 0614

Tel (09) 832 4777
or 0800 692 624 Outside Auckland
nzbnb4u@clear.net.nz
www.panoramaheights.co.nz

Double/Twin $180
Single $150
(Full breakfast)
Dinner by request
Visa MC accepted
2 Queen 1 Twin (3 bdrm)
Bathrooms: 3 Ensuite 1 Private

Paul & Allison invite you to visit and share our extremely special location high in the Waitakere Ranges with tranquility,privacy and magnificent panoramic views across Native Rainforest to Auckland City and Rangitoto Island beyond. Explore 250km walking/hiking trails in surrounding Regional Park, West Coast beaches(Piha,Karekare,Bethells, Muriwai) Wineries,2 Scenic Golf courses. Train to City is nearby. Excellent quality accommodation is here for you to Enjoy. Your hosts, who reside nextdoor encourage relaxation while we spoil you. Please Phone/Email for Bookings/Directions.

Ranui *15 km SW of Auckland*
The Garrett *B&B Homestay*

Alma & Rod Mackay
295 Swanson Road,
Waitakere City,
Auckland 0612

Tel (09) 833 6018
Fax (09) 833 6018
rod_alma_295@xtra.co.nz

Double/Twin $90
Single $60
(Continental breakfast)
2 King/Twin 1 King
2 Single (2 bdrm)
Bathrooms: 1 Ensuite

Just 15 minutes from Auckland City, 5 minutes from Henderson. The Garrett offers villa style accommodation with ensuite. Twin beds or king-size available. Accommodation for extra guests with folding beds on request; suitable for business people. High ceilings, period furniture and decor create a charming atmosphere in this delightful homestay, just minutes from Waitakere City. Attractions include wine trails, Art Out West - including Lopdell House Gallery, Waitakere Ranges, bush walks, Aratiki Centre, and golf courses. Westcity Shopping Centre, Lynn Mall and St Lukes.

Okura *20 km N of Auckland Central*
Okura B&B *B&B Separate Suite*

Judie & Ian Greig
20 Valerie Crescent,
Okura,
North Shore City,
Auckland

Tel (09) 473 0792
Fax (09) 473 1072
ibgreig@paradise.net.nz

Double/Twin $115
Single $90
(Full breakfast)
Visa MC accepted
1 Queen 1 Single (2 bdrm)
Both in separate suite
Bathrooms: 1 Private
Own shower and toilet

Situated on Auckland's North Shore, Okura is a small settlement bounded by farmland and the Okura River, an estuary edged with native forest. If you like peace, quiet, with only bird song nearby, estuary and forest views, then this is for you. Accommodation includes your own, not shared, TV lounge, tea-making facilities, fridge, shower and toilet. Nearby is a wide variety of cafes, shops, beaches, walks, North Shore Stadium, Massey University and golf courses. Okura - one of Auckland's best kept secrets.

Coatesville - Albany *7 km N of Albany*
Camperdown *B&B Farmstay*

Chris & David Hempleman
455 Coatesville/Riverhead Highway,
RD 3, Albany,
Auckland

Tel (09) 415 9009
Fax (09) 415 9023
chris@camperdown.co.nz
www.camperdown.co.nz

Double/Twin $150
Single $100
(Full breakfast)
Children $50
Dinner $50
Children and pets welcome
Internet Available
1 King/Twin 1 King
3 Queen 3 Single (6 bdrm)
Bathrooms: 2 Private 1 Guest share

We are only 20 minutes from Auckland City, relax in secluded tranquillity. Our home opens into beautiful gardens, native bush and stream offering the best of hospitality in a friendly relaxed atmosphere. On the farm we have sheep, cattle and pet lambs Our spacious guest areas consist of the entire upstairs. Guests may use our games room, play tennis on our superb court, row a boat on the lake, or just stroll by the stream. Camperdown is easy travelling to the main tourist route north.

Albany *5 km N of Albany*
Albany Country B&B *B&B*

Alan & Lorraine Danks
127 Potter Road,
Albany,
Auckland

Tel (09) 415 8951
or 022 600 6429
or 021 0253 0888
Fax (09) 415 8951
albanycountrybnb@yahoo.co.nz

Double/Twin $180 - $230
Single $160
(Full breakfast)
Children $60
Dinner $50
Children welcome
Internet available
2 King 2 Single (3 bdrm)
Bathrooms: 2 Ensuite
Bath hosts share

Relax in our secluded, peaceful location, set on 13 acres amidst lovely gardens and rural views. We are 5 mins from Albany restaurants, and shopping mall. 20 mins to Auckland central. Two ensuite rooms, one with a private lounge and one with a private deck. Guest lounge, pool table, WiFi, outdoor fireplace & dining area. On route to your Northland destination or as a relaxing base for your Auckland stay. Alan & Lorraine & Holly, our small dog, invite you to enjoy our friendly country hospitality.

Bayswater *5 km S of Takapuna*
Beresford B&B *B&B Homestay*

Lesley Brown & Gordon Storey
46A Beresford Street,
Bayswater, North Shore,
Auckland 0622

Tel (09) 445 3959
or 027 492 4462
beresfordhomestay@email.com
beresfordbandb.co.nz

Double/Twin $110 - $125
Single $85 - $100
(Continental breakfast)
Continental breakfast included
Cooked breakfast $10 pp
Visa MC accepted
Not suitable for children
Internet available
1 Queen (1 bdrm)
Bathrooms: 1 Private

We warmly welcome travellers to our comfortable, modern home in peaceful Bayswater where you can relax and feel at home but be within easy reach of all Auckland has to offer. Easy walk to ferry, downtown Auckland 10 minute trip away. 5-10 minute drive to motorway, Devonport or Takapuna, restaurants and shopping. On bus route. Light, airy, upstairs bedroom next to private bathroom, own TV lounge, tea & coffee making, internet, laundry, spa pool, generous continental breakfast included (cooked $10pp). One timid cat.

Please let your hosts know if you have to cancel.
They will have spent time preparing for you.

Devonport *4 km NE of Auckland Central*
Karin's Garden Villa
B&B self-cont. studio cottage and Apartment
Karin Loesch & Family
14 Sinclair Street, Devonport, Auckland 0624

Tel (09) 445 8689   Fax (09) 445 8689
stay@karinsvilla.com
www.karinsvilla.com

Double/Twin $155 - $185
Single $95 - $145 (Continental breakfast)
Children $25   Self-contained cottage $195
Prices are subject to change during September & October
Visa MC accepted   Internet Available
2 Double 1 Twin 1 Single (4 bdrm)
Bathrooms: 1 Ensuite 1 Private 1 Guest share

Tucked away at the end of a quiet cul-de-sac, Karins Garden Villa - a Devonport dream - offers real home comfort with its light cosy rooms, easy relaxed atmosphere and the warmest of welcome from Karin and her family.

A beautifully restored spacious Victorian villa surrounded by large lawns and old fruit trees. Karins Garden Villa has also been featured on NZ and Australian television advertising for its relaxed, peaceful setting. Just 5 minutes stroll from tree-lined Cheltenham Beach, sailing, golf, tennis, shops and restaurants and only a short drive or pleasant 10 minute walk past extinct volcanoes to the picturesque Devonport with its many attractions.

Your comfortable room offers separate private access through french doors, opening onto wide verandahs and cottage garden. And for those visitors wanting comfort and privacy, there is even a studio cottage with balcony and a kitchenette to rent. For longer stays enquire about our new open-plan Garden Apartment in the heart of Devonport. Sit down to a nutritious breakfast in the sunny dining room with its large bay windows overlooking everflowering purple lavender and native gardens.

Feel free to use the kitchen, laundry and internet. Karin comes from Germany and she and her family have lived in Indonesia. We have seen a lot of the world and enjoy meeting other travellers. Always happy to help you arrange island cruises, rental cars, bikes and tours. Come as Guest - leave as a friend.

Devonport *1.5 km N of Devonport*
Ducks Crossing Cottage *B&B Homestay*
Gwenda & Peter Mark-Woods
58 Seabreeze Road,
Devonport,
Auckland

Tel (09) 445 8102
or mob.027 278 1495
Fax (09) 445 8102
duckxing@xtra.co.nz

Double/Twin $100 - $140
Single $75 - $85
(Special breakfast)
Children $30
Pet free home
Children welcome
1 King/Twin 1 Queen
1 Single (3 bdrm)
Bathrooms: 1 Ensuite 2 Private

Welcome to our charming modern home in a garden setting. Peaceful, spacious, sunny bedrooms with television and clock radios. Tea, coffee and home-cooking available. We overlook Waitemata Golf Course and are 5 minutes from Narrow Neck Beach. Devonport Village, with cafes, restaurants and antique shops is 2 minutes by car or 15 minutes walk. Hosts are well travelled,informative and enjoy hospitality. Directions:airport door to door shuttle, or drive Route 26, Seabreeze Road, first house on left. Good off-street parking, courtesy ferry pick up on request.

Devonport *01 km E of Devonport*
Rainbow Villa *B&B*
Judy McGrath
17 Rattray Street,
Devonport,
Auckland

Tel (09) 445 3597
Fax (09) 445 4597
rainbowvilla@xtra.co.nz
www.rainbowvilla.co.nz

Double/Twin $150 - $180
Single $130 - $150
(Full breakfast)
Visa MC accepted
Pet free home
Not suitable for children
1 King 1 Queen 1 Twin
2 Single (3 bdrm)
3 elegant bedrooms
Bathrooms: 3 Ensuite

Welcome to our Victorian villa (1885) nestled in a quiet cul-de-sac on the lower slopes of Mt Victoria. 3 elegant spacious rooms with ensuites, Sky TV. Spa pool in the garden. We serve a delicious full breakfast, coffee and tea available at all times. Situated just 100 metres from historic Devonport Village, 5 minute walk to ferry, only 10 minute 'cruise' to downtown Auckland. Directions: Rattray Street is first on left past Picture theatre. Shuttles available at airport. Not suitable for children or pets.

Devonport *0.25 km E of Devonport Township*
The Jasmine Cottage *B&B Cottage with kitchenette*

Joan & John Lewis
20 Buchanan Street,
Devonport,
Auckland

Tel (09) 445 8825
Fax (09) 445 8605
joanjohnlewis@xtra.co.nz
www.photoalbum.co.nz/jasmine/

Double/Twin $120
(Full breakfast)
1 Queen (1 bdrm)
Bathrooms: 1 Ensuite

Welcome to our cosy smoke-free quiet and private guest cottage. We are right in the heart of historic Devonport Village with all its attractions, cafes, beaches, golf course, scenic walks. The ferry to Auckland City and the Hauraki Gulf is 3 minutes walk away. A breakfast basket is delivered to your door and provides fruit juice, cereals, home made muesli and yoghurt, a platter of seasonal fruits, breads, jams, spreads, free-range eggs, breakfast teas and freshly brewed coffee. TV, fax.

Devonport *0.5 km N of Devonport*
Mahoe *B&B Apartment with Kitchen*

Judith & David Bern
15B King Edward Parade,
Devonport, 0624

Tel (09) 445 1515
or 027 291 3727
Fax (09) 445 1515
info@mahoe.co.nz
www.mahoe.co.nz

Double/Twin $170 - $200
(Breakfast by arrangement)
Children by arrangement
Visa MC accepted
2 Queen 1 Double (3 bdrm)
1 Queen/1Double B&B, 1 Queen
Bathrooms: 1 Ensuite 1 Private

Mahoe is an old school house transported from Huntly in 1985. Situated on the Devonport waterfront up a driveway in a peaceful setting. The upstairs B&B has queen room with deck and double room with lounge. The bathroom is separate. Our B&B is suitable for one couple or 3 or 4 people who are family or friends. We can accommodate 3 couples by including the apartment, which has a separate entrance and is fully equipped.

Devonport *0.3 km N of Information Office*
Seasaw *Luxury B&B Cottage with Kitchen*

Kerry and Ramazan Semiz
1 Hastings Parade,
Devonport,
Auckland

Tel 09 445 9699
or 021 868 797
info@seasawbnb.com
www.seasawbnb.com

Double/Twin $120 - $150
(Continental breakfast)
Children welcome
Baby cot available
1 Queen 1 Single (1 bdrm)
Bathrooms: 1 Ensuite
with luxury bath

Welcome to Seasaw Bed & Breakfast. A private,stand alone sunny cottage situated in the heart of historic Devonport Village. Only ten minute ferry cruise to downtown Aucland city. Breakfast is delivered to your door which includes fresh juice, tropical and seasonal fruits served with our homemade muesli and yogurts, a selection of assorted breads, free range eggs with breakfast teas and freshly brewed coffee. You may enjoy your breakfast in the privacy of your room or served on the sunny deck.

Devonport *.3 km N of Devonport*
Abed in Devonport *B&B Apartment with Kitchen*

Mandie & Tony O'Neill
34 Hastings Parade, Devonport, 0624

Tel (09) 446 6157 or 021 0260 5886
patoneill@yahoo.co.nz
www.abedindevonport.net16.net

Double/Twin $110 - $300
Single $110 - $300
(Continental breakfast provisions)
Children welcome but please be
advised we have no childproofing
Cafes and restaurants within
close walking distance
Payment terms cash as we
have no credit card facilities
Pet free home Children welcome
1 Queen 1 Double 1 Twin (3 bdrm)
Apartment has double room and twin room
B&B has queen room with ensuite and separate entrance
Bathrooms: 1 Ensuite in B&B 1 Guest Share in Apartment

Minutes from the heart of Devonport and Auckland. Will suit singles to large groups. New, clean, modern and comfortable, located in a very quiet street. WiFi available. Continental breakfast. Own outside entrance and off-street parking. The B&B is has a queen bed with ensuite. There is also tea and coffee making facilities, a fridge and toaster. The apartment has a double room and a twin room. Prices from $110 per night. A discount is offered for stays of 6 days or longer.

Auckland - Ponsonby *1 km SW of Auckland Central*
The Great Ponsonby Arthotel *B&B Hotel*

Sally James & Gerard Hill
30 Ponsonby Terrace, Ponsonby, Auckland 1011

Tel (09) 376 5989 or 0800 766 792
Fax (09) 376 5527
info@greatpons.co.nz
www.greatpons.co.nz

Double/Twin $180 - $425
Single $180 - $350 (Full breakfast)
Visa MC Diners Amex Eftpos accepted
Children and dogs welcome
6 King/Twin 5 Queen (11 bdrm)
Bathrooms: 11 Ensuite

Come and stay at the Great Ponsonby, providing bed & breakfast in Auckland. Just two minutes stroll to Ponsonby's vibrant cafes, fashion, galleries and just five minutes by taxi to the harbour or city centre.

Our breakfasts are legendary--friendships have been forged in the dining room, egg benedict lingered over on the verandah. Eleven rooms of varying size and price. All rooms have everything you could need. All have modern and Pacific artworks. Courtyard studios are much bigger than the villas. The spacious suites and penthouse are twice as large again. Our sitting room is a place to read, listen to our extensive CD collection or have a drink with friends. There is no TV. The TVs are in the bedrooms.

Ponsonby, an urban village, is one of the earliest areas of Auckland and luckily many of the historic buildings still remain. It is the trendiest part of town, a place to come to eat, drink coffee and to have fun. It is very close to the city centre.

The Great Ponsonby, set in a large, beautiful garden is in the perfect place from which to explore Auckland. Great Ponsonby has an Enviro Gold award and Sally & Gerry are committed to sustainability. Hemi and Tom are the resident dog & cat.

Auckland CBD *0.5 km E of Auckland CBD*

Braemar on Parliament Street *B&B*

Susan Sweetman
7 Parliament Street,
Auckland City Central, 1010

Tel (09) 377 5463
or 021 640 688
Fax (09) 377 3056
braemar@aucklandbedandbreakfast.com
www.aucklandbedandbreakfast.com

Double/Twin $225 - $350
(Full breakfast)
Visa MC Diners
Amex Eftpos accepted
Children and pets welcome
3 Queen 1 Double (4 bdrm)
Bathrooms: 1 Ensuite 1 Private
1 Guest share 1 Family share

A lovingly restored late Victorian townhouse in the Auckland CBD, Braemar provides comfortable, elegant accommodation to the discerning traveller. All upstairs bedrooms have posturepedic beds. All bathrooms have large claw foot baths. Complimentary toiletries, tea & coffee. Children welcome. Pets by prior arrangement. Toy poodles and cat live on site. Wireless broadband. Qualmark Green Enviro GOLD.

Auckland - Remuera *7 km E of Auckland Central*

A Woodland Retreat *B&B*

Jude & Roger Harwood
18 Waiatarua Road,
Remuera,
Auckland 1050

Tel (09) 524 6990
jude.harwood@xtra.co.nz
www.travelwise.co.nz

Double/Twin $155 - $175
Single $125
(Special breakfast)
Visa MC accepted
Pet free home
Not suitable for children
1 King 1 Double 1 Twin
1 Single (3 bdrm)
Bathrooms: 1 Ensuite 1 Private

Guest book comments: 'Absolutely purr-fect.' 'Very comfortable with stunning food.' 'A lovely oasis of calm with wonderful breakfasts.' 'Peaceful retreat with excellent breakfasts.' Our breakfasts ARE special using seasonal fruit and produce The 3 guest bedrooms have tea/coffee facilities, heated towel rails, swimming towels and colour TVs. Fridge. Safe off-street carparking. Arrive a guest - leave a friend.

Auckland - Remuera *1.5 km E of Newmarket*
Green Oasis *B&B Homestay Apartment with Kitchen*

James & Joy Foote
25A Portland Road,
Remuera,
Auckland 1050

Tel (09) 520 1921
Fax (09) 522 9004
footes1@xtra.co.nz
www.babs.co.nz/greenoasis

Double/Twin $120
Single $80
(Full breakfast)
Children $65
Laundry, ironing -
small charge by arrangement
Visa MC accepted
Children welcome
1 Queen 1 Single (2 bdrm)
Bathrooms: 1 Private

Green Oasis, a secluded, tranquil location in a much loved garden of native trees and ferns, 10 minutes to city centre. Close to the museum, antique & specialty shops, restaurants & cafes. An informal home of natural timbers, sunny decks where you will find us relaxed, welcoming and sensitive to your needs. Your accommodation, entered from a private garden, is self-contained with kitchen/dining room, tea/coffee making facilities, washing machine, TV. Special breakfast of seasonal and home-made taste sensations!

All our B&Bs are non-smoking.

Auckland - Remuera *3 km E of Auckland Central*
Omahu Lodge *Luxury B&B*

Robyn & Ken Booth
33 Omahu Road, Remuera, Auckland 1050

Tel (09) 524 5648 or 021 954 333
Fax (09) 524 5648   info@omahulodge.co.nz
www.omahulodge.co.nz

Double/Twin $220 - $325 Single $160 - $200 (Full breakfast)
Walking distance to great restaurants -
Visa MC accepted
Pet free home Not suitable for children
Internet Available
1 King/Twin 1 King 2 Queen 1 Twin 1 Single (4 bdrm)
All ensuited with views and complimentary refreshments
Bathrooms: 4 Ensuite 1 Private
Plus luxurious separate bath suite

Omahu Lodge offers luxury Bed and Breakfast accommodation with total privacy in a peaceful residential setting. The Lodge is very spacious with beautifully appointed bedrooms all with ensuites, fine bed linen, heated towels, bathrobes, slippers, hair dryers, ironing and tea/coffee facilities. Rooms have views of Cornwall Park, Mt Hobson, Mt St John, the eastern suburbs or the pool and spa complex from the Poolside Suite. Relax with a complimentary drink and snacks in the large lounge amongst the antiques, in the separate entertainment room with a large plasma television, DVD and CD player or enjoy the solar heated pool, sauna or spa. Omahu Lodge is a boutique resort. The city centre and Auckland's renowned harbour are just 10 minutes away by car. Remuera, Parnell, Newmarket's exclusive shopping, restaurants, Epsom Showgrounds and public transport are easy walking distance. Walks in Cornwall Park, Mt Hobson and Mt St John add to the peaceful ambience of the suburban setting. A sumptuous breakfast is served in the conservatory overlooking the pool, on the patio beside the pool or room service is available. Check www.tripadvisor.com for Auckland B&B rating and guest comments.

Auckland - Mt Eden *2 km SW of Auckland Central*

Bavaria B&B Hotel *B&B*

Ulrike & Rudolf
83 Valley Road,
Mt Eden, Auckland 1024

Tel (09) 638 9641
Fax (09) 638 9665
bavaria@xtra.co.nz
www.bavariabandbhotel.co.nz

Double/Twin $155 - $169
Single $105 - $119 (Full breakfast)
Children over 2 years $25
Extra adult $ 60
Please inquire about our reduced
rates from May-September
Visa MC Amex Eftpos accepted
Children welcome Internet available
1 King/Twin 4 Queen 2 Double
2 Twin 2 Single (11 bdrm)
Bathrooms: 11 Ensuite

Charming small hotel in quiet, historic, residential surroundings. Close to city with excellent connections to town. Mt. Eden summit with panoramic views easily accessible, immaculate quality rooms with ensuites, phones; wireless internet access available, free use of guest computer in lounge, healthy breakfast buffet-style, complimentary tea/coffee/biscuits, sunny lounge and peaceful garden, good shopping, fine restaurants & cafes nearby, off-street parking, friendly and welcoming atmosphere. Ask us for advice on rental cars, tours etc.

Auckland - Epsom *5 km S of Auckland City Centre*

Millars Epsom Homestay *B&B*

Janet Millar
10 Ngaroma Road,
Epsom,
Auckland 1023

Tel (09) 625 7336
or 027 251 3817
jmillar@xtra.co.nz

Double/Twin $120 - $150
Single $70 - $80
(Full breakfast)
Children $10-$20
Pet free home
Children welcome
1 King 1 Queen 2 Twin (2 bdrm)
All beds have electric blankets
Bathrooms: 1 Ensuite 1 Private
2 showers, 1 bath

Our home, is set in a quiet suburb , 200 metres from Greenwoods Corner Village with its bank, post office, a variety of cafes and bus stop to the city of Auckland. A walk, the opposite direction takes you to One Tree Hill and Cornwall Park, one of Auckland's loveliest recreational parks,which is also the way to the Expo Centre and Greenlane Hospital. There are 2 areas - the Garden Suite for 4 people,and the other is a double room . We welcome guests to our home

Auckland - Orakei/Okahu Bay *4.8 km E of Auckland Central*
Nautical Nook/Free Sailing *B&B Homestay*

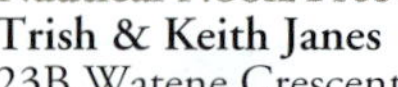

Trish & Keith Janes
23B Watene Crescent,
Orakei,
Auckland

Tel (09) 521 2544
or 0800 360 544
nauticalnook@bigfoot.com
www.nauticalnook.com

Double/Twin $151 - $162
Single $108
(Full breakfast)
Visa MC accepted
Children welcome
2 King/Twin (2 bdrm)
Bathrooms: 2 Ensuite

Friendly, relaxed beachside hospitality overlooking park/harbour, 4.8km from downtown. 100 metres from Okahu Bay. Gourmet breakfast. Stroll along picturesque promenade to Kelly Tarlton's Underwater World and Mission Bay beach. Bus at door to downtown, ferry terminal, museums and Eden Park (Rugby). Unwind for 2-3 day stopover. Complimentary sailing on the harbour on our 34' yacht. We have a wealth of local knowledge and international travel experience and can assist with sightseeing, travel planning. Welcome! Pay cash and deduct 7.5% off listed rates. Excellent website! Free Wireless Internet.

Auckland - Mission Bay *6 km SE of Auckland Central*
Cockell Homestay *Homestay*

Jean & Bryan Cockell
41 Nihill Cresent,
Mission Bay,
Auckland

Tel (09) 528 3809
cockells@xtra.co.nz

Double/Twin $105
Single $85
(Full breakfast)
Dinner $30 by arrangement
Visa MC accepted
Pet free home
Not suitable for children
1 Double (1 bdrm)
1 double bed
Bathrooms: 1 Private

We warmly welcome you to our comfortable split level home. The upper level is for your exclusive use including a private lounge. 5 minutes walk to Mission Bay beach, cafes and restaurants and 10 minutes scenic car or bus ride to down town Auckland and ferry terminal for harbour and islands in the Gulf. We are retired and look forward to sharing our special part of Auckland with you. Please phone for directions or airport shuttle to our door. Please no smoking.

Auckland - Mission Bay *7 km E of Auckland CPO*
Whitmour *Luxury B&B*

Christine & Stephen Olsen
20 Cullwick Road,
Mission Bay,
Auckland

Tel (09) 5281205
or (0274) 791000
stephenchristineolsen@gmail.com

Double/Twin $170 - $190
Single $150 - $170
(Full breakfast)
1 King (1 bdrm)
Additional bedroom with Queensize
bed available on request
Bathrooms: 1 Ensuite

We welcome you to enjoy a relaxing stay at one of Auckland's most popular beaches, Mission Bay. Share a breakfast of homemade bread & muesli, seasonal fruits & berries, or traditional English cooked breakfast while enjoying a panoramic view of the Regional Park & harbour. Guests have their own lounge, with tea & coffee making facilities, opening onto a loggia that enjoys all day sun. Stroll to a number of beautiful beaches, including 10kms of wide, flat promenade that follows the seashore to downtown Auckland.

Auckland - St Heliers *10 km SE of Auckland*
McPherson B&B *B&B*

Jill & Ron McPherson
102 Maskell Street,
St Heliers,
Auckland

Tel (09) 575 9738
Fax (09) 575 0051
ronjillmcpherson@xtra.co.nz

Double/Twin $130
Single $90
(Continental breakfast)
1 Queen 1 Twin (2 bdrm)
Bathrooms: 1 Private

Welcome to our modern home with off-street parking in a smoke-free environment. 1 group of guests is accommodated at a time. Having travelled extensively ourselves we are fully aware of tourists' needs. 8 minutes walk to St Heliers Bay beach, shops, restaurants, cafes, banks and post office. Picturesque 12 minutes drive along the Auckland waterfront past Kelly Tarlton's Antarctic and Underwater Encounter to downtown Auckland. Interests including all sports, gardening and Jill is a keen cross-stitch embroiderer. Not suitable for children/pets.

Auckland - St Heliers *12 km E of Auckland Central*
The Munro's *B&B Homestay*
Margaret and Don Munro
12 Emerson Street,
St Heliers,
Auckland, 1071

Tel (09) 528 0459
Fax (09) 528 0459
dmlmunro@xtra.co.nz

Double/Twin $120
Single $95
(Full breakfast)
Dinner by arrangement,
please inform of special dietary
needs at time of booking
Pet free home
Not suitable for children
Internet available
2 King/Twin 1 King (1 bdrm)
Bathrooms: 1 Ensuite

Our spacious guest room has a king/twin comfortable beds, ensuite, tea/coffee etc; private entry and off-street parking. Wireless internet access for use with your own laptop. Located only 2km from St Heliers Bay, beach shops restaurants. 10km scenic waterfront drive to CBD & Harbour. Tamaki Campus of Auckland University is 1.5km. Airport a 45min drive or a taxi/shuttle bus will bring you to our door. Convenient for travel to city by bus or train, or accessing North/South motorways.

Auckland - Howick *2 km N of Howick*
French Lavender *B&B*
Michael & Barbara Davis
40 McCahill Views,
Howick, 2010

Tel (09) 535 4910
enquiries@frenchlavender.co.nz
www.frenchlavender.co.nz

Double/Twin $100
Single $80
(Continental breakfast)
Family Rates Available
Visa MC accepted
Children welcome
Internet available
1 Queen 2 Single (2 bdrm)
Bathrooms: 1 Guest share

Set in a quiet cul-de-sac, French Lavender is a modern two storey home with the guest rooms on the upper level, sharing a private balcony overlooking the garden and 180-degree views. The guest lounge provides a separate spot for relaxation, peace and quiet. Your hosts have travelled extensively, enjoy meeting people, visiting local restaurants as well as gardening and an occasional round of golf. Stroll in the garden; watch the birds and fish or make friends with our two cats.

Auckland - Titirangi *15 km SW of Auckland Central*

Kaurigrove *B&B*

Gaby & Peter Wunderlich
120 Konini Road,
Titirangi,
Waitakere 0642,
Auckland

Tel (09) 817 5608
or 027 275 0574
kaurigrove@yahoo.co.nz

Double/Twin $110 - $120
Single $65
(Continental breakfast)
Visa MC accepted
Children welcome
1 Queen 1 Single (2 bdrm)
Bathrooms: 1 Private

Welcome to our home! Kaurigrove offers a tranquil location amidst kauri trees in a park-like setting yet close to shops, cafes and restaurants. Situated at Titirangi, we are near Auckland's historic west coast with its magnificent beaches and vast native bush with a wonder-world of walking tracks. Gaby and Peter, your hosts of German background, are keen travellers themselves and are happy to introduce you to the highlights of Auckland and its surrounding areas. Non-smoking inside residence.

Auckland Airport - Mangere Bridge *14 km S of Auckland Central*

Mangere Bridge Homestay *Homestay*

Carol & Brian
1 Boyd Ave,
Mangere Bridge,
Auckland

Tel (09) 636 6346
Fax (09) 636 6345
mangerebridgehomestay@xtra.co.nz

Double/Twin $110 - $130
Single $85 - $100
(Full breakfast)
Children $20, 12 & under
Dinner $35 by prior arrangement
2 King/Twin 1 Double (3 bdrm)
Bathrooms: 3 Ensuite

We invite you to share our home, which is within ten minutes of Auckland Airport, an ideal location for your arrival or departure of New Zealand. We enjoy meeting people and look forward to making your stay an enjoyable one. Full breakfast after 7am. We welcome you to join us for dinner by prior arrangement. Airport courtesy pick up or drop off. Off street parking available. Handy to public transport. Short stroll to waterfront. Please no smoking indoors. Our cat requests no pets. Inspection welcome.

Auckland - Mangere Bridge *12 km N of Mangere Bridge*
Domain Lane *B&B Separate Suite Apartment with Kitchen*

Martina
5 Domain Lane,
Mangere Bridge,
Auckland, 2022

Tel 021 755 523
or (09) 633 0033
Fax (09) 633 0034
martina@domainlane.co.nz
www.domainlane.co.nz

Double/Twin $130 - $220
(Continental breakfast provisions)
Visa MC accepted
Children welcome
Internet available
1 King/Twin 2 King
1 Queen (4 bdrm)
Bathrooms: 3 Ensuite 1 Guest share

Welcome to our 1860 historic homestead nestled on the slopes of one of Auckland's largest volcanic cones. Immaculate quality apartment accommodation or private rooms with satellite TV, WiFi, secure parking, private outdoor area, BBQ facilities and kitchen. This beautifully restored home is set in park like grounds with panoramic views of the harbour and Auckland's major landmarks. Take a leisurely stroll around the mountain or enjoy a water taxi on the harbour. Only 12 minutes from the Airport and 12km to the City. Short walk to shops and cafes.

Howick/Botany - Manukau *2 km S of Botany Town Centre*
Accent on Armstrong *Deluxe B&B/Apartment with Kitchenette*

**Angela Sutton & Ross Hill
& Marie Hickling**
41 Armstrong Farm Drive,
Botany Downs, 2016

Tel (09) 265 0202
or 027 537 7002
Fax (09) 265 0203
Angela.Sutton@xtra.co.nz

Double/Twin $145 - $160
Single $135 - $145
(Continental breakfast provisions)
Payment online in advance
of stay preferred
If you require a special diet kindly
advise when booking - Many thanks!
Not suitable for children
Internet available
1 Queen 1 Single (2 bdrm)
1 x generous double (with the queen bed),
1 x good-sized single (has king-single bed)
Bathrooms: 1 Private

Newly built, 2 bedroom apartment complete with bathroom, dining and lounge area, private outdoor patio and secure parking for 2 vehicles. Has separate driveway and access. Beautifully appointed - double glazed, underfloor heating throughout and landscaped gardens. This is luxurious, quiet accommodation for the discerning traveller.

Maraetai Beach *25 km E of Manukau*
Maraetai Views *B&B Apartment with Kitchen Separate suite*

Sue & Terry Jordan
42 Craig Road,
Maraetai Beach,
Manukau 2018

Tel (09) 536 5885
or 021 840 842
stjordan@vodafone.co.nz
www.maraetaiviews.co.nz

Double/Twin $130 - $130
Single $130 - $130
(Continental breakfast)
Extra guests $20 p.p.
Dinner not available
Special rates for longer stays available
Pet free home
2 King/Twin 1 King (2 bdrm)
Bathrooms: 1 Ensuite
Access other rooms

Sue & Terry welcome guests to the seaside village of Maraetai, the upper level of our home is for your exclusive use and you will enjoy 180 degree sea & island views. New home, spacious lounge/dining room, small kitchen, fridge, cooktop,microwave.Two bedrooms, bathroom - semi ensuite. Spacious deck with outdoor furniture and BBQ. Suit families or couples travelling together, you don't have to share accommodation with others. Maraetai is 20 mins drive from Howick, and Manukau, 35 mins from Auckland International Airport.

Auckland - Manurewa *2 km S of Manukau City*
Hillpark Homestay *B&B Homestay*
Katrine & Graham Paton
16 Collie Street,
Manurewa,
Auckland 2102

Tel (09) 267 6847 or 021 207 2559
Fax (09) 267 8718
stay@hillpark.co.nz
www.hillpark.co.nz

Double/Twin $100 - $110
Single $60 - $70
(Full breakfast)
Children $20-$25
Dinner $20 by arrangement
Visa MC accepted
Children welcome
Internet available
1 Queen 4 Single (3 bdrm)
Bathrooms: 1 Ensuite 1 Guest share

Welcome to our sunny, spacious home and meet our friendly tonkinese cat. We are 15 minutes from Auckland Airport, 20 minutes from Auckland City centre, on the route south and the Pacific Coast Highway. Nearby are restaurants, Auckland Regional Botanic Gardens, TelstraClear Pacific Events Centre, Tipapa Events Centre, Manukau City Shopping Centre, Manukau Superclinic and Surgery Centre. Our interests include teaching, classical music, painting, gardening, photography, Christian activities, reading and travel. We are a smoke-free home. Directions: please phone or visit our website.

Miranda *30 km SE of Bombay Hills Freeway*
Miranda Views B&B *B&B Cottage with Kitchen*

Millie & Wayne Taylor
1213 Miranda Road,
Miranda, 2473

Tel (09) 232 7800
or 027 4942 780
Fax (09) 232 7811
mill@xtra.co.nz

Double/Twin $200
Single $145
(Full breakfast provisions)
1 Queen 3 Single (2 bdrm)
Bathrooms: 2 Guest share

Our lifestyle farm is situated in the beautiful Miranda Valley; less than an hours drive south from Auckland Airport. Enjoy the panoramic views of our lush valley, the Firth of Thames and Coromandel Ranges in the background. Relax and unwind in your own private chalet, take in views on your own balcony, stroll around our farm, visit some of our local attractions, or just watch abit of TV. We along with our daughter Ashley and our 2 spoilt cats and 1 friendly dog welcome you.

Papakura *1.5 km SW of Papakura*
Campbell Clan House *B&B*

Colin & Anna Mieke Campbell
57 Rushgreen Avenue,
Pahurehure, Papakura

Tel (09) 298 8231 or 027 496 7754
Fax (09) 298 7792
colam@pl.net
www.campbellclan.co.nz

Double/Twin $135
Single $85
(Special breakfast)
Children negotiable
Dinner $30-$60 prior booking only
Discount for 3+ nights
Visa MC accepted
Pet free home   Children welcome
Internet available
2 Queen 2 Single (3 bdrm)
Bathrooms: 2 Ensuite 1 Private

We offer you above average facilities in a peaceful attractive location. Buses,trains,shops and restaurants are a short walk away. We are 2 minutes from the motorway and Karaka Bloodstock, 15 minutes from the domestic and international airports and enroute to the Firth of Thames and the Coromandel. Our separate upstairs guest accommodation includes 3 double bedrooms, large comfortable lounge with tea/coffee, tourist information, TV and private balcony overlooking estuary. We offer wireless internet access and laundry facilities and discount for 3+ nights.

Drury *3 km E of Drury*

The Drury Homestead *B&B*

Carolyn & Ron Booker
349 Drury Hills Road, Drury, South Auckland

Tel (09) 294 9030 or 021 157 6531
Fax (09) 294 9035 druryhomestead@gmail.com.nz

Double/Twin $140 Single $90 (Full breakfast)
Children negotiable Children welcome
3 Queen 1 Twin (4 bdrm)
Bathrooms: 3 Ensuite 1 Private

The Drury Homestead is a wonderful old colonial house, built in the 1860s and lovingly restored by your hosts Carolyn and Ron. With 4 beautifully decorated rooms to choose from where would you like to sleep? Upstairs looking out over the creek and bush is The River Room with queen-size bed and en suite. Dunedin has magnificent views across the countryside, a queen bed and en suite. Cape Reinga has twin king-single beds and it's own bathroom with shower, toilet, vanity and claw-foot bath and oh what views from the bath! Downstairs is The Lily Room, a self-contained studio with kitchen facilities , a queen size bed and en suite and own entrance and verandah. Ideal for a longer stay. We also have a cot and pull-out beds available for children. We offer a discount for those staying 3 nights or more. We are situated on a rural block, minutes from the motorway, 35 minutes from Auckland CBD and 20 minutes from the airport. Set amidst paddocks with surrounding bush and a stream, the only noise you will hear are the birds and the sound of the tumbling stream. We love our lifestyle here and would like to make your stay in New Zealand a truely memorable one. The guest lounge is the perfect retreat or somewhere you can get to know Ron!

Waikato,
King Country
Kopu
2
Mangatarata
27
Te Kauwhata
Huntly
1
Raglan
23
Hamilton
Tamahere
Cambridge
Ohaupo
1
Tirau
Te Awamutu
31
3
Otorohanga
Waitomo
0 Kilometres 20
Miles
0 12
Te Kuiti
Piopio
3
30

Mangatarata *13 km SW of Ngatea*
Clark's Country Touch *Farmstay*

Betty & Murray Clark
249A Highway 27,
Mangatarata, RD 6,
Thames 3576

Tel (07) 867 3070
or 021 808 992
Fax (07) 867 3070
bmclark@xtra.co.nz

Double/Twin $120
Single $85
(Continental breakfast)
Children discount
Dinner by arrangement
Visa MC accepted
Children welcome
1 Queen 1 Twin (2 bdrm)
Bathrooms: 1 Private Shower

We welcome you to our new home which is warm and spacious and in a quiet location with panoramic rural views. Our guestrooms are private and comfortable with bathroom between. A sliding door creates an ensuite to the queen-sized room. We are close to local cafes, the Hauraki Golf and Bowling clubs, seabird coast, Miranda hot pools, Ngatea township and Watergardens, Thames Coromandel coast, and are one hour south-east of Auckland airport. Warm country hospitality awaits you.

Raglan *20 km S of Raglan*
Matawha *Farmstay*

Jenny & Peter Thomson
61 Matawha Road,
RD 2, Raglan

Tel (07) 825 6709
Fax (07) 825 6715
jennyt@wave.co.nz

Double/Twin $120 - $140
Single $60
(Full breakfast)
Dinner $20
Cash or cheque only please
Not suitable for children
1 King 1 Double 4 Single (3 bdrm)
Bathrooms: 1 Private 1 Guest share
1 Family share

We live on the west coast and our family has farmed this land for 100 years. Come and enjoy our private beach, expansive garden, home-grown vegetables, spa, 1 cat and the peace of no other buildings or people for miles. Take bush or mountain walks, a scenic drive, go surfing or fishing, or maybe find the hot-water beach! Auckland 2.5 hours, Hamilton 1 hour, Raglan 30 minutes. We are the only B&B on the West Coast. Directions: take Hamilton/Raglan route 23, turn left at Bridal Veil Falls sign, right at Te Mata onto Ruapuke Rd, left onto Tuturimu Rd and follow to T-junction, straight ahead across to cattlestop - 61 Matawha Rd.

Hamilton *3 km N of Hamilton*

Kantara *Homestay*
Mrs Esther Kelly
7 Delamare Road,
Bryant Park,
Hamilton

Tel (07) 849 2070
or 027 263 9442
esther@slingshot.co.nz

Double/Twin $110 - $135
Single $80
(Full breakfast)
Dinner $25
Pet free home
Not suitable for children
1 Double 1 Twin (2 bdrm)
Bathrooms: 1 Ensuite 1 Private

I have travelled extensively throughout New Zealand and overseas and welcome tourists to my comfortable home. I live close to the Waikato River with its tranquil river walks and St Andrews Golf Course. My interests are travel, golf, Mah Jong. Tea/coffee making facilities are available. I look forward to offering you friendly hospitality. Directions: from Auckland - leave main Highway north of Hamilton at round intersection into Bryant Road (large Blue sign-St Andrews). Turn left into Sandwich Road and second street on right.

Hamilton *1.5 km E of Hamilton Central*

Matthews B&B *B&B Homestay*
Maureen & Graeme Matthews
24 Pearson Avenue,
Hamilton, 3214

Tel (07) 855 4269
or 027 474 7758
Fax (07) 855 4269
mgm@xtra.co.nz
www.matthewsbnb.co.nz

Double/Twin $100 - $140
Single $60 - $80
(Full breakfast)
Children half price
Pet free home
1 Double 1 Twin (2 bdrm)
Bathrooms: 1 Guest share
1 Family share

Welcome to our home 2 seconds off the city bypass on Routes 7 & 9 at Five Crossroads. We are adjacent to the Waikato Events Centre, Ruakura Research Station, handy to the university and only 3 minutes from central city. Our home is a lived-in comfortable home, warm in winter and cool in summer, with a pool available. We have been hosts for 20 years and still enjoy the new friendships formed with guests both from New Zealand and overseas.

Hamilton *3 km N of Hamilton Central*
Ebbett Homestay *B&B Homestay*

Glenys & John Ebbett
162 Beerescourt Road,
Hamilton

Tel (07) 849 2005
johnebbett@xtra.co.nz

Double/Twin $120
Single $85
(Full breakfast)
Dinner $30
Pet free home
Not suitable for children
2 single beds in 1 bedroom
Bathrooms: 1 Private

Only minutes from town centre, our 19 year old home has a spectacular view of the Waikato River (New Zealand's longest) and easy access to Hamilton's popular river walk. We enjoy sharing travel anecdotes, but also respect our guests' wish for privacy. Your room has its own tea/coffee facility and private bathroom. Only 85 minutes from Auckland International Airport, we appeal to tourists arriving or departing New Zealand. Our interests include people, music, sport, travel, gardening and community. 17 years of happy hosting.

Hamilton - Ohaupo *4 km SW of Hamilton*
Green Gables of Rukuhia *B&B*

Earl & Judi McWhirter
35 Rukuhia Road,
RD 2,
Ohaupo

Tel (07) 843 8511
or 021 583 462
Fax (07) 843 8514
judi.earl@clear.net.nz

Double/Twin $100 - $130
Single $60 - $75
(Continental breakfast)
Dinner by arrangement
Visa MC accepted
Children welcome
Wireless broadband available
2 Double 1 Twin (3 bdrm)
Bathrooms: 1 Guest share

Warm, comfortable smoke-free family home in a quiet rural setting, close to Hamilton, Airport and field days (Mystery Creek). Free pick-up/delivery airport, bus, train terminal all part of the friendly service. 5km to Vilagrad Winery; 2 minutes walk to Gostiona Restaurant. 2 storeyed house with guest bedrooms and lounge/kitchenette downstairs; dining and hosts upstairs. Continental breakfast with fresh home-baked bread. Judi lectures statistics, University of Waikato. Earl is a school teacher.

Hamilton *4 km S of Hamilton*
The Poplars *Homestay Home & Garden*

Lesley & Peter Ramsay
402 Matangi Road,
RD 4,
Hamilton

Tel (07) 829 5551
or 027 668 0985
plramsay@xtra.co.nz

Double/Twin $120
Single $90
(Full breakfast)
Dinner $40pp by arrangement
Visa MC accepted
Children and pets welcome
1 King 1 Twin (2 bdrm)
Bathrooms: 1 Private

Minutes from Hamilton, Mystery Creek and Cambridge, The Poplars offers a haven of peace and quiet. Set in a 3 acre garden with internationally acclaimed daffodils, 500 roses and water features. Guest rooms have tea and coffee making facilities, and TV. Solar heated swimming pool and jacuzzi are adjacent. Hosts Peter and Lesley, themselves seasoned travellers, offer you the charms of country living. A warm welcome shared with family cats awaits you. A unique place to stay Directions: Please phone.

Hamilton - Tamahere *10 km S of Hamilton*
Lenvor B&B *B&B Homestay*

Lenora & Trevor Shelley
540E Oaklea Lane,
RD 3,
Tamahere,
Hamilton

Tel (07) 856 2027
Fax (07) 856 4173
lenvor@clear.net.nz

Double/Twin $120 - $135
Single $75 - $85
(Full breakfast)
Children $10-$25
Dinner by arrangement
Children welcome
3 Queen 3 Single (4 bdrm)
Bathrooms: 1 Ensuite
2 Guest share 1 Family share

Lenora and Trevor warmly invite you to relax and to share the comfort of our home Lenvor, which is set in a rural area, down a country lane. Our 2 storeyed home has guest rooms and small lounge upstairs; dining, lounge and hosts downstairs. 10 minutes to Hamilton or Cambridge, 5 minutes to Mystery Creek or airport. Lenora's interests are floral art and cake icing. Trevor enjoys vintage cars. Centrally situated for day trips to Coromandel, Tauranga, Rotorua, Taupo and Waitomo Caves.

Hamilton - Ohaupo *15 km S of Hamilton*
Ridge House *B&B Homestay*

Margaret Birtles & Matthew Harris
15 Great South Road,
Ohaupo, 3803

Tel (07) 823 6555
or 021 260 6504
Fax (07) 823 6550
m.a.birtles@xtra.co.nz

Double/Twin $90 - $120
Single $70
(Continental breakfast)
Children $15
Dinner $20 by arrangement
Visa MC accepted
Children and pets welcome
2 Queen 1 Single (2 bdrm)
Ensuite, and double bedroom
Bathrooms: 1 Ensuite 1 Guest share

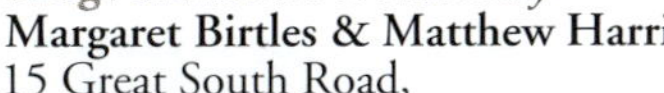

We welcome you to come and visit our home with its wonderful lake and pastoral views. We are just 6 minutes to Hamilton Airport and can arrange pick up from there and car storage ($10). This is an ideal base for trips to Hamilton, Te Awamutu, Waitomo Caves, Cambridge, Rotorua and Tauranga. Mystery Creek (home of the Field Days) and popular golf courses are close by. Games room, and garden to relax in.

Hamilton *12 km SW of Hamilton*
Uliveto Countrystay *Homestay Countrystay B&B*

Peter & Daphne Searle
164 Finlayson Road,
RD 10, Ngahinapouri,
Hamilton

Tel (07) 825 2116
or 027 755 8289
or 027 200 5320
uliveto@xtra.co.nz
www.uliveto.co.nz

Double/Twin $140
Single $110 - $140 (Full breakfast)
Dinner by arrangement
Visa MC accepted
Not suitable for children
2 Queen (2 bdrm)
Choose from either The Lavender
or The Olive Room
Bathrooms: 2 Private ensuite

Come and enjoy the peace and tranquility of the beautiful countryside with us and our chocolate labrador, Bella. Wander in our olive grove and gardens or relax on your private deck. Hamilton City,the airport and National Fieldays are 20 minutes away.Nearby attractions include - Waitomo Caves,lavender farm, golf course,horse treks/tramping tracks on Mt Pirongia, Bridal Veil Falls, Raglan beaches and cafes. To complete your day, share dinner and wine with us or relax in the guest lounge or our therapeutic spa.

Hamilton CBD *0.2 km N of Hamilton CBD*
Home Hospitality *B&B Homestay*

Diana & Fred Houtman
7A Hamilton Parade,
Hamilton

Tel (07) 838 1538
or 021 170 3210 (text only)
frediana@ihug.co.nz
www.accommodationinnewzealand.
co.nz//homehospitality

Double/Twin $120
Single $70 (Full breakfast)
Dinner $30 - advance notice required
Separate rate for special events -
Please enquire
Internet available Pet free home
Not suitable for children
1 Queen 2 Twin (2 bdrm)
1 Queen ; 1 Twin/King
Bathrooms: 1 Guest share

Comfortable self-contained accommodation in a quiet riverside cul-de-sac in the centre of Hamilton. Private sitting room for guests, with tea/coffee making facilities. Leave your car in our secure off-road parking area & walk to restaurants, shops, theatres, sports venues, conference centres - no parking hassles. A handy point from which to explore a large area of central NZ. Hosts are well travelled & enjoy meeting new people. Dutch spoken. Credit cards NOT accepted.

Hamilton - Matangi *10 km SE of Hamilton*
Kowhai Lodge *B&B Homestay*

Sheila and John
81 Butcher Road,
RD 4,
Hamilton, 3284

Tel (07) 829 6014
kowhai.lodge@yahoo.co.nz

Double/Twin $0 - $120
Single $0 - $95
(Full breakfast)
Dinner By arrangment
Pet free home
2 Queen 1 Twin (3 bdrm)
Bathrooms: 3 Ensuite

Sheila and John would like to welcome you to Kowhai Lodge, a new pet free home built in Matangi. Located 90 minutes from Auckland Airport and just 15 minutes from Hamilton city centre. A few minutes drive from State highway 1 & 1B, Matangi is centrally situated for Hamilton airport, Mystery Creek Event Centre and day trips to Rotorua, Tauranga or Waitomo Caves. Matangi is ideal for couples looking for the tranquility of the countryside in comfortable surroundings; rooms have tea/coffee making facilities and ensuites.

Cambridge *5 km SW of Cambridge*
Birches *Cottage with Kitchen Farmhouse Bed & Breakfast or Self Contained Cottage*

Sheri Mitchell & Hugh Jellie
263 Maungatautari Road,
PO Box 194, Cambridge

Tel (07) 827 6556
or 021 882 216
Fax (07) 827 3552
birchesbandb@xtra.co.nz
www.birches.co.nz

Double/Twin $150 - $175
Single $100
(Special breakfast)
Children by arrangement
Dinner by arrangement
Visa MC accepted
Children welcome
1 Queen 1 Double 1 Single (2 bdrm)
Bathrooms: 1 Ensuite 1 Private

Our character farmhouse offers open fires, tennis, swimming pool and hottub in country garden amongst renown horse studs. Proximity to Lake Karapiro makes Birches an ideal base for lake users. Hugh, a veterinarian, and I are widely travelled. We have farm pets and a cat. Cherry Tree Cottage is ideal for couples wanting privacy. The twin room in farmhouse has private bathroom with spa bath. We serve delicious farmhouse breakfasts alfresco or in dining room.

Cambridge *2 km S of Cambridge*
Glenelg *B&B Homestay*

Shirley & Ken Geary
6 Curnow Place,
Cambridge

Tel (07) 823 0084
glenelgbnb@ihug.co.nz
www.cambridge.co.nz

Double/Twin $120
Single $85
(Full breakfast)
Children $25
Dinner $25 by arrangement
Children and pets welcome
3 Queen 1 Twin (4 bdrm)
3 ensuites and 1 private
Bathrooms: 3 Ensuite 1 Private

Glenelg welcomes you to your home away from home. We offer spacious, quality accommodation, that is warm, quiet and private, overlooking Waikato farmland. There is plenty of off-street parking. Beds have electric blankets and woolrests. There are 200 rose bushes in the garden. Five minutes to Lake Karapiro. Mystery Creek, where NZ National Field Days and many other functions are held, is only 15 minutes away. Laundry facilities available. Homemade Kiwi dinners are available by arrangement.

Cambridge *2 km N of Town Centre*
Debevalmar *Homestay*
Val Massey
88 Hall Street,
Cambridge, 3434

Tel (07)827 0229
val.massey@xtra.co.nz

Double/Twin $110
Single $90
(Full breakfast)
Dinner $30pp by arrangement (BYO)
1 Twin 1 Single (2 bdrm)
Extra bed available on request
Bathrooms: 1 Guest share

Situated in one of Cambridge's most beautiful streets, 'Debevalmar' offers warm friendly home away from home accommodation. Central to Cambridge Raceway, Mystery Creek Events Centre and Lake Karipiro, 2 minutes to town centre, Lake Koutu and River Walkway. Guests can relax on the secluded deck with access from twin bedroom or watch the world go by on deck off Lounge. Bedrooms, in private wing, are warm and sunny. Guests share bathroom, adjacent to bedrooms.

Te Awamutu *2 km S of Te Awamutu*
Leger Farm *B&B Farmstay*
Beverley & Peter Bryant
114 St Leger Road,
Te Awamutu

Tel (07) 871 6676
Fax (07) 871 6679

Double/Twin $125 - $140
Single $85 - $100
(Full breakfast)
Dinner $35
1 Queen 1 Double 1 Twin
3 Single (4 bdrm)
Bathrooms: 1 Ensuite 1 Private
1 Guest share 1 Bath

Leger Farm is a private residence with country living at its finest. The discerning leisure traveller seeking quality accommodation, in peaceful, relaxing surroundings, will find warm hospitality and every comfort here. Spacious bedrooms share stunning views of surrounding countryside. Each bedroom has its own balcony with garden vistas. We farm cattle and sheep, and are centrally based for visiting Waitomo Caves and black water rafting, Rotorua with its thermal activity and NZ's dramatic West Coast and ironstone sands. Golf course nearby for relaxation. Smoke-free home.

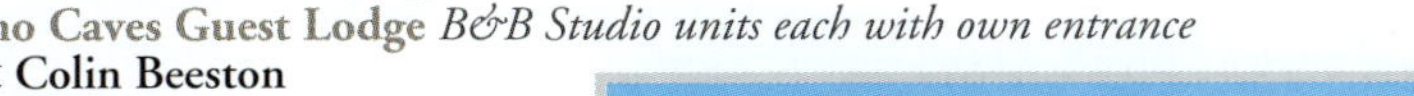

Waitomo Caves Village *15 km SW of Otorohanga*
Waitomo Caves Guest Lodge *B&B Studio units each with own entrance*

Janet & Colin Beeston
7 Te Anga Road,
Waitomo Caves Village, 3943

Tel (07) 878 7641
or Freephone 0800 465 762
Fax (07) 878 7466
waitomocavesguestlodge@xtra.co.nz
www.waitomocavesguestlodge.co.nz

Double/Twin $100 - $130
Single $80 (Continental breakfast)
Children 0 - 14 years $15
Extra adult $25
Visa MC Eftpos accepted
Children welcome
Internet available
7 Queen 1 Twin 9 Single (8 bdrm)
A variety of double, twin and family rooms
Bathrooms: 7 Ensuite 1 Private There is a bath in the private bathroom

Right in Waitomo Caves Village, opposite award-winning Huhu Café, next to the store and just a short walk to the Waitomo Glowworm Caves. Each ensuite studio unit has a private entrance and beautiful views of the cottage garden and surrounding hills. There is Wi-Fi access and a laptop computer available for use by guests. Expect a warm welcome from Gypsy, the family dog, as well as Colin and Janet, who can give you knowledgeable advice, make bookings for local activities and help with your itinerary.

Te Kuiti - Waitomo District *2 km N of Te Kuiti*
Simply the Best B&B *B&B Farmstay*

Margaret & Graeme Churstain
129 Gadsby Road,
RD 5,
Te Kuiti

Tel (07) 878 8191
or 027 666 9343
Fax (07) 878 5949
enquiry@simplythebestbnb.co.nz
www.simplythebestbnb.co.nz

Double/Twin $100 S
ingle $50 (Continental breakfast)
Children negotiable
Pet cats on property
Children welcome
2 Queen 1 Twin (3 bdrm)
Spacious and comfortable
Bathrooms: 1 Ensuite
1 Private 1 Guest share

Just 2.5hours from Auckland Airport our peaceful farmlet, signposted off SH3, northern end of Te Kuiti, we welcome you to 'Simply the Best' way to break a journey or to begin or end your New Zealand adventure. Happy to share our knowledge of the local area, Waitomo Caves, Blackwater rafting 10minutes away. Our comfortable 1 level home is unique for easy access from all rooms to decks overlooking stunning rural views. We offer secure parking, restaurants nearby, and 'above all' a place to remember.

Pio Pio - Waitomo District *19 km S of Te Kuiti*

Carmel Farm *B&B Homestay Farmstay*

Barbara & Leo Anselmi
1832 SH3, PO Box 93, Pio Pio

Tel (07) 877 8130
or 0800 877 813
Fax (07) 877 8130
Carmelfarms@xtra.co.nz

Double/Twin $120
Single $80
(Continental breakfast)
Dinner $25pp
Children and pets welcome
2 King/Twin 4 Single (4 bdrm)
Bathrooms: 1 Ensuite 1 Guest share

Barbara and Leo Anselmi operate a 2000 acre sheep, beef and dairy farm. You will be welcomed into an established homestead set in a picturesque limestone valley.

You will be treated to delicious home-cooked meals and the warmth of our friendship.

Whether mustering mobs of cattle and sheep, viewing the milking of 550 Friesian cows, driving around the rolling hills on the 4 wheeled farm-bike, basking in the sun by the pool or enjoying the gardens, you will feel relaxed and rejuvenated. Whether you seek excitement or tranquility, Carmel Farm is the perfect retreat.

We are ideally located for you to explore many other attractions. We are adjacent to a beautiful 18 hole golf course which welcomes visitors. The property is a short distance from black water rafting and canoeing activities, The Lost World Cavern, and the famous Waitomo Caves. Nearby are bush walks, waterfalls, and the home of the rare kokako bird. The Mangaotaki stream is a mecca for the trout enthusiast. We can help to arrange activities for people of all ages and interests; from garden visits to horse riding. (P.S. In the TV lounge there is Sky for those all-important rugby matches.) Please let us know your preference.

We are 140km from Rotorua/Taupo. Directions: Travel 19km south of Te Kuiti on SH3 towards Piopio. Carmel Farm is on the right. We can arrange to pick up from Otorohanga, Te Kuiti or Waitomo, if required.

Coromandel Peninsula
Waiheke Island
Coromandel
Kuaotunu
Opito Bay
Whitianga
Hahei
Cooks Beach
Hot Water Beach
Beachlands
Whitford
Clevedon
Papakura
Tairua
Te Puru
Kaiaua
Thames
25
Bombay
Whangamata
Mercer
2
Paeroa
Karangahake
Waihi
Waihi Beach
Kilometres
0   20
Miles
0   12
Coromandel

Thames *6.4 km E of Thames*
Mountain Top B&B *Homestay*
Elizabeth McCracken & Allan Berry
452 Kauaeranga Valley Road,
RD 2,
Thames

Tel (07) 868 9662
Fax (07) 868 9662
mountain.top@slingshot.co.nz

Double/Twin $115 - $120
Single $80
(Full breakfast)
Children half price
Dinner $30-$35
Visa MC Diners Amex accepted
Children and pets welcome
1 Queen 2 Twin (2 bdrm)
Bathrooms: 1 Guest share

Allan and I grow mandarins, native trees and raise coloured sheep on a small organic farm. Our private, peaceful, guest wing with lounge, TV and extensive library has bedrooms and decks with superb views overlooking river, forest swimming pools and mountains. Nearby Forest Park has wonderful walking tracks. We have a productive, rambly garden, Jack Russell Roly, cat Priscilla. No cell phone coverage - best to phone mornings or evenings. We love entertaining and cooking for people, mostly from farm produce. Let's look after you.
664

Thames *8 km E of Thames*
Huia Lodge *B&B*
Celia & Murray Newby
589 Kauaeranga Valley Road,
Thames

Tel (07) 868 6557
Fax (07) 868 6557
celian@wave.co.nz
www.thames-info.co.nz/HuiaLodge

Double/Twin $120
Single $80
(Full breakfast)
Extra person $40
Visa MC accepted
2 Queen 2 Single (2 bdrm)
Spacious suites ,
Queen and single beds, ensuite
Bathrooms: 2 Ensuite

Each unit has an ensuite and tea/coffee facilities. Relax and enjoy the tranquility of the valley, hike in the nearby Forest Park or circle the Peninsula to view the famous Coromandel scenery. We enjoy meeting travellers, love the rural lifestyle, grow fruit/vegetables, and enjoy the peace with our pet dog on our 3 acre paradise. Turn at BP corner (south end of township)into Banks Street then follow Parawai Road into the valley. We're 8km from BP. Just 1 1/2 hours from Auckland.
2309

Thames *3 km S of Thames*
Totara Valley Barns *B&B*

Shona & Bruz MacGregor
65 Totara Valley Road,
RD 1, Thames

Tel (07) 868 9730
or 027 310 3644
info@totarabarns.co.nz
www.totarabarns.co.nz

Double/Twin $125 - $155
Single $125
(Continental breakfast)
Dinner $35 Delicious Kiwi meals
or order a BBQ Box cook yourself
Visa MC accepted
Children welcome Internet available
2 Queen (2 bdrm)
Comfortable Queen beds
with own ensuite
Bathrooms: 2 Ensuite

Unique, quality accommodation in a beautiful mature garden setting. 90 minutes south of Auckland Airport, Totara Barns is perfect for a relaxing weekend or as a base to explore the Thames/Coromandels exciting attractions. Separate guest accommodation with ensuites and spacious guest lounge/kitchenette. Enjoy the quiet surroundings, safe off-road parking, a generous continental breakfast and largel garden to unwind in at days end. Evening meal available using home-grown produce. Your local hosts, Shona and Bruz, assure you of true Kiwi hospitality.

3389

Thames *1 km N of Information Centre*
Ocean View on Thames *B&B Homestay Apartment with Kitchen*

Julie & Steve McLellan
509 Upper Albert Street,
Thames, 3500

Tel (07) 868 3588
sjmclellan@xtra.co.nz
retreat4u.co.nz

Double/Twin $160 - $180
Single $160
(Full breakfast)
Extra persons in apartment $35 each
Visa MC Eftpos accepted
Pet free home
Children welcome
2 Queen 1 Twin (3 bdrm)
1 Queen in B&B
1 Queen, 1 Twin in apartment
Bathrooms: 2 Private
Private in home Private in apartment

Peace, tranquility, wonderful views and a very warm welcome await you at Ocean View, with its beautifully landscaped gardens and array of native birds. Thames is a great base from which to explore the stunning and varied scenery of the Coromandel Peninsula, or just enjoy a quiet relaxing break. Ten-minute walk to town centre, restaurants and the coast. Facilities include: off-road parking, laundry service, free WiFi, barbecue, outdoor spa pool with sea view, private lounge with TV/DVD, fridge, tea/coffee, safe, hairdryer.   4058

Thames *2.5 km SE of Post Office*
The Heights *Luxury B&B*
Vicky & Phil English
300 Grafton Road, Thames, 3500

Tel (07) 868 9925 or 0800 68 9925 (NZ)
info@theheights.co.nz
www.theheights.co.nz

Double/Twin $199 - $230
Single $189 - $215
(Full breakfast)
Dinner $50 - $60 per person by pre-arrangement
Free wireless internet
Visa MC Diners Amex accepted
Not suitable for children
2 King (2 bdrm)
2 King bedrooms, one can be reconfigured as 2 singles
Bathrooms: 2 Ensuite

Photos can't do justice to the breathtaking panoramic views of sea, mountains and countryside at The Heights.

Relax in luxury with your own private deck or patio, king bed, ensuite, tea making, fridge, SKY TV, DVD, Internet, and all the special touches for a memorable stay. Hosts Vicky and Phil love sharing with you all the best spots to visit, and our friendly cats add to the welcome.

The 100 km of views from the deck from Te Moana are worth the short climb of stairs, while garden-view Te Koru features its own fireplace.

Only 1.5 hours from Auckland International Airport, take time to pamper yourself at The Heights. Qualmark Enviro Silver award winner.
@ Home New Zealand Qualmark 4 1/2 stars Qualmark Enviro Silver award for our sustainability programme.3684

Thames *5 km S of Thames*
Thorold Country House *Luxury B&B Homestay Cottage with Kitchen*

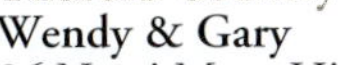

Wendy & Gary
36 Ngati Maru Highway, Kopu,
Thames, 3578

Tel 07 868 8480 or 021 253 6746
thorold@xtra.co.nz
www.thoroldcountryhouse.co.nz

Double/Twin $195 - $250
Single $150 (Full breakfast)
Dinner by prior arrangement,
Special diets catered for
Garden Cottage $250 double
Extra person $50, max 4
Visa MC accepted
Pet free home Children welcome
Internet available
2 Queen 2 Twin (4 bdrm)
Queen & Twin in Homestay and Garden Cottage
Bathrooms: 2 Private
Private bathroom in both Homestay and Garden Cottage

Relax in our private, peaceful, quality country home situated on 6 acres just 70 minutes from Auckland Airport. The ideal base to explore the beautiful Coromandel Peninsula. Views extend over the Coromandel Hills and Firth of Thames. Luxury guest rooms open onto wide verandas with private seating areas overlooking park like grounds. The Garden Cottage is a spacious home from home with large lounge, dining room, kitchen, bathroom, BBQ. Tennis court, secluded swimming pool set in subtropical gardens, WiFi, open log fire for cooler evenings.

Thames *1.5 km NW of THAMES*
Cotswold Cottage Country House *Luxury B&B Homestay*

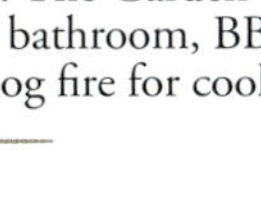

Graham & Jacqueline Hamlett
46 Maramarahi Road,
Totara, Thames

Tel (07) 868 6306
or Freephone 0800 111 175
Fax (07) 868 6202
cotswoldcot@gmail.com
www.cotswoldcottage.co.nz

Double/Twin $130 - $200
Single $100 - $165
(Full breakfast)
Not suitable for children under 10
Host dinners $40-$50 and small bar
Guest BBQ /special BBQ dinners
Visa MC accepted
Pet free home
Internet Available
3 Queen Double 1 Twin /Superking (4 bdrm)
Bathrooms: 3 Ensuite 1 Private Neatherwood suite private double spar bath, sitting area.

Relax and unwind in our lovingly restored 1920's villa just one hour from Auckland 3 minutes from historic Thames A very warm welcome awaits you from hosts who love to share local knowledge and help make your stay memorable . With breath taking sea, river and mountain views. Wi fi internet, laundry service, an outside hot spa pool and private off street car parking. Generous gourmet breakfasts and home baking inc. Host guest dinners and speciality BBQ nights by arrangement.   Heritage Inns Qualmark 4 1/2 stars   4235

Thames *0 km N of*
Miranda Homestead *B&B*
Ellie Vette
397 Front Miranda Road,
RD 6,
Thames, 3576

Tel (07) 867 3377
or 021 866 332
ellie.vette@hotmail.com

Double/Twin $150
Single $100
(Full breakfast by arrangement)
Dinner by arrangement
Visa MC accepted
Pet free home
Not suitable for children
Internet available
1 King 1 Queen 1 Twin

In a picturesque countryside an hour from Auckland, you are assured of an hospitable welcome from Ellie, who was an international flight attendant and is a registered nurse. From the Miranda Homestead you can explore the abundant bird life and flight of the godwit on the Seabird Coast; relax in the famous Miranda Hot Pools 2kms away; capture the character of Kaiaua; savour local fish and chips; walk the regional parks; discover the beautiful Coromandel Peninsula. Sky TV. Dinner Arranged at the Old Miranda Church.

Thames Coast - Te Puru *12 km N of Thames*
Te Puru Coast Bed & Breakfast *B&B Homestay Cottage with Kitchen*
Bill & Paula Olsen
2A Tatahi Street, Te Puru,
Thames Coast, Thames

Tel (07) 868 2866
or 027 656 6058
Fax (07) 868 2866
tepurucoastbnb@xtra.co.nz
www.tepurucoastbnb.co.nz

Double/Twin $120 - $140
Single $100 - $100
(Full breakfast)
Children $2 under 12
Dinner $35pp,
Includes New Zealand wine or beer
Cottage $140 (2 people)
Pet free home
Children welcome
1 Queen 1 Double 1 Twin 2 Single (3 bdrm)
2 bedrooms in B&B, 1 bedroom in cottage
Bathrooms: 1 Ensuite 2 Private

Welcome to the beautiful Thames Coast. Our modern comfortable home is 80 metres off the main coast road. Guest lounge has TV, books and tea & coffee facilities. You may choose a continental or cooked breakfast and evening meals are on request ($35.00pp) with complimentary New Zealand wine or beer. Our large deck is yours to enjoy or take a 2 minute walk to the beach. A warm welcome greets you on arrival with tea or coffee and homemade cookies.   @
Home New Zealand 1957

Coromandel *10 km S of Coromandel*
AJ's Homestay *B&B Homestay*
Annette & Ray Hintz
24 Kowhai Drive,
Te Kouma,
RD,
Coromandel

Tel (07) 866 7057
or 027 458 1624
Fax (07) 866 7057
rm.aj.hintz@actrix.co.nz

Double/Twin $125 - $145
Single $95 - $110
(Special breakfast)
Dinner $40-- $45
Visa MC accepted
Children welcome
1 King/Twin 2 Queen
1 Single (3 bdrm)
Bathrooms: 1 Ensuite 1 Private 1 Family share

AJ's Homestay with panoramic sea views overlooking the Coromandel Harbour, spectacular sunsets. A 5 minute walk to a safe swimming beach. Our games room has a billiard and table tennis table. Wireless internet available. Dinner by arrangement. Directions: Thames coast main road (SH25) approximately 50 minutes. At the bottom of the last hill overlooking the Coromandel Harbour. Turn sharp left, at the Te Kouma Road sign. Travel past the boat ramp, next turn left. Kowhai Drive, we are number 24.   1370

Coromandel *3 km S of Coromandel*
Jacaranda Lodge *B&B*
Robin Münch
3195 Tiki Road,
Coromandel, RD 1

Tel (07) 866 8002
or 021 252 6892
Fax (07) 866 8002
info@jacarandalodge.co.nz
www.jacarandalodge.co.nz

Double/Twin $125 - $165
Single $75 - $140
(Special breakfast)
Visa MC accepted
Pet free home
Not suitable for children
4 Queen 1 Twin 1 Single (6 bdrm)
Bathrooms: 2 Ensuite 1 Private
1 Guest share Spotlessly clean

Robin invites you to share her spacious home set on 6 acres of tranquil country paradise. Located 3km south of Coromandel Town, Jacaranda Lodge provides the perfect escape: relax in one of the guest lounges; stroll around the delightful gardens; experience Coromandel's walks, unique attractions and spectacular coastline. Delicious continental breakfasts include fresh organic produce from Jacaranda's orchard. Large, comfortable bedrooms. Wireless internet connection. Fully equipped guest kitchen (additional charge may apply). Special dietary needs can be catered for, including kosher. Sleep, eat, enjoy.   2010: Check that the surname has symbol above the 'u'.2206

Coromandel - Te Kouma *8 km S of Coromandel*
Te Kouma B&B *B&B Separate Suite Apartment with Kitchen*

Kurt & Jo Muller
50 Puriri Road,
Te Kouma,
Coromandel

Tel (07) 866 7971
or 021 263 5533
Fax (07) 866 7971
ko_jm_muller@xtra.co.nz

Double/Twin $130 - $150
Single $120 - $120
(Continental breakfast)
Children welcome
Lots of dinner options in Coromandel
Pet free home
Children welcome
2 Queen 2 Twin (3 bdrm)
Queens have ensuites
Twins share bathroom
Bathrooms: 2 Ensuite 1 Family share

Our well appointed home has the best views in the area. Kurt speaks German and makes delicious wholemeal breads, served for your breakfast with home preserved fruits and jams. Jo collects pacific seashells and old china. We live in a very tranquil place, abounding with bellbirds, tuis and pigeons, over looking Coromandel Harbour. Coromandel town 10 minutes North. Thames 45 minutes South.   3666

Coromandel Town *0.5 km S of Coromandel Town*
The Green House B&B *Luxury B&B*

Malcolm & Denise Stone
505 Tiki Road,
Coromandel Town

Tel (07) 866 7303
or 027 232 6396
Fax (07) 866 7303
m.d.stone@slingshot.co.nz
www.greenhousebandb.co.nz

Double/Twin $140 - $165
Single $100 - $125
(Special breakfast)
Visa MC accepted
Not suitable for children
Internet available
1 King/Twin 1 King 1 Queen
1 Double (3 bdrm)
2 Guest rooms are upstairs, 1 downstairs
Bathrooms: 3 New ensuite

This relaxed home has extremely comfortable facilities, stunning views over hills and sea, and is minutes walk to the excellent restaurants of Coromandel Town. Upstairs, the dedicated guest lounge has a lovely airy feeling with vaulted ceiling and the folowing facilities: complimentary tea/coffee, fridge, TV, computer + (Wi-Fi), book swap etc. The bedrooms, one with private deck, the other sea views, are separated by the guest lounge. Both rooms have excellent ensuite facilities. Generous hospitality is offered by Malcolm & Denise making your stay memorable.   @ Home New Zealand 170

Coromandel *0.5 km E of Coromandel*
Breakaway B&B *B&B Units Separated from House*

Michael & Ross
39 Whangapoua Road,
Coromandel

Tel (07) 866 8310
or 027 363 9960
Fax (07) 866 8310
info@breakaway-bb.co.nz
www.breakaway-bb.co.nz

Double/Twin $165 - $165
Single $165 - $165
(Continental breakfast)
Each extra person $25
Visa MC Eftpos accepted
Not suitable for children
Pets welcome
2 Queen 2 Twin (4 bdrm)
All units are seperate from the home and private
Bathrooms: 4 Ensuite 4 Private
Unit 2, twin,l arge shower room ideal for wheel chair use

Allow time in your travels to stop with us. Michael & Ross invite you to a quiet and relaxing stay in their rural country setting in park-like grounds. Just a 1 minute drive or a 10 minute level walk to Coromandel town which offers an excellent variety of restaurants and cafes. Also a good selection of quality craft shops. A continental breakfast is served in the conservatory overlooking the garden with views of the Coromandel Harbour. The fishing is great !!! Pets are welcome by arrangement.   471   Wheelchair logo

Kuaotunu *17 km NE of Whitianga*
Kaeppeli's *B&B Farmstay*

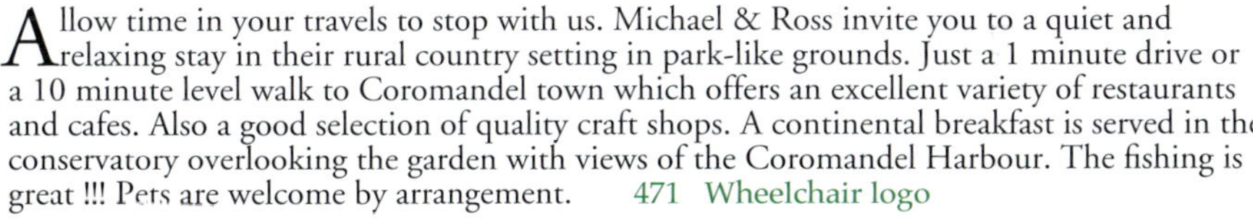

Jill Kaeppeli
40 Gray Ave, Kuaotunu,
Whitianga, 3592

Tel (07) 866 2445
or 027 656 3442
Fax (07) 866 2445
paradise@kaeppelis.co.nz
www.kaeppelis.co.nz

Double/Twin $130 - $190
Single $95 - $140
(Full breakfast)
Children negotiable
Dinner $40 by arrangement
Visa MC Eftpos accepted
Children and pets welcome
2 King 4 Single (4 bdrm)
Bright sunny cosy rooms with glorious views
Bathrooms: 4 Ensuite Bath & Shower with ocean views

Unique peaceful, secluded, haven with stunning sea, bush and rural views above the Pacific Ocean. Relax, unwind, enjoy the natural beauty that surrounds you. Comfortable sunny rooms with private decks and entrances. Dinner by arrangement using local mostly organic produce. Self catering option also available. Panoramic gazebo dining room. Clean, safe, sandy unspoilt beaches, kayaking, tennis, 2 hr bush walk from door, horsetrekking, fishing, golf, arts and crafts. Ideal for exploring Coromandel. Swiss/ German spoken. Children welcome. Pets to pamper. Our view? Simply the best.   @ Home New Zealand   513

Kuaotunu *16 km N of Whitianga*
@ The Peacheys *B&B Homestay Homestay*

Yvonne & Dale Peachey
15 Kawhero Drive,
Kuaotunu, RD 2,
Whitianga

Tel (07) 866 5290
or 027 206 7221
Fax (07) 866 4592
DYPeachey@xtra.co.nz
www.thepeacheys.co.nz

Double/Twin $140
Single $120
(Special breakfast)
Visa MC accepted
Not suitable for children
1 King/Twin 1 Queen
3 Single (2 bdrm)
Spacious rooms with comfortable beds
Bathrooms: 2 Ensuite

We welcome you to our piece of paradise on the Coromandel Peninsular. Seven safe beaches all close by, & ours is 100 metres from your spacious & well appointed room. Short & picturesque drives to Whitianga & Coromandel & local attractions, cafes & resturuants.. Laundry & Bicycles available. We have a very shy cat, Chelsey. We will enjoy meeting you & welcome you to our home.   649   Wheelchair logo

---

Kuaotunu *17 km N of Whitianga*
Drift In B&B *B&B Homestay*

Yvonne & Peppe Thompson
16 Gray Avenue,
Kuaotunu, RD 2, Whitianga

Tel (07) 866 4321
or 027 245 3632
driftin@paradise.net.nz
www.coromandelfun.co.nz/driftin

Double/Twin $135
Single $75
(Full breakfast)
Children negotiable
Dinner main and dessert $30
Visa MC accepted
Children welcome
1 Queen 2 Single (2 bdrm)
Reading lights, tea and coffee tray in
room comfortable beds
Bathrooms: 1 Guest share with bath and shower

Welcome is assured. This tranquil comfortable modern cedar home is designed to take full advantage of the sun and breathtaking island views by day and moonlit night. An unique beach theme pervades house and garden, small dog in residence. Just a minute stroll to white sand beaches for safe swimming and fossicking. Breakfast is a memorable occasion with sight and sounds of birds and sea complementing an excellent range of home cooking. Drift in, relax and enjoy this unique and special part of New Zealand.   1324

Opito Bay *27 km E of Whitianga*
At Opito *B&B*

Max & Bev
13 Stewart Place, Opito Bay,
RD 2, Whitianga
Tel (07) 866 0317
or 027 418 5588
max-bev@xtra.co.nz
www.atopito.co.nz

Double/Twin $165
Single $130
(Full breakfast)
Children $20
Dinner $35 by arrangement
Visa MC accepted
Pet free home Children welcome
1 Queen (1 bdrm)
Plus sofa bed in guest room
Bathrooms: 1 Private Shower over 'shub' (mini-bath)

A warm kiwi welcome awaits you with complimentary tea & coffee and home baking on the deck. Our clean comfortable B&B offers you your own entrance,queen room, bathroom, guest area with sofa-bed, fridge, toaster, electric jug etc. Enjoy soaking in our spa after a swim or walk along Opito's beautiful, safe, white sandy beach, just 2 minutes stroll away. Restaurants at Whitianga or Matarangi or join us for a home cooked dinner or you may choose to self-cater on the BBQ. Laundry facilities available.   @ Home New Zealand 4064

Whitianga *1 km S of Whitianga*
Cosy Cat Cottage *B&B Cottage with Kitchen*

Gordon Pearce
41 South Highway (town end),
Whitianga
Tel (07) 866 4488
cosycat@xtra.co.nz
www.cosycat.co.nz

Double/Twin $95 - $125
Single $80 - $90
(Full breakfast)
Cottage $90-$180
Visa MC accepted
Children welcome
Internet available
2 Queen 1 Double 1 Single (3 bdrm)
2 queen rooms and 1 single room
with caty decor
Bathrooms: 2 Ensuite 1 Private

Welcome to our picturesque 2 storied cottage filled with feline memorabilia! Relax with complimentary tea or coffee served on the veranda or in the guest lounge. Enjoy a good nights rest in comfortable beds and choose a variety of treats from our breakfast blackboard menu. You will probably like to meet Honey the cat or perhaps visit the cat hotel in the garden. A separate cottage is available with queen beds, bathrooms and kitchen. Friendly helpful service is assured - hope to see you soon!

Whitianga *4 km N of Whitianga*
At Parkland Place *Luxury B&B*
Maria & Guy Clark
14 Parkland Place, Whitianga, 3510

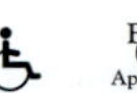

Tel (07) 866 4987
or 021 404 923
Fax (07) 866 4946
parklandplace@wave.co.nz
www.atparklandplace.co.nz

Double/Twin $165 - $200
(Continental breakfast)
Children negotiable
Dinner by arrangement
Visa MC accepted
Pet free home
Children welcome
Internet Available
1 King/Twin 4 King
2 Single (5 bdrm)
Bathrooms: 5 Ensuite

Enjoy European hospitality in Whitianga's most luxurious hotel style B&B. Maria, a ships chef from Poland and NZ husband Guy, a master mariner, will make your stay a memorable experience. A single level purpose built house with private entry for guests. Large luxuriously appointed rooms with ensuite, quality linen, TV and writing desk. Magnificent continental breakfast. Superb dinner or BBQ by arrangement. Sunny, private picturesque outdoor area with spa pool. Large guest lounge with refreshment bar & satellite TV.   180
Wheelchair logo

Cooks Beach *17 km NE of Tairua*
Mercury Orchard *B&B Cottage with Kitchen*
Heather and Barry Scott
141 Purangi Road,
Cooks Beach,
Whitianga

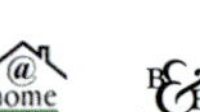

Tel (07) 866 3119
relax@mercuryorchard.co.nz
www.mercuryorchard.co.nz

Double/Twin $165 - $185
Single $120 - $140
(Full breakfast)
Children $20
Fig Tree Cottage $185
Paua Bach 185
Visa MC accepted
Children welcome
1 King 1 Queen 2 Single (3 bdrm)
Bathrooms: 2 Ensuite

Paua Bach and Fig Tree Cottage are nestled amongst 5 acres of peaceful country gardens and orchard. Self- contained country style luxury with french doors opening onto your private deck. Crisp cotton bed linen, bathrobes, fresh fruit, flowers and candles. Special to the Bach, an old fashioned outdoor bath. Enjoy a Mercury Orchard full breakfast while listening to the birdsong. Barbeque your evening meal Kiwi style. Hot Water Beach, Cooks Beach and Cathedral Cove are 7-8 minutes drive. We share our home with two small dogs.

Whitianga - Coroglen *14 km S of Whitianga*
Coroglen Lodge *B&B Farmstay Separate Suite*

Wendy & Nigel Davidson
2221 State Highway 25,
RD 1,
Whitianga, 3591

Tel (07) 866 3225
Fax (07) 866 3235
info@coroglenlodge.co.nz
www.coroglenlodge.co.nz

Double/Twin $120
Single $80
(Continental breakfast)
Visa MC accepted
Children welcome
2 Queen 2 Single (3 bdrm)
Bathrooms: 2 Guest share

Coroglen Lodge is situated on 17 acres of farmland with cattle, sheep and alpacas. Nestled in the hills with views of the Coromandel Ranges, this is rural tranquillity. Halfway between Whitianga township and Hot Water Beach there is easy access to both areas and all attractions. Guest area is separate, relaxed, and spacious with a large sunny lounge area for your comfort. Wendy spins and knits with wool from her sheep and alpacas, and Nigel has a collection of vintage tractors.
1200

Coromandel

Whitianga *6 km N of Whitianga*
On The Beach *B&B Homestay*

Gordon and Diana Barnaby
66 State Highway 25,
Wharekaho,
Simpson's Beach,
RD 2,
Whitianga, 3592

Tel 07 866 2433
or 027 245 7496
info@onthebeach
whitianga.co.nz
www.onthebeachwhitianga.co.nz

Double/Twin $120 - $180
(Continental breakfast)
Children up to 12 yrs free
Dinner by request
Visa MC Amex accepted
Children welcome
Internet available
2 King 1 Queen 1 Single (3 bdrm)
Fully equipt
Bathrooms: 3 Ensuite

Diana and Gordon look forward to exceeding your expectations when you choose to stay with them. They have travelled extensively and are aware of what their guests would expect when they are away from home. They look forward to making you welcome and to fulfil your needs.
@ Home New Zealand 4153 Wheelchair logo

Hahei *38 km S of Whitianga*
The Church *Separate Suite Cottage No Kitchen Cottage with Kitchen*

Richard Agnew & Karen Blair
87 Beach Road, Hahei,
RD 1, Whitianga

Tel (07) 866 3533 or 0274 596 877
Fax (07) 866 3055
info@thechurchhahei.co.nz
www.thechurchhahei.co.nz

Double/Twin $110 - $210
Single $110 - $210
(Breakfast by arrangement)
Children $10-$15
Extra Adult $20
Dinner Menu a la carte
Visa MC Eftpos accepted
Children and pets welcome
Internet available
14 Queen 1 Double 12 Twin 13 Single (15 bdrm)
Bathrooms: 11 Ensuite 1 Family share

The Church, Hahei's unique accommodation and dining experience. The Church building provides a character licensed restaurant for delicious evening meals.11 cosy,simple wooden cottages and house scattered through delightful bush and gardens offer a range of accommodation and tariffs. Ensuites,microwave,toaster, fridge, tea and coffee facilities. Some cottages and house fully self-contained with woodstoves for winter.Breakfast tray by arrangement. Conference facilities. Enjoy nearby wonders of Cathedral Cove, Hot Water Beach, and the Coromandel Peninsula. Seasonal rates.Winter specials. Smoking outside. 89
Wheelchair logo

Tairua *45 km E of Thames*
Harbour View Lodge *Luxury B&B*

Eve and Alan Roper
179 Main Road,
Tairua

Tel (07) 864 7040
or 0274 797 851
Fax 07 864 7042
info@harbourviewlodge.co.nz
www.harbourviewlodge.co.nz

Double/Twin $190 - $230
Single $160 - $200
(Full breakfast)
Visa MC accepted
Not suitable for children
Internet available
1 King/Twin 2 Queen (3 bdrm)
Bathrooms: 3 Ensuite

Peace & tranquility is yours when you stay in one of our luxury rooms with ensuite. Enjoy the swimming pool and garden,or try out our kayaks. Start your day with a sumptuous breakfast while enjoying the breathtaking views of Tairua Harbour & Paku Mountain. A short stroll will take you to cafes, restaurants, shops and safe beaches. We can also help you plan your daily activities. We have friendly pets for you to enjoy.
Qualmark 4 stars 4294

Whangamata *.2 km N of town centre*
Sandy Rose Bed & Breakfast *B&B*

Shirley & Murray Calman
122 Hetherington Road
(Corner Hetherington &
Rutherford Roads),
Whangamata 3620

Tel (07) 865 6911
sandyrose@whangamata.co.nz
sandyrose.whangamata.co.nz

Double/Twin $150
Single $110
(Special breakfast)
Visa MC accepted
Pet free home
Not suitable for children
2 King/Twin 1 Queen
1 Double (3 bdrm)
Bathrooms: 3 Ensuite

A charming B&B in the Coromandel Peninsula's popular holiday destination, we have 3 tastefully decorated guest bedrooms, all with ensuite bathrooms, comfortable beds and in-room TVs. Complimentary tea & coffee is available in the guest lounge. We are ideally located, close to Whangamata's shops, cafes and restaurants, and an easy stroll to the surf beach, harbour and wharf. Enjoy our extensive special breakfast and use our home as a base to relax and enjoy the natural attractions that Whangamata and area has to offer.
1481   Wheelchair logo

Whangamata *2 km S of Town Centre*
Kotuku *B&B Homestay*

Linda & Peter Bigge
422 Otahu Road,
Whangamata

Tel (07) 865 6128
or 027 358 1227
Fax (07) 865 6128
bookings@kotukuhomestay.co.nz
www.kotukuhomestay.co.nz

Double/Twin $100 - $140
Single $80 - $100
(Full breakfast)
Visa MC accepted
3 Queen (3 bdrm)
Bathrooms: 3 Ensuite

We offer comfortable homestay accommodation in a purpose built home. Rosie, our friendly dog and Elizabeth, the cat, will give you a warm welcome too! Relax in the spacious lounge or private patio, take an outdoor spa. Kotuku is situated at the quieter end of Whangamata, just a short stroll to the lovely Otahu Estuary Reserve; ideal for walking, swimming and kayaking. Golf courses(two), shops,cafes a short drive and the surf beach an easy ten minute walk. Do use our bikes and kayaks.
@ Home New Zealand 2174

Waihi *1 km S of Waihi*
West Wind Gardens *B&B Homestay*

Josie & Merv Scott
58 Adams Street,
Waihi 3610

Tel (07) 863 7208
westwindgarden@xtra.co.nz
www.athomenz.org.nz

Double/Twin $90
Single $50 (
Continental breakfast)
Children $20
Dinner $20
Visa MC accepted
Children welcome
1 Double 2 Single (2 bdrm)
Bathrooms: 1 Guest share

We offer a friendly restful smoke-free stay in our modern home and garden. Waihi is the gate way to both the Coromandel and the Bay of Plenty with its beautiful beaches. Waihi is a historic town with a vintage railway and a working gold mine discovered 1878 closed 1952. Reopened in 1989 as a open-cast mine. Beach 10 minutes away, beautiful walks, golf courses, trout fishing. Enjoy a home cooked meal or sample our restaurants. Our interests are gardening, dancing and travel.
@ Home New Zealand 326   Wheelchair logo

Waihi *2 km SW of Waihi*
Ashtree House *B&B rural b@bplus private unit*

Anne & Bill Ashdown
20 Riflerange Road,
Waihi

Tel (07) 863 6448
or 027 492 8915
Fax (07) 863 6443
ash.tree@clear.net.nz
ash.tree@clear.net.nz

Double/Twin $100
Single $60 (Full breakfast)
Children under 10 $10
Garden Unit $40pp
Children welcome
Smoking in Garden
Internet Available
1 Queen 1 Double 2 Single (3 bdrm)
Bathrooms: 2 Private 1 Guest share
One in house bathroom

Modern brick home set on the side of a hill with extensive views and access to trout river. Private guest wing comprising 2 double bedrooms, large private bathroom with shower and bath. Guest lounge with TV, stereo and large selection of New Zealand books. Laundry and separate toilet. 8 acres, large attractive garden and pond area. 1 house dog. Situated 2 minutes to centre of Waihi, complete privacy and quiet guaranteed. Self-contained unit with wheelchair facilities. 5 minutes to beautiful Karangahake Gorge.

Waihi *0.5 km SW of Waihi*
Chez Nous *B&B Homestay*

Sara Parish
41 Seddon Avenue,
Waihi, 3610

Tel (07) 863 7538
or 027 644 5562
sarap@slingshot.co.nz

Double/Twin $65
Single $45
(Continental breakfast)
Children $20
Dinner $20pp by arrangement
Visa MC accepted
Children welcome
Internet available
1 Queen 1 Twin (2 bdrm)
Bathrooms: 1 Guest share

Enjoy a relaxed and friendly atmosphere in a spacious, modern home in an attractive garden setting. Shops and restaurants are within easy walking distance. Discover past and present gold mining activities (tours available), sandy surf beaches, bush walks, 18 hole golf course, art, craft and wine trails. Waihi is an ideal stopover for the traveller who wants to explore the Coromandel Peninsula, Bay of Plenty and Waikato.
1605

Waihi *1 km NE of Waihi*
Dragonfly Garden Bed and Breakfast *B&B*

Bert and Kathy
11 Parry Palm Ave,
Waihi, 2981

Tel (07) 863 9034
or 027 236 1997
wattsdue@paradise.net.nz
www.dragonflygardenbnb.co.nz

Double/Twin $130 - $150
Single $90
(Full breakfast)
Dinner BBQ, outside garden oven
Not suitable for children
Pets welcome
1 Queen 1 Twin (2 bdrm)
Bathrooms: 2 Ensuite

Enjoy these charming and comfortable detached bedrooms with ensuites which are ideally situated amoungst 1 1/2 acres of mature trees and gardens with fishponds. We offer laundry facilities, outdoor garden oven, fireplace and BBQ area. Situated 1 minute from Waihi Centre, 8 minutes from Karangahake george and 15 minutes from the beach. This area offers something for everyone. Your friendly hosts Bert and Kathy and Roco (the Tibetan Terrier) look forward to looking after you.
3802

Waihi Beach *11 km E of Waihi*
Waterfront Homestay *Apartment with Kitchen*

Kay & John Morgan
17 The Esplanade
(off Hinemoa Street),
Waihi Beach

Tel (07) 863 4342
or 021 170 5058
Fax (07) 863 4342
k.morgan@xtra.co.nz

Double/Twin $120 - $150
(Breakfast by arrangement)
Self catering breakfast option
Visa MC accepted
Pet free home
Children welcome
1 Queen 3 Single (2 bdrm)
Bathrooms: 1 Private

Waterfront Homestay. Fully self-contained, 2 double bedrooms. Situated on beach at north end.Suitable for 2 couples or small family group. Unit is lower floor of family home. Walk from front door directly onto an uncrowded sandy beach. Safe ocean swimming, surfcasting, surfing and coastal walks. Restaurants within walking distance or use facilities provided with accommodation. Waterfront Homestay is situated close to popular scenic coastal walks to Orokawa and Homunga Bays. Tariff $120 - 150, bed and breakfast. Hosts John & Kay Morgan.

Waihi Beach *12 km N of Katikati*
The Candy's B&B *B&B Cottage with Kitchen*

Gloria & Neil Candy
43 Athenree Road,
Athenree,
Waihi Beach

Tel (07) 863 1159
Fax (07) 863 1196
neil.candy@vodafone.co.nz

Double/Twin $130 - $135
Single $80 - $100
(Continental breakfast)
Dinner $32pp
2 King 2 Twin (3 bdrm)
1 Bedroom Cottage self contained ,
2 at main house
Bathrooms: 1 Ensuite 1 Private
1 Guest share
Bath available at the B&B

Take time out: relax. Our modern home is on three acres, with beautiful harbour views: each room has a private patio. Walk to Athenree Hotpools, drive 3 minutes to Waihi Surf Beach, 10 minutes south to Katikati, 2 Local Golf Courses, Morton Estate Winery, . 10 minutes north to Waihi Goldmine, walks and excellent restaurants. Neil loves fishing, and Gloria loves crafts. Meals on request. This is paradise and our city pets agree. New 1 bedroom cottage self contained no meals supplied.

Waihi Beach *11 km E of Waihi*
Seagulls Bed & Breakfast *B&B*

Marie & Steve Quinlan
8 West Street
(off Pacific Road),
Waihi Beach, 3611

Tel (07) 863 4633
or 021 0290 9880
seagullsquinlan@clear.net.nz

Double/Twin $130 - $150
Single $110 - $120
(Full breakfast)
Children welcome
2 Queen 1 Single (2 bdrm)
Queen size with extensive sea
and beach views
Bathrooms: 1 Guest share
Large modern with bath and shower

Relax and unwind at beautiful Waihi Beach - gateway to Coromandel Peninsular, historic Karangahake Gorge, Orokawa/Homunga walkways and Bay of Plenty. Enjoy spectacular panoramic views of main beach (3minutes walk) and Mayor Island. Watch the sunrise, listen to tuis sing in bush on boundary. Modern spacious luxury home with your own TV lounge, tea/coffee facilities, bedrooms all with sea views. Excellent outdoor area, cafes/restaurants RSA closeby, swimming, surfing, fishing, beach and bush walks. Breakfasts include fresh seasonal fruits, homemade preserves, free range eggs.   2188

The difference between a B&B and a hotel
is that you don't hug the hotel staff when
you leave.

Bay of Plenty
Kilometres
0
40
Miles
0
24
aotunu
Hahei
ach
Coroglen
Tairua
25
es
Vhangamata
Waihi
Katikati
2
Omokoroa
Mt. Maunganui
Papamoa
Tauranga
Te Puke
Waihau Bay
Matata
Whakatane
Ohope
35
Ngongotaha
Lake Rotoiti
Opotiki
Rotorua
1
30
Ngakuru
5
2
Whatatutu
Waipaoa
Taupo
Ormond
1
Gisborne
Motuoapa
Waikaremoana
Turangi
Mahanga
Beach
Wairoa

Katikati *8 km N of Katikati*
Cotswold Lodge Countrystay *B&B*

Alison & Des Belsham
183 Ongare Point Road,
RD 1,
Katikati

Tel (07) 549 2110
Fax (07) 549 2109
relax@cotswold.co.nz
www.cotswold.co.nz

Double/Twin $165 - $175
Single $120
(Special breakfast)
Dinner by prior arrangement
Visa MC accepted
2 Queen 1 Twin (3 bdrm)
Quality furnished bedrooms
with ensuite bathroom
Bathrooms: 3 Ensuite

We offer warm hospitality and a little luxury, in our rural home, set amidst orchards, with views to Kaimai Ranges, and situated 8 mins north of Katikati and 15 mins from Waihi Beach. Welcoming afternoon tea on arrival. Yummy breakfast. Quality accommodation with ensuite bathrooms. Relax in the undercover hot-tub or play petanque in the garden. Short walk to Harbour. We have a friendly Labrador. We will look forward to meeting you.

Katikati *9 km N of Katikati*
B&B @ Panorama Country Lodge *Luxury B&B*

Barbara & Phil McKernon
901 Pacific Coast Highway (SH2),
RD 1,
Katikati

Tel (07) 549 1882
or 0211 655 875
Fax (07) 549 1882
mckernon@xtra.co.nz
www.panoramalodge.co.nz

Double/Twin $180 - $200
Single $140 - $150
(Special breakfast)
Visa MC accepted
Internet available
1 King 1 Queen 1 Twin (2 bdrm)
Bathrooms: 1 Ensuite 1 Private

Perfectly situated between beautiful Waihi Beach and Katikati. Nestling in the foothills of the Kaimai Ranges, magnificent ocean views from every room! Relax in spacious and peaceful guest suites, quality furnishings, french doors to swimming pool and terrace, TV, CD, DVD, slippers & robes, coffee & tea, delicious breakfasts, served: in-suite, terrace or dining room. Explore the grounds, orchards, paddocks and meet 'our boys' the alpacas, not forgetting our very friendly dog, Kaimai. Nearby: cafes, wineries, beaches, golf, bushwalks... 'We love it here...so will you!'

Katikati *5 km SE of Katikati*
Tranquility Lodge *B&B Homestay*
Gayle & Capt Reynold Alvins
325 Rea Road,
RD 2,
Katikati, 3178

Tel (07) 549 3581
or 027 452 2960
Fax (07) 549 3582
info@tranquilitylodge.co.nz
www.tranquilitylodge.co.nz

Double/Twin $170
Single $135
(Special breakfast)
Children by arrangement
Visa MC accepted
Children and pets welcome
2 King (2 bdrm)
Luxury King bedrooms
Bathrooms: 2 Ensuite

Nestled in a peaceful valley, warm kiwi hospitality and superior accommodation await you. Relax on your own private deck, view our farmyard pets & Maremma dogs, listen to the tune of birdsong & stream while viewing the Kaimai Ranges, or play Petanque. Each King suite is sumptuously furnished, with fine linens, bathrobes, slippers, toiletries & hairdryers. So get away from the crowds & discover Katikati. You will find golf, DaySpa, art, Winery, beaches, bushwalks & much more all within easy reach of our home.

Katikati *9 km SW of Katikati*
Burr-wood Countrystay *B&B Homestay*
Maureen and Alan Cook
449 Lund Road,
RD 2,
Katikati, 3178

Tel (07) 549 2060
Fax (07) 549 2061
nzjewellery@clear.net.nz

Double/Twin $135 - $140
Single $90 - $100
(Full breakfast)
Dinner $35 pp 2 courses plus wine
Visa MC accepted
Pet free home
Not suitable for small children
Internet available
1 Queen 2 Single (2 bdrm)
Bathrooms: 1 Private
We take one party only at a time

Burr-wood is set in a 2 1/2 acre garden and surrounded by native bush. An elevated situation, we overlook a panorama of land,sea, harbour and islands. Enjoy breakfast which includes homemade bread and jams; complimentary pre-dinner drinks. Dinner is available by arrangement. We are 5mins from SH2 and within easy reach of Bay of Plenty attractions We make unique N.Z. Native Timber jewellery. Only one party at a time. Home baking,tea/coffee on arrival. Bathrobes,tea/coffee in rooms. Laundry. Internet for emails.

Omokoroa *17 km N of Tauranga*
Seascape *B&B*

Sue & Geoff Gripton
5 Waterview Terrace,
Omokoroa

Tel (07) 548 1027
or 021 1711936
grippos@xtra.co.nz
www.seascapenz.com

Double/Twin $130 - $140
Single $90
(Full breakfast)
Visa MC accepted
1 Double 2 Single (2 bdrm)
Bathrooms: 1 Ensuite

Come share our stunning views of Tauranga Harbour and Kaimais. On our doorstep are beaches, walkways, golf, hot pools, boat ramps etc. Just halfway between Tauranga and Katikati, we offer a double room with ensuite and TV, twin room with shared bathroom, both with tea/coffee. Enjoy a cooked or continental breakfast with homemade bread and jams while gazing at view. Only 3 1/2 kilometres from SH2, left at third roundabout, 1st right, 1st left into Waterview Terrace. Geoff, Sue and our cat will welcome you.

Tauranga *2 km N of Tauranga Central*
Harbinger House *B&B*

Helen & Doug Fisher
209 Fraser Street,
Tauranga

Tel (07) 578 8801
or 027 236 8660
Fax (07) 579 4101
d-h.fisher@xtra.co.nz
www.harbinger.co.nz

Double/Twin $100 - $120
Single $85 - $105
(Continental breakfast)
Children half price
Dinner $35
Visa MC accepted
2 Queen 2 Single (3 bdrm)
Bathrooms: 1 Guest share

Harbinger House provides affordable luxury in the heart of Tauranga, being close to hospital, conference facilities, downtown and a new shopping mall 100 metres away. Our upstairs has been renovated with your comfort in mind, using quality furnishings, linen, bathrobes, fresh flowers, tea and coffee. Laundry facilities are available. The queen rooms have separate vanities and private balconies. Breakfast is continental using fresh local ingredients where possible. Complimentary pick up from public transport depots and off-street parking is provided.

Tauranga - Matua *3 km N of Tauranga*
Aramoana BnB *B&B*

Doreen Anderson
9 Seaway Terrace,
Matua, Tauranga, 3110

Tel (07) 576 3058
or 027 320 0203
Fax (07) 576 3758
andersondem@xtra.co.nz
www.aramoanabnb.co.nz

Double/Twin $120
Single $80
(Full breakfast)
Children $35
Eftpos accepted
Pet free home
Children welcome
1 Queen 1 Twin (2 bdrm)
Relax in comfort and warmth
Bathrooms: 1 Guest share

Relax in comfort by the sea with fabulous views of the harbour and Mt Maunganui. Watch the ships coming and going to the port. Enjoy the lights at night and the moonlight sparkling on the water. Walk along the beach to parks. Dine or shop in nearby Cherrywood village or drive to golf, the nearest course only 4 minutes away. Use Aramoana as your base to explore the bay. Your host has extensive knowledge of the area and will make you very welcome.

Omokoroa - Tauranga *15 km N of Tauranga*
Wildhaven Farm *Luxury B&B*

Robert & Bryony Cross
257 Whakamarama Road,
RD 6, Tauranga

Tel (07) 552 5484
or 021 618 201
Fax (07) 552 5484
roberthhcross@eol.co.nz
wildhaven.co.nz

Double/Twin $175
Single $150
(Full breakfast)
Children $25
3 course dinner with a complimentary glass of wine $45
Payment by cash/cheque/internet
Children welcome
1 Double (1 bdrm)
Luxury bedroom with en-suite facilities
Bathrooms: 1 Ensuite
Large shower room with heated towel rail and hair dryer

We warmly welcome guests to our little slice of paradise. Our 77 acre working farm has uninterrupted coastal views of Mount Maunganui, north to the Alderman Islands, which you can enjoy from the extensive landscaped gardens and heated swimming pool. We have one large air-conditioned double bedroom, a fold down sofa bed and a cot provides sleeping accommodation for children. Your hosts are, Robert & Bryony and their two children Emma (12) and Freddie (10) and their friendly dog, Murray.

Tauranga - Pyes Pa *18 km S of Tauranga*
Millers Haven Homestay *B&B Homestay*

Simon and Renu Miller
147 Belk Road South, RD 3,
Pyes Pa, Tauranga, 3173

Tel (07) 543 5335
or 021 258 8270
Fax (07) 543 5335
millershaven@actrix.co.nz
millershavenhomestay@kiwiweb.net.nz

Double/Twin $150 - $190
Single $100 (Full breakfast)
Dinner $25 pp by prior arrangement
Guest Lounge - TV,
Tea/Coffee facilities
Visa MC Eftpos accepted
Internet available
1 King/Twin 1 Queen (2 bdrm)
King bed can be made into 2 king single beds
Bathrooms: 2 Ensuite

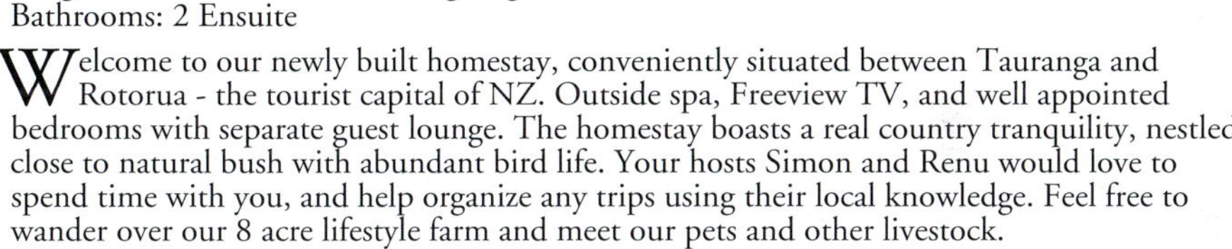

Welcome to our newly built homestay, conveniently situated between Tauranga and Rotorua - the tourist capital of NZ. Outside spa, Freeview TV, and well appointed bedrooms with separate guest lounge. The homestay boasts a real country tranquility, nestled close to natural bush with abundant bird life. Your hosts Simon and Renu would love to spend time with you, and help organize any trips using their local knowledge. Feel free to wander over our 8 acre lifestyle farm and meet our pets and other livestock.

Judea-Tauranga *0 km N of*
DellWay HideAway *B&B Homestay Cottage with Kitchen*

Rolf & Bernadette Remin
8 Dell Way,
Judea, 3110

Tel (07) 571 4451
or 021 148 6742
dellway@clear.net.nz

Double/Twin $80 - $100
Single $70 - $90
(Full breakfast)
Children $30
Dinner $25 pp
Pet free home
Children welcome
Internet available
2 Queen (2 bdrm)
1Q/1S cottage, 1Q in house
Bathrooms: 2 Ensuite

A delightful fully self contained modern cottage set in a private bush setting. Another guest area consisting of a Q/S bedroom, en-suite, lounge and deck is also available below hosts house. Both rooms have garden views and access to walkways and a stream. Rolf is a qualified chef and can cook meals for you at short notice and Bernadette is a kahuna massage therapist and healer. We offer a unique, peaceful oasis that is only minutes to downtown Tauranga, hotpools, and estuary walkways.

Mt Maunganui *9 km S of Mt Maunganui*
Pembroke House *B&B*
Cathy & Graham Burgess
12 Santa Fe Key,
Royal Palm Beach,
Papamoa/ Mt Maunganui

Tel (07) 572 1000
PembrokeHouse@xtra.co.nz
www.pembrokehouse.co.nz

Double/Twin $110
Single $80
(Full breakfast)
Children $40
Visa MC accepted
2 Queen 1 Twin (3 bdrm)
All bedrooms have own
ensuite or private bathroom
Bathrooms: 2 Ensuite 1 Private

A modern home. Cross the road to the Ocean Beach, where you can enjoy swimming, surfing and beach walks. Enjoy stunning sea views while dining at breakfast. Near Fashion Island and Palm Beach Shopping Plaza, restaurants and golf courses. Visit nearby attractions at Mount Maunganui, Tauranga, Rotorua and Whakatane. Separate guest lounge with TV and tea making facilities. Cathy, a schoolteacher, and Graham, semi-retired are widely travelled and enjoy meeting people. We share our home with Sheba - our Tonkinese cat. Unsuitable for pre-schoolers.

Mt Maunganui - Papamoa *9 km SE of Mount Maunganui*
Hesford House bed and breakfast *B&B*
Sally & Derek Hesford
45 Gravatt Road, Royal Palm Beach,
Papamoa 3118, Mt Maunganui

Tel (07) 572 2825
or 021 257 7384
info@hesfordhouse.co.nz
www.hesfordhouse.co.nz

Double/Twin $90 - $140
Single $75 - $100
(Full breakfast)
Children negotiable
Visa MC accepted
Pet free home
2 Queen 1 Twin (3 bdrm)
Light and airey,
Cool in summer, warm in winter
Bathrooms: 1 Ensuite 1 Guest share

Enjoy wonderful kiwi B&B hospitality. A short stroll to the fabulous Papamoa Beach for excellent patrolled swimming and surfing or enjoy fine dining at the Bluebiyou Restaurant. FREE WIRELESS INTERNET. Explore local shops, supermarket, cafes, restaurants and internet cafe opposite. Close to golf, fishing, walks etc. View our beautiful garden while sampling our delicious breakfast. Your spacious room includes TV, tea/coffee and small fridge. Enjoy day trips to Rotorua (50 mins drive) Whakatane (White Island) and the Coromandel (1hr). Courtesy pickup from public transport.

Mt. Maunganui *3.5 km SE of Mt. Maunganui Centre*
Beachside Bed & Breakfast *B&B with free wireless internet*

Lorraine & Jim Robertson
21B Oceanbeach Road,
Mt Maunganui, 3116

Tel (07) 574 0960
or 021 238 0598
info@beachsidebnb.co.nz
www.beachsidebnb.co.nz

Double/Twin $105 - $140
Single $85 - $100
(Full breakfast)
Visa MC accepted
Pet free home
1 King/Twin 2 Queen (3 bdrm)
Bathrooms: 2 Ensuite 1 Private

We are 30 seconds to NZ's most popular beach, but still close to the action and golf courses but far enough away to be quiet. Free wireless internet, off-street parking, courtesy transport to/from local airport/buses. Enjoy stunning sea views from our guest lounge while indulging in a generous cooked breakfast plus seasonal fresh fruit salad, home-baked bread & real expresso coffee. We are widely travelled, enjoy meeting and helping our guests. Use our B&B as a base to explore White Island, Rotorua & Coromandel Peninsula.

Te Puke *3.5 km S of Te Puke*
Aotea Villa *B&B Self Contained Bungalow*

Peter & Nanette Miller
246 Te Matai Road,
Te Puke 3188

Tel (07) 573 9433
Fax (07) 573 9433
Millerph@xtra.co.nz
www.aoteavilla.co.nz

Double/Twin $125
Single $95
(Full breakfast)
Children $35 up to 13yrs
Visa MC accepted
Children and pets welcome
Internet available
2 Queen 2 Single (2 bdrm)
Villa 1 double,
Bungalow 1 double, 1 single
Bathrooms: 1 Ensuite 1 Guest share
Villa guest share, bungalow has ensuite.

Welcome to our relaxing and comfortable 1910 villa situated in the heart of the Bay of Plenty in pictuesque kiwifruit and avocado countryside. We are minutes from Te Puke, 45 minutes from Whakatane and Rotorua and 20 minutes from Tauranga and Mount Maunganui. Relax on our wisteria covered verandahs and view our beautiful sunsets. Laundry and internet facilities. Guest lounge and games room. Stunning local restaurants, excellent golf course, bush walks and trout fishing close by. Visit our website for more information.

Matata *34 km SW of Whakatane*
Pohutukawa Beach B&B & Cottage *B&B Farmstay Cottage with Kitchen*

Christine & Jorg Prinz
693 State Highway 2,
RD 4,
Whakatane

Tel (07) 322 2182
joe@prinztours.co.nz
www.beachbnb.co.nz

Double/Twin $100 - $140
Single $100
(Continental breakfast)
 Self-contained cottage
(sleeps 4) $150-$200
Visa MC accepted
Children welcome
1 Queen 2 Twin (3 bdrm)
Bathrooms: 1 Ensuite 1 Private

Enjoy the fantastic views over the Pacific Ocean in this beautiful rural and cosy setting. We run an organic cattle farm and orchard. We are involved in health care and wellness and provide on site family counseling and health coaching for those guests in respite. One twin ensuite room. Self-contained or fully serviced guest house for four people. Relax at the pool, sauna or garden, cuddle the dogs and cats or 'have a chat' to the friendly farm animals. English and German spoken. You are welcome!

Matata - Pikowai *30 km NW of Whakatane*
Fothergills on Mimiha *B&B Farmstay Separate fully equipped Cottage*

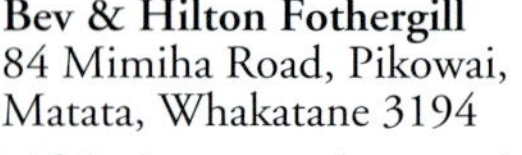

Bev & Hilton Fothergill
84 Mimiha Road, Pikowai,
Matata, Whakatane 3194

Tel (07) 322 2224 or 0274 605 958
Fax (07) 322 2224
bev@fothergills.co.nz
www.fothergills.co.nz

Double/Twin $150 - $160
Single $120 - $130 (Special breakfast)
Children $20 under 13,
Teens & extra adults $30
Dinner $50 each, with wine, b/a
Cottage 2-nights minimum $320,
Then $100p.n. double = $820p.w
Visa MC accepted Internet Available
Children and pets welcome
2 King/Twin 2 Queen 1 Twin (4 bdrm)
Two bedrooms in B&B suite + 2 bedrooms in cottage
Bathrooms: 1 Ensuite 2 Private One bathroom in each venue.

Just off SH2 and the beach, you'll find our stylish, comfortable, peaceful B & B suite and cottage, and us, your friendly, helpful, hospitable hosts. Breakfasts, served in house or garden, are garden-fresh, home-made and delicious. Mimiha Cottage, is fully equipped; a home-away-from-home. Stroll in our idyllic garden, play petanque, walk along the unspoilt beach, up the country road or climb the wonderful hills with our two fox terriers; feed the pig. After a busy day, soak in the outdoor spa. Come and enjoy this slice of heaven!

Whakatane *7 km NW of Whakatane*
Whakatane Homestay- Leaburn Farm *Farmstay Homestay on a dairy farm*

Kathleen & Jim Law
237 Thornton Road, RD 4, Whakatane 3194

Tel (07) 308 7487
or 021 21 21 196
Fax (07) 308 7437
info@whakatanehomestay.co.nz
www.whakatanehomestay.co.nz

Double/Twin $110 - $120
Single $85 - $100 (Full breakfast)
Children negotiable Dinner $25 - $35 negotiable
Visa MC accepted
Pet free home Pets welcome
Internet Available
1 Queen 2 Single (2 bdrm)
Large rooms - Single bedroom has handbasin only
Bathrooms: 1 Guest share

Looking for peace and quiet, or do you want to explore this sunshine coast? If stimulating conversation or a browse in an extensive library is something you enjoy, you are welcome here.

Other guests comments over the 27 years we have been home-hosting, include: ' 'Superb hospitality and very interesting talks' Les and Alison -NZ. 'Most relaxed homestay ever experienced.' -Joy and Peter UK. 'Lovely room, great breakfast and lovely people'-Bert and Tineke - Holland

As 'young oldies', we enjoy company, farming tales, travel, business interests, and your choice of topic. We are handy to the golf course, 7km to thriving Whakatane Township. Special interests of genealogy,

Lions Club,and bowls . Our queen-bed room is adjacent to a spa bathroom, separate shower and toilet, and is shared only with other guests if the twin bedroom is occupied. Be as busy as you like or enjoy restful country atmosphere. We live at 237 Thornton Road,(the old State Highway 2) We haven't shifted -the SH did.)Pamper yourselves at our place.

Whakatane *10 km S of Whakatane*
Baker's *B&B Homestay Cottage with Kitchen*

Lynne & Bruce Baker
40 Butler Road, RD 2, Whakatane

Tel (07) 307 0368
or 027 284 6996
Fax (07) 307 0368
bakers@world-net.co.nz
www.bakershomestay.co.nz

Double/Twin $120 - $140
Single $90 - $110
(Continental breakfast)
Children $20
Dinner $50 b/a (wine included)
Self-contained private cottage available
Visa MC accepted
Children and pets welcome
Internet Available
1 King/Twin 2 Queen 2 Single (4 bdrm)
Garden Room Queen lovely garden aspect
Bathrooms: 2 Ensuite 1 Private Fully tiled private ensuites

Friendly welcome to our lovely country home nestled amongst mature gardens croquet lawn and Avocado orchard. Enjoy our Swimming or spa pool Choose between our delightful fully self-contained 2 bedroom cottage or be pampered with bed & our special breakfast in our warm spacious home. Sky TV in our comfortable guest lounge Lynne & Bruce are keen outdoor hosts enjoying fishing,surfing, gardening and travel White Island tours, dolphin watching, fishing and diving activities can be arranged for your memorable stay.

Whakatane *1.5 km SE of Whakatane Central*
Crestwood Homestay *Luxury B&B Separate Suite one party booking only*

Janet & Peter McKechnie
2 Crestwood Rise,
Whakatane, 3120

Tel (07) 308 7554
or 0800 111 449
pandjmckechnie@xtra.co.nz
www.crestwood-homestay.co.nz

Double/Twin $140
Single $120
(Continental breakfast)
Dinner $50 per person by
pre- arrangement includes wine
Visa MC accepted
Children welcome
Internet available
1 Queen 2 Single (2 bdrm)
Rooms open onto balcony
Bathrooms: 1 Private Separate toilet

Hill top seclusion with spectacular sea views. Three minutes drive to town and jetty for White Island/dolphin watching tours. Trout fishing paradise with scenic bush and rivers nearby. Private upstairs suite with guest lounge, sunny balcony, tea-making facilities, fridge, tv, phone, wireless internet. Rooms are warm, comfortable and spacious. Suite is yours alone with guest entry and safe off road parking.Ideal for group of up to four travelling together. Interests are coastguard activities, flyfishing, bush walks and rugby.Home baking on arrival.

Whakatane *10 km S of*
Devand farmstay *B&B Homestay*

John & Gayle
108 Te Rahu Road,
Whakatane, 3193

Tel (07) 308 0571
or 027 473 6575
gayle@devand.co.nz
www.devand.co.nz

Double/Twin $85 - $110
Single $70 - $95
(Continental breakfast)
Children by arrangement
Dinner two or three course with
complimentary wine /beer
Picnic lunches by arrangement
1 King 1 Double 1 Twin (3 bdrm)
All with ensuites and heating
Bathrooms: 3 Ensuite
2 ensuites with showers, 1 ensuite with bath

Quiet, comfortable accommodation on a Red Devon stud farm. Relax on the decks, in the spa pool, by the fire in season or take an interest in the farm. We have a large garden with a pond and also grow olives and blueberries; we have a pet cat. Two and three course evenings meals made with local and free range produce (whenever possible) served with complimentary wine and/or beer. We are only 15 minutes to the CBD and boat ramp (parking for boat trailers).

Ohope Beach *8 km SE of Whakatane*
Oceanspray Homestay *Homestay Apartment with Kitchen*

Frances & John Galbraith
283A Pohutukawa Avenue,
Ohope, Bay of Plenty

Tel (07) 312 4112
or 027 286 6824
Fax (07) 312 4192
frances@oceanspray.co.nz
www.oceanspray.co.nz

Double/Twin $150 - $170
Single $80 - $100
(Full breakfast provisions)
Children negotiable
Visa MC accepted
3 Queen 2 Twin (5 bdrm)
3 Bedrooms in apartment,
2 bedrooms in cottage
Bathrooms: 1 Ensuite 2 Private
Apartment - ensuite & bathroom, Cottage - own bathroom

Welcome to our beachfront home. Wonderful sea views from our upstairs decks. Our modern downstairs 3 bedroom apartment is self-contained with own kitchen, lounge, two bathrooms (one ensuite). Adjacent to our house is a 2 bedroom, modern, self-contained cottage. Families welcome. Home comforts - Sky TV, books,/DVDs/toys for children. Continental breakfast provisions are supplied into your unit. John's pursuits are kayaking and longline fishing. Frances enjoys entertaining and providing excellent cuisine. Our very sociable cats,Barnaby & Cleo, will also greet you with a warm welcome.

Ohope Beach *8 km N of Whakatane*
The Rafters *Apartment with Kitchen*
Pat Rafter
261A Pohutukawa Avenue,
Ohope Beach

Tel (07) 312 4856
Fax (07) 312 4856
The_Rafters_Ohope@xtra.co.nz
www.wave.co.nz/pages/macaulay/The_Rafters.htm

Double/Twin $100
Single $85
(Accommodation only)
Children $10
Extra adult $20, limit 1
Children and pets welcome
1 King 1 Single (2 bdrm)
Bathrooms: 1 Ensuite

Breakfast is not supplied, Unit is self-contained. Minimum 2 night stay. Maximum 3 guests.

Sea views: White, Whale islands, East Coast. Safe swimming. Many interesting walks. Golf, tennis, bowls, all within minutes. Licensed Chartered Club Restaurant opposite. Trips to volcanic White Island, fishing, jet boating, diving, swimming with dolphins arranged. Full cooking facilities; private entrance, sunken garden, BBQ. Complimentary: tea, coffee, biscuits, fruit, newspaper, personal laundry service.

Pat's interests are: philosophy, theology, history, English literature, the making of grape wines and all spirits, golf, bowls, music and tramping. Courtesy car available. House trained animals welcomed. 4 restaurants and oyster farm within 5 minutes drive. I look forward to your company and assure you unique hospitality.

Directions: on reaching Ohope Beach turn right, proceed 2km to 261A (beach-side) name 'Rafters' on a brick letterbox with illuminated B&B sign.

Ohope *10 km SE of Whakatane*
Moanarua Beach Cottage *Luxury Cottage with Kitchen*

Miria & Taroi Black
2 Hoterini Street,
Ohope

Tel (07) 312 5924
or 021 255 6192
info@moanarua.co.nz
www.moanarua.co.nz

Double/Twin $125 - $155
Single $105 - $135
(Continental breakfast provisions)
Children 1 baby or small child
BBQ, hangi, or 3 course
meal by arrangement
Kayaks and boat trips
Pets welcome
1 King (1 bdrm)
Bathrooms: 1 Ensuite

Naumai, haere mai Miria and Taroi welcome you to a unique cultural experience in a romantic hideaway, a restful retreat nestled between the ocean and the harbour in sunny Ohope. Feel free to use BBQ, luxury spa and expansive decks with views of ocean and harbour. Chat with us about local history and Maori art works that adorn our home, cottage and garden. Kick back, relax in your private fully self-contained cottage or enjoy many local activities. Boat tours and kayaks available for hire.

Ohope Beach *7.5 km E of Whakatane*
Seaview Bed and Breakfast *B&B Homestay*

Lynnette and Ross Nicholson
33 Waterford Avenue,
Waterford Estate, Ohope

Tel (07) 312 6005
or 021 207 3838
Fax (07) 3126005
r.lnicholson@xtra.co.nz
www.seaviewbb.co.nz

Double/Twin $115 - $150
Single $100 - $130
(Special breakfast)
Children by negotiation
Dinner $35 pp by arrangement
Visa MC accepted
Pet free home
Children welcome
1 Queen 1 Double 1 Twin (3 bdrm)
Bathrooms: 1 Guest share

Relax and enjoy the quiet gated location of Seaview with the lovely Ohope Beach just metres away. Lovely views from our upstairs deck.br/> Guests have their own lounge downstairs - TV/Video, Tea/Coffee facilities, Microwave. Special picnic hampers can be ordered in advance. Home baking and preserves. Laundry available. Honeymoon Special is available - enquire now. Golf Club, Restaurants, Playground all close by. Lynnette and Ross, who are former farmers, have many interests including Sea/Lake Fishing, Reading, Sports, Cooking.

Opotiki *18 km E of Opotiki*
Coral's B&B *B&B Farmstay Cottage with Kitchen*

Coral Parkinson
Morice's Bay,
Highway 35,
RD 1,
Opotiki

Tel (07) 315 8052
or 021 299 9757
coral@xnet.co.nz

Double/Twin $95 - $130
Single $70 - $90
(Continental breakfast)
Children $15
Breakfast $10 pp by arrangement
Children and pets welcome
2 Queen 2 Single (3 bdrm)
Bathrooms: 1 Private

We provide self-contained accommodation located on our hobby farm. As well as pets and farm animals we collect varied memorabilia. Enjoy the beach and bird life; swim at nearby sandy surf beach. Fish, ramble over the rocks, explore caves. Our 2 storied cottage features lead-light windows, native timbers, large decks look out across the bay and native bush. 3 golf courses within an hours drive; covered parking, home-made bread and preserves. We have a classic English Daimler car Visit our local Marae.

Opotiki *12 km SW of Opotiki*
Tanglewood *B&B self contained with kitchenette*

Peter & Louise Maple
16 Ohiwa Harbour Road,
RD 2,
Opotiki, 3198

Tel (07) 315 4623
or 027 696 0147
peter-louise.maple@xtra.co.nz

Double/Twin $125
(Continental breakfast provisions)
Dinner with your hosts
by prior arrangement
Not suitable for children
Pets welcome
1 King (1 bdrm)
Kingsize or twin king
single arrangement
Bathrooms: 1 Ensuite

Enjoy fantastic views over the Waiotahi estuary and along the East Coast from your private deck during a peaceful stay in our modern self contained unit. Swim, fish or use our kayaks at nearby sandy Bryans Beach or the beautiful Ohiwa Harbour. Stroll round our five acres or try some of the local walks with spectacular bush and coastal views and plenty of associated birdlife. Peter and Louise provide generous continental breakfasts, free range eggs, home produce and dinner by arrangement. We have a friendly cat.

Opotiki - Waihau Bay *112 km N of Opotiki*
Waihau Bay Homestay *B&B Homestay Apartment with Kitchen*

Noelene & Merv Topia
10942 State Highway 35,
Oruaiti Beach Waihau Bay,
RD 3, Opotiki

Tel (07) 325 3674
or 0800 240 170
n.topia@clear.net.nz
www.waihaubayhomestay.co.nz

Double/Twin $85 - $120
Single $60 - $75
(Continental breakfast)
Children half price
Dinner $35
Visa MC Eftpos accepted
Children and pets welcome
Internet available
2 King 1 Queen 4 Single (3 bdrm)
Bathrooms: 3 Ensuite
All bathrooms are suitable for disabled

Surrounded by unspoiled beauty come and enjoy magnificent views, stunning sunsets, swim, go diving, kayaking (we have kayaks) or just walk along the sandy beach. You are most welcome to join Merv when he checks his craypots and his catches are our cuisine specialty. Fishing trips, horse treks and guided cultural walks are also available. We have 2 self-contained units with disabled facilities, and a double room with ensuite. Our cat Tosca and our small dog Kaykay enjoy making new friends.

Rotorua *2 km N of Rotorua centre*
Rotorua Lakeside Homestay *Homestay*

Ursula & Lindsay Prince
3 Raukura Place,
Rotorua, 3010

Tel (07) 347 0140
or 0800 223 624
Fax (07) 347 0107
the-princes@xtra.co.nz

Double/Twin $110 - $120
Single $90 - $100
(Special breakfast)
1 King/Twin 1 Queen (2 bdrm)
Bathrooms: 1 Ensuite 1 Private

We invite you to share our spacious, modern home in its tranquil lake setting. Hosts since 1988, our interests include world affairs and environmental issues. We enjoy outdoor activities - feel free to use our Canadian canoe. Now retired, we have lived overseas and still travel extensively. At breakfast (home-made goodies) we'll help you plan activities and arrange bookings. Minimum stay 2 nights. Directions: From Lake Road turn into Bennetts Road, then first left into Koutu Road, then first right into Karenga Street. Turn RIGHT into Haumona Street, a left turn at the end brings you down Raukura Place to our door. $5.00 discount off per night for three or more nights.

Rotorua *4 km SW of Rotorua*

Hunts Farm *Farmstay*

Maureen & John Hunt,
363 Pukehangi Rd, Rotorua (Home 1: Top Photo)
Tel (07) 348 1352 or 027 486 3477
Sonya Hunt & Dave Cronshaw
359 Pukehangi Rd, Rotorua (Home 2: Bottom 2 Photos)
Tel 07 348 2874 or 027 486 3477
sonyahunt@xtra.co.nz

Double/Twin $125
Single $80
(Full breakfast)
Children $30
Children welcome
Home 1: 1 King/Twin 1 Queen 2 Single (2 bdrm)
Home 2: 1 Queen 1 Double 2 Single (2 bdrm)
Bathrooms: 3 Ensuite

Come and relax in our neighbouring new homes as we help you plan your itinerary and book your local tours. Explore our 150 acre scenic farm running beef and deer. Views of farm, lake, forest and city are uninterrupted panoramic and magical. Guest areas have private entrances, lounges with tea/coffee facilities and fridges.

Home 1 (363) Maureen and John Hunt: Single story ranch style home, private guest wing with TV. Two triple rooms each with ensuite and private terrace. 1 Queen with Single and ensuite, 1 King Twin with single and ensuite.

Home 2 (359) Sonya Hunt and Dave Cronshaw: Upstairs private guest wing available to one group at a time only. Well suited for family groups. Enjoy our 12 m swimming pool and spacious lawns and gardens. At 359 the family includes 2 children and cat. 1 Queen 1 double 2 single with ensuite. Complementary high speed wireless internet available.

Rotorua - Ngakuru *32 km S of Rotorua*
Te Ana Farmstay *Farmstay Cottage No Kitchen*

The Oberer Residence:
Heather Oberer
Poutakataka Road,
Ngakuru, RD 1, Rotorua

Tel (07) 333 2720
or 021 828 151
teanafarmstay@xtra.co.nz
www.teanafarmstay.co.nz

Double/Twin $120 - $150
Single $95
(Special breakfast)
Children negotiable
Dinner by prior arrangement
Children welcome
2 Queen 4 Single (4 bdrm)
2 homestead rooms, garden views;
2-roomed cottage
Bathrooms: 2 Ensuite 1 Family share

Te Ana, The Oberer family sanctuary since 1936, offers peace and tranquility in a spacious rural garden setting affording magnificent views of lake, volcanically-formed hills and lush farmland. Enjoy a leisurely stroll before joining host for a very generous country breakfast. Ideal base from which to explore the Rotorua and Taupo attractions, Waiotapu and Waimungu Thermal Reserves, Waikite Thermal mineral swimming pool and Tamaki Tours Hangi. Families welcomed by Jack, our loyal Jack Russell. Farm tour and fishing rod available.

Rotorua *4 km S of Rotorua*
Serendipity Homestay *B&B Homestay*

Kate & Brian Gore
3 Kerswell Terrace,
Tihi-o-Tonga, Rotorua

Tel (07) 347 9385
or 027 609 3268
b.gore@clear.net.nz
www.serendipityhomestay.co.nz

Double/Twin $150 - $160
Single $90
(Full breakfast)
Children under 12 $40
Dinner $40 by arrangement
Visa MC accepted
Pet free home
Children welcome
1 Queen 2 Single (2 bdrm)
Electric blankets and wool underlay ensure your comfort
Bathrooms: 1 Private spa bath plus shower

Marvel at unsurpassed views of geysers, city, lakes and beyond. Relax in all day sun, on the deck, in the conservatory or in the privacy of our garden. Indulge in comfort, home-cooked cuisine and the friendly folk who have been enjoying hosting for many years. Our interests are, golf, tramping, travel, the environment, antiques and sharing our extensive local and national knowledge with you. Let us advise you on the 'must see' list while in Rotorua and other highlights of our beautiful country. Welcome!

Rotorua Central *0.2 km E of Post Office*
Central Classic Tresco Thermal Oasis B&B *Luxury B&B Cottage*

Trinka & Trevor
3 Toko Street off Victoria Street,
Rotorua

Tel (07) 348 9611
or Freephone TRESCO (0800 873 726)
Fax (07) 348 9611
trescorotorua@xtra.co.nz
www.trescorotorua.co.nz

Double/Twin $150 - $180
Single $80 - $130
(Full breakfast)
Double/Triple $180-$250
Visa MC Eftpos accepted
Pet free home
Children welcome
Internet available
1 King 3 Queen 1 Double 1 Twin 1 Single (5 bdrm)
Bathrooms: 3 Ensuite 1 Private 2 Guest share

We all come to Rotorua for this rare Geothermal activity and Tresco has the only real geothermal hot pool [Maori call 'Healing Waters'] from the volcano, with the prestigous Qualmark [excellent] 4 Stars Award. Urprivate pool and cooked breakfast included - Yes free. Enjoy Tresco Art+ Origami gallery. Why stay outside Rotorua spending time driving? Forget urcar - park in rgarden. 2 minutes walk [not by helicopter!] from City. Laundry. Internet. 'Lonely Planet Guide' recommended. Summer and Winter, 100% Pure Tresco's warmest welcome awaits.

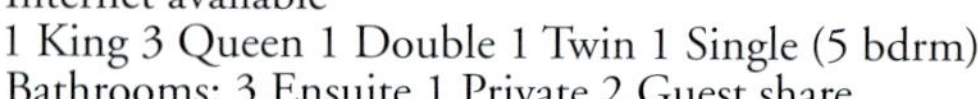

Rotorua *14 km NE of Rotorua*
Brunswick *B&B*

Joy & Lin Cathcart
99 Brunswick Drive,
RD 4,
Rotorua 3074

Tel (07) 350 1472
or mob 021 256 5355
Fax (07) 350 1472
joylin@clear.net.nz

Double/Twin $125
Single $85
(Full breakfast)
Visa MC accepted
Pet free home
Not suitable for children
1 King (1 bdrm)
Bathrooms: 1 Private
Bathroom is adjacent to the bedroom

With peaceful surroundings and beautiful views over Lake Rotorua 'Brunswick' is 15mins from Rotorua City centre and 5mins from Rotorua Airport. Having retired from dairy farming Lin now enjoys his golf: Joy plays bridge and gardening is a shared hobby. Our guest room has TV, hot drink facilities, refrigerator and balcony. The bathroom has both bath and separate shower. We are smoke free. Joy's home baking and a warm welcome await you!

Rotorua *5 km SE of Rotorua*
Walker Homestay & B&B *B&B Homestay Self contained Cottage*

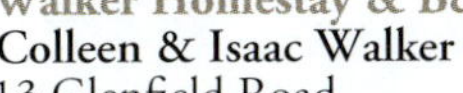

Colleen & Isaac Walker
13 Glenfield Road,
Owhata, Rotorua 3010

Tel (07) 345 3882
or 021 050 9633
colleen.walker@clear.net.nz

Double/Twin $110 - $130
Single $70 - $110
(Continental breakfast)
Children half price
Dinner $25 - $40 by arrangement
Extra guest $20
Visa MC accepted
Children welcome
1 Queen 1 Double 1 Twin (3 bdrm)
Two in cottage One in house
Bathrooms: 1 Ensuite 1 Private
Cottage has own bathroom Room in house has ensuite

Two bedroom cottage in own garden area has lounge, kitchen, bathroom,and laundry. Guest room in house has ensuite; tea/coffee facilities; microwave; separate entrance; access to hosts living area. Complete privacy or become one of the family. Colleen is a business administration tutor and Isaac (Ike), a NZ Maori, is a coach driver with a background of farming and paper industry, keen fisherman and golfer. Both are Lions. 2 friendly dachshunds will welcome you. 24 hours notice for Dinner. Off-road parking.

Rotorua *3 km SW of Rotorua*
West Brook *B&B Homestay*
Judy Bain
378 Malfroy Road,
Rotorua

Tel (07) 347 8073
Fax (07) 347 8073

Double/Twin $100
Single $50
(Continental breakfast)
Children under 12 half price
Dinner $25
Visa MC accepted
Children welcome
4 Single (2 bdrm)
Bathrooms: 1 Family share

Judy, a Rotorua Host Lion Member with years of hospitality involvement lives 3km from city on western outskirts. Interests include meeting with the people, the farming scene, International and local current affairs. Assistance with sight seeing planning and transport to and from tourist centre available. Both well appointed comfy guest rooms are equipped with electric blankets. The friendly front door welcome and chatter over the meal table add up to my motto: home away from home.

Rotorua - Ngongotaha *17 km N of Rotorua*
Clover Downs Estate *Luxury B&B Homestay Farmstay*
Lyn & Lloyd Ferris
175 Jackson Road, RD 6, Ngnogotaha, Rotorua, 3096
Tel (07) 332 2366 or 021 712 866   Fax (07) 332 2367
reservations@cloverdowns.co.nz
www.accommodationinrotorua.co.nz

Double/Twin $250 - $350
Single $235 - $335 (Special breakfast)
Children negotiable Internet Available
Visa MC Diners Amex accepted
2 King/Twin 1 King (3 bdrm)
Super-king size rooms, with ensuite bathrooms
Bathrooms: 3 Ensuite Governor's Suite has bath and shower

Welcome to Clover Downs Estate, a luxury bed & breakfast retreat in stunning rural surroundings near Rotorua. Enjoy the comfort of superior accommodation while experiencing New Zealand farm life. Clover Downs is a unique place to stay situated just 15 minutes north of Rotorua city centre in the secluded country setting of Ngongotaha it is a B B farmstay like no other.

Large comfortable king-size suites comprising of ensuite bathroom, tea & coffee facilities, refrigerator, TV, stereo, wireless internet and individual outdoor decks to provide you with a place to rest and relax in peace and tranquility Take our complimentary farm tour 9am each morning and feed ostriches by hand see trained sheep dogs rounding up sheep, pat a deer and get within a few feet of our magnificent elk stag. In the evenings, enjoy a glass of wine on your own private verandah overlooking the lush pasture.

Your hosts, Lyn & Lloyd and our 4 friendly dogs will ensure that your retreat is comfortable and memorable. We can also help arrange other activities so that you can experience all that Rotorua has to offer, geothermal wonderlands with geysers and bubbling mud pools and the rich Maori culture, excellent fishing, sightseeing and other exciting pursuits. For dining out, the city has an impressive array of cafes and restaurants which offer cuisine from all over the world to tempt the palate or maybe indulge in a traditional hangi feast. We strive to exceed our guest's expectations through an ineffable blend of warmth, generosity and detail.

Directions: Take State Highway 5 to roundabout. Travel thru Ngongotaha village on Hamurana Road, go over railway line then take 3rd left into Central Road. Turn 1st right into Jackson Road, Clover Downs Estate is number 175 on left hand side.

Rotorua *4 km E of Rotorua*
Aroden B&B Homestay *B&B Homestay*

Leonie & Paul Kibblewhite
2 Hilton Road,
Lynmore,
Rotorua, 3010

Tel (07) 345 6303
or 027 696 4211
Fax (07) 345 6353
aroden@xtra.co.nz
www.aroden>co>nz

Double/Twin $130 - $145
Single $90 - $110
(Full breakfast)
Children negotiable
Visa MC accepted
Internet available
2 Queen (2 bdrm)
Bathrooms: 1 Ensuite 1 Private

Agreat central location with character, style and comfort! Thermal and lakes nearby, Whakarewarewa Forest adjacent (glow-worms), city 5 minutes drive. You are welcome to all downstairs: 2 lounge areas, well-appointed rooms with comfortable beds and fine linen, kitchen, central heating/open fire, patio, spa, a private and luxuriant garden. Paul, scientist, and Leonie, teacher, are fourth generation Kiwi with real knowledge of this remarkable area. Meet Taupo, Paul's delightful guide dog. Breakfast is special - this couple enjoys food! Leonie parle francais.

Rotorua *10 km NE of Rotorua*
Ngongotaha Lakeside Lodge *B&B Homestay*

Lyndsay & Graham Butcher
41 Operiana Street,
Ngongotaha,
Rotorua

Tel (07) 357 4020
or 0800 144 020
Fax (07) 357 4020
lake.edge@xtra.co.nz
www.lakesidelodge.co.nz

Double/Twin $180 - $250
Single $150 - $220
(Full breakfast)
Visa MC accepted
Children over 10 welcome
Internet available
1 King 1 Queen 3 Single (3 bdrm)
Bathrooms: 3 Ensuite

Arrive, settle in and make yourselves at home in our Award Winning Lakeside Bed & Breakfast. Enjoy stunning panoramic views, well appointed rooms with all the comforts of home, fly fishing, bird watching, great food and warm, friendly, relaxed, hospitality. Quiet, peaceful, close to major tourist attractions, and away from the sulphur fumes. Come, stay awhile, relax and enjoy. We promise you a great stay!

Rotorua Central *1 km SW of Rotorua Central*
Innes Cottage *B&B Homestay*

Gill Innes
18A Wylie Street,
Rotorua Central

Tel 0800 24 30 30
or (07) 349 1839
Fax (07) 349 1890
gill@clican.com
www.innescottage.co.nz

Double/Twin $145
Single $100
(Continental breakfast)
Children POA
Dinner N/A
Visa MC accepted
Children welcome
2 Queen 2 Single (3 bdrm)
Bathrooms: 2 Ensuite 1 Private

Centrally situated, within flat walking distance to restaurants and the city, set in a treelined quiet neighborhood only 100 metres from the main road. Close to Te Puia Thermal area and major tourist attractions are easily accessible.My rooms are warm and comfortable with queen beds and ensuite bathrooms. Let me assist and advise you on the most popular and 'must see' attractions and other highlights of our beautiful country.

Rotorua *10 km N of Rotorua centre*
Lake Okareka B&B *B&B Homestay Apartment with Kitchen*

Patricia & Ken Scott
10 Okareka Loop Road,
RD 5, Rotorua

Tel (07) 362 8245
patricia.scott@xtra.co.nz
www.lakeokarekabnb.co.nz

Double/Twin $150
Single $120
(Special breakfast)
Visa MC accepted
Pet free home
3 Queen (3 bdrm)
Each room has an ensuite,
fridge, microwave, dinner set
Studio has kitchen, dining area,
lounge suite, ensuite
Bathrooms: 3 Ensuite

A very warm welcome awaits you at tranquil Lake Okareka, one of the most beautiful Lakes in the area. Our modern home captures magnificent Lake views and beyond to Mt Tarawera. Stroll along the waters edge, enjoy the native bush, ferns and birdlife. Use our local knowledge on all nearby hot pools, fishing, scenic, thermal, adventure and cultural activities. Excellent swimming, complimentary kayaks available. Our environment is quiet and peaceful yet only ten minutes from Rotorua. The perfect retreat with space, privacy and home comforts.

Rotorua *Rotorua Central*
Robertson House *B&B*
John Ballard
70 Pererika Street,
Rotorua

Tel (07) 343 7559
Fax (07) 343 7559
info@robertsonhouse.co.nz

Double/Twin $140 - $190
Single $110 - $155
(Continental breakfast)
Extra person $50
Pets welcome
1 King/Twin 2 Queen
2 Double 2 Single (5 bdrm)
Bathrooms: 5 Ensuite

Our historic home, only 2 minutes drive from city centre, was built by one of Rotoruas forefathers, in 1905. Under the auspices of the Historic Places Trust it has been carefully renovated, retaining its colonial charm. Relax in its warm comfortable atmosphere, or take time out on the verandah and enjoy our old English cottage garden resplendent with colour and fragrance, citrus trees and grape vines. Our friendly hosts are happy to assist with information and bookings for Rotorua's Maori cultural and sightseeing attractions.

Rotorua - Lake Rotoiti *20 km NE of Rotorua*
Lakestay Rotoiti *B&B*
Graeme & Raewyn Natusch
173 Tumoana Road,
Lake Rotoiti,
RD 4,
Rotorua

Tel (07) 345 4089
or 027 418 8404
Fax (07) 345 4089
lakestayrotoiti@xtra.co.nz

Double/Twin $120 - $150
(Full breakfast)
Dinner $35
Self-contained studio $120-$150
Off season rates May-Oct
Visa MC accepted
2 Queen (2 bdrm)
Bathrooms: 2 Ensuite

Lakestay Rotoiti, a very special destination for the discerning couple or individual travellers both summer and winter with friendly informative hosts and siamese cat. One of just 3 lakefront properties in a beautiful secluded sandy bay surrounded by native bush, forest and stunning lake views from all living and guest bedrooms. Excellent swimming, trout fishing, walking tracks and natural rejuvinating hot baths nearby. Guests enjoy complimentary use of kyaks, dingy, windsurfer and bicycles. Wonderful evening dinner by arrangement. Directions are essential. A truely unique experience.

Rotorua *2 km N of Rotorua centre*
Rotorua's Legend on the Lake Homestay *B&B Homestay Apartment with Kitchen*

Murray & Heather Watson
33 Haumoana Street, Koutu, Rotorua
Tel (07) 347 1123 or 027 492 7122
Fax (07) 347 1313
muzzandheb@kol.co.nz
www.troutnz.co.nz
Double/Twin $150
Single $150 (Full breakfast)
Children $20
Dinner $45 per person by arrangement
Additional Adults $30/night per person
Visa MC accepted Pet free home
2 Queen 1 Double 1 Single (3 bdrm)
Bathrooms: 1 Ensuite 1 Private
Yes available with the private facility.

On arrival you will be greeted with our magnificent, quiet and secluded lakes-edge view and a genuine Kiwi welcome. Please join us beside the lake for refreshments as we would love to help you plan your stay by sharing our local knowledge of the area and its many attractions.

Hearing the tranquil lapping of the lake you will find it hard to believe you are only 3 minutes drive from the city centre. You will find your self-contained apartment to have all the comforts of home (washing machine, TV, DVD, video, stereo, oven, micro-wave and dishwasher). Separate bedroom (queen) and living area/kitchen with ensuite access from both rooms. Free email access.

Our smoke-free apartment ensures a freshness you will enjoy. Breakfast includes fruit, yoghurt, cereal, juice and tea/coffee followed by a cooked breakfast - all this and you can choose the time you would like to have it served. Breakfast is a great time to get to know us and for us to help you make best use of your time in this volcanic thermal paradise.

We are more than happy to assist with local bookings and recommend you sample some of the strong local Maori culture. Murray operates a trout fishing charter business on Lake Rotorua from our Lakeside jetty.Special rates apply.We have both travelled extensively, internationally and throughout New Zealand and enjoy meeting people from all over the world. We have been running homestays for the last 15 years and really know how to make your time here enjoyable and comfortable.

Feel free to sit on the lawn and watch the spectacular sunsets we are lucky enough to enjoy almost every night. We hope you will arrive as our guests and leave as our friends.'Humble luxury here'

Rotorua - The Redwoods *4 km E of Rotorua*
B&B @ The Redwoods *Luxury B&B Homestay*

Vivien & Peter Cooper
3 Awatea Terrace, Lynmore - Rotorua

Tel (07) 345 4499
or 027 270 3594
Fax (07) 345 4499
bnb@theredwoods.co.nz
www.theredwoods.co.nz

Double/Twin $145 - $195
Single $130 - $160
(Full breakfast)
Single bed avail. for child to share room
Dinner $45 Host experience in
hospitality industry and silver service
Visa MC accepted
Pet free home
Children welcome
2 Queen 1 Single (2 bdrm)
New Luxurious Ensuite Bedrooms
Bathrooms: 2 Ensuite Excellent shower

Secluded yet central! Two new luxurious ensuite guestrooms with private entrance, guest-only lounge, dining and outdoor living. Decor is simple yet stylish, lounge opens onto courtyard and garden. We live upstairs in split level home; enjoy our company or privacy of your own space. We combine interaction with discretion. Redwood Forest on your doorstep, city and lakes 5 minutes with Rotorua's many attractions very accessible. Safe off-street parking. Free internet access. All our guests have enjoyed our personal service and quality recommendations.

Rotorua *6 km NW of City*
Westminster Accommodation *B&B Farmstay Cottage Self contained Units*

Gillian and Barry Gillette
58A Mountain Road,
Rotorua, 3201

Tel (07) 348 4273
or 0800 937 864
Fax (07) 348 4205
westminster@slingshot.co.nz
www.westminsterlodge.co.nz

Double/Twin $120 - $160
Single $110 - $120
(Breakfast by arrangement $10 pp)
Children $20 per child under 14
Visa MC Eftpos accepted
Children and pets welcome
Internet available
3 Queen 2 Twin 2 Single (4 bdrm)
2 bedrooms in cottage 6 in lodge
Bathrooms: 2 Ensuite 1 Private
Cottage has shower over bath and units walk in showers

Westminster Accommodation has an English Tudor style cottage and studio units nestled on the slopes of Mt Ngongotaha overlooking the city of Rotorua. So country, yet only 6 minutes to the city centre. Panoramic views in the day and fairy land at night. We have miniature cows friendly sheep, chickens, and Mrs Pig. Our house pets are a cockatoo Paulie, and Holly and Benji our little dogs. All the animals are friendly and can be hand

Rotorua - Ngongotaha *12 km N of Rotorua*

A Panoramic Country Homestay *Luxury B&B Homestay Farmstay*

David Perry & Christine King
144 Fryer Road, Hamurana, RD 7, Rotorua 3097

Tel (07) 332 2618 or 021 610 949 Fax (07) 332 2618
panoramahomestay@xtra.co.nz
panoramahomestay.co.nz

Double/Twin $190 - $290 Single $125 - $155 (Special breakfast)
Dinner by arrangement   Discount for over 2 nights stay
Visa MC accepted   Pet free home   Internet Available
1 King 1 Queen (3 bdrm)
1 Superking/Twin
Bathrooms: 2 Ensuite 1 Private
Large plunge bath in Queen room

Aptly named Panorama is your ideal base to stay near Rotorua's many attractions. Take in the magnificent views overlooking Lake Rotorua and legendary Mokoia Island, Mt Tarawera and surrounding country side.

Feel the peace and tranquility as you relax under the stars in the outdoor heated massage spa pool, then curl up in front of the log fire in winter to stay cosy and warm. You may prefer to enjoy an energetic game of tennis on the championship sized court or take in many of the fantastic walks then come home and stretch out on the extra large beds in Panorama's peaceful surrounds for a perfect nights sleep.

The three spacious, luxury bedrooms have private bathrooms/ensuites containing, toiletries, heated towel rails, hairdryers, shaving points and heaters. The large comfortable inner spring beds are warmed with electric blankets, woollen underlays and feather quilts in winter. In the living area, the formal lounge has a native timber, cathedral ceiling, and an open fire where you can relax with a book and listen to soft music.

The large house is centrally heated, screened and wheelchair accessible. Only 15min from Rotorua, Panorama is situated on the northern side of the lake away from the sulphur smells. There is ample room for safe off street parking and helicopter access. Pet lambs and sheep can be fed by hand. Dave and Chris welcome you to spend a few days at Panorama where hospitality is ensured in their country home. They have lived in Rotorua for many years and have a wealth of knowledge to assist you in enjoying your stay and the local attractions. They would be happy to help you with any bookings you may require.

Rotorua - Rerewhakaaitu *45 km S of Rotorua*
Ashpit Place *B&B Homestay Farmstay*

Alison & Scott Marshall
815 Ashpit Road,
Rerewhakaaitu,
Rotorua, 3073

Tel (07) 366 6709
or 021 117 0317
Fax (07) 366 6710
samarshall@clear.net.nz
www.ashpitplace.co.nz

Double/Twin $190
(Continental breakfast)
Dinner $35 pp
Visa MC accepted
1 King/Twin 1 Queen (2 bdrm)
Bathrooms: 2 Ensuite
Spa bath in one suite

Relax and enjoy the panoramic views of Lake Rerewhakaaitu and Mt Tarawera with farming and forestry vistas from the lounge and dining areas. We have some of the best sunsets in the world. The property is in a quiet rural area which is at lakes edge where you can walk at your leisure. We are in between the thermal areas Waiotapu and Waimangu, central to Rotorua and Taupo and on the way to Whirinaki National Park.

Rotorua - Hamurana *20 km N of Rotorua*
Lakeview Heights *B&B Farmstay*

Liz & John Dentice
269 Te Waerenga Road,
Rotorua, 3096

Tel (07) 332 3570
or 021 022 42513
Fax (07) 332 3570
john-lizdentice@xtra.co.nz
www.lakeviewheightsnz.co.nz

Double/Twin $130 - $180
Single $100 - $150
(Full breakfast)
Dinner by arrangement
Visa MC accepted
Children and pets welcome
Internet available
2 Queen 2 Twin 2 Single (3 bdrm)
Family room with Queen & 2 singles, 2 Queen rooms
Bathrooms: 1 Ensuite 1 Private 1 Guest share

Our country home has three guest rooms with superb views across the lake to the city and the volcanic Mount Tarawera in the distance. We are bordered by a Scenic Reserve with native trees,ferns Tuis and Bell birds. John & Liz are well travelled with farming backgrounds and would be delighted to give you a tour of Arab horses, sheep and calves. Fluff the house cat and two Cavalier King Charles Spaniels will make you welcome. Trout fishing, golf course and Rotorua's arttractions all nearby.

Taupo *2.5 km S of Taupo*
B&B @ Number Ten *B&B*

Ann & John Page
10 Coprosma Crescent,
Taupo, 3330

Tel (07) 378 6823
or 021 237 2405
Fax (07) 378 6823
ajpage@nettel.net.nz
www.bnb-at-number-ten.co.nz

Double/Twin $175 - $195
Single $150
(Full breakfast)
Visa MC accepted
Pet free home
Internet available
1 King/Twin 1 Queen (2 bdrm)
Bathrooms: 2 Ensuite

A friendly welcome and refreshments await you at our relaxed and comfortable home. We look forward to making your time with us memorable and fun. Our sunny guest rooms open onto individual courtyards with peaceful views of Lake Taupo. Bedrooms are well appointed with television, tea and coffee making facilities, heatpump/airconditioning units, hair dryers, wireless internet and iron/ironing board. Guest refrigerator and microwave available. The view from our upstairs dining room will encourage you to get out and explore the beauty of Taupo.

Taupo *3 km E of Central Taupo*
Hill Top Park Homestay *B&B Homestay*

Colleen & Bob Yeoman
61 Puriri Street,
Taupo, 3330

Tel (07) 377 0283
Fax (07) 377 4683

Double/Twin $140
Single $80
(Full breakfast)
Children $40
Dinner $40 by arrangement
Children welcome
1 Queen 1 Twin (2 bdrm)
Bathrooms: 1 Ensuite 1 Guest share
We take only one party at a time

B ob and I have enjoyed hosting for many years, our lovely new home in Hill Top Park with beautiful mountains views from our living area makes our guests' stay in Taupo very special. All attractions are nearby, golf courses, thermal pools, Huka Falls and fishing. We are retired sheep and cattle farmers, who enjoy travelling and meeting other travellers. Bob excels at golf and is in charge of cooked breakfasts. Home-made jams and marmalade are my specialty. Please phone for directions. Good off street parking

Taupo - Acacia Bay *6 km SW of Taupo*
Leece's Homestay *Homestay*

Marlene Leece
98 Wakeman Road,
Acacia Bay,
Taupo, 3330

Tel (07) 378 6099
or 021 0243 9190
Fax (07) 378 6092

Double/Twin $110 - $120
Single $80
(Continental breakfast)
1 King 1 Queen 2 Single (2 bdrm)
Bathrooms: 1 Ensuite 1 Guest share

Your host Marlene & Jaspa (my Birman cat) extend a warm welcome to our large wood interior home with woodfire for winter and north facing sunny deck from guest bedroom. Also magnificent view of Lake Taupo from lounge and front deck. There are bush walks and steps down to lake to swim in summer with an extended new piece of road. Easy walking and different view. Awaiting your arrival with anticipation of making friends. Please phone for directions.

Taupo *1 km NW of Taupo*
Pataka House *B&B Homestay Separate Suite*

Raewyn & Neil Alexander
8 Pataka Road,
Taupo

Tel (07) 378 5481
Fax (07) 378 5461
pataka-homestay@xtra.co.nz
www.patakahouse.co.nz

Double/Twin $140
Single $100
(Full breakfast)
Children $40 up to 13 years
Separate suite $150
Visa MC accepted
Children welcome
2 Queen 2 Single (3 bdrm)
Extra comfortable beds in all rooms
Bathrooms: 1 Ensuite 1 Private
1 Guest share All renovated bathrooms

Pataka House is highly recommended for its hospitality. We assure guests that their stay lives up to New Zealand's reputation as being a home away from home. We are easily located just 1 turn off the lake front and up a tree-lined driveway. Our garden room is privately situated, has an appealing decor and extremely popular to young and old alike. Stay for 1 night or stay for more as Lake Taupo will truly be the highlight of your holiday. Mika, a burmese, loves visitors.

Taupo *1 km N of Taupo Central*
Lakeland Homestay *Homestay*
Lesley & Chris
11 Williams Street,
Taupo

Tel (07) 378 1952
or 0274 877 971
Fax (07) 378 1912
lakeland.bb@xtra.co.nz

Double/Twin $130 - $140
Single $70
(Continental breakfast)
Visa MC accepted
1 Queen 2 Twin (2 bdrm)
Bathrooms: 1 Ensuite 1 Family share

Nestled in a restful tree-lined street, a mere 6 minutes stroll from the lake's edge and shopping centre Lakeland Homestay is a cheerful and cosy home that enjoys views of the lake and mountains. Keen gardeners, anglers and golfers Chris and Lesley work and play in an adventure oasis. By the way we have two cats, Caddy and Monica. Laundry facilities are available and a courtesy car is available for coach travellers, there is off-street parking. Please phone for directions.

Taupo *15 km N of Taupo*
Brackenhurst *B&B Homestay Farmstay Separate Suite Cottage with Kitchen*
Barbara & Ray Graham
801 Oruanui Road,
RD 1, Taupo

Tel (07) 377 6451
or 0274 456 217
Fax (07) 377 6451
rgbg@xtra.co.nz

Double/Twin $110 - $150
Single $75 - $75
(Full breakfast)
Children $40
Dinner $50
GST Registered
Visa MC accepted
Pet free home
Children and pets welcome
2 Queen 1 Double 4 Single (4 bdrm)
Bathrooms: 2 Ensuite 2 Private

Brackenhurst is a modern Lockwood home on 14 acres of peaceful countryside with fantails, tuis and bellbirds in the large garden. highland cattle and sheep. A warm welcome with peace and tranquility. . We are half a kilometre from SH1 and close to Huka Falls, geothermal activities, golf courses a days outing to Rotorua, Waitomo Caves or Napier. Private guests wing in the house or separate annex offer away from home comforts. Breakfast to suit, continental style or full English. Dinner available by arrangement.

Taupo *15 km N of Taupo*
Maimoa House *B&B Homestay Farmstay Separate Suite Apartment*

Margaret & Godfrey Ellis
41 Oak Drive,
off Palmer Mill Road, Taupo

Tel (07) 376 9000
or 021 233 4640
mewestview@xtra.co.nz
www.maimoahomestay.co.nz

Double/Twin $140 - $150
Single $95
(Special breakfast)
Children $30 ages 5-14
Dinner by arrangement
10% discount for 3 nights or more
Visa MC accepted
Children and pets welcome
1 King/Twin 1 Queen 1 Twin (3 bdrm)
Our rooms are airy & spacious with great views
Bathrooms: 1 Ensuite 1 Guest share
Large Spa bath, seperate shower, toilet

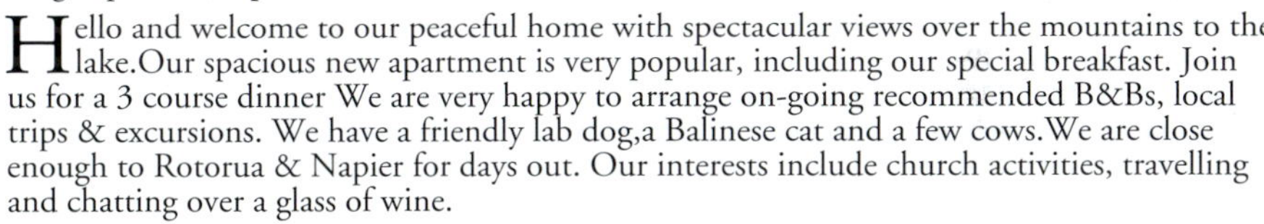

Hello and welcome to our peaceful home with spectacular views over the mountains to the lake.Our spacious new apartment is very popular, including our special breakfast. Join us for a 3 course dinner We are very happy to arrange on-going recommended B&Bs, local trips & excursions. We have a friendly lab dog,a Balinese cat and a few cows.We are close enough to Rotorua & Napier for days out. Our interests include church activities, travelling and chatting over a glass of wine.

Taupo *1 km S of Taupo*
Above The Lake - Taupo *B&B*

Angela & Bruce Christoffersen
46 Rokino Road,
Taupo, 3330

Tel (07) 378 8738
windsor-charters@xtra.co.nz
www.taupostay.com

Double/Twin $160 - $215
Single $150 - $205
(Full breakfast)
Visa MC accepted
Pet free home
1 King 2 Queen (3 bdrm)
Bathrooms: 1 Ensuite
1 Private 1 Guest share

On arrival, relax and enjoy magical lake, mountain and Taupo town views. Your supremely comfortable accommodation is centrally located in the heart of Taupo. Easy to find, and just a short stroll to the lake and own, hot water beach. Walking distance to award winning restaurants. On arrival, join your hosts for coffee or a glass of wine. Make use of our extensive local knowledge to plan your Taupo experience.

Taupo - Acacia Bay *5 km SW of Taupo*
The Loft *B&B*

Jane Redfern and John de Latour
3 Wakeman Road,
Acacia Bay, Taupo

Tel (07) 377 1040 or 027 485 1347
Fax (07) 377 1049
book@theloftnz.com
www.theloftnz.com

Double/Twin $155 - $185
Single $100 - $130
(Full breakfast)
Children $50 - $75
Dinner $50 - $65 pp
Washing available   POA
Visa MC accepted
Children welcome
Internet available
3 Queen 3 Single (3 bdrm)
Well apppinted rooms with view of native bush
Bathrooms: 3 Ensuite

Situated five minutes from Taupo township and a few minutes walk to the lake and a very good restaurent. The Loft is set in a cottage garden adajacent to a native bush reserve. Hosts Jane & John look forward to your visit. Enjoy a scrumptious breakfast of fresh fruit salad, orange juice, wonderful poached or scrambled eggs with bacon mushrooms and our own delicious tomatoes when in season. Tea and coffee making facilities on landing upstairs. Lovely outdoor seating area.

Taupo *1.5 km N of Taupo*
Rive Gauche *Luxury Homestay studio apartment*

Lynne Fauchelle & Jim Veitch
128 Ferndale Way,
RD 1, Taupo 3377

Tel (07) 377 6167 or 021 050 6735
lynnejim4@clear.net.nz
www.rivegauchetaupo.co.nz

Double/Twin $175 - $225
Single $150 - $175
(Continental breakfast)
Children negotiable
Rollaway bed available
Restaurant 5 minutes walk away
Lynne parle français
Visa MC accepted
Pet free home
Internet available
2 King 1 Queen 1 Single (3 bdrm)
Wifi access. Satellite TV and heat pump/air con. in studio.
Bathrooms: 3 Ensuite All fully-tiled with underfloor heating

Set on a 1 hectare site on the left bank of the Waikato River just 3 minutes from Taupo town centre, Rive Gauche was purpose-built in 2007 to offer quality lodge-style B&B accommodation. We have 3 options: a separate studio with lovely river views, a queen room and a king plus king single. Our B&B rooms have access to a kitchenette with fridge. Facilities include air conditioning, satellite TV and Wifi. We love to travel and can advise you on your itinerary. Fluent French spoken.

Taupo *13 km N of Taupo*
Bellbird Ridge Alpaca Farm *B&B Farmstay Cottage with Kitchen*

Rex and Donna Ferrall
68 Tangye Road, RD 1, Taupo

Tel (07) 377 1996 or 027 552 2055
Fax (07) 377 1992
info@bellbirdridge.co.nz
www.bellbirdridge.co.nz

Double/Twin $180 - $180
Single $150 - $150
(Full breakfast)
Children $50 under 12
Dinner 1 course $30, 2 courses $40
or 3 courses $50 BYO beverages
or purchase from hosts
Visa MC Eftpos accepted
Children and pets welcome
Internet available
1 King/Twin 2 Queen 1 Single (4 bdrm)
Bathrooms: 1 Ensuite 1 Private

Take a break and unwind in our charming and secluded self-contained one bedroom cottage, enjoy our beautiful garden and friendly alpacas, and labradoodle located only 10 mins from Taupo. The cottage has a separate queen bedroom, kitchen/dining/lounge area & deck with BBQ. Generous breakfast provisions are provided. Also available in a separate guest wing in the homestead, where you would be our only guests, are a super king, 1 queen, 1 queen & a single bedrooms with your own bathroom with full breakfast cooked for you.

Taupo *1 km S of Taupo*
Moselle *B&B Separate Suite Apartment with Kitchen Self Contained*

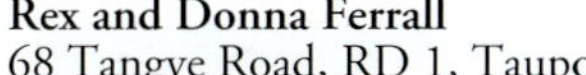

Grahame & Anne Velvin
3 Te Hepera Street,
Taupo, 3330

Tel (07) 377 2922
or 021 072 9975
Fax (07) 377 2290
ragevelvin@xtra.co.nz
moselletaupo.com

Double/Twin $180
Single $150
(Full breakfast)
Children welcome
Visa MC Amex accepted
Children and pets welcome
1 King/Twin 1 King 2 Single
(3 bdrm plus sofa bed)
Bathrooms: 3 Ensuite 3 Private
1 spa bath

Moselle has a S/K bed and top quality linen New ensuite,Laundry and fully self contained. Sky TV video and fresh breakfast food supplied daily to your requirements. A four minute drive to the Taupo Golf Club two minutes drive to Thermal Hot Pools & 5 minutes drive to the Taupo Township, walking distance to the Lake. Private parking. 90 minutes to Ski Field.

Turangi *1 km SW of Turangi Information Centre*
Brown Trout House *B&B Homestay*

Bruce & Nita Wilde
11 Kokopu Street,
Turangi, 3334

Tel (07) 386 0308
or 027 253 3415
Fax (07) 386 0308
kohinoor@xtra.co.nz
www.browntrouthouse.co.nz

Double/Twin $130 - $140
Single $90
(Full breakfast)
Children negotiable
Lunches and dinner
by prior arrangement
Visa MC accepted
1 King/Twin 1 Queen
2 Twin (3 bdrm)
Bathrooms: 1 Private 1 Guest share

Welcome to Brown Trout house overlooking the Tongariro River in Turangi, halfway between Auckland and Wellington. Your bedroom opens on to the spacious deck. Have refreshments or step out our gate on to the Tongariro River Walkway or in to world famous fishing pools. Bruce is a keen fisherman willing to share his knowledge. Shuttle pickup for the Tongariro Crossing arranged. Choose walks, golf, skiing or a hot swim 5 mins drive away. Friendly experienced hosts willing to give genuine kiwi hospitality.

Turangi *15 km SW of Turangi*
Omori Lake House *Luxury Lodge*

Niel & Raewyn Groombridge
31 Omori Road,
Omori

Tel (07) 386 0420
or 021 667 092
stay@omorilakehouse.co.nz
www.omorilakehouse.co.nz

Double/Twin $175
Single $165
(Special breakfast)
Dinner by arrangement
Visa MC accepted
Pet free home
Not suitable for children
2 King (2 bdrm)
Bathrooms: 2 Ensuite

Our new boutique accommodation high above Omori has stunning views across to Taupo. There are two en-suite guest rooms with king beds, tea/coffee facilities and private deck. Raewyn loves to cook and eating well is part of the experience. Enjoy barbeques or meals with kiwi classics Omori on the menu. We are close to a variety of activities including fly-fishing, The Tongariro Alpine crossing, bush walks, thermal pools and ski slopes.

Turangi *54 km SW of Taupo*
Founders@Turangi *B&B*

Peter & Chris Stewart
253 Taupahi Road,
Turangi, 3334.

Tel (07) 386 8539
Fax (07) 386 8534
chris@founders.co.nz
www.founders.co.nz

Double/Twin $180
Single $120
(Special breakfast)
Visa MC Eftpos accepted
Pet free home
Not suitable for children
Internet available
2 King/Twin 3 Queen (4 bdrm)
Bathrooms: 4 Ensuite

Welcome to Turangi and to our home where 4 ensuite guest bedrooms open onto the veranda. A myriad of outdoor activities are available at this place for all seasons, with the Tongariro River, the volcanoes of Tongariro National Park and magnificent Lake Taupo on our doorstep. Breakfast each morning, in our sunny dining room. We happily cook early breakfasts for Tongariro Alpine Crossing adventurers! Enjoy the views at lakeside restaurants or walk to dinner in town. We love to share this beautiful place with visitors.

Omori - Turangi *16 km NW of Turangi*
Wills' Place *B&B*

Jill & Brian Wills
145 Omori Road, Omori, 3381

Tel (07) 386 7339
or 027 228 8960
Fax (07) 386 7339
b.g@willsplace.co.nz
www.willsplace.co.nz

Double/Twin $140 - $160
Single $110 - $130
(Full breakfast)
Children negotiable
Dinner by arrangement
Visa MC accepted
Pet free home
Children welcome
Internet available
2 Queen 2 Single (2 bdrm)
Private suite with 2 bedrooms
Bathrooms: 1 Private Bath with shower over

A lakeside home and superior guest suite with wonderful views. Fishing, boating, swimming, walks. Off the beaten track, yet only 10-15 minutes to shops, restaurants, thermal pools, Tongariro River, rafting, etc. 40 minutes to World Heritage Tongariro National Park. Private suite with two bedrooms, full size bathroom with bath and shower, living area, tea-making facilities, fridge, microwave, television, laundry, email access. Private patio overlooking the lake. Suite yours alone with separate entry and safe parking. Discount for three or more nights.

Turangi *2 km N of Turangi*
At the Tongariro Riverside B & B *B&B Homestay*

Leslie & Maryke Wilson
72 Herekiekie Street, Turangi, 3334

Tel (07) 386 7447
or 027 781 0488
info@bytheriver.co.nz
www.bytheriver.co.nz

Double/Twin $125
Single $125
(Special breakfast)
Dinner $45 pp with wine,
by arrangement
Visa MC accepted
Internet available
1 King/Twin (1 bdrm)
Overlooks the world famous
Tongariro River
Bathrooms: 1 Ensuite

Location! Location! Location! Right alongside the world famous Tongariro river. Trout fishing - just metres from your king/twin ensuite bedroom (latest tiled walk-in shower). Double glazing and under floor heating. Wonderful sunsets in a peaceful and tranquil setting. Situated halfway between Auckland and Wellington with secure on- site parking. Leave your car with us for the Tongariro Alpine Crossing - (Shuttles arranged). Skifields just 40 minutes away. Free WiFi, Air-Conditioning, Flat screen TV, DVD, Radio, CD, i-Pod charger, Tea/ Coffee making facilities and fridge. Generous continental breakfast (fresh fruit and cheese etc). Restaurants just a stroll away.

Turangi *0.5 km E of Turangi*
Ika Lodge *B&B Apartment with Kitchen*

Margaret & Kenneth Toon
155 Taupahi Road,
Turangi, 3334

Tel (07) 386 5538
or 027 292 5023
ikalodge@ika.co.nz
www.ika.co.nz

Double/Twin $155 - $170
Single $140
(Full breakfast)
Dinner on request
Visa MC Diners Eftpos accepted
Pet free home
Children welcome
4 Queen 1 Single (4 bdrm)
2 B&B Suites
2 Bedroom Apartment
Bathrooms: 2 Ensuite 1 Guest share
2 ensuites, apartment 1 shared.

Ika Lodge offers superior bed and breakfast homestay suites and a 2 bedroom apartment on the banks of the Tongariro River minutes from some of the worlds best trout fishing. A perfect base for the Tongariro National Park ski fields and the famous Tongariro Crossing trek all in a tranquil garden setting.

Gisborne
Waihau Bay
Te Kaha
araenui
35
Tolaga Bay
2
Waipaoa
Gisborne
2
0   Kilometres   20
0   Miles   12
Gisborne

Tolaga Bay *3 km N of Tolaga Bay*
Papatahi *Homestay Separate Suite*
Nicki & Bruce Jefferd
427 Waiapu Rd,
Tolaga Bay

Tel (06) 862 6623
or 021 283 7178
Fax (06) 862 6623
nickibrucej@xtra.co.nz

Double/Twin $120
Single $70
(Full breakfast)
Children half price
Dinner $35pp
Children welcome
1 Queen 1 Double 2 Single (3 bdrm)
Bathrooms: 1 Ensuite 1 Guest share

Papatahi Homestay... easy to find being just 3km north of the Tolaga Bay township, on the Pacific Coast Highway. We have a comfortable, modern, sunny home set in a wonderful garden. Papatahi offers separate accommodation with ensuite. A golf course, fishing charters, the Tolaga Bay Cashmere Co. and several magnificent beaches are all just minutes away. Daily farm activities are often of interest to our guests. Friendly farm pets add to the experience! Great country meals and good wine are a speciality. Inspection will impress!

Waipaoa *20 km N of Gisborne*
The Willows *Farmstay*
Rosemary & Graham Johnson
Waipaoa,
RD 1,
Gisborne

Tel (06) 862 5605
or 027 483 7365
waipaoa@bordernet.co.nz

Double/Twin $90
Single $60
(Full breakfast)
Children 10% discount
Dinner $30 by arrangement
2 Queen 2 Single (3 bdrm)
Bathrooms: 1 Private 1 Guest share

Our home is situated on a hill amid a park-like garden with some wonderful trees planted by our forefathers. We enjoy the amenities available in the city and also the country life on our 440 acre property involving cattle, sheep, grapes and cropping. We now offer a double bedroom with a private bathroom. The bedroom has its own access so you can enjoy privacy if you so desire. We are situated 20km north of Gisborne on SH2 through the scenic Waioeka Gorge.

Gisborne *0.5 km N of Gisborne Central*
Sea View *B&B Homestay*

Raewyn & Gary Robinson
68 Salisbury Road,
Gisborne

Tel (06) 867 3879
or 021 031 1514
raewyn@regaleggs.co.nz

Double/Twin $100 - $120
Single $100
(Continental breakfast)
Children welcome
1 Queen 1 Double
1 Twin 1 Single (3 bdrm)
Bathrooms: 2 Private

Luxury, comfort and a friendly welcome always at our beachfront Bed & Breakfast. Seaview is situated on the foreshore of Waikanae beach with unsurpassed panoramic views of Young Nicks Head and Poverty Bay. Just 50 metres from front door to golden sand, and warm blue waters. Only 2 minutes drive to the city (easy walking distance) and visitor information centre. Enjoy safe swimming and great surfing. 5 minutes to international golf course and Olympic pool complex. We offer 2 double bedrooms and twin room. 2 private bathrooms. Internet facilities available.

Gisborne *5 km NE of Gisborne*
Beach Stay *B&B*

Peter & Dorothy Rouse
111 Wairere Road,
Wainui Beach,
Gisborne

Tel (06) 868 8111
Fax (06) 868 8162
pete.dot@xtra.co.nz

Double/Twin $90 - $110
Single $60
(Full breakfast)
Children $10
Dinner $25 pp
Pets welcome
1 Queen 2 Single (2 bdrm)
Bathrooms: 1 Ensuite 1 Private

We welcome you to our home which is situated right on the beach front at Wainui. The steps from the lawn lead down to the beach, which is renowned for its lovely clean sand, surf, pleasant walking and good swimming. Gisborne can also offer a host of entertainment, including golf on 1 of the finest golf courses, charter fishing trips, wine trails, Eastwood Hill Arboretum etc, or you may wish to relax on the beach for the day.

Gisborne *14 km SW of Gisborne*
Fairlight *B&B*

Kay and Don Orchiston
52 Saddler Road,
RD 2,
Gisborne 4072

Tel (06) 862 8499
or 027 440 9556
orchiston@clear.net.nz
www.cmrn.co.nz/fairlight.htm

Double/Twin $120
Single $80
(Full breakfast)
Children by arrangement
Dinner by arrangement
Children and pets welcome
1 King 1 Queen 1 Double
3 Single (4 bdrm)
Bathrooms: 1 Private
1 Shower as well

Our home is situated on a hill with expansive views of the sea, city and rural wine region. We are 14 kms south of the city. Gisborne has beautiful beaches, scenic walks, restaurants and excellent sport facilities. We have 2 friendly sheep dogs and 2 elusive bengal cats. Visitors welcome to experience handling sheep and cattle. Trout fishing and deep sea fishing by prior arrangement. Please see http://www.cmrn.co.nz/fairlight.htm

Gisborne *2.0 km NE of Gisborne*
Thistles *Homestay*

Barrie & Lesley Munday
137 Riverside Road,
Gisborne, 4010

Tel (06) 868 8900
or 021 035 0587
thistles137@gmail.com

Double/Twin $130
Single $95
(Full breakfast)
Children by arrangement
Pet free home
Children welcome
1 Queen 1 Double (2 bdrm)
Bathrooms: 1 Private

Thistles quiet location offers comfortable modern homestyle hospitality. An ideal base for exploring the Historic East Coast, the first landing sites of Captain Cook and the Chardonnay Capital of New Zealand. Tours of local vineyards and wineries can be arranged. Unwind in the spa bath before savouring the delights of the many restaurants in Gisborne. French, German and Scottish dialect spoken! Secure parking available.

Taranaki, Wanganui, Ruapehu, Rangitikei
Te Awamutu
Otorohanga
Waitomo
Te Kuiti
Piopio
3
4
Taumarunui
43
Piriaka
Owhango
47
Tura
New Plymouth
43
Egmont National Park
Stratford
3
Ohakune
Raetihi
4
Taihape
Waitotara
3
Wanganui
Marton
Fielding
Colyton
Newbury
Woodville
Oroua Downs
Palmerston North
Tokomaru
Pahiat
Foxton
Eketahuna
Ki
Levin
Otaki
Te Horo
Kilometres
0
40
Miles
0
24

Taranaki, Whanganui, Ruapehu, Rangitikei

New Plymouth *25 km N of New Plymouth*
Cottage by the Sea *Cottage with Kitchen Garden studios with kitchens*

Nancy & Hugh Mills
66 Lower Turangi Road,
RD 43, Waitara

Tel (06) 754 4548
or (06) 754 7915
cottagebythesea@clear.net.nz
www.cottagebythesea.co.nz

Double/Twin $175 - $215
Single $165 - $205
(Breakfast by arrangement)
Restaurant and takeaway nearby
Extras $40 each/per night
Visa MC accepted
Not suitable for children
1 King/Twin 3 Queen
2 Double (4 bdrm)
Cottages sleep 2-4; Studios sleep 2
Bathrooms: 4 Ensuite (1 per accommodation)

Find yourself, lose yourself - the choice is yours. Peacefulness and privacy are our specialty - a perfect place to unwind. Enjoy the everchanging seaviews, discover our tranquil sunken garden, wander down 100 handcrafted steps to the secluded blacksand beach. Two 1-bedroom cottages and two, open-plan studios, nestled in their own gardens with kitchens and ensuites. Minutes from cafes, coastal walks, gardens and Mt Taranaki. Two small, cheeky poodles may greet you. See our website for more photos and details.

New Plymouth *5 km NW of New Plymouth centre*
Whaler's Rest *B&B*

Maureen & Denis Whiting
86A Barrett Road,
New Plymouth 4310

Tel (06) 751 4272
or 027 328 0268
whalersrest@clear.net.nz
www.whalersrest.co.nz

Double/Twin $110
Single $90
(Continental breakfast)
Children $20
Children and pets welcome
1 Double 1 Twin (2 bdrm)
Bathrooms: 1 Ensuite 1 Private

Large double bedroom with ensuite, and your own deck for drinks, plus twin room with private bathroom. Tea and coffee facilities in your room. Breakfast, continental. We are on the gateway to Surf Highway, 10 minutes to Oakura beach and 5 minutes to New Plymouth City featuring the Wind Wand, coastal walkway, Puke Ariki Museum and Pukekura Park. Your hosts Maureen and Denis who love their tennis and garden welcome you. We have a very sociable labrador Stella, and 2 cats, Tuffy and Biscuit. Please phone for bookings and directions.

New Plymouth *0.5 km SW of New Plymouth*
Airlie House *B&B Apartment with Kitchen*

Gabrielle Masters
161 Powderham Street,
New Pymouth

Tel (06) 757 8866
or 021 472 072
Fax (06) 757 8866
email@airliehouse.co.nz
www.airliehouse.co.nz

Double/Twin $0 - $155
Single $0 - $120 (Full breakfast)
Children negotiable
Studio $155 double
Visa MC Eftpos accepted
Internet available
1 King/Twin
2 Queen 2 Single (3 bdrm)
Bathrooms: 1 Ensuite 2 Private
1 claw bath

Airlie House is a 110 year old character home nestled among mature trees and garden. This beautiful home provides 2 guest bedrooms with ensuites or private bathrooms, plus a studio apartment with its own kitchen and private bathroom. Located in central New Plymouth Airlie House is an easy 5 minute walk from shops, restaurants, the sea front, parks and many other local attractions. All rooms have many amenities available for your comfort, including Sky Digital TV, broadband and wireless internet access.

New Plymouth *0.01 km N of New Plymouth City*
Timata Ora *Luxury B&B Luxury B&B 5 min walk from CBD*

Carol & Rodney Hall
55 Gover Street,
New Plymouth

Tel (06) 757 9917
or 0274 523 885
Fax (06) 759 1654
carol_rodney@iconz.co.nz
www.timataora.com

Double/Twin $130 - $145
Single $120 - $135 (Full breakfast)
Family suite when both
bedrooms used $230
Visa MC Eftpos accepted
4 Queen 1 Twin (5 bdrm)
All large with own bathrooms,
TV, coffee, tea & extras
Bathrooms: 4 Ensuite
All suites each have own bathroom

We warmly welcome guests to our fully refurbished central city home. A 1920's heritage home, Timata Ora offers 4 luxurious queen suites (1 with 4 Poster) each with own bathroom, TV, fridge, hair drier, iron/ironing board, heated towel rails, complimentary beverages and in room treats. The family suite has an additional twin bedroom along with the queen bedroom. Gregarious cat Murphy (the Butler) shares Timata Ora. Breakfast in your suite, dining room, in the conservatory or on the terrace.

New Plymouth *0.5 km E of New Plymouth CBD*
Courtenay Villa *B&B Homestay*
David & Marilyn McDonald
240 Courtenay Street, New Plymouth, 4312

Tel (06) 759 1515 or 021 847 888
courtenayvilla@actrix.co.nz

Double/Twin $120 Single $80 (Full breakfast)
Dinner 3 courses $35, by prior arrangement
Gluten-free options.
Discounts available for stays longer than 3 nights
Visa MC accepted
Pet free home   Internet available
1 Queen 1 Twin (2 bdrm)
Bathrooms: 2 Private

We're delighted to welcome you to Courtenay Villa, our authentically preserved 1902 home, with two relaxing lounges and a sunny patio surrounded by roses. Our accommodation comprises two rooms (one queen, one twin) which are warm and bright with very comfortable beds, electric blankets, feather duvets, and well-stocked bookcases. Each room has its own private bathroom, both of them with massage showers and one with a traditional claw-foot bathtub.

We offer warm hospitality and delicious meals that include home-made bread and gluten-free options. Help yourself to tea and coffee in the kitchen at any time. Dinner (pre-arranged) is served with New Zealand wine, although several restaurants are within 3-10 minutes' walk. Wireless broadband internet access is available free, as is the transfer of your photos from digital camera to CD.

We're located just off State Highway 3 in the centre of New Plymouth -- less than 8 minutes' walk to the Coastal Walkway and 5 minutes to the beautiful Te Henui bush track.

New Plymouth *2 km NE of Post Office*
The Grange *B&B*

Rachael Nielsen and Alan Clarke
44B Victoria Road,
Brooklands,
New Plymouth

Tel (06) 759 8004
or 0274 345 680
grangebandb@xtra.co.nz

Double/Twin $120 - $140
Single $80 - $90
(Full breakfast)
Visa MC Diners Amex accepted
Pets welcome
Internet Available
1 King/Twin 2 Queen (3 bdrm)
1 Queen room has patio,
over looking bush
Bathrooms: 3 Ensuite

Come and stay in our modern award-winning home built with the privacy and comfort of our guests in mind. With unique bush views and a house designed to take full advantage of the sun, our guests can enjoy relaxing in the lounge or the extensive tiled courtyards and listen to the sounds of the native birds. The Grange is centrally heated, security controlled and located adjacent to the renowned Pukekura Park and Bowl of Brooklands. The city is 10 minutes walk. Laundry available.

New Plymouth - Bell Block *7 km SE of New Plymouth*
K & J's Bed and Breakfast *B&B*

Keith and Joy Hosking
94 Parklands Avenue,
Bell Block, 4312

Tel (06) 755 4199
or 027 294 9682
Fax (06) 755 4199
kjhosking@xtra.co.nz

Double/Twin $110
Single $80
(Continental breakfast)
Not suitable for children
2 Queen (2 bdrm)
1 downstairs and 1 upstairs
Bathrooms: 1 Ensuite 1 Private

Lovely sea and mountain views very close to airport. 10 minutes to central New Plymouth. Restaurant, Bank and shopping facilities in walking distance. Able to walk to the beach. Situated in quiet street. 2007 winner of 'Supreme House of the Year' award. Broadband and Wireless available. Very close to Golf Course.

New Plymouth *1 km E of Fitzroy Shops*
Mountain View Bed & Breakfast *B&B*

Colin & Pauline Christie
14 Chatswood Grove, Fitzroy,
New Plymouth, 4312

Tel (06) 769 6971
or 027 481 7954
Fax (06) 769 6973
mountainmeadows@xtra.co.nz

Double/Twin $120
Single $75
(Continental breakfast provisions)
Children $30
Visa MC accepted
Children and pets welcome
Internet available
1 Queen 1 Double 1 Twin (2 bdrm)
1Queen room, 1 Twin room,
Double sofa bed in guest lounge
Bathrooms: 1 Guest share

We welcome you along with our two Shih Tzu's to our home. Guest lounge has Sky TV, Wireless Internet, Fridge, Microwave, etc. Relax in the Garden, have a Barbeque or refreshing Spa. Close to Fitzroy Shops, Fitzroy Beach, Coastal Walkway, Lake Rotomanu, Golf Course, Valley Mega Shopping Centre, Cafes, Restaurants and CBD. 10 mins to airport.

New Plymouth *4 km E of New Plymouth*
Astron Dales Deer Farm *B&B Farmstay Apartment with Kitchen*

Bob & Daphne
149 Smart Road,
New Plymouth, 4372

Tel (06) 757 9853
or 0274 313 123
Fax (06) 757 9853
pestfree1@xtra.co.nz

Double/Twin $150
Single $100
(Continental breakfast provisions)
Children up to 15 years $35
Children and pets welcome
1 Queen 1 Double (1 bdrm)
1 Queen in bedroom
1Bed settee in lounge
Bathrooms: 1 Private

Set in tranquil surroundings, Astron Dales Deer Farm offers a seperate, modern and comfortable apartment with all amentities. Ideally located on the city boundary only 1km from the main highway, and 1.5km to the new Waiwhakaio shopping complex. The views over the gently rolling farmland with quietly grazing deer and on to the sea beyond offers relaxation, and a 'sense of away from it all'. We and our pets offer a warm welcome and an enjoyable stay. Your house trained pet is also welcome.

Stratford *0.1 km N of Stratford*
Stratford Lodge B&B on Stallard Farm *B&B Homestay Farmstay*

Billieanne & Corb Stallard
3514 State Highway 3,
Stratford, 4394
(600 metres N of PO)

Tel (06) 765 8324
Fax (06) 765 8325
stallardbb@infogen.net.nz
www.stratfordlodge.co.nz

Double/Twin (any two people) $98
Single $60 (Full breakfast)
Children age 5-15 $20
Visa MC accepted Pet free home
Children welcome
Internet available
2 Double 2 Twin 2 Single (4 bdrm)
Antique romantic
Bathrooms: 4 Ensuite 1 Guest share

Graceful 'Upstairs Downstairs' comfort. A down to earth gardeners rest Aga cooked or continental breakfast included. Free self-catering kitchen, tea, coffee, biscuits. Homely or private. Own key. Optional separate lounge. Restaurants, taverns, shops nearby. Rooms are antique, romantic with TV, heaters, electric blankets, serviced daily. Gardens, BBQ, row boat, bush bath, river walks. 15 minutes to Mt Egmont ski fields, tramping. Centrally located easy distance to New Plymouth, museums, famous gardens, tourist attractions. Interests include gemstones travel, art. Welcome. AA accredited.

If you need any information ask your hosts
they are your own personal travel agent and guide.

Egmont National Park *9 km SW of Stratford*
Anderson's Alpine Lodge *B&B Homestay Farmstay*

Berta Anderson
922 Pembroke Road
RD 21, Stratford, 4391

Tel (06) 765 6620
or 0274 412 372
andersonsalpinelodge@xtra.co.nz
www.andersonsalpinelodge.co.nz

Double/Twin $160 - $190
Single $160
(Full breakfast)
Visa MC accepted
Children and pets welcome
1 King/Twin 1 Double
1 Twin (3 bdrm)
Secluded , romantic rooms
with Swiss alpine ambiance
Bathrooms: 3 Ensuite

Swiss style lodge rests in 5 acres of native bush capturing majestic views of Mount Egmont/Taranaki. Landscaping includes New Zealand natives, lakes, waterwheel and bushwalks. Home of abundant native birds and a great place for photography. Three charming rooms with ensuite, one with spa bath. Specially crafted wooden interior, logs and stonework on the outside, log fire and beautiful views from every floor level. Egmont National Park opposite front gate. 5km to spectacular walking tracks, summit climb (guides available) and skiing. Helicopter rides by request. Trout streams, gardens and museums nearby. 9km to Stratford. Berta Anderson has lived on the mountain since 1976.

Waitotara - Whanganui (Formerly Wanganui)
29 km SW of Whanganui
Ashley Park
Farmstay Cottage with Kitchen
Wendy Pearce
State Highway 3,
Box 36,
Waitotara,
Wanganui

Tel (06) 346 5917
Fax (06) 346 5861
ashley_park@xtra.co.nz
www.ashleypark.co.nz

Double/Twin $100 - $140
Single $100
(Full breakfast)
Dinner $30
Visa MC Eftpos accepted
Internet available
1 Queen 4 Single (3 bdrm)
Bathrooms: 1 Ensuite 1 Guest share

We have a 500 acre sheep and cattle farm and live in a comfortable home, set in an attractive garden with a swimming pool and tennis court. Also in the garden is an antique shop selling Devonshire teas. 100 metres from the house is a 4 acre park and lake, aviaries and a collection of hand fed pet farm animals. We welcome guests to have dinner with us. Self-contained accommodation is available in the park.

Whanganui (Formerly Wanganui) *2 km NW of Whanganui*

City centre

Kembali *B&B Homestay*
Marylyn & Wes Palmer
26 Taranaki Street,
St Johns Hill, Wanganui

Tel (06) 347 1727
or 027 741 7517
wespalmer@xtra.co.nz

Double/Twin $110 - $125
Single $80 - $95 (Full breakfast)
Small charge for laundry facilities
Visa MC accepted
Pet free home
Not suitable for children
Internet available
1 Queen 1 Twin (2 bdrm)
Firm beds, attractive decor,
centrally heated
Bathrooms: 1 Private

Kembali is a modern, centrally heated, sunny home in a quiet street overlooking trees and wetlands. Situated upstairs are guest bedrooms, bathroom and lounge (with TV, fridge, tea/coffee) for 1 party/groups exclusive use. Retired, children married, we offer a restful stay. We have many varied interests including church activities. Parking and laundry available. Guests compliment us on our delicious breakfasts. 5 minutes drive to city, heritage buildings, restored paddle steamer, restaurants, museum, art gallery and walks. We look forward to welcoming you.

Whanganui (Formerly Wanganui) *.5 km N of Whanganui centre*

Braemar House *B&B Guest House*
Clive Rivers
2 Plymouth Street, Wanganui

Tel (06) 348 2301
Fax (06) 348 2301
contact@braemarhouse.co.nz
www.braemarhouse.co.nz

Double/Twin $80 - $120
Single $75 - $90
(Full breakfast)
Children $20
Dinner $25 by arrangement
Visa MC Eftpos accepted
Not suitable for children
4 Queen 1 Double 3 Twin (8 bdrm)
Individually period designed
Bathrooms: 4 Guest share
Deluxe sized bath Powerful Showers

Welcome to 'Olde Worlde Charm'. This restored historic Homestead, nestled alongside the Wanganui River, has a homely ambience making your stay restful and enjoyable. The graceful entrance leads to eight centrally heated, period-designed bedrooms, drawing room and dining room. Laundry, wireless internet, fully equipped kitchen available. Off-street parking set in beautiful gardens. Close to the city and tourist attractions, The paddle steamer Waimarie passes daily in front of the Homestead. We look forward to you visiting Braemar House.

Whanganui (Formerly Wanganui) *20 km N of Marton*
Te-Aunui Farmstay *B&B Farmstay Cottage with Kitchen Guest House*

Mike & Marg Webster
RD 11,
Wanganui

Tel (06) 327 3821
TE-AUNUI@xtra.co.nz
www.te-aunuifarmstay.co.nz

Double/Twin $130
Single $75
(Special breakfast)
Children $25
Dinner $40 by arrangement
Children and pets welcome
1 King 1 Queen 2 Single (3 bdrm)
Bathrooms: 1 Private

Te-Aunui is a 300 acre sheep and beef farm. We offer a fully self-contained 3 bedroomed homestead fr guests to explore the farm from or join Marg and I as we work our way through the farm year, shearing, rearing calves, lambing etc. Farm tours and home cooking a speciality. Te-Aunuiis an ideal base to tour the Rangitikei from with one of Marg's picnic hampers. TV, phone and internet access but no cell phone coverage in the valley.

Taumarunui *5 km NE of Taumarunui*
Matawa Country Home *Farmstay*

Shirley & Allan Jones
213 Taumarunui Road,
Taumarunui

Tel (07) 896 7722
Fax (07) 895 6927
costleyj@farmside.co.nz

Double/Twin $100 - $120
Single $70 - $80
(Full breakfast)
Children half price
Dinner by arrangement
Visa MC accepted
Children welcome
1 King 1 Twin (2 bdrm)
Bathrooms: 1 Guest share

Our spacious home is situated 5km from the centre of Taumarunui surrounded by a peaceful one acre garden with a native bush backdrop filled with NZ native birds. The bedrooms open on to a large verandah. Laundry available. A stream runs along one boundary of the 80 acre property suitable for walks and summertime swimming. A golf course is located within 2 km, along with guided mountain walks, canoeing, hot pools, scenic flights, skiing, trout fishing and white-water rafting are all within an hours drive.

Taumarunui - Owhango *15 km S of Taumarunui*
Fernleaf *B&B Farmstay Cottage No Kitchen*

Carolyn & Melvin Forlong
58 Tunanui Road,
RD 1,
Owhango

Tel (07) 895 4847
or 0800 FERNLEAF
Fax (07) 895 4837
fernleaf.farm@xtra.co.nz
www.fernleaffarmstay.co.nz

Double/Twin $100 - $150
Single $85 - $100
(Full breakfast)
Dinner $30
Visa MC Diners Amex accepted
Children welcome
2 Queen 1 Double 1 Twin (4 bdrm)
Bathrooms: 2 Ensuite 1 Guest share

Relax in the tranquil Tunanui Valley just 500 metres from SH4. Close for convenience, far enough away for peace and quiet. We are the third generation to farm Fernleaf and our Romney sheep flock has been recorded every year for ninety years . The views from various vantage point on the farm are awesome, taking in the mountains: Ruapehu, Ngaruahoe, Tongariro and Taranaki. Enjoy our generous country hospitality, wonderful breakfast, a beautiful dalmatian Sally, and friendly cats. Other meals by arrangement. 'River Fishing' nearby.

Raetihi *0.5 km N of Raetihi*
Log Lodge *Luxury B&B*

Jan & Bob Lamb
5 Ranfurly Terrace,
Raetihi, 4632

Tel (06) 385 4135
Fax (06) 385 4835
Lamb.Log-Lodge@Xtra.co.nz

Double/Twin $120
Single $65 - $75
(Full breakfast)
Children under 14 $40
Spa $5 per person
Visa MC accepted
Pet free home
1 Queen 1 Double 4 Single
(1 open plan room)
Bathrooms: 2 Private
We only accept 1 booking at a time

A unique opportunity to stay in a modern authentic log home sited high on 7 acres on the edge of town. Completely private accommodation, with own bathroom. All sleeping on mezzanine, your own lounge with wood fire, snooker table, TV/video, stereo and dining area, opening onto large verandah, with swimming pool and spa available. Panoramic views of Mts Ruapehu, Ngauruhoe and Tongariro. Tongariro National Park and Turoa Skifield are a half hour scenic drive.

Ohakune *6 km SW of Ohakune*
Mitredale *Homestay Farmstay*

Audrey & Diane Pritt
Smiths Road, RD, Ohakune

Tel (06) 385 8016
or 027 453 1916
Fax (06) 385 8016
mitredale@ihug.co.nz

Double/Twin $120
Single $65
(Continental breakfast)
Dinner $35pp by arrangement
Visa MC accepted
Pets welcome
Internet available
1 Double 2 Single (2 bdrm)
Comfortable, cosy,
electric blankets on all beds
Bathrooms: 1 Guest share 1 Family share

We farm sheep, empty dairy cows and run a boarding kennel in a beautiful peaceful valley with magnificent views of Mt Ruapehu. Tongariro National Park for skiing, walking, photography. Excellent 18 hole golf course, great fishing locally. We are members of Ducks Unlimited (a conservation group)and our local wine club. We have 3 labradors. We offer dinner traditional farmhouse (Diane, a cook book author with new kitchen), or breakfast with excellent home-made jams. Take Raetihi Road, at Hotel/BP Service Station corner. 4km to Smiths Road. Last house 2km.

Taihape *6 km S of Taihape*
Grandvue *Homestay*

John & Dianne McKinnon
110 Wairanu Road,
RD 4, Taihape 4794

Tel (06) 388 1308
or 027 244 1309
Fax (06) 388 1308
grandvue@xtra.co.nz

Double/Twin $110
Single $75
(Special breakfast)
Children 9 and under $25
Dinner by arrangement
Visa MC accepted
Children and pets welcome
Internet available
1 Queen 2 Twin (2 bdrm)
Portacot available
Bathrooms: 1 Guest share
Tiled shower/Spa bath

Relax in comfort in our cosy modern home situated in the heart of the Rangitikei on 90 acres of farmland. Only 6 minutes south of Taihape, 2 minutes off State Highway 1. Our home situated in spacious grounds boasts magnificent views of mountains and ranges. One hour to Mt Ruapehu, two hours to Taupo and three to Wellington with many local activity options available. Comfortable beds with electric blankets. Paddock facilities available for travelling animals.

Taihape - Rangitikei *26 km NE of Taihape*
Tarata Fishaway *Luxury River Retreats & Farmstay*
Stephen & Trudi Mattock
925 Mokai Road, RD 3, Taihape

Tel (06) 388 0354 or 027 279 7037
Fax (06) 388 0954   fishaway@xtra.co.nz
www.tarata.co.nz

Double/Twin $130 - $220
Single $70 - $110 (Full breakfast)
Children under 12 half price
Dinner $45 pp by arrangement   3 Private spa pools
Visa MC accepted
Children and pets welcome
4 King/Twin 5 Queen 1 Double 3 Single (9 bdrm)
Awesome views
Bathrooms: 5 Ensuite 1 Guest share
Honeymoon suite has spa bath

We are very lucky to have a piece of New Zealand's natural beauty. Tarata is nestled in bush in the remote Mokai Valley where the picturesque Rangitikei River meets the rugged Ruahine Ranges. With the wilderness and unique trout fishing right at our doorstep, it is the perfect environment to bring up our 13 year old daughter, Mikayla. Stephen offers guided fishing and scenic rafting trips for all ages. Raft through the gentle crystal clear waters of the magnificent Rangitikei River, spot the many trout, visit Middle Earth and a secret waterfall, stunning scenery you will never forget. Our spacious home and large garden with amazing views allow guests plenty of space to relax and unwind. Come on a farm tour meeting our many friendly farm pets including Panda the llama and Teddy the Alpaca. Stay in our Homestead, Tree House or River Retreat and relax on the large decking amidst native birds and trees. Soak in your own private spa pool with million dollar views of the Rangitikei. Peace, privacy and tranquillity at its best! We will even deliver a candle light dinner to your door. We think Tarata is truly a magic place and we would love sharing it with you.
Directions: Tarata Fishaway Lodge is 26 scenic kilometres from Taihape. Turn off SH1, 6km south of Taihape at the Gravity Canyon Bungy and Ohotu signs. Follow the signs (14km) to the bungy bridge. We are 6 km past bungy, 925 Mokai road. Features & Attractions Honeymoon Retreat, Trout Fishing, Scenic Rafting, Visit LOTR, Bungy, Mini Golf with a difference, swimming pool, spa pools, bush walks, spotlight safaris, campouts and farm pets.

Taihape *1 km S of Taihape*
Llanerchymedd *Luxury B&B Apartment with Kitchen*

Alan & Jan Thomas
10 Dixon Way,
Taihape

Tel (06) 388 0283
or (06) 388 0666
Fax (06) 388 0683
alajan@xtra.co.nz

Double/Twin $90
(Continental breakfast provisions)
Children $20
Additional charge $20 per head
Children welcome
1 Queen 1 Double
2 Single (1 bdrm)
Bathrooms: 1 Ensuite

We are a married couple with two children and two cats. LLanerchymedd is a quiet residence, with established gardens. We are two minutes from Taihape and are easily located, 1km south of the town with panoramic views of Mt Ruapehu. A tranquil walk up into the gardens is well rewarded with fantastic views. Take a glass of wine with you and relax in the top gazebo - you will feel on top of the world.

Marton *45 km N of Palmerston North*
Rea's Inn *B&B Homestay*

Keith and Lorraine Rea
12 Dunallen Avenue,
Marton 4710

Tel (06) 327 4442
or 027 479 9589
Fax (06) 327 4442
keithandlorraine@xtra.co.nz

Double/Twin $95
Single $55
(Continental breakfast)
Children half price
Dinner $30
Visa MC accepted
Children welcome
Internet available
1 Queen 1 Twin (2 bdrm)
Bathrooms: 1 Guest share

We have a warm comfortable home offering hospitality, peace and tranquility. Situated in quiet cul-de-sac with a private garden setting. Guests stay in separate wing of home. Close to Nga Tawa and Huntley Schools. Ideal for weekend retreat or stopover. (Only 2 hours from Wellington Ferry). Your comfort and pleasure are important to us. Clients enjoy our homemade hot bread served at breakfast. Our birman cat likes people too, and we all welcome you to come, relax and enjoy the friendly atmosphere at Rea's Inn.

Hawkes Bay
Tiniroto
Mahanga Beach
Wairoa
Mahia Beach
2
5
Eskdale
Bay View
Napier
Taradale
Hastings
Havelock North
50
2
Otane
Waipawa
Waipukurau
2
52
Kilometres
0
40
Miles
0
24

Hawkes Bay

Mahia Peninsula - Mahanga Beach *50 km N of Wairoa*
Reomoana *B&B Apartment with Kitchen Bunkroom for children*

Louise Schick
629 Mahanga Road,
RD 8,
Mahanga Beach,
Mahia,
Hawkes Bay, 4198

Tel (06) 837 5898
Fax (06) 837 5990
reomoana@paradise.net.nz
www.reomoana.co.nz

Double/Twin $130 - $150
Single $75
(Continental breakfast)
Children $30
Visa MC accepted
Children and pets welcome
2 Queen 1 Twin 1 Single (4 bdrm)
Bathrooms: 1 Ensuite 1 Private

Reomoana - The voice of the sea. Overlooking the Pacific with breathtaking views this rustic home with handcrafted features combines New Zealand and Hungarian creativity. Situated on a hillside the property is grazed by sheep and cattle, where walks may be enjoyed through QE 2 convenanted native bush. 5mins. walk to 8Kms. of white sandy beach, a recreational paradise for swimming, surfing and fishing. Attractions:- Morere Hot Springs, Marae visits, Golf-course and fishing charters. 6Kms. to Cafe Mahia and Sunset Point Restaurants.

Wairoa *95 km S of Gisborne*
The Bank Gallery *B&B Homestay Guest House*

Jill Cameron
208 Marine Parade,
Wairoa, 4108

Tel (06) 838 8553
jill@bankgallery.co.nz
www.bankgallery.co.nz

Double/Twin $100
Single $75
(Continental breakfast)
Dinner by arrangement
Internet available
1 Queen 1 Double 2 Single (3 bdrm)
1 bedrooms sleeps 3 people,
1 bedroom sleeps 2
Bathrooms: 1 Guest share

The Bank Gallery B&B is on the top floor of an Art Gallery very recently established in the charming small town of Wairoa. The elegant historic building started life just 100 years ago as the Union Bank of Australasia and is as beautiful today as it must have been then. The rooms overlook the river and the building has been very recently renovated without losing its original charm. Downstairs houses the Gallery with many works from talented local and guest artists on display. Step outside and you are in town, walking distance to everything.

Bay View - Napier *12 km N of Napier*

Kilbirnie *Homestay*

Jill & John Grant

84 Le Quesne Road, Bay View, Napier, 4104

Tel (06) 836 6929 or 027 234 7363

jill.johng@xtra.co.nz

www.bnb.co.nz/kilbirnie.html

Double/Twin $95 - $120 (Special breakfast)
Dinner $40pp by arrangement
Visa MC accepted   Not suitable for children
2 Queen (2 bdrm)
Bathrooms: 1 Ensuite 1 Private

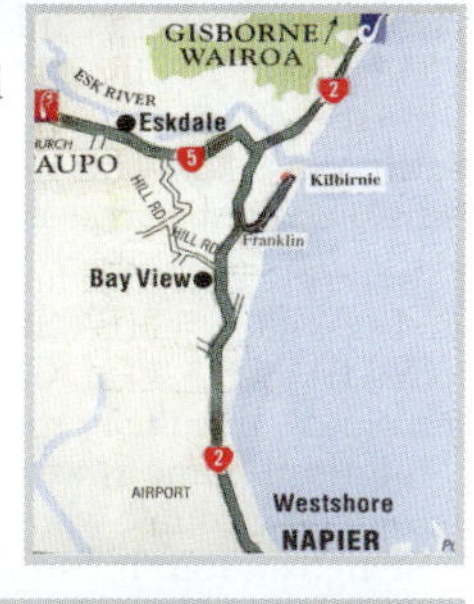

We moved with our dog in 1996 to the quiet end of an unspoiled fishing beach by the Esk River, attracted by the beauty and position away from the traffic, while only 15 minutes from a full range of harbourside restaurants north of Napier.

Kilbirnie is near the Taupo Road intersection with the Pacific Highway to Gisborne, with off-road parking. Upstairs, air-conditioned guest rooms have restful views of the Pacific Ocean one side or vineyards on the other, private bathrooms, excellent showers, abundant hot water, comfortable firm beds and small room with TV tea making and ironing facilities,guests also welcome in family room.

Special breakfast overlooking the ocean is an experience which makes lunch seem superfluous. We are retired farmers with time to share good company, fresh imaginative food and juice, real coffee, an eclectic range of books, who invite you to enjoy our hospitality in modern surroundings. We have 20 years home hosting experience and are non-smokers. season Oct. to April inclusive.

Directions: from Taupo first left after intersection Highways 2 & 5. Franklin Road to Le Quesne, proceed to far end beachfront. From Napier first right after Mobil Station (approx 1 K). Prior contact appreciated.

Bay View - Napier *12 km N of Napier*
The Grange *B&B Farmstay Self-contained Lodge*
Roslyn & Don Bird
263 Hill Road, Eskdale, Hawkes Bay,
PO Box 136 Bay View, Hawkes Bay, 4149

Tel (06) 836 6666 or 027 28 15738
Fax (06) 836 6456   thefarmstay@xtra.co.nz
www.thefarmstay.com

Double/Twin $110 - $140 Single $85 - $95 (Full breakfast)
Dinner $55pp 3 course with wine
LODGE: Dbl from $140, sgl $100, extras $30pp, opt breakfast
Visa MC accepted   Children welcome   Internet Available
1 King/Twin 1 King 2 Double 2 Single (3 bdrm)
2 in farmstay, 1+ Loft in Lodge
Bathrooms: 1 Private 1 Guest share
Farmstay guest max 4 share luxury bathroom, separate toilet

Enjoy genuine kiwi hospitality at our tranquil countryside escape overlooking the picturesque Esk Valley.'THE GRANGE'our delightfully modern 'FARMSTAY' and superior SELF-CONTAINED 'LODGE' offers private,sunny, spacious accommodation in relaxing peaceful surrounds. Breathe in spectacular farm, valley vineyard, coastal and city VIEWS. Feel the comforts of home as we tempt you with fine wine, farm produce, baking, and preserves. We're an outgoing couple who really enjoy the company of guests. Experience our FARM life with Roslyn, Sam (our friendly 'Huntaway' farm dog), and Allie (resident cat). Feed sheep(Petal and Rose etc), cows (especially Snowy), pigs (Bubble and Squeek), chickens, dairy goats (try milking Nan) or bottle-feeding a lamb (seasonal). Its a winelovers paradise! Don a third generation Hawkes Bay WINEMAKER with more than 30 years experience is passionate about the wine industry and happy to share his knowledge over dinner or help plan your personalized WINERY ADVENTURE. Explore the world's ART DECO Capital NAPIER 12 MINUTES drive away and Hawke's Bay's many regional attractions within 30 minutes. Experience the thrill of MOUNTAIN BIKING at Eskdale mtb park, discover the FISHING waters of the beautiful Esk river or just relax visiting art studios, wineries and rural cafes. We have it all within 5 minutes of home. We are always happy to advise on any tours or special requests as our knowledge, information and contacts throughout Hawkes Bay are invaluable. Unwind on the Deck to the soothing chorus of native birds in the surrounding gardens and trees and at day's end spend time romancing over our wonderful night sky. Email access available. We also offer our Taupo (Kinloch) cottage to those wishing to stay in that area.

Napier *1 km N of Napier*
Spence Bed & Breakfast *B&B Homestay*

Kay & Stewart Spence
17 Cobden Road,
Bluff Hill,
Napier, 4110

Tel (06) 835 9454
or Freephone 0800 117 890
Fax (06) 835 9454
ksspence@actrix.gen.nz
www.spencebnb.co.nz

Double/Twin $160 - $170
Single $120 - $140
(Full breakfast)
Visa MC accepted
Pet free home Children welcome
Internet available
1 Queen 1 Single (1 bdrm)
Bathrooms: 1 Ensuite

Welcome to our comfortable near new home. Quiet area, 10-15 minutes walk from Art Deco City centre. Guest suite opens outside to patio, and colourful garden. Lounge includes double bed settee, wireless internet access, TV, kitchenette with tea making facilities, fridge and microwave. Bedroom has queen and single beds, ensuite bathroom. We have hosted for over 10 years and enjoy overseas travel. Able to meet public transport. Directions: port end Marine Parade, Coote Road, right into Thompson Road, left into Cobden Road opposite water tower.

Napier *1.5 km N of Post Office*
A Room with a View *B&B Homestay*

Robert McGregor
9 Milton Terrace,
Napier

Tel (06) 835 7434
or 027 249 2040
Fax (06) 835 1912
roomwithview@xtra.co.nz

Double/Twin $130
Single $100
(Continental breakfast)
Visa MC accepted
Surcharge on credit card payments
1 Queen (1 bdrm)
Spacious bedroom with
panoramic view
Bathrooms: 1 Private with bath &
shower, directly oppposite bedroom

After 10 years hosting with my late wife, I'm continuing to enjoy companionship, conversation and laughter with guests. Fourth generation property, 130 year old garden, spacious room, panoramic sea view. 15 minute walk to restaurants at historic Port Ahuriri or our world famous Art Deco city centre. Private bathroom. Free laundry facilities, pick-up service, internet. Off-street parking. Smoke-free inside please. I'm interested in travel, gardening, the arts, and especially local history, as until retirement I was Chief Executive of the Art Deco Trust.

Napier *1.2 km N of Napier Central*
Hillcrest *B&B Homestay*
Nancy & Noel Lyons
4 George Street,
Hospital Hill,
Napier

Tel (06) 835 1812
lyons@inhb.co.nz
www.hillcrestnapier.co.nz

Double/Twin $110 - $115
Single $85 - $90
(Continental breakfast)
Visa MC accepted
Pet free home
Not suitable for children
1 Double 2 Single (2 bdrm)
Bathrooms: 1 Guest share

If you require quiet accommodation just minutes from the city centre, our comfortable home provides peace in restful surroundings. Relax on wide decks overlooking our garden, or enjoy the spectacular sea views. Explore nearby historic places and the botanical gardens. Your own lounge with tea/coffee making; laundry and off-street parking available. We have travelled extensively and welcome the opportunity of meeting visitors. Our interests are travel, music, bowls and embroidery. We will happily meet you at the travel depots. Holiday home at Mahia Beach available.

Napier *5 km S of Napier*
Snug Harbour *B&B Homestay*
Ruth & Don McLeod
147 Harold Holt Avenue,
Napier, 4112

Tel (06) 843 2521
Fax (06) 843 2520
donmcld@clear.net.nz
www.snugharbour.co.nz

Double/Twin $100 - $130
Single $90
(Full breakfast)
Dinner $40 by arrangement
Visa MC accepted
Pet free home
1 Queen 1 Twin (2 bdrm)
Twin room has super single beds
Bathrooms: 1 Ensuite 1 Family share

Ruth & Don welcome you to their comfortable home with its rural outlook and sunny attractive patio. The garden studio with ensuite and tea making facilities has its own entrance. We are situated on the outskirts of Napier City, the art deco city of the World, and in close proximity to wineries and many other tourist attractions. We both have a background in teaching, with interests in travel, gardening and photography.

Napier *1 km N of Napier on hill above city*
The Coachhouse *Cottage with Kitchen*

Jan Chalmers
9 Gladstone Road,
Napier

Tel (06) 835 6126
or 021 251 5847
janchalmers@paradise.net.nz
www.thecoachhouse.co.nz

Double/Twin $100
Single $80
(Continental breakfast provisions)
Children $25 - babies free
$140 for 3, $160 for 4
Visa MC accepted
Children and pets welcome
1 Queen 2 Single (2 bdrm)
Bathrooms: 1 Private

On the hill over-looking a gorgeous Mediterranean garden and sea views, the historic Coach-house is tastefully renovated and totally self-contained. It contains 2 bedrooms, open plan kitchen, dining, living rooms, bathroom and separate loo. The breakfast supplies include homemade jam and marmalade. TV and radio included and fresh flowers in all rooms. The sunny deck has a table and chairs and gas barbecue. Off-street parking and easy access plus peace and privacy complete the picture.

Napier - Taradale *10 km SW of Napier*
Otatara Heights *B&B Apartment with Kitchen*

Sandra & Roy Holderness
57 Churchill Drive,
Taradale, 4112

Tel (06) 844 8855
Fax (06) 844 8855
sandroy@clear.net.nz

Double/Twin $100
Single $75
(Continental breakfast)
Extra guest $40
1 Queen 1 Double (1 bdrm)
Bathrooms: 1 Private

Comfortable, quiet apartment in the heart of our foremost wine producing area. Superb day and night views over Napier and local rural scenes. 10 minutes drive to the art deco capital of the world. 2km to Taradale Village. Safe off-street parking. Top quality restaurants and wineries nearby. We are a friendly couple who have enjoyed B&B overseas and like meeting people. Our interests are travel, theatre, good food and wine. Bella, our cat, keeps to herself. Handy to EIT and golf course.

Napier - Marine Parade *0.1 km N of Napier*
Mon Logis *B&B*
Gerard Averous
415 Marine Parade, Napier
PO Box 871, Napier

Tel (06) 835 2125
or 0274 725 332
Fax (06) 835 8811
monlogis@xtra.co.nz
www.monlogis.co.nz

Double/Twin $120 - $240
Single $120 - $180
(Full breakfast)
Visa MC Diners Amex accepted
Not suitable for children
2 King/Twin 2 King (4 bdrm)
Bathrooms: 3 Ensuite 1 Private

A little piece of France nestled in the heart of the beautiful wine-growing region of Hawkes Bay. Built as private hotel in 1915, this grand colonial building is a few minutes walk from the city. Now lovingly renovated Mon Logis will cater to a maximum of 8 guests. Downstairs, an informal guest lounge invites relaxation, television viewing or a quiet time reading. Guests can help themselves to coffee/tea and home-made biscuits at any time.

Napier *1 km N of Napier*
Cobden Garden Homestay *Luxury B&B Homestay*
Rayma and Phillip Jenkins
1 Cobden Crescent,
Bluff Hill, 4110

Tel (06) 834 2090
or 0800 426 233
Fax (06) 834 1977
info@cobden.co.nz
www.cobden.co.nz

Double/Twin $210 - $230
Single $180 - $200
(Full breakfast)
Children negotiable
Visa MC Diners Amex
Eftpos accepted
Internet available
2 King/Twin 1 King
1 Single (3 bdrm)
Bathrooms: 3 Ensuite

We invite you to our sunny, quiet, colonial villa high on Bluff Hill. Enjoy spacious bedrooms comfortably furnished with; quality bedding, lounge furniture, TV with DVD player, refreshments, robes, hairdryer. Relax in the garden, on the veranda or in a guest lounge. Check emails on the guest computer with wireless access. Join us for complimentary tasting of local wine and hors- d'oeuvres each evening. Choose breakfast from a selection of homemade and local foods. Your stay will be memorable. Three unobtrusive cats in residence.

Napier *1 km N of Napier*
Maison Béarnaise *B&B Homestay*

Christine Grouden &
Graham Storer
25 France Road,
Bluff Hill,
Napier 4110

Tel (06) 835 4693
or 0800 624 766
Fax (06) 835 4694
info@maisonbearnaise.co.nz
www.maisonbearnaise.co.nz

Double/Twin $160 - $220
Single $120 - $170
(Full breakfast)
Visa MC accepted
Not suitable for children
Internet available
2 Queen (2 bdrm)
Bathrooms: 2 Ensuite

Christine, Graham & Brewster (shy cat), welcome you to our attractive, peaceful oasis. Walk to city centre, restaurants, Bluff lookout. Off-street parking, wireless email access, laundry service available. Large bedrooms have views, comfortable beds, electric blankets, and DVD-television. Relax with tea / coffee in your room or guest lounge where newspapers, magazines, books are at your disposal. Delicious breakfasts including home grown and local produce served in dining room or colourful courtyard. Friendly adult retreat. Christine, Napier born, happily shares her wealth of local knowledge.

Napier *0.5 km N of Napier Central*
Seaview Lodge *B&B Homestay*

Catherine & Evert Van Florenstein
5 Seaview Terrace,
Napier

Tel (06) 835 0202
or 021 180 2101
cvulodge@xtra.co.nz
www.aseaviewlodge.co.nz

Double/Twin $150 - $170
Single $120 - $130
(Continental breakfast)
Visa MC accepted
Pet free home
Not suitable for children
1 King/Twin 1 King
1 Single (3 bdrm)
Bathrooms: 1 Ensuite 2 Private

Seaview Lodge is a lovingly renovated, spacious late Victorian home. This inner city, beachside bed and breakfast offers a warm welcome and spectacular views. Enjoy breakfast on the lower verandah while watching the waves break on the shore. In the evening relax in the spacious guest lounge or on the upstairs balcony. Situated across the road from the beach, hot pools and conference complex and a three minute stroll to the city centre. The 2008/2010 edition of the 'Lonely Planet' guide promoted Seaview Lodge as their pick for Napier.

Villa Vista B&B *B&B*
Anna Roulston & Tim Barker
22A France Road,
Bluff Hill, Napier

Tel (06) 835 8770
or 027 435 7179
Fax (06) 835 8770
accommodation@villavista.net
www.villavista.net

Double/Twin $140 - $150
Single $115 - $125
(Special breakfast)
Children negotiable
Visa MC accepted
Children welcome
3 Queen 1 Single (3 bdrm)
Spacious, comfortable, relaxed
Home baking provided
Bathrooms: 3 Ensuite

A grand Edwardian villa blessed with fantastic views over the sea to Cape kidnappers from every large and private bedroom. Ensuite, air-conditioning, television, tea/coffee making facilities & home baking in each bedroom. Selection of continental and cooked breakfasts are served in the spacious dining room. Amicable children and pets residing. Welcome to Napier.

Napier *3 km S of Napier*
Art Deco Te Awa *B&B*
Kay & Rod Goodspeed
19 Te Awa Avenue,
Napier

Tel (06) 835 1618
or 027 211 0023
Fax (06) 835 3689
kaypat1@xtra.co.nz

Double/Twin $140 - $160
(Full breakfast)
Pet free home
1 Queen 1 Double
1 Twin (3 bdrm)
Bathrooms: 3 Ensuite

Art Deco Te Awa is spacious, executive quality accommodation. Ideal for visiting NZ's Art Deco City. Breakfast includes locally grown fresh fruit, home made muesli and preserves. Quality beds with fine linen. Guest rooms include one spacious double room with ensuite bathroom, one queen with ensuite bathroom and one twin with ensuite bathroom, all with heated towelrail, hairdryer and complimentary toiletries. Five minutes to city centre. Ten minutes to airport. Walking distance to the beach and 18 hole golf course. Easy access to Hawke's Bay's wineries.

Napier *2.5 km SW of City*
Logan B & B *B&B Homestay*

Pam & John Thompson
15 Logan Avenue,
Napier, 4110

Tel (06) 843 7558
or 027 660 6982
Fax (06) 843 7569
pam.john@xtra.co.nz

Double/Twin $130 - $130
Single $110 - $110
(Continental breakfast)
1 Queen (1 bdrm)
Beautifully appointed
in Art Deco style
Bathrooms: 1 Private
Spacious with spa bath &
shower right next to room

We are Art Deco enthusiasts living in an iconic home in Napier's renowned Art Deco suburb. A simple 'walk around the block' enables you to complete much of the 'Marewa Meander' Art Deco tour. Better still, you are just 5 minutes drive from Napier's inner city which is packed with more Art Deco interest, cafes, and shopping. Winery tours are readily available and we have good local knowledge. Excellent off-street parking. 2 friendly cats and our small dog Molly will add to your warm welcome.

Hastings City *1 km N of Hastings Central*
McConchie Homestay *Homestay*

Barbara & Nina McConchie
115A Frederick Street,
Hastings, 4122

Tel (06) 878 4576
or 0274 784 576
barbaramcconchie@xtra.co.nz
www.bnb.co.nz

Double/Twin $110
Single $70 (Full breakfast)
Children $30
Dinner $30 pp by arrangement
Visa MC accepted
Children welcome
1 Queen 2 Single (2 bdrm)
Bedroom with 2 single beds
opens out to a deck
Bathrooms: 1 Guest share

Enjoy our peaceful garden back section, no traffic noises, yet central to Hastings City. My 2 cats say 'Hi'. Nearby are parks, golf courses, wineries, orchards and the best icecream ever. Short trips take you to spectacular views, Cape Kidnapper's gannet colony, or Napier's art deco, hot pools, or just relaxing and enjoying great hospitality. Directions: from Wellington, arriving Hastings City, turn left into Eastbourne Street, right into Nelson Street, right into Frederick Street, cross Caroline Road. Driveway on right. 115A first house off driveway.

Hastings *14 km NW of Hastings*
Grandvue Country Stay *B&B Homestay*

Dianne & Keith Taylor
Grandvue, 2596 State Highway 50, RD 5 Hastings 4175

Tel (06) 879 6141 or 027 668 0252   homestays@xtra.co.nz
www.bnb.co.nz/grandvuehomestay.html

Double/Twin $110 - $130 Single $70 (Full breakfast)
Children negotiable Dinner $30 pp
Visa MC accepted   Pet free home   Children welcome
1 King/Twin 1 Queen (2 bdrm)
Bathrooms: 1 Ensuite 1 Family share

Recently retired and moved from our farm but still the same genuine and caring hospitality. Enjoy with us in a relaxed atmosphere in our extensive private garden the wonderful views over vineyards in the Gimlett Gravels and Ngatarawa area, and to Havelock North hills in the distance.Comfortable beds with firm mattresses make for a good nights sleep (electric blankets in winter.) Sit and chat when time allows over a generous breakfast cooked or continental with homemade preserves and goodies - inside or alfresco. Dinner available on request.

Our interests include tramping, bushwalks, gardening, travel and genealogy. Having travelled extensively we do enjoy meeting local and overseas visitors. Let us advise you on all the wonderful things to do and see while in our lovely Hawkes Bay. There are many wineries close by with restaurants, Safari trips to the Gannet Colony, Orchard tours, Trout fishing, 6 golf courses, Panoramic views from Te Mata Peak, Havelock North with it's boutique shops and cafes and Napier the Art Deco City of the world are just a few.

We can arrange tours for you too, and also advise you on your travels through New Zealand. After more than 22 years of hosting we have an ever increasing circle of friends with many returning. Please read our guests comments on our B&B Book website. Guests are welcome to use our swimming pool in summer and the tennis court. Dianne has a certificate in Homestay Management. We look forward to meeting you - our aim is to make your stay memorable. No pets inside please. Arrive as a guest and leave as our friends. Easy access and plenty of parking

Havelock North - Hastings *16 km S of Havelock North*
Wharehau *Homestay Farmstay*

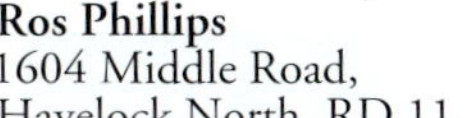

Ros Phillips
1604 Middle Road,
Havelock North, RD 11,
Hastings, 4178

Tel (06) 877 4111
or 021 0271 9215
Fax (06) 877 4115
ros.phillips@xtra.co.nz
www.wharehau.co.nz

Double/Twin $120
Single $60 (Full breakfast)
Children half price
Dinner $30
Beach bach $130 - $150
Visa MC accepted
Children welcome
2 Queen 2 Twin 1 Single (4 bdrm)
Bathrooms: 1 Guest share 1 Family share

Wharehau is in the beautiful Tuki Tuki valley -a great base for Hawkes Bay experience. Quarter of an hour travel from Hastings or Havelock North in the midst of Wine Country. Close to golf courses, Splash Planet, gannets and art deco. Or enjoy the peace and space on the farm. Weather permitting a farm 4WD tour is available. Walks available locally. Trout fishing (local guide can be hired) in the Tuki Tuki River. Comfortable beach bach at Kairakau Beach is available for rent.

Havelock North *1.5 km S of Havelock North*
The Loft Art Studio and Bed and Breakfast *Premium Boutique B&B*

Iris and John
10 Woodford Heights,
Havelock North, 4130

Tel Landline: (06) 877 5938
or Mobile 021 474 729
Fax (06) 877 5938
theloft@hawkesbayaccommodation.com
www.hawkesbayaccommodation.com

Double/Twin $149 - $200
(Special breakfast)
Dinner in romantic setting by
arrangement $65 pp or as arranged
Rates seasonal
Visa MC accepted Pet free home
1 King 1 Queen (2 bdrm)
King room with ensuite, Queen
room with ensuiteBathrooms: 2
Ensuite King room has spa bath & shower; Queen has shower

Come and be pampered in our paradise. We, Iris and John, 4th generation New Zealanders will welcome you with complimentary refreshments. Our architectural art filled home has many unique features and superb views of Hawke's Bay. Use the courtyard and /or deck. Delicious breakfasts. Soak luxuriously in the spa bath and view the stars through the glass ceiling. Luxury linen, comfortable beds. John is an artist with a house studio to visit. We are close to our best attractions and can advise you on excursions. Cycles available.

Havelock North *2 km NE of Havelock North*
'Options' *B&B Homestay*
Rosemary & Graham Duff
92 Simla Ave,
Havelock North, 4130

Tel (06) 877 0257
or 027 653 7270
Fax (06) 877 0257
gr.duff@xtra.co.nz

Double/Twin $130 - $150
Single $100 - $120
(Full breakfast)
Children negotiable
Dinner by arrangement
Visa MC accepted
Pet free home
Internet Available
1 King 1 Queen 1 Twin
1 Single (3 bdrm)
Bathrooms: 1 Ensuite 1 Private

Options offers: Near Te Mata Peak; Views; 5 minutes to Havelock North village; Wine, gannets and Art Deco all within 30 minutes; Swimming pool and spa; Private sheltered patios; Pet free home; Wireless internet connection; Breakfast inside or outside depending on the weather; Optional evening meal at an additional cost; A home away from home.

Havelock North *1 km NE of Havelock North Village Centre*
The Whitehouse Homestay B&B *Luxury Homestay B & B*
Doug Henderson & Karin Campbell
14 Woodford Heights,
Havelock North, 4130

Tel 06 877-0522
or 021 143 8109
info@thewhitehousebandb.co.nz
www.thewhitehousebandb.co.nz

Double/Twin $145 - $215
(Full breakfast)
Children by arrangement
Dinner by arrangement with soft music and candlelights
Hire car - Mazda MX5 Roadster
Visa MC Amex accepted
Pet free home Children welcome
1 King 2 Queen (3 bdrm)
Bathrooms: 2 Ensuite 1 Private

Welcome to THE WHITEHOUSE, an adventure with a difference. We offer luxury homestay B&B in the heart of Havelock North, only minutes from cities, Hastings & Art Deco Capital, Napier. These locations offer boutique shopping and casual or fine dining, also short drive to wonderful wineries that makes this region so very special. We offer 3 luxury suites, 'Woodford', 'Hereworth',& 'Iona', refreshments, homebaking on arrival, relax on the decks & soak up the stunning views. Hire Mazda MX5 Roadster enjoy Wineries, Golf, Art Deco,Cape Kidnappers.

Otane - Central Hawkes Bay *8 km N of Waipawa*
Ludlow Farmstay/B&B *Luxury B&B Farmstay Cottage with Kitchen*

Gwen and Neil White
53 Drumpeel Road,
RD 1, Otane/Waipawa

Tel (06) 856 8348
or 027 441 8354
ludlow.white@xtra.co.nz
www. ludlowfarmstay.co.nz

Double/Twin $160
Single $100
(Full breakfast provisions)
Children $20-$30 Cot/highchair
Dinner $35 by arrangement
Internet available
1 King/Twin 1 Queen
1 Double 2 Twin (3 bdrm)
Twin room can be made as a king
Bathrooms: 1 Private Shower only

Ludlow is a Working 555 hectare extensive cropping farm, growing mainly wheat and barley, squash pumpkins, sweetcorn and peas with lamb and beef finishing. Enjoy luxury accommodation in our renovated shearers' cottage which is situated in private surroundings, 150 metres from main homestead, with full kitchen facilities, laundry, open fire and views over the Drumpeel Valley Farmland, with stock grazing alongside the cottage. Swimming pool and Astrograss tennis court available for guests' use. Farm tour available on request. Expect a warm welcome from Ellymae the Jack Russell terrier.

> Just as we have variety of B&Bs
> you will also be offered a variety of breakfasts,
> and they will always be generous.

Hawkes Bay

Waipawa *1 km NE of Waipawa*
Abbot Heights *Luxury B&B*
Jacqui & Charlie Hutchison
6 Parkland Drive,
Waipawa

Tel 027 433 0146
or (06) 857 8585
Fax (06) 857 8580
chipper.c@xtra.co.nz

Double/Twin $150
Single $100
(Continental breakfast)
Not suitable for children
2 Queen (2 bdrm)
Crisp, modern, clean airy,
spacious luxurious rooms
Bathrooms: 1 Ensuite 1 Private
Private bathroom has spa bath

Welcome to Abbot Heights. Your friendly hosts (and cat Myrtle) look forward to your stay at their stunning modern manor set in 12 acres of private park and gardens. Enjoy tea or coffee on arrival or relax in your spacious room. Facilities include a splendid private lounge small library, luxury goose down duvets, plush bathrobes,electric blankets and private entrance.Read a book by the fire in winter or find a shady spot in the garden or courtyard in summer. It's all about your comfort.

Waipukurau *3 km S of Waipukurau*
Hineiti Homestay *Luxury B&B Homestay*
Caroline & Dan von Dadelszen
11 JG Wilson Drive,
Hatuma Heights,
RD 1

Tel Mobile 021 264 0307
or Landline - refer website
caroline@hinerangi.co.nz

Double/Twin $180
Single $120
(Full breakfast)
Dinner by arrangement $40pp,
wine included
Internet Available
2 Queen (2 bdrm)
2 Ensuite

Hineiti Homestay is a spacious newly home built on 1.55 hectares, with a rural outlook and views over Hatuma lake and surrounding countryside Local activities include several golf courses, trout fishing, and beaches and wineries within an hours drive. We have recently moved from the farm, but are not retired, so if guests are interested and Dan is available, farm tours can be arranged over Hinerangi Station, a working sheep and cattle farm. Guests are most welcome to join us for dinner.

Waipukurau *2 km S of Waipukurau*
Woburn Homestead *Luxury B&B*
Heatha Edwards & Philip Allerby
216 Hatuma Road, RD 1, Waipukurau

Tel (06) 858 9668
or 0274 529 112
heatha.woburnhomestead@xtra.co.nz
www.woburnhomestead.co.nz

Double/Twin $250 - $300
Single $0 - $150 (Special breakfast)
Dinner available by prior arrangement
Visa MC accepted
Not suitable for children
Internet Available
3 Queen (3 bdrm)
3 with queen beds and 1 queen has
an extra king single in the room
Bathrooms: 3 Ensuite

Welcome to Woburn Homestead, an exquisite 7 bedroom home with 6 bathrooms, built in 1893 and listed with the NZ Historic Places Trust.

Heatha and Philip adore sharing their home, and there are 2 tubby Labradors, who relentlessly patrol the grounds for any stray snacks or crumbs!

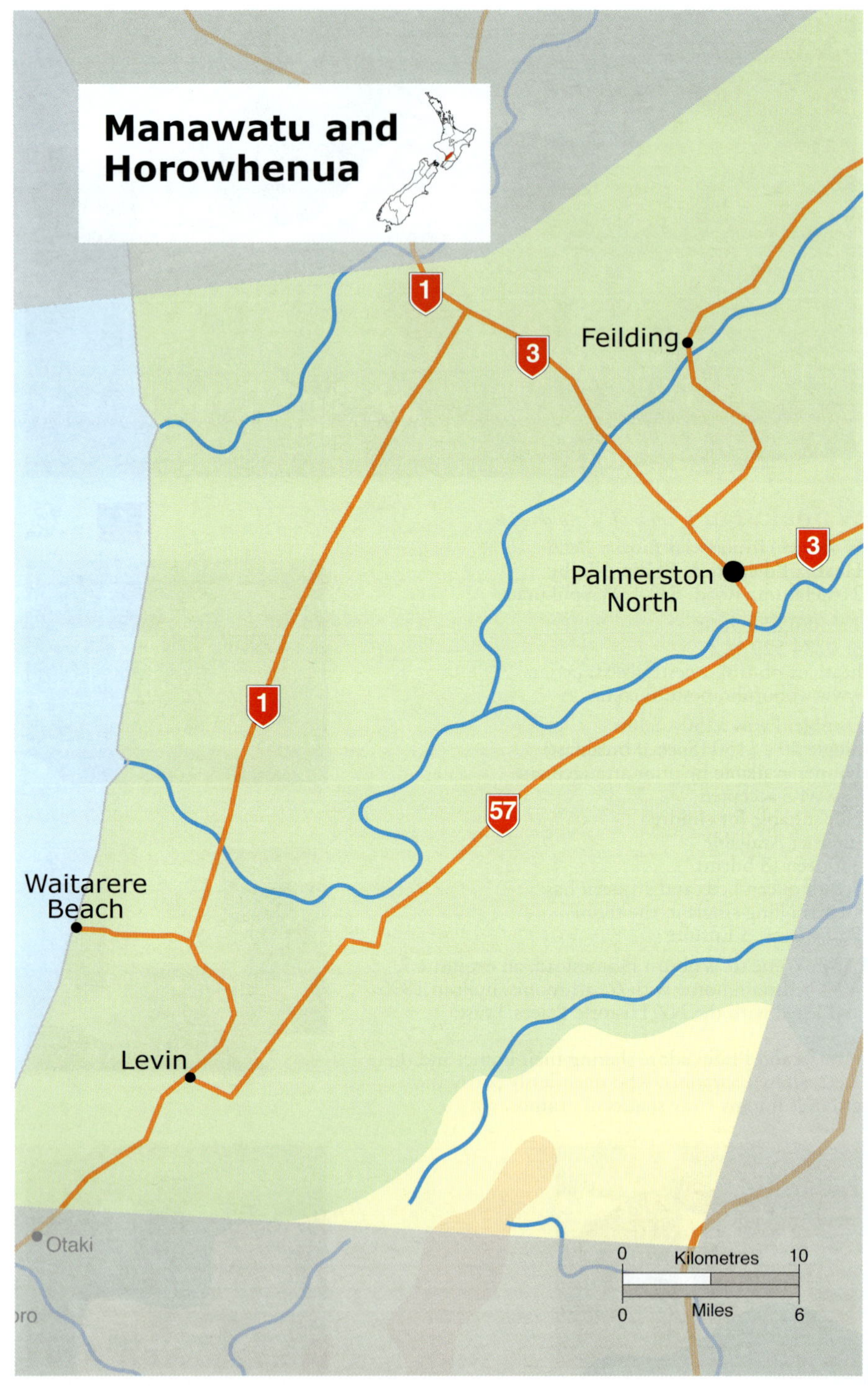

Manawatu and Horowhenua
1
3
Feilding
3
Palmerston North
1
57
Waitarere Beach
Levin
Otaki
0 Kilometres 10
0 Miles 6

Feilding *0.25 km N of Feilding Central*

Avoca Homestay *Homestay*

Margaret Hickmott
12 Freyberg Street,
Feilding

Tel (06) 323 4699
margh-avoca@inspire.net.nz

Double/Twin $110
Single $85
(Full breakfast)
Dinner $30 by arrangement
1 Queen 2 Twin (2 bdrm)
Bathrooms: 1 Ensuite 1 Family share

Enjoy a break in friendly Feilding, 14 times winner of New Zealand's Most Beautiful Town Award. You are assured of a warm welcome and an enjoyable stay in a comfortable smoke-free home set in an attractive garden with mature trees and a colourful shrubbery. Off-street parking is provided for your vehicle. The main bedroom has a queen-size bed, ensuite and an outside entrance for your sole use. We are within easy walking distance of the town centre and well situated for the Manfield Park complex.

Feilding *1 km E of Feilding Town Centre*

Feilding Mahoe B&B *Guest House Self contained B&B*

David & Lesley Klue
171 South Street,
Feilding, 5301

Tel (06) 323 0311
or 027 277 0235
purplepear@xtra.co.nz

Double/Twin $120 - $180
Single $70 - $100
(Continental breakfast provisions)
Dinner by arrangement
Off street parking,
Full cooking and laundry facilities
Eftpos accepted
Children and pets welcome
1 Queen 1 Single (1 bdrm)
Extra beds available
Bathrooms: 1 Ensuite

We enjoy our semi rural lifestyle with our three children, small dog, cat, four sheep and pig nestled amongst old native and fruit trees. Your privacy is assured in the guest house, separate from the main house, with views to gardens and a swimming pool. Situated just 1km from Manfield Park, and the town centre - you can enjoy great shopping and cafes, or alternatively, Palmerston North city is only a 15min drive. Welcome to Mahoe, your stay would be our pleasure.

Palmerston North *3 km SW of Palmerston North*

Andellen *Farmstay Guest House*

Kay and Warren Nitschke
580 Kairanga Bunnythorpe Road,
RD 8, Palmerston North

Tel 027 244 1393
or (06) 355 4155
Fax (06) 355 4155
kw@inspire.net.nz

Double/Twin $120
Single $70
(Continental breakfast provisions)
Children $20 under 12
Dinner $30pp by arrangement
Visa MC accepted
Children and pets welcome
2 Queen 2 Single (3 bdrm)
Electric blankets on all beds
Bathrooms: 1 Ensuite 1 Private
Gorgeous spa bath in large bathroom

Welcome to ANDELLEN. Enjoy your very own separate modern three bedroom house with both a private and tranquil setting looking out over the farm.

Kay, Warren and Libby (13 years)would love to have you stay. Set on 70 acres with lovely native gardens and plenty of room for children to run around or play on the trampoline or jungle gym.

We offer guests the opportunity to relax in an elegant, tranquil country setting. Accomodation includes private lounge, TV and gorgeous spa bath. Seasonal farm activities available. Children very welcome. City 3km away. We have a small pet dog and cat and generally there are horses, sheep and cattle on the farm. Dinner by arrangement. Plenty of parking for cars, trucks and trailers. The Airport and hospital are only a few minutes away. Cattle or horses are welcome as yarding and paddock facilities are available.

Palmerston North *3 km NW of Palmerston North Centre*
Bradgate *B&B Homestay*

Frances
3 Celtic Court,
Roslyn,
Palmerston North

Tel (06) 355 5956
or 021 0241 1864
Fax (06) 355 5956
bradgate@xtra.co.nz

Double/Twin $90
Single $50
(Full breakfast)
Dinner $30
1 Queen 1 Double 1 Twin (3 bdrm)
Bathrooms: 1 Guest share

Welcome to Bradgate, a four bedroomed brick townhouse located in a quiet cul-de-sac. 34 years ago my husband and I came to New Zealand. We owned a restaurant opposite Virginia Lake Wanganui, after retiring we ran a bed & breakfast overlooking the river. Having shifted to Palmerston North it was time to open up our home again. I have a Labrador named Crunchy. I enjoy playing golf, gardening and meeting people. Close to airport, will pick up if required. Non-smoking house, dinner by arrangement.

Palmerston North *13 km E of Palmerston North*
Country Lane Homestay *B&B Homestay*

Fay & Allan Hutchinson
52 Orrs Road,
RD 1, Aokautere,
Palmerston North

Tel (06) 326 8529
or 027 448 5833
Fax (06) 326 9216
countrylane@xtra.co.nz

Double/Twin $100 - $140
Single $75 - $95
(Full breakfast)
Dinner $25-$30
Not suitable for children
1 King/Twin 1 King 1 Queen
1 Double 1 Single (3 bdrm)
Bathrooms: 1 Ensuite
2 Private 1 Family share

Luxury country living, short distance from Palmerston North, near Manawatu Gorge, below wind farm. 10km from Pacific College and 2km from Equestrian Centre. Excellent stop over en route to/from Wellington or East Coast. Our home is newly decorated, with antiques in a country traditional style surrounded by our garden. Sawmill on the property, coloured sheep, horses and calves. Manawatu River borders our property. It is our pleasure to provide home-cooked meals with some local produce. Directions: please phone. A brochure with map is available.

Waitarere Beach *14 km NW of Levin*
Dunes *B&B Homestay*

Robyn & Grant Powell
10 Ngati Huia Place,
Waitarere Beach, 5510

Tel (06) 368 6246
or 027 285 3643
sand.dunes@xtra.co.nz
waitarere.dunes.googlepages.com

Double/Twin $135
Single $100
(Continental breakfast)
Dinner $30
Visa MC accepted
2 Queen (2 bdrm)
Bathrooms: 2 Ensuite

Robyn & Grant Powell welcome you to our absolute beachfront retreat. Enjoy beach walks and magnificent views of Kapiti and Mounts Taranaki and Ruapehu. We offer 2 queen-size bedrooms with own private entrance and deck areas, ensuites, own living areas with TV, tea/coffee making facilities - continental breakfast provided. Situated 14km north west of Levin, approximately 1 and a half hours from Wellington and 35 minutes from Palmerston North. Laundry facilities, off-street parking, non-smoking. Dinner by arrangement.

If you would like dinner
most hosts require 24 hours notice.

Levin *1 km E of Levin*

Fantails Accommodation *B&B Cottage with Kitchen Self-contained cottages*

Heather Watson
40 MacArthur Street,
Levin 5510

Tel (06) 368 9011
Fax (06) 368 9011
fantails@xtra.co.nz
www.fantails.co.nz

Double/Twin $145 - $165
Single $130 - $150
(Special breakfast)
Dinner by arrangement
Self-contained cottages $140-$190
Visa MC accepted
Children and pets welcome
1 King 2 Queen 1 Twin
4 Single (4 bdrm)
Bathrooms: 3 Ensuite 1 Private

Your hostess provides a high standard Bed & Breakfast service to 3 elegant rooms plus has 2 self-contained modern cottages set in a beautiful sustainable garden, including flower beds, lawns, vegetables and century old trees which attract a variety of birds. The tone achieved is tranquil and welcoming aiming for a quiet, warm and comfortable stay. The unique setting also has internet, secure parking, a gift gallery, a massage spa area, a laundry service and is close to golf, the Tararuas for tramping and beaches.

Levin - Ohau *5 km S of Levin*

Ardo Highland Haven B&B *B&B Farmstay*

Malcolm & Rachel Phillips
170 McLeavey Road,
RD 20, Levin 5570

Tel (06) 368 7080
or 021 506 990
Fax (06) 368 7080
ardo@farmside.co.nz
or info@ardohighlandhaven.co.nz
www.ardohighlandhaven.co.nz

Double/Twin $130 - $140
Single $100 (Full breakfast)
Dinner by arrangement $35
Visa MC accepted
Children welcome, cot and
highchair available
Internet available
2 Queen 1 Single (3 bdrm)
Bathrooms: 1 Private
We host one party only at a time

Travelling to or from Wellington? A warm welcome awaits you at Ardo, our country home on 10 acres,5km south of levin. Upstairs is for you alone as we host one party only at a time. We have a dairy farming background, and now breed highland cattle and friendly sheep. Excellent restaurants nearby. Hosting is wonderful - such interesting guests from many countries. Just Mandy, our Australian Terrier, and Lola, our tabby cat at home with us now! Please take time to read our Guest Reviews.

Wairarapa
Colyton
elding
ewbury
Palmerston North
Oroua Downs
Tokomaru
Foxton
Levin
Eketahuna
Otaki
Te Horo
Waikanae
paraumu
kariki
Masterton
Carterton
Upper Hutt
retaunga
Martinborough
3
2
2
53
0 Kilometres 20
0 Miles 12

Eketahuna *45 km N of Masterton*

Brookfields Lodge *B&B Licensed restaurant and separate self catering cottage*

Terry and Corinna Carew
31 Alfredton Road, Eketahuna, 4900

Tel (06) 375 8686
or 021 214 7039
terry@brookfieldslodge.co.nz
www.brookfieldslodge.co.nz

Double/Twin $120 - $180
Single $120 - $140
(Full breakfast)
Dinner available in the
attached restaurant
Cottage price on application
Visa MC Eftpos accepted
Children welcome
3 Queen (3 bdrm)
Stylish, relaxing en suite
accommodation
Bathrooms: 3 Ensuite
1 bathroom in self catering

Brookfields is ideally situated halfway between Wellington and Napier providing the discerning traveller with a relaxed friendly place to stay overnight or longer. Originally built as a 3 bedroom villa in 1910, this grand old home has been tastefully restored to provide comfortable en-suite accommodation in the heart of the Tararua District. The emphasis is on good food, comfortable surroundings and pleasant company.

Masterton *10 km SW of Masterton*

Tidsfordriv *B&B Homestay*

Glenys Hansen
54 Cootes Road,
Matahiwi, RD 8,
Masterton, 5888

Tel (06) 378 9967
Fax (06) 378 9957
ghansen@contact.net.nz

Double/Twin $110
Single $70 (Full breakfast)
Children $30 under 13 years
Dinner $25 by arrangement
includes pre-dinner drink
Visa MC accepted
Children welcome
Internet Available
1 Queen 2 Single (2 bdrm)
1 Queen room, 1 twin room
Bathrooms: 1 Private

A warm welcome awaits you at 'Tidsfordriv' - a 64 acre farmlet - seven kilometres off the main bypass route. Enjoy the comforts of a modern home set in parklike surroundings with large gardens & lakes. Bird watch with ease and enjoy the peaceful serenity of this 'Rural Retreat'. Glenys invites you to join her for dinner and enjoy good conversation about gardening, conservation, travel & local history. Stay more than one night and enjoy visits to Pukaha Mount Bruce Wildlife Centre, Castlepoint and other Wairarapa attractions.

Masterton *1 km E of Masterton*
Mas des Saules *B&B Homestay*

Mary & Steve Blakemore
35A Pokohiwi Road,
Homebush, 5810

Tel (06) 377 2577
or 027 620 8728
Fax (06) 377 2578
mas-des-saules@wise.net.nz

Double/Twin $125
Single $85 (Full breakfast)
Children $40 Dinner $40
Visa MC accepted
Children and pets welcome
Internet Available
2 Queen (2 bdrm)
Double bedrooms, central heating,
two windows and double wardrobes
Bathrooms: 1 Guest share

Hidden down a tranquil country lane, discover our authentic French Provencal farmhouse with its landscaped garden, stream, and courtyard. Swimming and trout fishing in nearby river. Our children have departed, leaving us with two cats, our small dog, and cattle on our small farm. Guest lounge and bathroom with bath and shower. Open fire and central heating. Enjoy farmhouse cooking with fresh vegetables from our large country garden, barbecues and picnic lunches. We are a well-travelled couple who enjoy helping guests discover the unspoilt Wairarapa.

Masterton *1 km NW of Urban Boundary*
Llandaff *B&B Farmstay*

Elizabeth & Robin Dunlop
183 Upper Plain Road Masterton

Tel (06) 378 6628
or 021 359 562
Fax (06) 378 6628
llandaff@xtra.co.nz
www.llandaff.co.nz

Double/Twin $110 - $130
Single $70 - $120 (Full breakfast)
Children $25 Dinner $35
Children welcome
1 King 2 Queen 1 Double
1 Twin (5 bdrm)
Decotated in the style
of the historic house
Bathrooms: 1 Ensuite 3 Guest share
Ensuite shower only

Elegantly restored, the homestead boasts beautiful native NZ timbers throughout, wood panelled rooms, polished floors, old pull-handle toilets, a 'coffin' bath, open fireplaces and cosy woodburning kitchen stove. Explore the historic stables, washhouse, produce shed, gardener's shed, pavilion and dove cote. See the vintage farm machinery. Relax in the majestic garden beneath 130 year old trees, or wander the farm and see the animals. Bike riding, croquet and petanque are available to guests. Enjoy a cooked breakfast with dinner available on request.

Masterton *8 km E of Masterton*
Vista Homestay *B&B Homestay*

Carol and Quenten Hansen
339A Te Ore Ore Settlement Rd,
RD 6, Masterton, 5886

Tel (06) 370 8919
or 027 360 6499
cqhansen@xtra.co.nz

Double/Twin $120
Single $70
(Continental breakfast)
Children $25 under 12
Dinner $35 per adult,
includes pre dinner drink
Visa MC accepted
Pet free home
Children welcome
Internet available
1 Queen 2 Single (2 bdrm)
Bathrooms: 1 Private
1 party per booking

From the moment you arrive you will be made to feel welcome. The smell of fresh flowers and home cooking awaits you along with stunning views from inside our modern home to the outdoors. Vista Homestay is a genuine slice of the Wairarapa. To make your visit memorable we invite you to join us for dinner.

Homebush - Masterton *2 km E of Masterton*
The Landing *B&B Homestay*

Robin & Marianne Hercock
35B Pokohiwi Road,
Homebush,
Masterton

Tel (06) 370 2428
or 027 237 7013
info@thelanding.net.nz
www.thelanding.net.nz

Double/Twin $120 - $180
Single $110 - $170
(Full breakfast)
Dinner by arrangement
Visa MC accepted
Not suitable for children
Internet available
2 King 2 Queen (4 bdrm)
Bathrooms: 2 Ensuite 2 Private

This elegant Country House and Venue is set among shady oaks and citrus in the heart of 'The classic NZ Wine Trail', 12km East of Masterton. While having all the modern facilities including wireless broadband, swimming pool and tennis court, The Landing is all about making guests feel welcome and relaxed. Delicious breakfasts are prepared with homegrown and local produce where possible. For a romantic relaxed weekend getaway or break in a NZ road trip, The Landing is a perfect place.

Carterton *3 km S of Masterton*
Pinnacle Grove *Homestay Farmstay*

Alma & Ad van der Tol
240 Norfolk Road,
RD 1,
Carterton, 5791

Tel (06) 370 3309
avdt@pinnacle-grove.walnuts.co.nz
www.walnuts.co.nz

Double/Twin $150
Single $125
(Continental breakfast)
Visa MC accepted
Children welcome
Internet available
2 King (2 bdrm)
Bathrooms: 1 Guest share

Pinnacle Grove Homestay is situated in Carterton District at a short distance from Masterton township on the road to the Tararua Forest Park and Mt Holdsworth recreation area. Jessie, our Jack Russel terrier will welcome you enthusiastically and so will Alma and Ad in our modern, comfortable home situated on 28 acres of walnut plantation in a relaxed and friendly atmosphere. Linger and relax on the verandah, walk in the Tararua Forest Park or enjoy the wine, arts and craft of the Wairarapa.

Martinborough *0.5 km NW of Martinborough*
Oak House *B&B*

Polly & Chris Buring
45 Kitchener Street,
Martinborough

Tel (06) 306 9198
Fax (06) 306 8198
chrispolly.oakhouse@xtra.co.nz
buringswines.co.nz

Double/Twin $120 - $140
Single $60 - $70
(Special breakfast)
Children by arrangement
Dinner by arrangement
Visa MC accepted
Children welcome
2 Queen 2 Single (3 bdrm)
Bathrooms: 1 Ensuite 1 Guest share

Our characterful 80 year old Californian bungalow offers gracious accommodation. Our spacious lounge provides a relaxed setting for sampling winemaker Chris's wonderful products. Our guest wing has its own entrance, bathroom (large bath and shower) and separate toilet. Our new bedroom has ensuite facilities. Bedrooms enjoy afternoon sun and garden views. Breakfast features fresh croissants, home-preserved local fruits and conserves. Creative cook Polly matches delicious dishes (often local game) with Chris's great wines. Tour our onsite winery with Chris. Meet our multi-talented cats.

Martinborough *1 km SW of Martinborough*
The Old Manse *B&B Homestay*

Sandra & John Hargrave
Corner Grey & Roberts Streets,
Martinborough

Tel (06) 306 8599
or 0800 399 229
Fax (06) 306 8540
info@oldmanse.co.nz
www.oldmanse.co.nz

Double/Twin $170 - $210
(Full breakfast)
Visa MC Diners Amex
Eftpos accepted
Not suitable for children
Internet available
5 Queen 1 Twin (6 bdrm)
Bathrooms: 6 Ensuite

In the heart of the wine district, a beautifully restored Presbyterian Manse, built 1876, has been transformed into a boutique homestay. Spacious, relaxed accommodation in a quiet, peaceful setting. 1 twin, 5 queen-size bedrooms all with their own ensuites. All day sun. Off-street parking, open fireplace. Amenities include spa pool, petanque, billiards. Enjoy breakfast or wine overlooking vineyard. Walking distance to Martinborough Square with selection of excellent restaurants. Close to vineyards, antique and craft shops, adventure quad bikes and golf courses. Qualmark 4+

Martinborough *1 km S of village square*
The Martinborough Connection *B&B*

David & Lorraine Murray
80 Jellicoe Street,
Martinborough, 5711

Tel (06) 306 9708 or 027 438 1581
Fax (06) 306 9706
martinboroughconnection@xtra.co.nz
www.martinboroughconnection.co.nz

Double/Twin $135 - $145
Single $115 - $120 (Full breakfast)
Children in room with extra bed $15
Additional adult in room
with extra bed $30
Visa MC Eftpos accepted
Pet free home Children welcome
Internet available
4 Queen 1 Single (4 bdrm)
Bathrooms: 4 Ensuite

Bed & breakfast accommodation situated within the Martinborough wine village. Originally built in 1889 the property has been fully restored retaining its original character. Open your bedroom door to a sunny verandah & garden. Start the day with a scrumptious breakfast, before visiting Martinboroughs wineries,or Cape Palliser with its spectacular coastline,lighthouse,& furseal colony. Relax in the guest lounge with its open fire or outside in the lovely gardens. We look forward to hosting you.

Wellington
Kapiti Island
Kapiti Coast
Manaka
Otaki
Te Horo
Waikanae
1
Paraparaumu
Raumati
Plimmerton
Paremata
2
Upper Hutt
1
Tawa
2
Stokes Valley
Lower Hutt
Oharju Valley
Johnsonville
See
Wellington City
next page
Petone
Aro Valley
Brooklyn
Mt. Victoria
Hataitai
Vogeltown
Mt. Cook
Mornington
Karaka Bay
Melrose
Seatoun
Island Bay
Breaker Bay
Palmer Head
Wellington
International
Airport
Wainuomata
Eastbourne
0
Kilometres
10
0
Miles
6

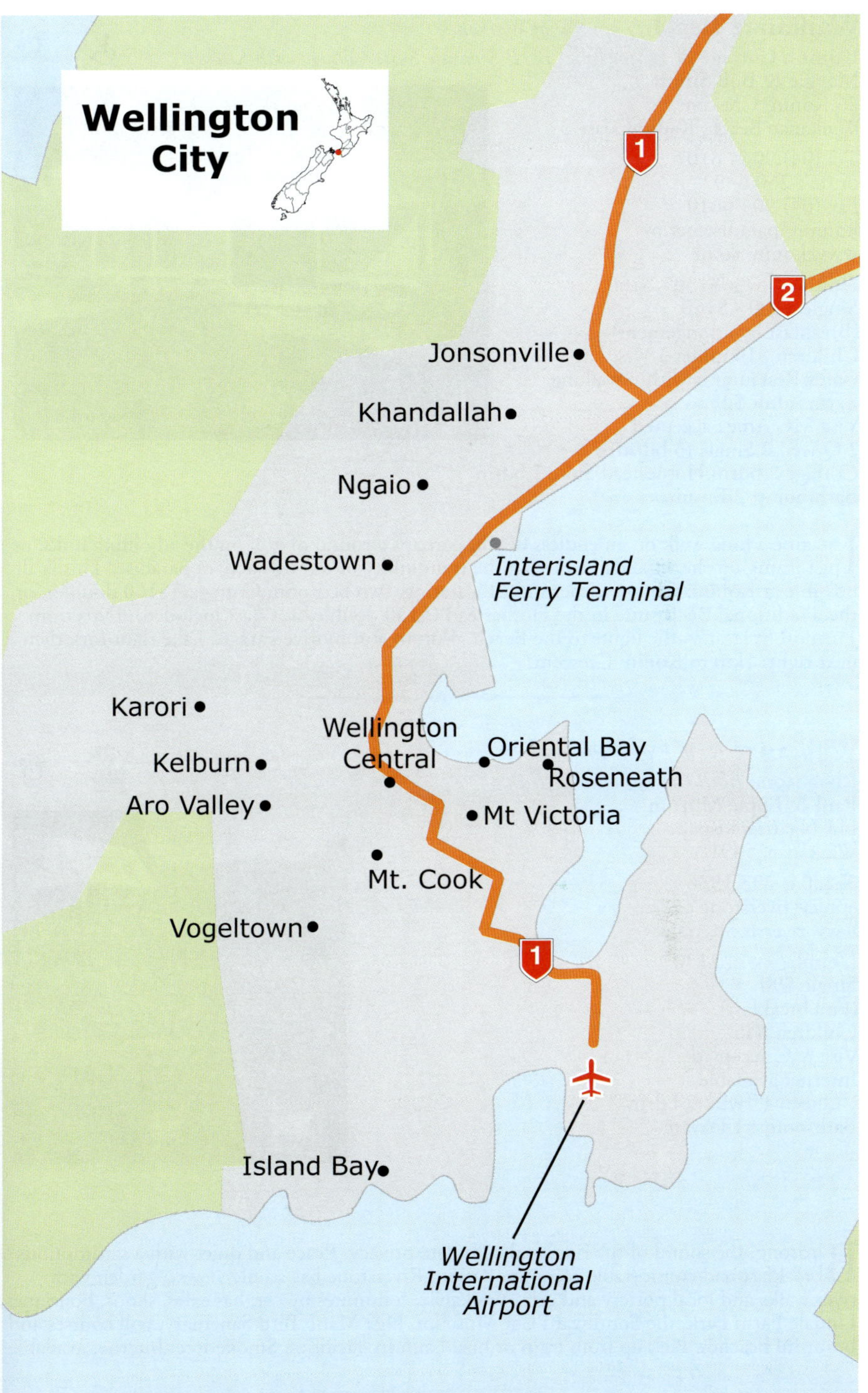

Wellington
City
1
2
Jonsonville
Khandallah
Ngaio
Wadestown
Interisland
Ferry Terminal
Karori
Wellington
Central
Oriental Bay
Roseneath
Kelburn
Aro Valley
Mt Victoria
Mt. Cook
1
Vogeltown
Island Bay
Wellington
International
Airport
Wellington

Waikanae Beach *5 km SW of Waikanae*
Konini: Cottage & Homestead *B&B Separate Suite Cottage with Kitchen*

Maggie & Bob Smith
26 Konini Crescent,
Waikanae Beach, Kapiti Coast

Tel (04) 904 6610
or 027 260 6492
Fax (04) 904 6610
konini@paradise.net.nz
www.konini.co.nz

Double/Twin $130 - $160
Single $100 - $160
(Breakfast by arrangement)
Children $10 under 13yrs.
Cafes/Restaurants within walking
Extra Adult $25
Visa MC Amex accepted
2 Queen 2 Single (3 bdrm)
Cottage 2 bdrm Homestead Suite 1 bdrm
Bathrooms: 2 Ensuite

Imagine a long walk on an endless beach, perhaps a round of golf on the adjoining links, or just lazing on the verandah enjoying the tranquillity of our one acre of paradise. This is all possible at Konini. Choose either the self catering, two bedroom Cottage, ($160 double), or the Traditional B&B suite in the Homestead ($130 double breakfast included). Direction: Turn off SH1 at traffic lights to the Beach. 4km to automotive garage. Take right fork then next right. 1km to Konini Crescent.

Waikanae *6 km E of Waikanae*
RiverStone *B&B Cottage with Kitchen*

Paul & Eppie Murton
111 Ngatiawa Road,
Waikanae, 5391

Tel (04) 293 1936
eppie@riverstone.co.nz
www.riverstone.co.nz

Double/Twin $130
Single $90
(Full breakfast)
Children $45
Visa MC accepted
Internet available
1 Queen 1 Twin (2 bdrm)
Bathrooms: 1 Private

Birdsong, the sound of the river and complete privacy. Peace and quiet with a scrumptious breakfast and comfortable accommodation. Riverstone has scenic views a garden with river walks and local pottery and cafe. Waikanae, 5 minutes by car, has cafes, shops, boutiques, Lindale Farm Park, the Southward Car Museum, Nga Manu Bird Sanctuary, golf courses and beautiful beaches. Pick up from train or bus. Laundry facilities. Smoke-free. Internet available.

Waikanae *45 km N of Wellington*
Waimoana *B&B Homestay*
Elizabeth and Bryan Couchman
63 Kakariki Grove,
Waikanae 5036,
Kapiti Coast

Tel (04) 293 2005
or 021 0222 0217
relax@waimoana.co.nz
www.waimoana.co.nz

Double/Twin $150
Single $120
(Continental breakfast)
Visa MC accepted
1 Queen (1 bdrm)
Bathrooms: 1 Ensuite

Waimoana is a purpose built quality homestay. Enjoy majestic sea views over Kapiti from the sundeck or pool. Living rooms radiate from a glass-roofed atrium featuring an indoor swimming pool, garden and waterfall. Our guest room has its own private entrance, parking and ensuite facilities. Local activities include native bush walks, beaches, first-class restaurants and cafes, craft and mosaic shops, bird sanctuaries and golf courses. A warm welcome awaits you from our three sons and cat Tabitha.

Waikanae *1 km E of Waikanae*
Te Rimu B & B *B&B*
Barbara Baylis
11 Hira Street,
Waikanae, 5036

Tel (04) 293-2535
or 021 118-9845
enquiries@terimu.co.nz

Double/Twin $120 - $150
Single $80 - $100
(Full breakfast)
Dinner by prior arrangement
Visa MC accepted
Pet free home
Not suitable for children
1 King/Twin 1 Double (2 bdrm)
1 King/twin room, 1 double room
Bathrooms: 1 Guest share

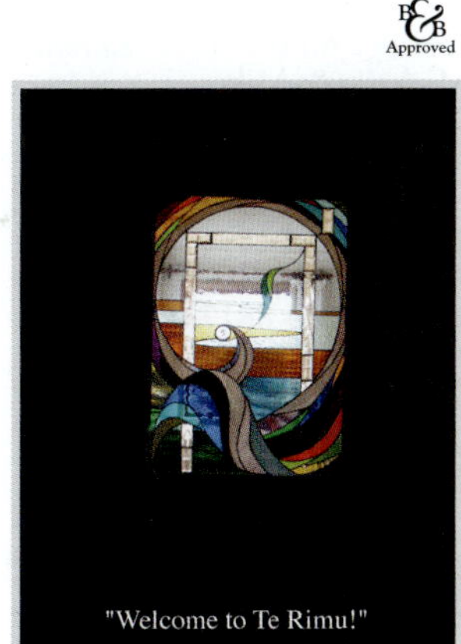

Join me in my beautiful home set among trees, tuis and tranquility on the eastern slopes of the hill in Waikanae. I enjoy good company and good food and will endeavour that you do also. As I work away from home forward bookings would be appreciated, so I can give you great hospitality.

Raumati Beach *3 km SW of Paraparaumu*
Sea Haven *B&B Homestay*

Jan & Laurie Bason
325 Rosetta Road,
Raumati Beach,
Paraparaumu

Tel (04) 902 0047
or 021 0279 8803
jan-laurie@paradise.net.nz

Double/Twin $120
Single $95
(Continental breakfast)
Visa MC accepted
Pet free home
Not suitable for children
Internet available
1 Queen (1 bdrm)
1 single inflatable bed if required
Bathrooms: 1 Private

Welcome to our spacious smoke-free home. Our guest room opens to a small garden, with seating amongst native trees. Private access to the beach. 250 metres from village shops, restaurants, swimming pool, bowling green and Marine Gardens. Kapiti Miniature Railway is situated at Marine Gardens with various locomotives running on Sunday afternoons. Golf courses in the area. Laurie, a railway enthusiast, has a miniature locomotive and collection of railway memorabilia. We enjoy overseas travel, and travelling throughout NZ in our Motorhome.

Paremata *5 km N of Porirua*
Cottage on the Inlet *Self contained cottage*

Michelle & Mike
300a Paremata Road,
Paremata,
Wellington

Tel (04) 234 1699
or 021 305 342
Fax (04) 234 8817
mdykes@dykesassoc.co.nz
www.cottageontheinlet.co.nz

Double/Twin $160 - $180
Single $160 - $180
(Breakfast by arrangement)
Children 2 and under - no charge
Dinner not provided
Rates are for the entire cottage
Children and pets welcome
1 Queen 2 Single (2 bdrm)
Bathrooms: 1 Private

Are you looking for a private peaceful retreat? Located just north of Wellington on the Pauatahanui Inlet with unrestricted views of the water, the Cottage on the Inlet could be just what you need. The self contained cottage is nestled in an old fruit orchard and is part of a larger property built in the early 1900s. The cottage has recently been renovated and is spacious yet cosy whilst still retaining that 'country cottage' feel. Come and enjoy your retreat today.

Lower Hutt *1 km N of Lower Hutt Centre*
Judy & Bob's Place *Homestay*
Judy & Bob Vine
11 Ngaio Crescent,
Woburn, Lower Hutt

Tel (04) 971 1192
or 021 510 682
Fax (04) 971 6192
bob.vine@paradise.net.nz
www.bobvine.gen.nz/

Double/Twin $140
Single $70
(Full breakfast)
Dinner $40
Visa MC Diners Amex accepted
Pet free home
Internet available
1 Queen 2 Single (2 bdrm)
Bathrooms: 1 Private
Limit: 1 booking a time to obviate bathroom sharing

Located in Woburn, a picturesque and quiet central city suburb of Lower Hutt, known for its generous sized houses and beautiful gardens. Within walking distance of the Lower Hutt downtown, 15 minutes drive from central Wellington, its railway station and ferry terminals; airport 25 minutes; 3 minutes walk to Woburn Rail Station. Private lounge and TV. Love to entertain and share hearty Kiwi style cooking with good New Zealand wine. Laundry facilities. Transfer transport available. High speed Internet connections.

Lower Hutt *0.5 km SE of Lower Hutt*
Rose Cottage *B&B Homestay*
Maureen & Gordon Gellen
70A Hautana Street,
Lower Hutt,
Wellington

Tel (04) 566 7755
or 021 481 732
Fax (04) 566 0777
gellen@xtra.co.nz

Double/Twin $115 - $130
Single $95 - $115
(Full breakfast)
Dinner $35 by arrangement
Visa MC accepted
Not suitable for children
1 King/Twin 1 Queen (2 bdrm)
Bathrooms: 1 Ensuite 1 Family share

Relax in the comfort of our cosy home which is just a 5 minute walk to the Hutt City Centre and 15 minutes to ferries. Originally built in 1910 the house has been fully renovated. Interests, travel, sports and live theatre. As well as TV in guest room there's coffee and tea-making facilities. Breakfast will be served in our dining room at your convenience. Unsuitable for children. We look forward to welcoming you into our smoke-free home which we share with Scuffin our cat.

Lower Hutt - Harbourview *1.5 km SW of Lower Hutt*
Harbourcity View B & B *B&B Homestay*

Mary Quayle
14 City View Grove,
Harbourview,
Lower Hutt, 5010

Tel (04) 586 0557
or 027 688 3306
harbourcityview@xnet.co.nz
www.harbourcityviewbnb.com

Double/Twin $120 - $200
Single $75 - $150
(Full breakfast)
Dinner $25 pp by arrangement
Visa MC accepted
Not suitable for children
2 Super King 1 Single (3 bdrm)
Bathrooms: 1 Ensuite 1 Family share

Welcome to my home in a peaceful setting surrounded by a bush reserve with panoramic views of Wellington harbour and Hutt River. 15mins by train or car to central Wellington to visit Parliament, Botanical Gardens, Cable Car, Te Papa, Zealandia. Alternatively hike in the Regional Parks or play golf on nearby courses. At the end of the day relax in the garden with a view to the sea. Enjoy tea/coffee facilities with home baking in the conservatory. Tours arranged, Airport/Ferry transfers. Laundry available, Off street parking.

Lower Hutt *1 km SE of Lower Hutt i-site*
Hallcroft Homestay *B&B Homestay*

Lynley Hall
2 Miro Street,
Woburn,
Lower Hutt, 5010

Tel (04) 938 1686
or 021 253 4131
lyndavid@paradise.net.nz

Double/Twin $60 - $120
Single $60 - $60
(Continental breakfast)
Children by arrangement
Cash or NZ cheque only
Children and pets welcome
1 Queen 2 Twin (2 bdrm)
Bathrooms: 1 Guest share

A smoke free, wheelchair accessible home and facilities. Off road parking. One queen bedroom. One twin bedroom. Shared Guest Bathroom. Cot and high chair available. Radio, TV and hairdryers, tea & coffee making facilities in rooms. Continental breakfast. 3 mins walk to railway station, 20 mins by train to Wellington station. Easy walk to local eating places. One small dog lives inside.

Lower Hutt - Stokes Valley *15 km N of Lower Hutt*
Rambling Brook *Cottage with Kitchen*

Mal & Nina
30 Tawhai Street,
Stokes Valley,
Lower Hutt

Tel (04) 563 8716
malboandnina@yahoo.co.nz

Double/Twin $130 - $160
Single $120 - $135
(Breakfast by arrangement)
Children $35
Gluten & dairy free
breakfasts available
Children welcome
1 Queen (1 bdrm)
Double pullout couch in lounge
Bathrooms: 1 Ensuite

Welcome to Rambling Brook B&B. Come and enjoy our hospitality while relaxing in our private garden beside the stream, with birds singing during the day and the sounds of moreporks and frogs in the evening. We offer a private self contained cottage with off street parking. We have a range of DVD movies to watch and board games to play. 20 minutes to Lower Hutt or Upper Hutt. Close to Golf Course and driving range. Our three cats will also love to meet you.

Lower Hutt - Stokes Valley *08 km SW of upper hutt*
Myrian House *B&B Homestay*

Myra Moon & Ian Lawson
435 Stokes Valley Road,
Stokes Valley,
Lower Hutt, 5019

Tel (04) 938 1143
or mobile 021 159 4441
myrianhouse@paradise.net.nz

Double/Twin $120 - $130
(Special breakfast)
Seasonal discounts May to October
Pet free home
Internet available
2 Queen (2 bdrm)
Bathrooms: 1 Guest share

Myra & Ian welcome you to Myrian House @ 435 Stokes Valley rd; with complimentary Devonshire tea on arrival. .Surrounded by bush and birdsong ,you will feel relaxed and comfortable. Only a short drive from CBD,Kapiti coast or wine country. Whether you enjoy a game of golf, bushwalks,beach ,theatre or shops we have it all. Free wireless internet, cable/sky TV, dinner by arrangement. As your hosts we are committed to make your stay with us memorable.

Moores Valley - Wainuiomata *8 km NE of Lower Hutt*
Moores Valley Retreat *B&B Farmstay Cottage with Kitchen*

Chuni & Jaya
303 Moores Valley Road,
Lower Hutt. Wellington, 5373

Tel (04) 564 7504
or 021 986 504
Fax (04) 5647508
mooresvalley@ihug.co.nz

Double/Twin $120 - $150
Single $95
(Continental breakfast provisions)
Children $30
Dinner by arrangement
Visa MC accepted
Pet free home Children welcome
Internet available
2 Queen 1 Single (3 bdrm)
Bathrooms: 1 Private

Welcome to our idyllic countryside homestay, set in 10 beautiful acres of farmland. Located close to Wellington's CBD, and minutes from the local village. This private and comfortable homestay has spacious guest rooms, a fully equipped kitchen, Sky TV, DVD, BBQ, laundry, and bathroom. You'll enjoy access to our very own private and natural stream with bridge. Located close to Rimataka reserve, scenic bush walks, and local golf courses. This is the perfect rural holiday retreat located within easy reach of the capital.

Eastbourne - York Bay *3 km N of Eastbourne*
Bush House *Homestay*
Belinda Cattermole
12 Waitohu Road,
York Bay,
Eastbourne

Tel (04) 568 5250
or 027 408 9648
Fax (04) 568 5250
belindacat@paradise.net.nz

Double/Twin $100
Single $80
(Special breakfast)
Dinner by arrangement
1 Double 1 Single (2 bdrm)
Bathrooms: 1 Private 1 Family share

Come and enjoy the peace and tranquility of the Eastern Bays. You will be hosted in a restored 1920's settler cottage nestled amongst native bush and looking towards the Kaikoura mountains of the South Island. My love of cordon-bleu cooking and the pleasures of the table are satisfied through the use of my country kitchen and dining room. Other attractions: A Devon Rex cat. Eastbourne is a small seaside village across the harbour from Wellington City with a range of attractions.

 www.bnb.co.nz

Eastbourne - Days Bay *12 km E of Wellington*
FernTree Hideaway *B&B Apartment with Kitchen Boutique*

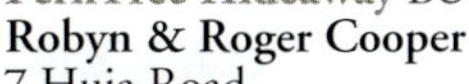

Robyn & Roger Cooper
7 Huia Road,
Days Bay, Eastbourne

Tel (04) 562 7692
or 027 616 9826
Fax (04) 562 7690
relax@ferntreehideaway.co.nz
www.ferntreehideaway.co.nz

Double/Twin $185 - $215
Single $160 - $180
(Continental breakfast provisions)
Children $32   Extra adults $45
Visa MC accepted
Children welcome
Internet Available
1 King (1 bdrm)
1 king bedroom, 2 sofabeds in lounge
Bathrooms: 1 Private

Ride our private cable car through native bush to FernTree Hideaway. Self-contained romantic retreat overlooking Wellington harbour. Enjoy sparkling sea views and bellbird song; breakfast on your garden patio; relax with books, TV, DVDs, CDs. Open plan lounge/dining/kitchenette, luxury bath/shower, free Wi-Fi, phone. 200 metres to beach, cafes, galleries. Days Bay ferry to Central Wellington (20 minutes) berths near Te Papa and The Stadium. Interisland ferry 20 minutes. 'This place is Dreamland - a Kiwi Shangri-la.' Self-catering optional.

Eastbourne *20 km E of Wellington*
The Anchorage *B&B*

Bet & Wal Louden
107 Marine Parade,
Eastbourne,
Lower Hutt 5013

Tel (04) 562 8310
or 021 049 5169
betandwal@paradise.net.nz

Double/Twin $140
Single $110
(Continental breakfast)
Extra guests $60
Visa MC accepted
Children welcome
Internet available
1 Queen 1 Single (2 bdrm)
1 queen,1single/lounge-sofa
bedBathrooms: 1 Private

Welcome to our waterfront property, wonderful views of Wellington Harbour and city. One minute walk to Eastbourne Village and wharf, supermarket, cafes, restaurants, pub, antique shops and art gallery. We offer for the more adventurous a choice of guided bush walks from an easy 2 hours to a demanding 7 hours (bookings essential; Mon-Friday only), outstanding beech, northern rata and podocarp forests. Coastal walks (mountain bike rides) to Pencarrow Lighthouse. Kayak trips also available. Labrador, Splash on property. Wireless broadband. Single party bookings only.

Eastbourne *2 km S of Eastbourne Village*
The Walnut Tree *Luxury B&B*
Jasmin & Alan Macdonald
335 Muritai Road,
Eastbourne, Wellington, 5013

Tel (04) 562 8768 or 027 439 3886
Fax (04) 562 8763
jasmin@thewalnuttree.co.nz
www.thewalnuttree.co.nz

Double/Twin $160
Single $120 (Full breakfast)
Children $25
Not suitable for mobile pre-schoolers
Dinner Casual/ Family $20 pp
Special/private $40 pp
Visa MC accepted
1 King/Twin 1 Queen 1 Single (3 bdrm)
1Queen, 1King/Twin, 1Single
Single party bookings only
Bathrooms: 1 Private private semi-ensuite

Enjoy glorious views, birdsong and total privacy from the top storey of our renovated multi-level country character home. We offer delicious food, three charming Bedrooms, a sumptuous upstairs Lounge with widescreen tv, garden balcony and outdoor spa. Easy stroll to the beach and bush, or cafes and boutiques in Eastbourne village. The Wellington bus stops right at the front gate. Our two teenagers and two spoilt Siamese cats live with us too. The welcome mat is out, the croissants are hot- we'd love your company!

Eastbourne - Days Bay *10 km S of Petone*
Ruru Lane Bed & Breakfast *B&B*
Les Maiden & Nicky Long
12 Korimako Rd,
Days Bay, 5013

Tel Landline (04) 562 8970
or Mobile 021 628 617
info@rurulane.co.nz
www.rurulane.co.nz

Double/Twin $160 - $180
Single $140 - $160
(Continental breakfast)
Children $30 extra
Visa MC Amex accepted
Internet available
1 King 1 Double (2 bdrm)
Rooms have sofas, writing tables,
tea and coffee facilities
Bathrooms: 1 Private Single party bookings only

Ruru Lane is a large, gracious house with luxurious accommodation surrounded by an abundance of trees, ferns and flowering plants. Two generous bed sitting rooms adjoin the guest entrance hall. Both rooms have sofas, writing tables, tea and coffee making facilities and delightful views. Enjoy the spacious bathroom with clawfoot bath, shower and a generous range of toiletries. Breakfast is continental with fresh juices, seasonal fruit, organic yoghurt, homemade cereal and preserves. Choose from a range of breads or items from the bakery.

Wellington - Johnsonville *8 km S of Wellington*
Paparangi Homestay *B&B Homestay*

Joy and Autry Kawana
145 Helston Road,
Johnsonville,
Wellington, 6037

Tel (04) 478 1747
or 027 485 6432
autry.joy@xtra.co.nz

Double/Twin $100 - $110
Single $60 - $70
(Full breakfast)
Children negotiable
Dinner with family $25
Children welcome
Internet available
1 Queen 1 Twin 1 Single (2 bdrm)
Bathrooms: 1 Ensuite 1 Family share

Paparangi Homestay is a 100 year old restored cottage set in 1 acre of peaceful cottage gardens with abundant birdlife. Bedrooms have TV/Radio, heaters, electric blankets and garden views. We are 10 min from ferry and city and 2km from train station which takes you straight to stadium and city. Bus stop at top of drive to city. Free wireless internet access. Homemade muesli, bread, preserves and free range hens. Autry and Joy enjoy the company of all nationalities and our home is your home while you are with us.

Wellington - Khandallah *7 km N of Wellington*
Clothier Homestay *Homestay*

Sue & Ted Clothier
22 Lohia Street,
Khandallah,
Wellington

Tel (04) 479 1180
or 027 246 6158
sclothier@xtra.co.nz

Double/Twin $110
Single $90
(Continental breakfast)
Not suitable for children
1 Twin (1 bdrm)
Bathrooms: 1 Ensuite

This is a lovely, sunny and warm open plan home with glorious harbour and city views. A quiet easily accessible street just 10 minutes from the city and 5 minutes from the ferry. Close to Khandallah Village where you can make use of the excellent local restaurant, cafe or Monteiths pub. We are a non-smoking household. Another family member is an aristocratic white cat called Dali. We enjoy sharing our home with our guests.

Wellington - Khandallah *7 km N of Wellington*
The Loft in Wellington *B&B Separate Suite*

Phillippa & Simon Plimmer
6 Delhi Crescent,
Khandallah,
Wellington

Tel (04) 938 5015
or 021 448 491
plimmers@paradise.net.nz

Double/Twin $120
Single $95
(Continental breakfast provisions)
Visa MC accepted
Pet free home
Not suitable for children
1 Queen (1 bdrm)
Bathrooms: 1 Ensuite

The Loft in Wellington offers comfort and style in a beautifully appointed self-contained studio (no cooking facilities). Enjoy complete privacy with your own entrance. Cable TV, off-street parking and laundry facility available. 10 minutes from downtown Wellington. Close to ferry terminal. 300 metres to local train and bus. 15 minutes train ride direct to Westpac Stadium. 500 metres from Khandallah Village and local restaurants. Studio not suitable for pets. We have 3 young children.

Take time to enjoy your journey
and the company of your hosts.
Sometimes less is more.

Wellington - Ngaio *7 km N of Wellington*

Ngaio Homestay *B&B Homestay Apartment with Kitchen*

Jennifer & Christopher Timmings
56 Fox Street, Ngaio, Wellington 6035
Tel (04) 479 5325 Fax (04) 479 4325
enquiries@ngaiohomestay.co.nz   www.ngaiohomestay.co.nz
Double/Twin $160 - $180 Single $100 - $140 (Continental breakfast)
Children negotiable   Dinner $35pp by arrangement
Self-contained $180double, extra person $45
Visa MC accepted   Pet free home Internet available
1 Queen 1 Double 2 Twin 3 Single (5 bdrm)
1 queen, 1 twin, 1 double 2 singles
Bathrooms: 3 Ensuite 1 Private
Shower& bath in apartments, shower in ensuite B&B

Welcome to Wonderful Wellington! Share your visit with us and enjoy helpful personal hospitality! Our unusual multi-level open plan character home [built1960] is in the suburb of Ngaio. Guests may leave their car here and take the train to CBD [10 minutes] We are 5 minutes by car to InterIsland Ferry terminal.

Our double room has tea/coffee facilities, quality bedding, tiled ensuite and french doors opening onto a deck and private jungle garden. Breakfast is continental. Evening meals an optional extra.

2 self-contained apartments, 1 queen, 1 twin, adjacent to our property, are comfortable, convenient, tastefully furnished and recently re-decorated. Each apartment also has a couch with a fold-out bed in lounge, fully equipped kitchen, shower, bath, laundry facilities, cable TV, phone and internet [small fee] There is a large garden with trees, birds and views. Perfect for business, holiday or relocating.

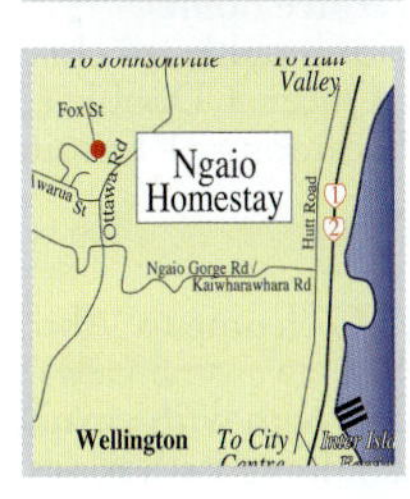

Jennifer plays harp at home and live piano music daily in NZ's top department store.

Compliment from guest: 'This is a home where there is beautiful music, art and love.' Do come and share! Please phone before 11am or after 3pm or fax or email. Bookings essential.

Wellington - Wadestown *2 km N of Wellington*
Harbour Lodge Wellington *B&B*

Lou & Chris Bradshaw
200 Barnard Street,
Wadestown,
Wellington

Tel (04) 976 5677
or 021 032 6497
lou@harbourlodgewellington.com
www.harbourlodgewellington.com

Double/Twin $180 - $270
(Continental breakfast)
Children negotiable
Visa MC Amex accepted
Children welcome
4 King (4 bdrm)
Bathrooms: 4 Ensuite

Let your stresses be gently lulled away in the luxurious comfort of this beautiful lodge. Admire the fabulous views of Wellington Harbour from the large sunny deck. Take a spa. Laze in the comfort of a large guest lounge with stunning harbour views. All this is only a few minutes drive from central Wellington, ferry terminal or Wellington Stadium. Children of all ages welcome, no pets please.

Wellington - Wadestown *2 km NW of C.B.D*
Ahu Mairangi *B&B*

James and Helen
128 Weld Street,
Wadestown, 6012

Tel landline (04) 473 7157
or freephone 0800 678 031
james.quinn@xtra.co.nz

Double/Twin $140 - $160
Single $100 - $120
(Continental breakfast)
Dinner 48 hrs notice
Neg.rates for longer stays
Pet free home
Not suitable for children
1 Queen 1 Double (2 bdrm)
Bathrooms: 1 Ensuite 1 Private

Welcome to 'Ahu Mairangi' Located high up on the hills above Wellington City for awesome views and maximum sun. Our recently modernised home has a large guest bedroom with ensuite which has both bath and shower. Also a second double bedroom with adjoining bath room and separate w.c. Both rooms have peaceful bush views so come and enjoy a relaxing stay in our beautiful city. As we adjoin the town belt there are some great walks for the fitter guests. Dinner optional extra

Wadestown - Wellington *1 km S of Post Office*
The Garden Room *B&B Guest House*

Sarah Playne Caughley
5 Rankin Street,
Wadestown, Wellington, 6012

Tel (04) 473 0191
or 0274 419 998
sarah.reviresco@xtra.co.nz
www.thegardenroom.co.nz

Double/Twin $120 - $150
Single $120
(Full breakfast)
Dinner in special circumstances
Children welcome
1 Queen 1 Single (1 bdrm)
1 large living/bedroom
Bathrooms: 1 Ensuite

Guest house set in charming garden in keeping with 1904 Villa. Pure cotton linen. Tea and coffee facilities. 20 minute walk down hill to CBD. 5 minute walk to enter into Wellington Town Belt. Family home of Garden designer and lawyer with 3 older children 1 currently living at home, 2 Jack Russells, 1 Cat.

Wellington - Karori *4 km SW of Wellington CBD*
Bristow Place *Apartment with Kitchen*

Helen & Tony Thomson
8 Bristow Place,
Karori,
Wellington

Tel (04) 476 6291
or 021 656 825
Fax (04) 476 6293
h.t.thomson@xtra.co.nz

Double/Twin $180
(Breakfast provisions first night)
Long stay by arrangement
Visa MC accepted
Children welcome
Internet available
1 Queen 1 Double (1 bdrm)
Separate bedroom (queen) plus
fold-out double in lounge
Bathrooms: 1 Private

We offer a private, fully self-contained apartment, able to sleep up to 4, on a self-catered, self-serviced basis. Enjoy Sky TV, electric blankets, bathrobes, heated towel rails, etc. Full laundry facilities. Wireless internet access available. German spoken. Inner suburb location with ample parking, good transport and local shops and restaurants.

Wellington - Karori *5 km SW of Wellington*
Campbell Homestay *Homestay*
Murray & Elaine Campbell
23 Parkvale Road, Karori 6012, Wellington

Tel (04) 476 6110 or 0274 535 080
Fax (04) 476 6593   ctool@ihug.co.nz
bnb.co.nz

Double/Twin $110 Single $75 (Continental breakfast)
Children half price (under 12)   Dinner $35 by arrangement
Visa MC Eftpos accepted   Children and pets welcome
1 Queen 1 Twin 1 Single (2 bdrm)
Bathrooms: 1 Guest share
Separate toilet, full bathroom/shower next to bedrooms.

Welcome to our home right in the village of Karori, but only ten minutes from the central city. Dine with us, or eat out at the local taverns, cafes, enjoy our local village shopping centre,library, Post Office and other amenities all within a few minutes walking distance. As we are on the main bus route, guests,can park their car off street and take the bus into the city. We are happy to pick you up from ferry, train, bus or airport terminals and of course make sure you do not miss your onward connection. We are situated close to the Karori Wildlife Sanctuary, Botanic Gardens and Otari-Wilton's Bush, Cable Car, historic Thorndon's boutique shopping centre and restaurants, Katherine Masefield's birthplace, the Westpac Stadium 'Absolutely Positively Wellington' is a dynamic ever changing compact city making it easy to walk from one place to the next and with simply the most friendly helpful people. Take advantage of Wellington's cultural events: orchestra, ballet, opera, galleries and theatres. Visit our fabulous modern museum Te Papa or take a shuttle ferry across the harbour. We have two guest bedrooms, 1 Queen and 1 Twin which can also be a single. Guests have the sole use of a separate toilet and a full sized bathroom next door to the bedrooms. Relax and make yourself at home - use our laundry, garden, lounge, email/internet facilities. Children of all ages welcome. Our home is perfect for business folk or families relocating as it is so close to all the village amenities and schools. Weekly rates on application Evening meals are an optional extra, $35.00 per person. From the motorway, when coming into Wellington from the north, take the Hawkestone Street/Karori exit off the motorway and follow the signs up past the Botanic gardens, through the tunnel, up the hill past the Marsden shops and down to the Karori village. Turn right at the lights into Parkvale Road (first turn past the Shopping Mall), then turn left down the drive to No 23 where a big welcome awaits you.

Wellington - Karori *2 km N of the central city*

B&B and Homestay *B&B Homestay Separate Suite*

Judit & Julian Farquhar
15 Nottingham Street,
Wellington, 6011

Tel (04) 976 8144
or 021 1810 8064
Fax (04) 976 8144
judit.farquhar@gmail.com
farquharsbedandbreakfast.blogspot.com

Double/Twin $120 - $130
Single $80 - $90
(Full breakfast provisions)
Children welcome at lower rates
Dinner by arrangement $20-35
Major currencies accepted
Children welcome
1 Queen 2 Single (1 bdrm)
Bathrooms: 1 Private

Welcome to our 100-year-old eco colonial home in the Wellington suburb of Karori with a beautiful mature organic garden, 5 minutes from the central city. We are a well-travelled Hungarian-Kiwi couple with our 10-year-old daughter. There is music, art and technology inside. Good transport, local shops and restaurants. We offer a separate guest-room for 2-4 people with its own WC and washbasin. There is also a self-contained, private apartment with kitchen to accomodate up to 4 people for longer period, by arrangment.

Wellington - Kelburn *1 km N of city centre*

Above Town Bed and Breakfast *B&B*

Maria and Michael Phelan
23 Rimu Road,
Kelburn,
Wellington, 6012

Tel (04) 971 5737
abovetownbnb@paradise.net.nz
www.abovetownbnb.co.nz

Double/Twin $155 - $180
Single $135 - $155
(Full breakfast)
Visa MC accepted
1 King/Twin 1 Double (1 bdrm)
Guest room
Bathrooms: 1 Ensuite

Enjoy our spacious guest room situated in a quiet central city suburb. Nearby Wellington's cable car to central city locations and harbourfront. Walk to Victoria University and Botanic Gardens. Te Papa, downtown entertainments and Westpac Stadium are easily reached. Knowledgeable hosts, Maria and Michael, can provide information to help you explore Wellington. Relax in your stylish room with sitting area, TV, coffee/tea making, airconditioning and fridge. Double futon for extra guests; quality linen; separate entrance and roadside parking. Friendly pet dog in residence.

Wellington - Aro Valley *2 km SW of Information Centre*
Millie's Bed & Breakfast *B&B Homestay*

Miriam Busby
33 Holloway Road,
Aro Valley, Wellington, 6021

Tel (04) 381 2968
or 021 254 7308
Fax (04) 381 2969
miriam.busby@paradise.net.nz
www.milliesbb.co.nz

Double/Twin $130
Single $90 (Full breakfast)
Children $40
Dinner $25 for
Colonial cottage cuisine
Children welcome
1 Double 1 Single (2 bdrm)
1 double/ queen sized bed and
1 single room available
Bathrooms: 1 Family share
One bath & shower available for guests to use

Named after Millie, the pet cat, at Millie's you awake to the sound of native birdsong. The house is nestled in a bushy valley near the Karori Sanctuary. Situated on a heritage trail, Millie's is close to a bus-stop, Aro Street cafes, restaurants and shops. 20 minutes walk to city. Free off-street parking available. Complimentary breakfast. 1 extra divan bed in kitchen. Deck with BBQ. Dinner, scenic drives, walks & therapeutic art sessions are extra services available.

Wellington - Mt Cook *2 km SE of Wellington*
Apartment One *B&B Homestay*

Jim & Colleen Bargh
1/2 King Street,
Mt Cook,
Wellington

Tel (04) 385 1112
or 027 247 8145
apartmentone@yahoo.co.nz

Double/Twin $130 - $140
Single $90 - $100
(Full breakfast)
Visa MC accepted
Pet free home
Not suitable for children
Internet available
2 Queen (2 bdrm)
Bathrooms: 2 Ensuite

Experience apartment living in the city. We moved off the farm into our converted warehouse to try city life. We love its ever-changing beauty and the people are simply the best. Come try it for yourself. Buses depart every few minutes. 2 minutes walk to the Basin Reserve and 10-15 minutes walk to Courtenay Place (Wellington's restaurant, cafe and theatre district). Less than 10 minutes drive to the ferry terminal and airport. We serve a deluxe breakfast to get you through your eventful day.

Wellington - Mt Victoria *0.5 km E of Central Wellington*
Villa Vittorio *B&B Homestay*

Annette & Logan Russell
6 Hawker Street, Mt Victoria, Wellington

Tel (04) 801 5761 or 027 432 1267
Fax (04) 801 5762
villa@villavittorio.co.nz
www.villavittorio.co.nz

Double/Twin $195 - $235 Single $135 (Full breakfast)
Dinner by arrangement
Visa MC Diners Amex accepted
1 Double (1 bdrm)
Bathrooms: 1 Private

WELCOME TO VILLA VITTORIO. Centrally located close by Courtenay Place. Short walk to restaurants, theatres, shopping, conference centres, Te Papa Museum, Parliament & Stadium. Guest bedroom with TV, tea & coffee facilities. Adjoining sitting room with balcony overlooking city. Bathroom with show- and bath.

Breakfast served in Italian styled dining room or outside in courtyard. We enjoy having guests, having travelled extensively ourselves. Transport and gourmet dinner by arrangement. Garaging and laundry at small charge. No children or pets.

Directions: phone, fax, email or write.

Wellington - Mt Victoria *0.5 km E of Courtenay Place*
Austinvilla B&B Apartment with Kitchen

Zarli & Mark
11 Austin Street,
Mt Victoria,
Wellington

Tel (04) 385 8334
info@austinvilla.co.nz
www.austinvilla.co.nz

Double/Twin $190 - $230
(Continental breakfast)
Visa MC Eftpos accepted
Not suitable for children
2 Queen (2 bdrm)
Bathrooms: 2 Ensuite

Top location: Set amongst beautiful gardens in one of Mt Victoria's elegant turn-of-the-century villas, Austinvilla is within minutes walk of theatres, restaurants, Oriental Bay and Te Papa. Close to public transport and short drive to airport, ferries, and Westpac Stadium. 2 self-contained apartments with individual entrances come equipped with queen bed, ensuite (bath and shower), kitchen, living/dining area, cable TV, phone and wireless internet access. Both offer privacy, sun and city views with one having its own patio/garden. Laundry facilities and off-street parking available.

Wellington - Oriental Bay *1 km E of Wellington Central*
Trieste B&B Homestay
Hilda & Geoff Stedman
3/346 Oriental Parade,
Oriental Bay,
Wellington, 6011

Tel (04) 803 3451
or 021 0386 351
h.stedman@hotmail.com

Double/Twin $230
Single $150
(Full breakfast)
Visa MC accepted
Internet available
1 King/Twin (1 bdrm)
Bathrooms: 1 Private

Welcome to our modern comfortable apartment on Oriental Parade. Centrally located, a pleasant walk to nearby restaurants, shops and Te Papa. Also on the bus route, and close to the Airport and Ferries.

Wellington - Roseneath *2 km E of Central city*

Panorama *B&B*

Peg Mackay
1 Robieson Lane,
Roseneath

Tel (04) 801 8691
or 021 801 869
pegmackay@hotmail.com
www.wellingtonpanorama.co.nz

Double/Twin $140 - $170
Single $100 - $120
(Continental breakfast)
Children by arrangement
Evening meals by arrangement
Long term rates on application
2 Queen (2 bdrm)
With harbour views
Bathrooms: 1 Private
1 Guest share 1 Guest bath

Lie in bed and enjoy the panorama of ships, ferries and tugs and enjoy the sun, peace and privacy of our warm modern home above Oriental Bay. You have your own deck and sitting room with TV and refreshments. 5 min walk up to Mt Victoria or 15-20 minute walk down to Oriental Bay, the city, theatres, galleries and Te Papa: the Museum of New Zealand. Taste NZ in the many nearby cafes and restaurants. Ferry/Airport 10 minutes, city 5 minutes drive. AND you can park right at our door! Wireless Internet available.

Wellington - Roseneath *1 km E of Wellington CBD*

Maida Vale *B&B*

Bessie Sutherland
6 Maida Vale Road,
Roseneath, Wellington

Tel 027 332 1570
or (04) 970 5184
bess.sutherland@clear.net.nz
www.maidavalebnb.co.nz

Double/Twin $150 - $180
Single $60
(Continental breakfast)
Children negotiable
Weekly rates negotiable
Visa MC Amex accepted
Children welcome
Internet available
1 King 1 Single (2 bdrm)
Main room is spacious with harbour views
Bathrooms: 1 Ensuite

Our centrally located home has spectacular views across the harbour to the city centre. The larger room has an ensuite. Both rooms are on the ground floor and have their own entrance (our family lives above). The city centre, restaurants, theatres and museums are a 5 minute drive away or, alternatively, a 20 minute walk along the waterfront. The airport and ferry terminals are 10-15 minutes away. The family will greet you with a warm welcome as will Zoe, the Jack Russell terrier.

Wellington - Roseneath *2 km SE of Central City*
Crescent Point *B&B*

Bobbi & John Gibbons
18 The Crescent,
Roseneath,
Wellington 6011

Tel (04) 972 3464
or 027 485 0846
Fax (04) 972 3465
gibbonsjg@paradise.net.nz
www.crescentpoint.co.nz

Double/Twin $180
Single $125
(Full breakfast)
Dinner by arrangement
Visa MC accepted
Children and pets welcome
1 Queen (1 bdrm)
Bathrooms: 1 Private
Ensuite with spa bath

We welcome you to sunny Crescent Point, a spacious modern home with panoramic views overlooking the harbour above Oriental Bay. We offer two bedrooms with ensuites, cable TV. One with kitchenette, own entrance and carpark, the other a spa bath. Take a 5 min bush walk to Oriental Bay beach, then a pleasant 10 min walk to the City entertainment area, with restaurants, theatres and Te Papa. 10-15 min drive to Central City and Ferry. 10 mins to Wellington Airport. There is a cat in residence.

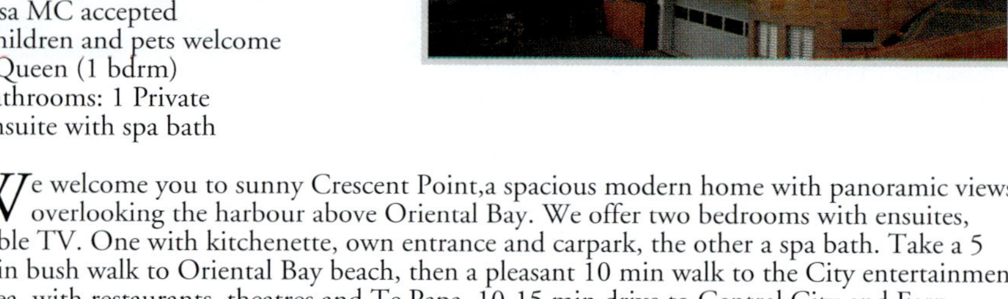

Wellington - Roseneath *1 km NE of Wellington*
Carlton Gore *Luxury B&B*

Brent & Janice Davies
17 Carlton Road,
Roseneath,
Wellington

Tel (04) 385 8508
or 027 284 0983
Fax (04) 385 8548
janibrent@xtra.co.nz
www.carltongore.co.nz

Double/Twin $140 - $250
(Full breakfast)
Visa MC accepted
Children welcome
4 Queen (4 bdrm)
Bathrooms: 2 Ensuite
1 Private 1 Guest share

Location, Location. Welcome to our luxury character 1900's home with all the modern conveniences, sea, sun and views (ground floor). We offer central heating, sat TV (ensuite rooms only), DVD, wireless internet access, continental or full breakfast, quality linen, own entrance, lounge and dining room to relax in. On-site parking, take a five minute ride to central city from the bus stop at door or fifteen minute scenic walk along Oriental Bay. Ten minutes to Wellington airport.

Wellington - Vogeltown (South Mt Cook)
3 km S of Wellington CBD

Finnimore House *B&B Homestay*
Willie & Kathleen Ryan
2 Dransfield Street,
Vogeltown, Wellington

Tel (04) 389 9894
Fax (04) 389 9894
w.f.ryan@xtra.co.nz
www.finnimorehouse.co.nz

Double/Twin $100 - $130
Single $90 - $110 (Full breakfast)
Children $30 Twin rate $120-$140
Extra person $30
Seaonal rates vary
Visa MC accepted
Children welcome
Wireless Internet available on request
3 Queen 2 Single (3 bdrm)
Bathrooms: 1 Private 1 Guest share

Welcome to our historical manor 5 minutes drive from downtown Wellington. Willie and Kathleen Ryan, offer warm Irish hospitality, spacious Victorian rooms with tea/coffee/fridge facilities, full cooked breakfast at your convenience. Willie offers enthusiastic guidance to Wellington's attractions. Our location is close to: airport, ferries, restaurants, Basin Reserve, hospital, zoo, Massey University, National School of Dance and Drama. Secure private parking on-site, convenient public transport. Laundry facilities free if staying 3 nights or more (otherwise a charge applies). Special rates may apply to major events.

Wellington - Island Bay *4 km S of Courtenay Place*
Buckley Homestay *B&B Homestay Separate Suite*
Mrs Wilhelmina Muller
51 Buckley Road, Southgate,
Island Bay, Wellington 6023

Tel (04) 934 7151
or 021 112 3445
Fax (04) 934 7152
willy.muller@paradise.net.nz
www.buckleyhomestay.co.nz

Double/Twin $120 - $140
Single $110
(Continental breakfast)
Children negotiable
Dinner by arrangement
Visa MC accepted
Pet free home
Children and pets welcome
1 King/Twin 1 Queen 3 Single (2 bdrm)
Large with views
Bathrooms: 2 Private 1 Family share

Large 2 storey sunny home with spectacular scenery and beautiful views over Wellington. New tastefully decorated, private entrance, 1 bedroom, self-contained suite with private balcony, TV, conservatory. Handy to hospitals. We are interested in food, wine, travel, relaxing and meeting people. Willy is a nurse, enjoys cooking, gardening and speaks Dutch. No pets or children at home. Off-street parking, complimentary refreshments, dinner by arrangement. On bus route. Handy to all tourist attractions, and airport.

Wellington - Island Bay *6 km S of Wellington City Central*
The Lighthouse & The Keep *Self-contained*

Bruce Stokell
326 The Esplanade & 116 The Esplanade,
Island Bay, Wellington

Tel (04) 472 4177
or 027 442 5555
bruce@thelighthouse.net.nz
www.thelighthouse.net.nz

Double/Twin $180 - $230
(Full breakfast provisions)
Visa MC accepted
Not suitable for children
1 Queen (1 bdrm)
Bathrooms: 1 Private

Island Bay - 10 minutes city centre, 10 minutes airport, 20 minutes ferry terminal.

The Lighthouse is on the south coast and has views of the island, fishing boats in the bay, the beach and rocks, the far coastline, the open sea, the shipping and, on a clear day, the South Island. There are local shops and restaurants.

The Lighthouse has a basic kitchen and bathroom on the first floor, the bedroom/sitting room on the middle floor and the lookout on the top. Romantic.

The Keep is a stone tower just 2 minutes from The Lighthouse. It has a lounge/basic kitchen on 1 level and a bed with ensuite on the next level. Also a spa bath in the bedroom. It is very cosy and has excellent views of the sea, especially in a storm. Stairs from the bedroom lead to a hatch which opens on to the roof.

Wellington - Island Bay *3 km S of Courtenay Place*

Ma Maison *B&B Boutique B&B*

Margo Frost

9 Tamar Street, Island Bay, Wellington

Tel (04) 383 4018 or 027 2429 827
Fax (04) 383 4018
bedandbreakfast@paradise.net.nz
www.nzwellingtonhomestay.co.nz

Double/Twin $160
Single $130 (Full breakfast)
 Visa MC accepted
2 Queen (2 bdrm)
Bathrooms: 1 Ensuite 1 Private

Luxury in a warm, comfortable home at a realistic price, our 1920s home is decorated with a French flavour. Drive to door, lovely garden.

The brown guest room has it's own entrance and ensuite, the blue room has private bathroom. Both rooms have queen posturepedic beds and are equipped with everything to make your stay as comfortable as possible.

Island Bay is a popular seaside suburb with excellent local restaurants. We are 8 minutes by car to the city and very handy to great bus service.

A full delicious breakfast is served at a time to suit you. Resident family cat.

Wellington - Island Bay *7 km S of Wellington City Central*

Nature's Touch Guest House *Luxury B&B*

Maarten & Natsuko Groeneveld

25A Happy Valley Road, Owhiro Bay, Wellington

Tel (04) 383 6977 or 027 559 0966
info@naturestouchguesthouse.com
naturestouchguesthouse.com

Double/Twin $135 - $170
Single $110 - $140 (Full breakfast)
Children $15-$45 per child
Japanese Dinner $40pp, European Dinner $35pp
Wireles broadband available,
bring your own computer
Visa MC accepted   Children welcome
1 King 1 Double (1 bdrm)
Luxury Bedroom with sea views
Bathrooms: 1 Private

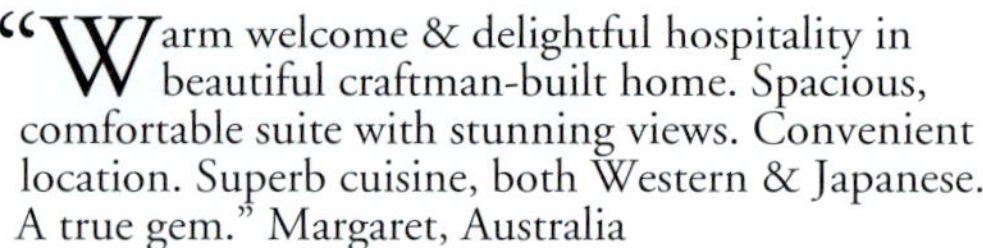

"Warm welcome & delightful hospitality in beautiful craftman-built home. Spacious, comfortable suite with stunning views. Convenient location. Superb cuisine, both Western & Japanese. A true gem." Margaret, Australia

"Nature's Touch Guest House was the best B&B that we experienced in New Zealand during our trip in March 2008. ...the food was amazing. The breakfasts outdid any other B&B by a long shot, and the Japanese meal was great. Thank-you Natsuko and Maarten for making our vacation memorable with a stay at your home." Don and Julie, Canada

A warm welcome from us and baby Lina! We are nautical themed B&B and just a short stroll to the beach. Only 10 minutes drive to the city, 15 minute drive (almost straight line) to the ferry terminal and the airport driving along the coast. Upper Boat Bedroom (Luxury suite) is for you to enjoy whole of upstairs and elevated views as well as privacy. Enjoy tranquillity.

Marlborough
French Pass
Pelorus Sound
Kenepuru Sounds
Queen Charlotte Sound
Mahau Sound
Anakiwa
Picton
6
Rapaura
Blenheim
63
Renwick
1
ble Bay
0 Kilometres 20
0 Miles 12

Marlborough

Picton *1 km E of Picton Central*
Retreat Inn *B&B Homestay*
Alison & Geoff
20 Lincoln Street,
Picton, 7220

Tel (03) 573 8160
or 021 143 2224
alisonandgeoff@retreat-inn.co.nz
www.retreat-inn.co.nz

Double/Twin $135 - $145
(Continental breakfast)
Room rate $135 - $145
Not suitable for children
2 Queen 2 Single (2 bdrm)
Bathrooms: 1 Ensuite 1 Private

Set in peaceful bush surroundings, Retreat Inn Homestay/B&B offers you comfort, rest, quietness. A choice of guest bedrooms - ground floor queen room (ensuite, bath and shower)with outside access to fern/seating area. Upstairs - queen(or twin)room, adjacent private bathroom. Marlborough province is diverse, unforgettable - come stay 2 or 3 nights and explore what we have to offer. Flat off-street parking. A happy 2 person/1 cat/1 hen household!

Picton *0.5 km SE of Picton Central*
Grandvue *B&B Homestay Apartment with Kitchen*
Rosalie & Russell Mathews
19 Otago Street,
Picton 7220

Tel (03) 573 8553
or 0800 49 1080
Fax (03) 573 8556
enquiries@grandvuepicton.co.nz
www.grandvuepicton.co.nz

Double/Twin $130 - $140
Single $75 - $100
(Continental breakfast)
Children $45
Visa MC accepted
Pet free home Internet available
2 Queen 1 Twin 1 Single (3 bdrm)
1 in Apartment, 2 in homestay
Bathrooms: 1 Ensuite 1 Family share

On the hills above Picton, Grandvue is a quiet haven in a secluded garden with a grand-view. It's a 5 minute walk to the shopping area, restaurants, the waterfront & bushwalks. Russell, retired, enjoys boating, fishing & gardening. Rosalie an enthusiastic quilter, loves cooking & gardening. Both enjoy meeting people. The accommodation is spacious, warm, quality & self-contained with kitchen & ensuite. Other rooms available in our home. Feast on magnificent views from our conservatory while enjoying a wholesome breakfast. Courtesy transport, parking & laundry facilities.

Picton *0.25 km SE of Picton*
Rivenhall *B&B Homestay*

Nan & Malcolm Laurenson
118 Wellington Street,
Picton,
Marlborough, 7220

Tel (03) 573 7692
rivenhall@kol.co.nz
www.rivenhall.co.nz

Double/Twin $140
Single $100
(Full breakfast)
Visa MC accepted
Pet free home
Children welcome
1 Queen 1 Double (2 bdrm)
Bathrooms: 2 Private

Rivenhall at the top of Wellington Street, is a gracious home with all the warmth, comfort and charm of days gone by, overlooking Picton with its background of surrounding hills. Rivenhall's location is perfect for Travellers overnighting in Picton, Tourists visiting Marlborough's local sites and attractions, or preparing to walk the Queen Charlotte track. And of course a courtesy pick up from the ferry, bus or train. The Marlborough Sounds start at the bottom of our street.

Picton - Kenepuru Sounds *80 km NE of Havelock*
The Nikaus *B&B Farmstay*

Alison & Robin Bowron
86 Manaroa Road,
Waitaria Bay, RD 2,
Picton, 7282

Tel (03) 573 4432
or 027 454 4712
Fax (03) 573 4432
info@thenikaus.co.nz
www.thenikaus.co.nz

Double/Twin $130
Single $65
(Full breakfast)
Dinner $35
Visa MC accepted
1 Queen 4 Single (3 bdrm)
1 Queen & 2 twin
Bathrooms: 1 Guest share

The Nikaus sheep & cattle farm is situated in Waitaria Bay, Kenepuru Sound, 2 hours drive from Blenheim or Picton. We offer friendly personal service in our comfortable spacious home. Large gardens contain rhododendrons, roses, Camellia, lilies and perennials, big sloping lawns and views out to sea. House pets Minny (Jack Russel-cross)Honey (Lab)+ 4cats, Other animals include the farm dogs, donkeys, pet wild pigs, turkeys, hens and peacocks. Country meals, home-grown produce. Operators available for fishing trips, launch charters, golf and various walks.

Picton - Queen Charlotte Sounds *16 km SW of Picton*
Tanglewood B&B Homestay Separate Suite Apartment with Kitchen

Linda & Stephen Hearn
1744 Queen Charlotte Drive,
The Grove, RD 1,
Picton

Tel (03) 574 2080
or 027 481 4388
Fax (03) 574 2044
tanglewood.hearn@xtra.co.nz

Double/Twin $155 - $185
Single $120 - $140
(Full breakfast)
Dinner $50
Self-contained $195 - $250
Visa MC accepted
2 King/Twin 1 Queen
2 Single (4 bdrm)
Bathrooms: 4 Ensuite

Modern architectural home nestled amongst the native ferns overlooking Queen Charlotte Sounds. Enjoy our luxury Super King/Twin ensuite rooms with balcony and views; or a self contained guest wing which includes Queen and two Single beds (with ensuites), lounge, kitchen and sunny balcony/BBQ area. Relax in our jacuzzi surrounded by beautiful native garden and birds or view the glow-worms. Substainal breakfast provided before your day's pursuits, swimming, fishing, kayaking, walking the Queen Charlotte Walkway or exploring Marlborough Wineries. Fifth generation Kiwi hospitality at its best.

Pelorus - Mahau Sound *33 km SW of Picton*
Ramona B&B Homestay

Phyl & Ken Illes
460 Moetapu Bay Road,
Mahau Sound, Marlborough

Tel (03) 574 2215
or 027 247 6668
illes@clear.net.nz

Double/Twin $130
Single $90 (Continental breakfast)
We can accomodate 3 children
3 course dinner served with
local wine by arrangement
Tea & coffee in conservatory
Visa MC accepted
Pet free home Children welcome
1 Queen 2 Twin 1 Single (2 bdrm)
All beds have electric blankets
Bathrooms: 1 Private
Hair dryer in bathroom

Our waterfront home on the beautiful Mahau Sound has been designed for you to share. Our guest floor has its own conservatory, here you can view the passing water traffic. Awake to the call of bellbirds and tuis, and after breakfast stroll around our large garden, or fossick on the beach. We are 15mins from the south end of Queen Charlotte Walkway. Phyl's interests include writing, quilting and gardening. Ken is a retired builderinterested in meeting people. We host only 1 party at a time.

Picton - Queen Charlotte Sound *11 km SW of Picton*
Waterfront Bed & Breakfast *B&B Homestay*

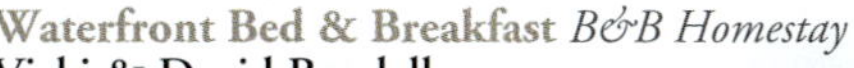

Vicki & David Bendell
Queen Charlotte Drive,
2383 Little Ngakuta Bay,
RD 1,
Picton

Tel (03) 573 8584
or 027 748 4172
waterfront@farmside.co.nz
www.picton.co.nz/waterfront

Double/Twin $165 - $185
(Full breakfast)
Dinner with notice $50pp - BBQ
or fish followed by cheese platter
Diners accepted
Children welcome
2 Queen (2 bdrm)
Bathrooms: 1 Ensuite 1 Private

Our waterfront accommodation is as close to the water as you can get. Seperate from our cottage are the aptly named and themed Boatshed and Pacific rooms with ensuite, private bathroom and Italian cotton linens. A long jetty outfront is ideal for swimming, fishing or an evening stroll to see the water fluoresce. Please join us for a meal on the deck over-looking the water. We have a young family and dog - not just another B&B but an accommodation experience with a NZ family.

Picton *0.5 km E of Picton*
Glengary *B&B*

Glenys & Gary Riggs
5 Seaview Cresent,
Picton

Tel (03) 573 8317
or 027 498 6388
g.riggs@xtra.co.nz
www.glengary.co.nz

Double/Twin $130 - $140
Single $80
(Continental breakfast)
et free home
Not suitable for children
2 King/Twin 2 Queen (3 bdrm)
Bathrooms: 2 Ensuite 1 Private

Located a short drive from Picton Ferry Terminal and a few minutes walk to the town centre. Inner harbour across the road. Whether you are interested in visiting wineries, fishing, bush walking, cruising, sea kayaking or simply relaxing in idyllic surroundings Glengary Bed & Breakfast is ideally located to explore the Marlborough area. Your friendly hosts will provide you with the best service to ensure your stay in the beautiful Marlborough Sounds is relaxing and enjoyable. Ferry pick up. 2 night stay recemended.

Picton *3 km NE of Picton*

Michiru *B&B*

Rosemary & Paul Royer
247B Waikawa Road, Waikawa, Picton

Tel (03) 573 6793
or (mob) 021 212 1689
Fax (03) 573 6793
relax@michiru.co.nz
www.michiru.co.nz

Double/Twin $140 - $160
Single $90 (Special breakfast)
Dinner $50 by arrangement
Visa MC accepted   Children welcome
1 King 1 Queen 2 Single (3 bdrm)
Bathrooms: 1 Ensuite 2 Private

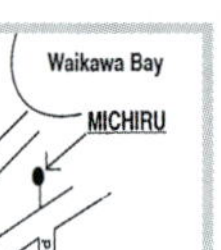

We only have one aim - to give you the finest and most memorable experience that we are able to provide. We overlook Waikawa Bay and the beautiful Queen Charlotte Sounds so you can watch the ferries and cruise ships pass while enjoying breakfast: and all of this is only 3km from Picton town centre.

The bright and sunny rooms are all located on the ground floor with a lovely private guest lounge and garden patio. Guests have the use of laundry facilities. We invite you to join us for Rosemary's delightful 3 course dinners with a glass of wine (by arrangement). We will of course meet or drop you at the ferry terminal, especially if you are walking the Queen Charlotte Track and don't have your own transport. There is a waterside restaurant and a cafe/bar within 5 minutes walk of the house. You'll love this location!

Walk the Queen Charlotte Track, kayak or sail the Queen Charlotte Sounds, take half or whole day winery tours, daily dolphin watch tours, re-live The Edwin Fox experience (she's the world's ninth oldest ship), visit the fascinating Seahorse World, and finally our favourite place Karaka Point historical site. Superb accommodation for the discerning guests!

Picton- Queen Charlotte Sound - Anakiwa *22 km SW of Picton*

Queens View B&B *B&B Separate Suite Apartment with Kitchen*

Ann & John McGuire
259G Anakiwa Road,
Anakiwa - Picton, RD1

Tel (03) 574 2363
or 021 0229 2864
enquiries@queensview.co.nz
www.queensview.co.nz

Double/Twin $145 - $180
Single $90 - $120
(Full breakfast)
Dinner by arrangement -
BBQ Facilities Available
Local Hotel 6 mins drive
Visa MC accepted
Pet free home
Children welcome
2 Queen 1 Twin (3 bdrm)
Bathrooms: 1 Ensuite 2 Private

Our elevated deck over the top of the Punga trees offers guests argueably some of the best views off the Queen Charltte Sound. The shoreline no more than a 3 min walk. The Queen Charlotte Track (10 mins walk),the holiday town of Picton (30 mins), the marina & mussel town of Havelock (25 mins)and the winery district of Blenheim (40 mins). So if your holiday is walking, swimming, boating, fishing, kayaking or exploring the many wineries then Queensview BnB is the ideal central location.

Picton *.25 km SW of Post Office*

Marineland Heritage House B & B *B&B Guest House*

Rosemary Baxter & Peter Broad
28 Waikawa Road,
Picton, 7250

Tel (03) 5736 429
or Freephone: 0800 616 429
Fax (03) 5737 634
marineland@xtra.co.nz
www.marinelandaccom.co.nz

Double/Twin $90 - $135
Single $85 - $135
(Continental breakfast)
Visa MC Amex Eftpos accepted
Not suitable for children under 13
1 King 1 Queen 5 Double
3 Twin 1 Single (11 bdrm)
Bathrooms: 5 Ensuite 6 Guest share

Enjoy Marineland Heritage House B & B, built in 1925 for the local Doctor. All downstairs rooms have ensuites, upstairs rooms have shared bathrooms. Rooms have electric blankets & tea/coffee making facilities. A comfortable lounge with Broadband Internet access & SKY TV. Adjacent to the lounge is the breakfast room for our 'Picton Breakfast', a wheat & gluten free option is available. We offer a laundry & parking. In-ground swimming pool. We are a few minutes walk from town centre & water front.

Picton *0.2 km S of Picton*
Echo Lodge *B&B Homestay*
Sharon & Russell Hooker
5 Rutland Street,
Picton

Tel (03) 573 6367
or 0274 213 359
echolodge@xtra.co.nz
www.echolodge.co.nz

Double/Twin $130 - $140
Single $95
(Continental breakfast)
Twin from $130
Children welcome
3 Queen 1 Twin 1 Single (3 bdrm)
Bathrooms: 3 Ensuite

Sharon, Russell and Chloe (our cat) welcome you to Echo Lodge. Overlooking the Picton Marina, Echo lodge is an easy 5 minute stroll from the town centre with its many cafes, restaurants and tour operators and a 2 minute walk from the many bush and waterfront walks in the area. Come and enjoy our home comforts, including a continental breakfast featuring fresh bread, locally made jams and homemade yoghurt served in our guest lounge. A large garden offers many areas to sit and relax. Courtesy transfer from Picton airport, bus train or Ferry Terminals.

Picton *0.5 km SE of Picton*
Palm Haven B&B *B&B*
Denise Heaps
15 A Otago Street,
Picton, 7220

Tel (03) 5735644
or 027 475 5178
Fax (03) 573 5648
palmhaven@xtra.co.nz
www.palmhaven.co.nz

Double/Twin $135 - $145
Single $85
(Continental breakfast)
Visa MC Eftpos accepted
Pet free home
Not suitable for children
2 Queen 1 Twin 1 Single (3 bdrm)
One triple, one double, one twin
Bathrooms: 2 Ensuite 1 Private

Palm Haven is a modern purpose built home designed for your comfort and convenience. Overlooking Picton and Mt Freeth, it is just a few minutes walk to the shopping center,cafes, restaurants and waterfront where guided walks, kayaking and a variety of boating, fishing and winery tours are available. Guest rooms, two with ensuites and one with private bathroom, accomodating triple, double or single occupancy all have tea and coffee making facilities, TV and bar fridge. Courtesy pickup from ferry, bus or train is provided.

Picton *9.1 km NE of Picton*
Charlotte House *B&B*
Peter Hill
432 Port Underwood Road,
Picton

Tel (03) 573 8969
or 027 444 8011
charlothouse@kol.co.nz
www.charlottehousemarlboroughsounds.co.nz

Double/Twin $160
Single $90
(Continental breakfast)
Visa MC Diners accepted
Pet free home
Not suitable for children
1 Queen (1 bdrm)
Bathrooms: 1 Ensuite

Enjoy the magnificence of the Queen Charlotte Sounds from your secluded, private suite where a uniquely tranquil and restful environment awaits you. A private deck runs the full length of the suite, with its own private entrance, air conditioned comfort with amazing sea views from every room. Lazy boy chairs, LCD TV, CD and DVD players with a selection of disks, wool underlay on bed. A home away from home. As one of our guests put it 'An absolutely beautiful haven, wish were staying longer'.

Please let others know how you enjoyed your
B&B experience.
Add a comment to the listing on the internet.
www.bnb.co.nz.

Blenheim *1 km SW of Blenheim Central*
Beaver B&B *Homestay Cottage with Kitchen*

Jen & Russell Hopkins
60 Beaver Road,
Blenheim

Tel (03) 578 8401
or 021 626 151
Fax (03) 578 8401
rdhopkins@xtra.co.nz
marlborough.co.nz/beaver/

Double/Twin $100
Single $70
(Continental breakfast)
Visa MC accepted
Not suitable for children
1 Queen (1 bdrm)
Bathrooms: 1 Ensuite

Our self-contained unit has its own entrance and off-street parking-5 minutes drive from central Blenheim and 10 minutes drive from the wineries and the Aviation Heritage Centre. The bed is queen-size. The mini-kitchen has a microwave,small sink and fridge containing items for a self-serve continental breakfast to have at your leisure. The bathroom has a large bath and a separate shower and toilet. 2 cats live with us .

Blenheim *2.5 km N of Blenheim*
Philmar *B&B Homestay*

Wynnis & Lex Phillips
9 Maple Close,
Springlands,
Blenheim

Tel (03) 577 7788
Fax (03) 577 7788
philmar9@xtra.co.nz

Double/Twin $80 - $100
Single $60 - $80
(Continental breakfast)
Dinner $20pp by arrangement
2 Queen 1 Twin (3 bdrm)
Bathrooms: 1 Ensuite 1 Guest share

Welcome to our home 2.5 km from the town centre. Guests can join us in our spacious sunny living areas. We both enjoy all sports on TV and our other interests include wood turning, handcrafts and the Lions organisation. Blenheim has many wineries, parks, craft shops, art galleries and golf courses. Not far from Picton, Nelson & Kaikoura whale watching. We share our home with our pets, Lucy-Lu and Louie. Smoking is not encouraged. Just phone to be picked up at airport, bus or train.

Blenheim *2 km N of Blenheim*
The Willows *B&B Homestay*
Millie Amos
6 The Willows,
Springlands,
Blenheim

Tel (03) 577 7853
Fax (03) 577 7853

Double/Twin $112
Single $70
(Continental breakfast)
Payment by cash or cheque
1 Queen 2 Twin (2 bdrm)
Bathrooms: 1 Private

Only 2km from the centre of town. The Willows is a spacious and modern home in close proximity to shops, restaurants and wineries. Peaceful location surrounded by lovely gardens. I welcome you to my home, so please phone first.

Blenheim *1 km N of Blenheim Central*
Maxwell House *Homestay*
John and Barbara Ryan
82 Maxwell Road,
Blenheim

Tel (03) 577 7545
Fax (03) 577 7545
mt.olympus@xtra.co.nz

Double/Twin $140
Single $100
(Full breakfast)
Visa MC accepted
Children welcome
1 Queen 1 Twin (2 bdrm)
Bathrooms: 2 Ensuite

Welcome to Marlborough. We invite you to stay at Maxwell House, a grand old Victorian residence. Built in 1880 our home has been elegantly restored and is classified with the Historic Places Trust. Our large guest rooms are individually appointed with ensuite, lounge area, television and tea & coffee making facilities. Breakfast will be a memorable experience, served around the original 1880's kauri table. Set on a large established property Maxwell House is an easy ten minute walk to the town centre. Non-smoking.

Blenheim *30 km S of Picton*
ParkView B&B *B&B*

Geoff & Shirley Cant
30 Solway Drive,
Blenheim, Marlborough

Tel (03) 578-4492
or 0800 78-4492
parkviewbb@xtra.co.nz
www.parkviewbb.co.nz

Double/Twin $135 - $145
Single $115 - $115
(Continental breakfast,
cooked by arrangement)
Children $45
Visa MC accepted
Pet free home
Internet available
3 Queen 1 Single (3 bdrm)
En-suited bedroom overlooks park
Bathrooms: 1 Ensuite 1 Private 1 Family share Bath & shower in en-suite

ParkView is a modern quality residence in a quiet Blenheim suburb adjacent to Harling Park & Japanese Garden and Wither Hills Farm Park. You can enjoy walking or cycling in Harling Park and the magnificent Wither Hills Farm Park and borrow our cycles and visit some of the many local wineries. Relax on ParkView's verandah overlooking the Japanese Garden with a glass of local wine. We offer free of charge: Wireless broadband internet Laundry & BBQ Complimentary transfer service to airport, bus, train or restaurant.

Blenheim *0.0 km NW of central Blenheim*
Henry Maxwell's B&B *Luxury B&B*

Diana and Graham Westenra
28 Henry Street, Blenheim

Tel (03) 578 8086
or 0800 436 796
graymere@xtra.co.nz
www.henrymaxwells.co.nz

Double/Twin $120 - $140
Single $80 - $90 (Full breakfast)
Children free
Visa MC Eftpos accepted
Pet free home Children welcome
Internet Available
3 Queen 1 Double 1 Twin
1 Single (5 bdrm)
3 large comfortable rooms, one
small single, 1 small double
Bathrooms: 4 Ensuite 1 Private
Bath in the large bathroom

Welcome to Henry Maxwell's Bed & Breakfast and Accommodation. A gracious 90 year old home, Guests have spacious quiet rooms, 4 with ensuites, 1 with a private bathroom. Comfortable beds and chairs, TV, tea, coffee, and complimentary port.Breakfast in the unique dining room (maps and charts)is memorable, kitchenette facilities. Guest laundry, wireless, library. 5 minutes stroll to town, restaurants, shops, theatre. Off-street parking.Very suitable for extended stays,conference and wedding parties. Discounts. Affordable luxury.

Blenheim *7 km N of Blenheim*
Blue Ridge Estate Vineyard Homestay *B&B Homestay*

Lesley & Brian Avery
50 O'Dwyers Road,
RD 3,
Blenheim 7273

Tel (03) 570 2198
stay@blueridge.co.nz
www.blueridge.co.nz

Double/Twin $200 - $255
Single $200 - $255
(Full breakfast)
Visa MC accepted
Not suitable for children
2 Queen 2 Twin (3 bdrm)
Bathrooms: 1 Ensuite 2 Private

Set on a 20 acre vineyard, Blue Ridge Estate, 2002 Marlborough Master Builders' 'House of the Year', enjoys a rural setting with stunning views across vineyards to the Richmond Range and is close to many of Marlborough's fine wineries, restaurants and gardens. Our home has proven popular with all visitors. Share our home with Bella our friendly labrador, where comfort and privacy will ensure your Marlborough visit is indeed a memorable one. Wireless Internet access available. This property is not suitable for children

---

Blenheim *9 km NW of Blenheim*
Stonehaven Vineyard Homestay *B&B Homestay*
Paulette & John Hansen
414 Rapaura Road,
RD 3, Blenheim, 7273

Tel (03) 572 9730
or 027 682 1120
Fax (03) 572 9730
stay@stonehavenhomestay.co.nz
www.stonehavenhomestay.co.nz

Double/Twin $185 - $280
Single $165 - $260 (Full breakfast)
Children suitable 10 years and over
Three course dinner $68pp
by arrangement, wine available
Guest bike hire $30 pp
Visa MC accepted
1 King 1 Queen 1 Twin (3 bdrm)
Vineyard and mountain views from all guest rooms
Bathrooms: 2 Ensuite 1 Private Twin room private bathroom is downstairs

Stonehaven is surrounded by beautiful gardens and vineyards in Marlborough's premium grape growing area. Spacious and comfortable, our home with commanding views over vineyards to the Richmond Ranges is close to some of NZ's most outstanding wineries. Our delicious breakfasts are often served in the summerhouse overlooking the pool. Dinner available by arrangement. Wireless internet available. We have an outdoor cat. Book-A-Bike operates from Stonehaven. Cycling is a great way to tour the wineries. Book at book-a-bike.co.nz

Blenheim Central *0.1 km E of Blenheim*
Brickweld House *B&B*
Julie Yonge
5 Weld Street,
Blenheim

Tel (03) 577 9915
or 027 686 5891
info@brickweldhouse.co.nz
www.brickweldhouse.co.nz

Double/Twin $140 - $160
Single $70 - $100
(Full breakfast)
Dinner by arrangement
Visa MC accepted
Not suitable for children
2 King/Twin 2 Queen (3 bdrm)
Bathrooms: 1 Ensuite 1 Private
1 Guest share

Your sanctuary after discovering the treasures of Marlborough Enjoy the convenience of a 10 minute stroll to the town centre where you will find many dining options or dine in by arrangement (24 hours notice required). In a peaceful garden setting, relax in the friendly atmosphere; sleep under the luxury of pure silk duvets; breakfast in the garden. Tea and coffee making facilities in rooms; separate guest lounge. Famous wineries just minutes away. Off-street parking. Join me for a glass of world acclaimed Marlborough Sauvignon blanc at the end of your day of adventure. You will also meet Lizzie, my very affectionate cat.

Renwick *10 km SW of Blenheim*
Clovelly *B&B Homestay*
Don & Sue Clifford
2A Nelson Place,
Renwick,
Marlborough, 7204

Tel (03) 572 9593
or 027 695 1614
Fax (03) 572 7293
clifford@actrix.co.nz
www.clovelly.co.nz

Double/Twin $140
Single $100
(Special breakfast)
Visa MC accepted
Children welcome
1 King/Twin 1 Queen (2 bdrm)
Bathrooms: 2 Private

Our colonial style home is set in lovely private grounds in the heart of vineyard country. We overlook organic orchards and out to the Richmond Range. Complimentary tea and coffee with home made baking. Visit the quaint local English pub. Dine in the village or vineyard restaurants. We are close to a number of prestigious vineyards. Complimentary bicycles are available for guests to cycle the vineyards and surrounds. Don, Sue and our Scottish terriers Chloe and Phoebe and cat Sophie, will welcome you most warmly.

Renwick - Blenheim *10 km SW of Blenheim*
Olde Mill House B&B & Cycle Hire *B&B Homestay*
Diane Sutton
9 Wilson Street,
Renwick, Marlborough

Tel (03) 572 8458
or 0800 653 262
Fax (03) 572 8458
info@oldemillhouse.co.nz
www.oldemillhouse.co.nz

Double/Twin $145
Single $110 (Continental breakfast)
Children under 12 $40
Extra adult in room $72
Visa MC Amex Eftpos accepted
Children welcome Internet Available
2 King/Twin 1 Queen (3 bdrm)
Room can be King or twin single
Bathrooms: 3 Ensuite
Heritage room ensuite with bathtub

Welcome to our elevated character bungalow, refurbished for your comfort whilst retaining its olde world charm. Our property consists of an extensive spa/bbq, garden area for you to relax in and enjoy views to the Richmond Ranges. We provide complimentary cycles for you to enjoy the local wine trail, a complimentary transfer service to local vineyard restaurants for evening dining. We also provide a wireless broadband internet service. We both enjoy gardening, motorcycling and our Border Collie dog Rosie.

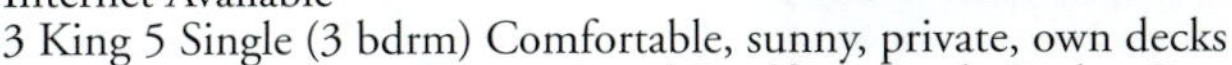

French Pass - Pelorus Sounds *110 km NE of Nelson*
Ngaio Bay Ecostay B&B *B&B Cottage with Kitchen*
Jude and Roger Sonneland
Ngaio Bay, French Pass Road,
Pelorus Sounds

Tel (03) 576 5287
Fax (03) 576 5287
welcome@ngaiobay.co.nz
www.ngaiobay.co.nz

Double/Twin $180 - $260
Single $135 - $210 (Special breakfast)
Children $80 3-12years,
under 2 $30 all inclusive
Dinner $40pp, children 3-12 years $15
Lunch $20pp, picnic $15 pp,
$8 per child 3-12 years
Visa MC Eftpos accepted
Internet Available
3 King 5 Single (3 bdrm) Comfortable, sunny, private, own decks
Bathrooms: 1 Ensuite 2 Private R and D selfcontained, Garden Cottage bathroom in main house

Remote and beautiful, Ngaio Bay is 2 hours scenic drive from Nelson or Blenheim. Jude and Rog offer an authentic Kiwi experience, near the awesome waters of French Pass. Garden Cottage, Rose & Dolphin and Seabreeze Cottage are comfortable, private, overlooking sea, garden, bush. Great sunsets. Guests enjoy scrumptious food and good conversation, open fire for cool evenings. Organic vegetable, flower garden and orchard, eco-composting toilets. Swim, walk, relax; your choice.! Private fireheated bath on beach. Special. 2 loveable labradors, Joe and Oscar. Directions when booking.

Nelson, Golden Bay
Pakawau
Collingwood
Parapara
Takaka
60
Abel Tasman National Park
Marahau
Kaiteriteri
Riwaka
Motueka
Motueka Valley
Ruby Bay
Atawhai
Mapua
Upper Moutere
6
Nelson
Richmond
Wakefield
Brightwater
0 Kilometres 20
0 Miles 12
6
63
Murchison
65
Nelson Lakes
St Arnaud

Nelson *2 km SW of Central Nelson*
Harbour View Homestay B&B *B&B or Self-contained house*

Judy Black
11 Fifeshire Crescent,
Nelson

Tel (03) 548 8567
or 027 247 4445
Fax (03) 548 8667
harbourview-homestay@xtra.co.nz

Double/Twin $150 - $165
Single $130 - $150
(Continental breakfast)
Enquire about available discounts
Visa MC accepted
2 Queen 2 Single (3 bdrm)
Bathrooms: 2 Ensuite 1 Private

Nelson
Golden Bay

Our home is above the harbour entrance. Huge windows capture spectacular views of beautiful Tasman Bay, Haulashore Island, Tahunanui Beach, across the sea to Abel Tasman National Park and mountains. Observe from the bedrooms, dining room and decks, ships and pleasure craft cruising by as they enter and leave the harbour. If you can tear yourself away from our magnificent view, within walking distance along the waterfront there are excellent cafes and restaurants. Judy, David and Possum the cat welcome you for a memorable stay.

Nelson - Atawhai - Marybank *6 km NE of Nelson*
Mike's B&B *B&B Homestay*

Mike Cooper &
Lennane Cooper-Kent
4 Seaton Street,
Nelson, 7010

Tel (03) 545 1671
mikecooper@actrix.co.nz
www.bnb.co.nz/hosts/kent

Double/Twin $85 - $90
Single $85 - $85
(Full breakfast)
Dinner $40 pp with prior notice
Visa MC accepted
Internet available
2 Queen (2 bdrm)
Bathrooms: 2 Ensuite
Showers in ensuite bathroom

5 minutes NE of Nelson City we welcome you to our comfortable home in a quiet neighbourhood with extensive views out over Tasman Bay to the mountains beyond. Our guests' accommodation is almost self contained and includes ensuite bedrooms, a kitchenette with a fridge/freezer, microwave and complimentary tea and coffee making facilities, a small lounge with TV and part of our collection of books. Laundry facilities, internet access and off street parking are available. Our interests include travel, education, and volunteer work abroad.

Nelson *5 km SW of Nelson*
Arapiki *B&B Apartment with Kitchen B&B Self-contained Homestay Units*

Kay & Geoff Gudsell
21 Arapiki Road,
Stoke,
Nelson

Tel (03) 547 3741
bnb@nelsonparadise.co.nz
www.nelsonparadise.co.nz

Double/Twin $90 - $125
Single $70 - $90
Continental breakfast
optional $7.50pp
Visa MC accepted
Internet available
1 Queen 1 Double
1 Single (2 bdrm)
Bathrooms: 2 Ensuite

Enjoy a relaxing holiday in the midst of your trip. The quality smoke-free units in our large centrally located home offer comfort, privacy, offstreet parking and Wireless Internet Access. The larger Unit 1 in a private garden setting opens on to a deck with outdoor furniture. It has an electric stove, microwave, Sky TV, auto washing machine and phone. Unit 2 has a balcony with seating to enjoy sea and mountain views. It has a microwave, hotplate, TV and phone. We have two Tonkinese cats.

Nelson *3 km E of Nelson*
Brooklands *B&B Homestay*
Lorraine & Barry Signal
106 Brooklands Road,
Atawhai,
Nelson

Tel (03) 545 1423
Fax (03) 545 1423
barry.lori@xtra.co.nz

Double/Twin $120 - $165
Single $85 - $100
(Full breakfast)
Children by arrangement
Dinner $50
Visa MC accepted
Pet free home
Children welcome
1 King 1 Queen 1 Double
1 Twin (3 bdrm)
Bathrooms: 1 Ensuite 1 Guest share spa bath

Spacious, luxurious 4 level home with superb sea views. Spacious well furnished king room on top level. Next level has 2 bedrooms sharing large bathroom with spa bath for 2. 1 bedroom has a private balcony. Spacious indoor/outdoor living areas. We enjoy sports, travel and outdoors. Lorraine makes dolls and bears and enjoys crafts, gardening and cooking. We are close to Nelson's attractions - beaches, crafts, wine trails, national parks, lakes and mountains. We enjoy making new friends. Smoke-free.

Nelson *0.75 km SW of Nelson Central*
Peppertree B&B *B&B Separate Suite*
Richard Savill & Carolyn Sygrove
31 Seymour Avenue,
Nelson 7010

Tel (03) 546 9881
or (03) 021 0746540
Fax (03) 546 9881
c.sygrove@clear.net.nz

Double/Twin $135
Single $135 (Continental breakfast)
Children $25
Dinner $40-$50 by arrangement
Extra adult $35
Visa MC accepted
Internet available
1 Queen 1 Double 1 Single (1 bdrm)
Separate master bedroom adjoining
private lounge
Bathrooms: 1 Ensuite

Enjoy space and privacy in our heritage villa, only 10 minutes riverside walk from Nelson's city centre. The master bedroom has an ensuite bathroom and walk-in wardrobe. Your private adjoining rooms include a large lounge with double innersprung sofabed, single bed, heat pump, Sky TV, fridge, microwave, kettle etc. Also sunroom with cane setting and private entrance. Wireless internet and off-street parking available. Children are welcome. We have 2 daughters aged 16 and 14.

Nelson - Tahunanui *4.5 km SW of Nelson*
Lamont B&B *B&B*
Pam & Rex Lucas
167A Tahunanui Drive,
Tahunanui,
Nelson

Tel (03) 548 5551
or 0274 351 678
Fax (03) 548 5501
rexpam@xtra.co.nz

Double/Twin $125
Single $95 or by arrangement
(Full breakfast)
Children by arrangement
Dinner (2 courses) $30
(24 hrs. notice required)
Visa MC accepted
Children welcome
1 Queen 1 Double (2 bdrm)
Bathrooms: 1 Private 1 Guest share

We are in a position to offer high standard accommodation having 2 double bedrooms with own toilet and bathroom facilities. Our house is on a private property in Tahunanui Drive opposite the Nelson Surburban Club where it is possible to get an evening meal. A 2 minute drive to Tahuna Beach and 5 minutes to a number of waterfront restaurants gives plenty of variety and choice. We are a few minutes from the airport. Pick-up from airport and bus if required. 1 cat in residence.

Nelson
Golden Bay

Nelson - Atawhai *4 km N of Nelson*

A Culinary Experience B&B at Sea Watch Estates *Luxury B&B*
Kay & Joe Waller
15 Seawatch Way, Atawhai, Nelson

Tel (03) 545 1886 or 0800 891 886   Fax (03) 545 1869
stay@a-culinary-experience.com
www.a-culinary-experience.com

Double/Twin $299 - $350 Single $280 - $330
(Special breakfast) Not suitable for young children
Join your hosts for a 3-course gourmet dinner
Cooking Classes and Therapeutic Massage can be booked
Visa MC accepted   Internet Available
2 King/Twin 2 King (2 bdrm)
Pure luxury with amazing seaview
Bathrooms: 2 Ensuite - Choose the double spa bath with
separate shower or a romantic enormous double shower.

Welcome to our lovely home filled with laughter, amazing views, original art and fabulous food. Completed in 2010 this purpose-built 5 star Luxury Bed and Breakfast was designed with you, the discerning traveller, in mind. Joe, a Naturopathic Doctor, provides therapeutic massage. Kay, cookbook author and cooking school owner, provides delightful dinners or cooking classes. Let us pamper you! Indulge yourself with a soak in the spa, relax in the infrared sauna, have a massage and feel rejuvenated.

Enjoy the sea and mountain views from your private balcony or patio, the vineyard or olive and lavender garden or feed our lovely alpacas. Sip a complimentary glass of wine in the wine cellar served with yummy appetizers baked in our wood-fired pizza oven. Read in the sculpture garden and quaff the aroma of fresh herbs, fruit, and organic produce that we grow for our gourmet meals. Book one of our luxurious rooms: king-size beds, heated tile ensuites (bathrooms) with 2 person shower or double spa bath, tea facilities, refrigerators and Wifi. Guest computer and media centre are located in the library. With so much to do, a stay of 3 or more nights is recommended.

Nelson *1 km E of Nelson Central*

Sussex House Bed & Breakfast *B&B*

Victoria & David Los
238 Bridge Street,
Nelson

Tel (03) 548 9972
or 0800 868 687
Fax (03) 548 9975
reservations@sussex.co.nz
www.sussex.co.nz

Double/Twin $150 - $180
Single $110 - $150
(Full breakfast)
Children $20
Visa MC Amex Eftpos accepted
Children welcome
5 Queen 3 Twin 3 Single (5 bdrm)
Bathrooms: 4 Ensuite 1 Private

Experience the peace and charm of the past in our fully restored circa 1880s B&B, one of Nelson's original family homes. Situated beside the beautiful Maitai River, Sussex House has retained all the original character and romantic ambiance of the era. It is only minutes' walk from central Nelson's award-winning restaurants and cafes, the Queens Gardens, Suter Art Gallery and Botanical Hill (The Centre of NZ) and many fine river and bushwalks.

The five sunny bedrooms all have TVs and are spacious and charmingly furnished. All rooms have access to the verandahs and complimentary tea and coffee facilities are provided. Breakfast includes a variety of fresh and preserved fruits, hot croissants and pastries, home-made yoghurts, cheeses and a large variety of cereals, rolls, breads and crumpets.

Other facilities include: wheelchair suite; free email/internet station; fax; courtesy phone; laundry facilities; separate lounge for guest entertaining; complimentary port; tea & coffee facilities; very sociable cat (Riley). We have lived overseas and have travelled extensively. We speak French fluently.

Nelson *1 km E of Nelson Cathedral*
Te Maunga - Historic House *B&B & Homestay & Apartment with Kitchen*

Anne Kolless
15 Dorothy Annie Way
@ 82 Cleveland, Nelson City

Tel (03) 548 8605
or 021 201 2461
temaungahouse@xtra.co.nz
www.nelsoncityaccommodation.co.nz

Double/Twin $90 - $135
Single $75 - $90
(Continental breakfast)
Children negotiable
Self-catered $140
Visa MC accepted
Pet free home Children welcome
Internet available
2 Double 1 Twin 1 Single (3 bdrm)
all with great views & comfort
Bathrooms: 2 Private 1 Guest share showers & tub-shower

Anne welcomes you to her family's 1930's registered Heritage House. Only 5 mins to downtown this stunning unique Arts & Crafts style, native woods example is mostly original with modern facilities. Te Maunga sits on a knoll, in rambling gardens, giving commanding views over Nelson, sea and valleys. Your special continental style breakfast includes local produce, home-made breads, and preserves. Relax and enjoy your aperitif, while taking in the amazing views. Self-catered unit next door! NZQA Food Safety Cert. Free Wireless Broadband link.

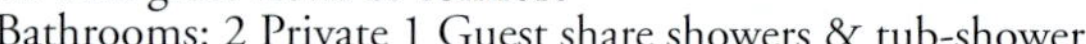

Nelson *3 km N of Nelson*
Havenview Homestay *B&B Homestay*

Shirley & Bruce Lauchlan
10 Davies Drive,
Nelson, 7010

Tel (03) 546 6045
or 027 420 0737
havenview@paradise.net.nz
www.havenview.co.nz

Double/Twin $140 - $160
(Full breakfast)
Dinner 2 course with
a glass of wine $35 pp
Visa MC accepted
Pet free home
Not suitable for children
Internet available
2 Queen (2 bdrm)
Large Queen ensuite sea view
Other Queen room garden view
Bathrooms: 1 Ensuite with shower 1 Private with shower and double spabath

Built for the magnificent views, our sunny modern home is on the northern entrance to Nelson, and only three minutes to the city and rugby venue. Relax with a complimentary wine while enjoying panoramic views overlooking the Miyazu Gardens and Tasman Bay. Enjoy dinner with us, or dine at a local restaurant; then relax in our lounge with Sky TV / Internet available. We are well travelled New Zealanders; play golf, and feel sure we can make your stay a pampered experience.

Nelson - Enner Glynn *5 km SW of Nelson*
Double View *B&B*

Judy Sisam
142 Panorama Drive,
Enner Glynn, 7011

Tel (03) 547 7292
or 027 411 8594
Fax (03) 547 7638
judy@doubleview.co.nz
www.doubleview.co.nz

Double/Twin $170
Single $150 (Full breakfast)
Children by arrangement
Dinner by prior arrangement
Visa MC accepted
Pet free home
1 King 1 Queen (2 bdrm)
Beautifully appointed
Superior & Junior Suite
Bathrooms: 2 Ensuite

Double View has spectacular views over Tasman Bay located 10 minutes from Nelson Airport and 15 minutes by vehicle from Nelson township. The Superior Suite is well appointed with spacious luxury Super King accommodation. The Junior Suite has own ensuite and queen bed. Guests are welcome to use laundry. Host Judy previously owned a cooking school and provides a great gourmet selection for breakfast. Dinner available by prior arrangement. Judy welcomes you to Double View to use as your base while exploring the region.

Nelson East *0.7 km E of Cathedral*
Annick House *B&B Separate Suite Apartment with Kitchen*

Ann and Nick James
29 Cleveland Terrace,
Nelson, 7010

Tel (03) 5480554
or 021 134 2808
Fax (03) 548 0505
nick.james@xtra.co.nz
www.annickhouse.co.nz

Double/Twin $180 - $220
Single $140 - $180
(Full breakfast)
Children over 12 are charged full rate
Dinner by arrangement only
Visa MC accepted
Children welcome
Internet available
2 Super king/Twin 1 Single (3 bdrm)
Bathrooms: 2 Private

Annick house offers two private self contained studio units in a secluded garden setting eight minutes walk to the city centre. Our Out of Africa unit is 50sq/m. The A Touch Oriental unit is 40sq/m and has a separate lounge. Both are tastefully furnished and have a private entrances and bathrooms. They are equipped with kitchen facilities, cooking essentials and a BBQ. We offer a continental or cooked breakfast tray. Expect a welcome from our two Tokinese cats.

Richmond *1 km E of Richmond*
Antiquarian Guest House *B&B*

Robert & Joanne Souch
12A Surrey Road,
Richmond,
Nelson

Tel (03) 544 0253
or (03) 544 0723
Fax (03) 544 0253
souchebys@clear.net.nz
souchebys@clear.net.nz

Double/Twin $95 - $125
Single $85
(Full breakfast)
Children $10
Visa MC accepted
Children and pets welcome
1 King 1 Queen 1 Twin (3 bdrm)
Bathrooms: 1 Ensuite 1 Guest share

Bob & Joanne Souch welcome you to their peaceful home only 2 minutes from Richmond (15 minutes drive south of Nelson) - excellent base for exploring National Parks, beaches, arts/crafts, ski fields etc. Relax in the garden, beside the swimming pool or in our large TV/ guest lounge. Tea/coffee facilities, home-baking and memorable breakfasts. Our family pet is Gemma (friendly border collie). As local antique shop owners we know the area well.

Richmond *12 km SW of Nelson*
Idesia *B&B*

Jenny & Barry McKee
14 Idesia Grove,
Richmond,
Nelson 7020

Tel (03) 544 0409
or 0800 361 845
Fax (03) 544 0402
idesian@xtra.co.nz
www.idesia.co.nz

Double/Twin $120 - $150
(Full breakfast)
Dinner by arrangement
Visa MC accepted
Pet free home
1 King/Twin 1 Queen (2 bdrm)
Bathrooms: 1 Ensuite 1 Private

You are assured of a warm welcome and quality service at Idesia Bed & Breakfast. Our home, elevated for sun and views is in a quiet grove easily accessible from State Highway 6. Breakfast is served with fresh seasonal fruits and a sizzling cooked selection. Join us for dinner, however Richmond's restaurants are close by. We offer broadband wireless network, off-road parking, information/booking Abel Tasman National Park. With our proven B&B experience we aim to give service and hospitality so you enjoy our regions attractions.

Richmond *12 km S of Nelson*
Lansfield Bed & Breakfast *B&B*

Dianne & Malcolm Tillier
6 Hugh Brown Place,
Richmond,
Nelson

Tel (03) 544 8166
or 021 131 3415
Fax (03) 544 8165
stay@lansfieldbedandbreakfast.co.nz
www.lansfieldbedandbreakfast.co.nz

Double/Twin $130 - $150
Single $120
(Full breakfast)
Dinner $40 pp by arrangement
1 King/Twin 1 Queen (2 bdrm)
Quality linen, garden views
Bathrooms: 2 Ensuite

Situated in the foothills of Richmond, close to Nelson, our home offers commanding views of the Waimea Plains and Tasman Bay. Expect a warm welcome, home baking and a wonderful breakfast. We use chemical free ENJO cleaning fibres throughout our home. Our interests include Tango, classic cars and gardening. We have a friendly Burmese cat, Pheobe. Close by are vineyards and restaurants, and you are welcome to join us for a meal if arranged prior. We look forward to meeting you.

Brightwater *10 km NW of Richmond*
Westleigh *B&B Homestay Farmstay Separate Suite*

John and Dell
Westleigh,511
Waimea West Road,
Brightwater,
Nelson, 7091

Tel (03) 542 3654
westleigh@paradise.net.nz
www.westleigh.co.nz

Double/Twin $130 - $140
Single $100 - $100
(Continental breakfast)
Dinner 3 course with wine $40pp
Visa MC accepted
Internet available
1 Queen with ensuite
1 Twin (2 bdrm)
Bathrooms: 1 Ensuite
1 Private 1 Guest share

Country home in 27 acres of privacy. House dates from c1860, now updated. 10 minutes to Richmond, golf and beach. Good local restaurants, but most guests eat with us,- more sociable and the food is ok too. A place for RnR, and central to all Nelson attractions. One cat. Directions: From Nelson, R6 past Richmond, turn off right at Brightwater, stay on that road c 5K. Westleigh sign prominent lhs. Or phone!

Wakefield *17 km S of Richmond*
Bushwalk B&B & Homestay *B&B Homestay*

Bruce & Sandra Monro
15 Hunt Terrace,
Wakefield, Nelson 7025

Tel (03) 541 9615
info@bushwalk.co.nz
bushwalk.co.nz

Double/Twin $140 - $160
Single $130 - $140
(Full breakfast)
Children $50 - $60 per child
(15 years and under)
3 course dinner by arrangement $30pp
Single twin rates $130+,
Single person $70 - $75
Visa MC accepted Children welcome
1 King 1 Double 1 Twin (3 bdrm)
Three large double rooms. Two have access onto decks.
Bathrooms: 1 Ensuite 1 Family share Ensuite has shower, family share bath only

Our home is in the trees adjacent to Faulkner's Bush Reserve surrounded by Totara, Beech, Pungas and ferns. It is only a ten minute stroll through the bush to the local shops and restaurants. Relax on the elevated deck or the courtyard with Missy the cat and the native birds. With a pottery and workshop on site you can be taught how to make a pot on the wheel, with your host, Bruce. Our interests are travel, music, singing, art, golf, pottery and furniture making.

Mapua Village *30 km N of Nelson*
Accent House Boutique Bed & Breakfast *Luxury Boutique Bed & Breakfast*

Wayne & Jacqui Rowe
148 Aranui Road,
Mapua Village,
Nelson 7005

Tel (03) 540 3442
or 027 540 3442
info@accentbnb.co.nz
www.accentbnb.co.nz

Double/Twin $195
Single $175 (Full breakfast)
Visa MC Amex Eftpos accepted
Pet free home
Internet available
2 King 1 Queen 1 Twin (4 bdrm)
Designed for your
comfort and pleasure
Bathrooms: 4 Ensuite
Heated white fluffy towels and heated undefloor tiles

Welcome to our new award winning home set on 1.5 acres overlooking our lagoon rich with local birdlife and drenched in Tasman Bay sunshine. Stroll to Mapua Village, cafes, shops and dine at our local restaurants. Check out the original local arts and crafts studios and the many local wineries all within a few minutes drive. 30 min drive to Nelson City and Abel Tasman National Park. 2hrs from Picton Ferry. 20 min from Nelson Airport. Private guest entrance, guest lounge with outdoor access overlooking Lagoon & tea/coffee making facilities.

Mapua *4 km SW of Mapua*

Kimeret Place Boutique B&B *Luxury B&B Apartment with Kitchen Cottage with Kitchen Guest House*

Gill & Ian Knight
78 Bronte Road East (off SH60),
Near Mapua, Nelson

Tel (03) 540 2727
Fax (03) 540 2726
stay@kimeretplace.co.nz
www.kimeretplace.co.nz

Double/Twin $225 - $355
Single $200 - $320
(Special breakfast)
2 bedroom cottage $400
Visa MC Eftpos accepted
Children welcome
Internet available
4 King/Twin (4 bdrm)
2 luxury suites, 1 apartment and 1 studio
Bathrooms: 4 Ensuite Suites have jacuzzi baths

A tranquil coastal setting in the heart of the wine & craft region with stunning views, heated swimming pool and spa. Just 4km to restaurants and 40 minutes to Abel Tasman National Park. A range of accommodation all with ensuite facilities, (2 with spa-baths), TV, DVD, Hi-fi, tea/coffee, fridge, sitting area and views from either balcony or deck. The 2 bedroom cottage also has a kitchenette and dining area. Light meals, laundry and internet are also available. Dog-lovers may wish to meet our golden retriever Alice.

Ruby Bay *20 km SW of Nelson*

Broadsea B&B *B&B*

Rae & John Robinson
42 Broadsea Avenue,
Ruby Bay,
Nelson

Tel (03) 540 3511
Fax (03) 540 3511
raer@clear.net.nz

Double/Twin $130 - $135
Single $125
(Full breakfast)
Not suitable for children
1 Queen (1 bdrm)
Tastefully furnished
Bathrooms: 1 Ensuite 1 Private

Beach front accommodation, with lovely walks on beach and reserve; cafes and tavern close by, as are wineries and restaurants. We are 15 minutes from Richmond and Motueka, 30 minutes from Nelson and the airport. Abel Tasman and Kaiteriteri are within 40 minutes drive. We want our guests to feel at home and have their privacy in a peaceful and private setting. Coffee, tea and old fashioned home-made biscuits available. Our Birman cat Bogart will greet you when you arrive.

Ruby Bay *32 km SW of Nelson*
Sandstone House *B&B*

John and Jenny Marchbanks
30 Korepo Road, Ruby Bay, Mapua
Tel (03) 540 3251 or 027 514 0652
Fax (03) 540 3251
sandstone@rubybay.net.nz
www.rubybay.net.nz

Double/Twin $265 Single $230 (Full breakfast)
Visa MC accepted   Not suitable for children
Internet Available
2 Queen (2 bdrm)
Bathrooms: 2 Ensuite

Welcome to Sandstone House - the ideal place to relax, stay a few days and explore this delightful region. We enjoy a maritime and semi-rural situation, ideally situated midway between Nelson and Motueka. We are handy to all the fine attractions that this region has to offer - National Parks, wineries, award winning restaurants, beaches, arts and crafts, the famous Mapua Wharf and lots lots more. We have 35 years local knowledge and are happy to assist you to make the most of your holiday and can help with any other forward bookings or reservations you may require. We are keen for you to have the best stay and trust you will enjoy our relaxed and homely atmosphere - our place is your place. Feel free to enjoy a drink, snack or a BBQ on either the front deck or the back verandah - depending on the weather, and if its winter time, enjoy some time out by the fire. Feast on the fabulous views anytime. We offer delicious homemade breakfasts with fresh free range eggs, baking, jams and preserves, and other local seasonal produce. Internet and laundry facilities are complimentary, and there is plenty of off street parking available. We hope you have a safe journey and look forward to sharing a 'welcome' drink with you when you arrive.

Tasman - Upper Moutere *5 km SE of Motueka*
The Estuary B&B *B&B Cottage with Kitchen*

Lynette Fischer/ Paul Leahy
59 Easton Loop,
RD 2,
Upper Moutere, 7175

Tel (03) 526 6213
or Mobile 027 526 6213
Fax (03) 526 6213
theestuarybandb@xtra.co.nz
theestuary.net.nz

Double/Twin $110 - $130
(Full breakfast)
Visa MC Eftpos accepted
Not suitable for children
Pets welcome
Internet available
2 Queen 1 Double (4 bdrm)
+ Studio with Queen Bed
Bathrooms: 3 Ensuite
Studio with bathroom

Hosts are Lyn And Paul. The estuary B&B overlooks the Kina estuary on the tasman coastal highway 2klm from Tasman village. Each room has views of the estuary. All rooms are ensuited. We have one teenage son. We also have a small friendly dog and a lovely cat living on the property as part of our family.

Motueka Valley *26 km S of Motueka*
Doone Cottage Country Homestay *B&B Homestay*

Glen & Stan Davenport
2281 Motueka Valley Highway,
Rural District No 1,
Motueka 7196

Tel (03) 526 8740
Fax (03) 526 8740
doone-cottage@xtra.co.nz
www.doonecottage.co.nz

Double/Twin $160 - $190
Single $110 - $160 (Full breakfast)
Dinner by arrangement
Nearest restaurants
5-20 minutes away
Visa MC accepted
Not suitable for children
2 King/Twin 1 Queen (3 bdrm)
Bathrooms: 3 Ensuite

Charming 130yr old cottage welcoming guests for 30 years. Secluded native flora & flower gardens in mountain setting overlooking Motueka River Valley. 5 Trout rivers - Guiding available. In-house Guestrooms plus Private Garden Chalet. Enjoy countrystyle B & B, homemade breads, preserves, free range eggs etc. Sheep, chickens, ducks, donkeys. Woolcraft. Short distance Abel Tasman, Kahaurangi, Nelson Lakes. Or just relax & soak up the country atmosphere of yesteryear in this special place. Nelson 45 mins. Motueka 20 mins. Picton 2 and a half hours Westcoast 3 hours.

Motueka Valley - Pokororo *25 km S of Motueka*

The Kahurangi Brown Trout *B&B Homestay Farmstay*

David Davies & Heather Lindsay
2292 Motueka River West Bank Road,
Pokororo, RD 1, Motueka

Tel (03) 526 8736 or 022 648 4401
Fax (03) 526 8736
enquiries@kbtrout.co.nz
www.kbtrout.co.nz

Double/Twin $160 Single $130 (Full breakfast)
Child in your room $25 or $100 for extra room
Dinner $6 pp includes salad, fresh bread, wine, dessert
Our gardens are 100% organic
Visa MC accepted
Children and pets welcome
Internet Available
2 King/Twin 2 King 1 Queen 3 Single (3 bdrm)
3 rooms with courtyard entrances and mini kitchen facilities
Bathrooms: 3 Ensuite

Enjoy the sound of the beautiful Motueka River. Step across the road for trout fishing, or a refreshing swim. Come 'home' for a delicious meal made with our home grown organic fruit and vegies. Enjoy the unique garden. Comments from last years visitors book say it all: Makes you feel invigorated just staying in such a wonderful place. Your gardens are an inspiration. The food really does taste better. We have loved every moment of our stay in your home. We are still laughing and joking as we leave. We wish we could have stayed longer. Dinner and breakfast were so delicious. I am so glad we found you at the end of our holiday and now return home with some extra special memories. As a conveniently located platform for exploring Kahurangi and Abel Tasman (parks) this place can't be beat. We aim for a relaxing atmosphere with time to socialize with our guests. Meals are timed to fit into your schedule as much as possible. Avi the Border Terrier assists with entertaining visitors. We are a little off the beaten track, and central to the Abel Tasman, Kahurangi and Nelson Lakes National Parks. You will want to stay a few days to fit it all in.

Motueka Valley *20 km SW of Motueka*
Vistara Bed and Breakfast *B&B Homestay Farmstay*

Bruce & Guruvati Dyer
2035 Motueka River Valley,
RD 1, Motueka, 7196

Tel (03) 526 8288
or 021 079 7919
Fax (03) 548 7284
info@vistara.co.nz
www.vistara.co.nz

Double/Twin $95
Single $75
(Continental breakfast)
Children $15 Dinner $15
Visa MC accepted
Children and pets welcome
Internet available
1 Queen 1 Double 2 Single (3 bdrm)
Polished floors & charming decor
Bathrooms: 2 Guest share

We welcome you to Vistara a relaxed peaceful haven situated on our 7 acre property adjacent to the Motueka River. Attractions include great river swimming, native birds and bush, a beautiful garden, mountain scenery and Jess our Jack Russell dog. Bedrooms feature polished floors and charming decor. Guests have their own lounge, tea and coffee facilities and are welcome to use the meditation room. Enjoy a delicious breakfast of home-made preserves, yoghurt, muesli and fresh organic fruit. Meals are organic, vegetarian and lovingly prepared.

Motueka *1.4 km E of Motueka*
Williams B&B *B&B Homestay Apartment with Kitchen*

Rebecca & Ian Williams
186 Thorp Street,
Motueka

Tel (03) 528 9385
Fax (03) 528 9385
info@Motueka-Homestay.co.nz
www.motueka-homestay.co.nz

Double/Twin $130 - $150
Single $75 - $90
(Full breakfast)
Children $20
Dinner by arrangement
Apartment with Kitchen - from $200
Visa MC accepted
Children welcome
Internet available
3 Queen 1 Double 2 Single (4 bdrm)
2 Bedroom Apartment with Kitchen, Sleeps 4 or 5
Bathrooms: 2 Ensuite

We are 1.4km to Motueka shopping centre and 1.2km to 18 hole golf course. A spacious 2 bedroom self contained apartement + 2 bedrooms both with own ensuite. The guest lounge has tea & coffee making facilities and fridge. Motueka is the stop-over place for visitors to explore Abel Tasman and Kahurangi National Parks. Golden Bay and Kaiteriteri golden sands beach is 10km away. We have a Jack Russell dog. Visa and Mastercard accepted.

Motueka *2 km S of Motueka*

Grey Heron - The Italian Organic Homestay *B&B Homestay*
Sandro Lionello & Laura Totis
110 Trewavas Street, Motueka 7120

Tel (03) 528 0472 or 021 0229 3547
Fax (03) 528 0472 sandro@greyheron.co.nz
www.greyheron.co.nz

Double/Twin $100 - $140
Single $65 - $85 (Continental breakfast)   Children welcome
Dinner $28pp Main + dessert or $40pp typical 3course italian dinner
3 Queen 1 Single (4 bdrm)
Bathrooms: 1 Ensuite 1 Private 1 Guest share

We are a couple from Northern Italy, much travelled and keen on tramping, mountaineering and motorbiking. We welcome you to our private hideaway and birdwatchers' paradise on the tidal estuary.

Pleasant beach-walks at the door-steps, far enough from the noise of the main road and yet only 5 mins drive to shops and restaurants. Or you can relax here after your exploring day, join us for dinner and taste our italian organic cuisine overlooking a beautiful sunset behind the mountains and enjoying Sandro's huge collection of Jazz records.

The Abel Tasman NP is 25mins drive; 45 mins drive to the alpine, easy accessible, Kahurangi NP and to Nelson city. The Guest Accommodation includes both ensuite/private and shared-facilities with toilet room and bathroom each separate (4-5 guests max capacity in the shared area). Basic tea-coffee facilities and secure off-street parking.

We serve a generous Continental breakfast including home-made breads and jams, fresh fruit and juice, yogurt and muesli. As keen walkers and mountaineers we can give helpful hints to maximize your exploration of the area. We also offer guided walks thanks to Sandro's experience as geologist and to our interest in the local flora and fauna. Rock-climbing and Italian Language lessons by arrangements.

Water-Taxi ticketing service and Kayak Tours booking service available. We are conveniently located just around the corner from the reliable and well-known 'Sea Kayak Company'. 'Benvenuti tutti gli amici italiani!'

Motueka *2 km SW of Motueka*
The Queen Vic *B&B Separate Suite Orchardstay*

Clare and Graham Ryder
199 Queen Victoria Street,
Motueka, 7120

Tel Landline (03) 528 8963
or Mobile 027 449 9180
Fax (03) 528 8963
clare@motuekabedandbreakfast.co.nz
motuekabedandbreakfast.co.nz

Double/Twin $0 - $135
(Full breakfast)
Visa MC accepted
Internet Available
1 Queen (1 bdrm)
Large room with ensuite
Bathrooms: 1 Ensuite

You will be assured of a warm welcome when you stay at The Queen Vic. Your room, separate from the house and overlooking the orchard is private and spacious with it's own ensuite. Soak in the spa pool in the garden, pick fruit fresh off the trees and on arrival, sample a jug of our own apple juice. Continental or cooked breakfast and home baking is provided. 20 mins to the Abel Tasman National Park and beaches. Well behaved Jack Russell called Flynn.

Abel Tasman - Riwaka Wharf *5 km N of Motueka*
Tasman Bay B&B *B&B*

Pauline & John Skelton
54 Wharf Road,
RD 3
Riwaka, 7198

Tel (03) 528 4992
or 027 345 4440
stay@tasmanbaybandb.co.nz
www.tasmanbaybandb.co.nz

Double/Twin $130 - $160
Single $100 - $120
(Continental breakfast)
Visa MC accepted
Pet free home
Internet available
2 King 2 Twin 3 Single (2 bdrm)
Bathrooms: 2 Ensuite
with spa baths and showers

Welcome to our waterfront home in Riwaka. New, purpose built B&B, idyllically situated on the shores of Tasman Bay, five minutes from cafes, restaurants and Motueka Information Centre. A recreational Paradise for walking, swimming, kayaking and just minutes from the Abel Tasman National Park, Kaiteriteri and Marahau. We can assist with kayak/activity bookings. Rooms have TVs, tea/coffee facilities, microwaves, separate guest entrances and outdoor areas. Relax in our guest lounge and sheltered outdoor courtyard. Enjoy generous continental breakfasts and genuine hospitality.

Kaiteriteri *12 km N of Motueka*
Bayview *B&B*

Tim Rich
2 Bayview Heights,
Kaiteriteri, RD 2,
Motueka 7197

Tel (03) 527 8090
or 027 454 5835
Fax (03) 527 8090
book@kaiteriteribandb.co.nz
www.kaiteriteribandb.co.nz

Double/Twin $175 - $205
(Full breakfast)
Visa MC accepted
Pet free home
Not suitable for children
1 King/Twin 1 King 1 Twin (2 bdrm)
Spacious rooms purpose built
Bathrooms: 2 Ensuite

Welcome to a piece of paradise. This modern house has huge windows with outstanding sea views overlooking Kaiteriteri Beach out to Abel Tasman National Park. Large, beautifully furnished guest rooms have every convenience you could want. Enjoy delicious home cooked breakfast in the dining room with your host who has an intimate knowledge of the area. Laundry, wireless broadband and booking facilities for boat trips, walking and kayaking are available. A two day minimum stay in this unique area recommended.

Kaiteriteri *13 km NE of Motueka*
Everton B&B *B&B*

Martin & Diane Everton
Kotare Place,
Little Kaiteriteri,
RD 2, Motueka

Tel (03) 527 8301
or 021 527 830
Fax (03) 527 8301
everton@xtra.co.nz
www.evertonbandb.co.nz

Double/Twin $140 - $160
Single $120 - $120
(Continental breakfast)
Visa MC accepted
Pet free home
Wireless internet available
1 King/Twin 1 King
1 Queen 1 Twin (3 bdrm)
Bathrooms: 1 Ensuite 2 Private

With wonderful sea views we are 2 minutes walk from beautiful Little Kaiteriteri Beach. Continental breakfast may include fresh bread or muffins. Nearby are excellent restaurants for evening dining. Our interests include Rotary, Toastmasters, golf, tennis, music, travel, and boating. The Abel Tasman National Park is right here where you can kayak, walk and water taxi. Martin is licensed to take you on a personalised trip in our boat. We offer email access and wireless internet. We have no pets and are non-smokers.

Kaiteriteri - Tapu Bay *12 km N of Motueka*
Maison Luc *B&B Cottage with Kitchen*

Angie & Martin Lucas
Tapu Bay,
410 Riwaka-Kaiteriteri Road,
RD 2, Motueka

Tel (03) 527 8247
or 0800 468 815
Fax (03) 527 8347
info@maisonluc.co.nz
www.maisonluc.co.nz

Double/Twin $100 - $130
Single $115 - $120
(Continental breakfast)
Cottage Single $115
Double $140 Extra guest $15
Visa MC accepted
Children welcome
1 King/Twin 2 Queen 1 Double (4 bdrm)
2 in B&B, 2 in cottage
Bathrooms: 2 Ensuite 1 Private

Maison Luc is centrally located to the Abel Tasman National Park and 1km to the golden sands of beautiful Kaiteriteri beaches. Relax by our sun trapped pool or walk 2 mins to local beaches. We have a fully self contained cottage set in a peaceful organic fruit garden. We offer a choice of two B&B rooms with ensuites and private entrance. (Complementary tea, coffee & homebaking). Enjoy wholesome breakfasts on our deck which overlooks the bay. We offer a relaxed family atmosphere and genuine kiwi hospitality.   Angie, Martin and Lu (dog).

Kaiteriteri *12 km N of Motueka*
Kaiteriteri Heights *Luxury B&B Separate Suite Apartment with Kitchen*

Mary & Richard Shee
28 Cederman Drive,
Kaiteriteri Heights,
RD 2, Motueka 7197

Tel (03) 527 8662
or 027 229 1698
Fax (03) 527 8662
info@KaiteriteriHeights.com
www.kaiteriteriheights.com

Double/Twin $180
Single $110 (Full breakfast)
Visa MC Eftpos accepted
Pet free home
Not suitable for children under 8
Internet available
2 Queen (2 bdrm)
Also one rollaway bed
Bathrooms: 2 Ensuite

Kaiteriteri's Premier Bed & Breakfast located in the hills overlooking Tasman Bay and the Riwaka Estuary. On the doorstep of the magnificent Abel Tasman National Park. Take the gentle 5-minute stroll down to Little Kaiteriteri beach, with its golden sands and safe swimming. Full privacy, or interact as part of the family. Shared facilities include the outdoor deck with barbeque area, coffee/tea facilities, spa pool, the main lounge area with TV with Sky.

Abel Tasman National Park - Marahau *18 km NW of Motueka*
Abel Tasman Bed & Breakfast *B&B Cottage with Kitchen Motel*

George Bloomfield
Abel Tasman National Park,
Marahau, Nelson Region

Tel (03) 527 8181
abel.tasman.stables.accom@xtra.co.nz
www.abeltasmanstables.co.nz

Double/Twin $125 - $165
Single $85 - $105
(Continental breakfast)
Dinner by prior arrangement
Cottage $155 (sleeps 4)
Visa MC accepted
Pet free home Children welcome
3 Queen 2 Double 4 Single (6 bdrm)
B&B 2 bedrooms, cottage 2
bedrooms, one in each motel
Bathrooms: 5 Ensuite 1 Private
1 Family share Showers

Great views, hospitality, peaceful garden setting are yours at Abel Tasman Stables accommodation. Closest ensuite facility to Abel Tasman National park. Guests comments include: 'I know now that hospitality is not just a word', TH, Germany. 'Wonderful place, friendly hospitality. The best things for really special holidays. We leave a piece of our hearts', P&M, Italy. 'The creme-de-la-creme of our holiday. What a view', MN & JW, England. Homestay bed & breakfast or self-contained options. Cafe close by.

Abel Tasman National Park *17 km NW of Motueka*
Split Apple Rock Homestay *B&B Homestay*

Thelma & Rodger Boys
116 Tokongawa Drive,
Split Apple Rock,
RD 2,
Motueka

Tel Landline (03) 527 8182
or Mobile 021 137 9145
splitapplerock@hotmail.com
www.splitapplerock.com

Double/Twin $150 - $180
Single $130 - $165
(Full breakfast)
Dinner $45 pp by arrangement
Visa MC accepted
Children welcome
1 Queen 1 Twin (2 bdrm)
Bathrooms: 2 Ensuite

Enjoy 180 degree panoramic sea views of Tasman Bay and Abel Tasman National Park. Our Eco-log home rooms have private entrances and decking. We are within walking distance of golden sand beaches, 5 minutes drive to Marahau and the start of Abel Tasman National Park where walking, kayaking, boating, swimming and more are available. 2 cats in residence. Directions: on the Marahau/Kaiteriteri Road take the Tokongawa Drive turn-off, 1.2km up Tokongawa Drive the 'Split Apple Rock Homestay' sign is on your right.

Abel Tasman National Park - Marahau *Motueka km N of*
Split Apple Lodge B&B Luxury Lodge *B&B Luxury Lodge*

Bert & Paulette Stannard
370 Kaiteriteri-Sandy Bay Road,
Marahau, 7197

Tel (03) 527 8502
or 027 439 4009
info@splitapplelodge.co.nz
www.splitapplelodge.co.nz

Double/Twin $180 - $210
(Continental breakfast)
Dinner in Winter
Visa MC Eftpos accepted
Pet free home
Not suitable for children
Internet available
6 Queen (6 bdrm)
Bathrooms: 6 Ensuite
Wet Floor Showers

Peacefully sitting amongst five acres of bush Split Apple Lodge offers spectacular sea or mountain views from every window. We have six spacious bedrooms with ensuites, a large guest lounge, dining area and deck. A pet and child free environment is maintained for the comfort of our guests. Fishing charters and horse riding are offered by the lodge and ten minutes away is the Abel Tasman National Park, hiking, kayaking, mountain biking and trout fishing. Come and enjoy this peace of paradise.

Takaka - Patons Rock Beach *10 km SW of Takaka*
Patondale *Cottage with Kitchen*

Vicki & David James
177 Patons Rock,
RD 2, Takaka 7182

Tel (03) 525 8262
or 0800 306 697 (NZ only)
Fax (03) 525 8262
patondale@xtra.co.nz
www.patonsrockbeachvillas.co.nz

Double/Twin $0 - $150
Single $130
(Breakfast provisions first night)
Children $20
Visa MC accepted
Pet free home
Children welcome
4 King 8 Single (8 bdrm)
All units 2 bedroom,
1King & 2 Single
Bathrooms: 4 Private

Four sunny, spacious, deluxe self-contained units, own attached carports. 2 bedrooms. Peaceful rural setting at the seaward end of our dairy farm yet only a few minutes walk to beautiful Patons Rock Beach. Central location, approx. 5mins to Mussell Inn. Simply the Best. Your Kiwi hosts, David & Vicki invite you to be our guests.

Takaka - Tata Beach *15 km NE of Takaka*
The Devonshires *B&B Homestay*
Brian & Susan Devonshire
32 Tata Heights Drive,
Tata Beach,
RD 1,
Takaka,
Golden Bay

Tel (03) 525 7987
Fax (03) 525 7987
devs.1@actrix.co.nz

Double/Twin $100
Single $70
(Full breakfast)
Children not suitable
Dinner $25-$30 by arrangement
Visa MC accepted
1 Queen (1 bdrm)
Bathrooms: 1 Ensuite

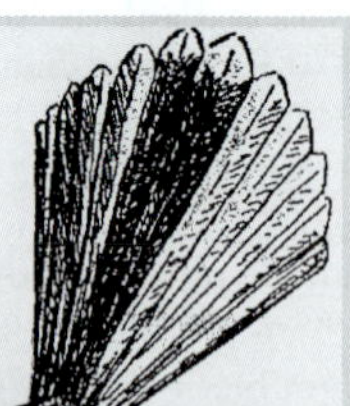

The Devonshires live at Tata Beach and invite you to enjoy their comfortable home and stroll to the nearby beautiful golden beach. A tranquil base for exploring the truly scenic Golden Bay, the Abel Tasman Walkway, Kahurangi National Park, Farewell Spit, amazing coastal scenery, fishing the rivers or visiting interesting craftspeople. Brian, an educator, wine and American Football buff is a keen fisherman. Susan enjoys crafts, painting, gardening and practising her culinary skills. Charlie Brown and Hermione are the resident cats. Longer visits welcomed.

Parapara *20 km NW of Takaka*
Hakea Hill House *B&B*
Vic & Liza Eastman
PO Box 35,
Collingwood 7054

Tel (03) 524 8487
Fax (03) 524 8487
vic.eastman@clear.net.nz

Double/Twin $130
Single $90
(Full breakfast)
Children $50
Family dinner by arrangement
Visa MC accepted
Children and pets welcome
2 Queen 6 Single (3 bdrm)
2 bedrooms have large balconies
Bathrooms: 2 Guest share
Bathtub and shower

Hakea Hill House at Parapara has views from its hilltop of all Golden Bay. The 2 story house is modern and spacious. Two guest rooms have large balconies; the third for children has bunk beds and a cot. American and New Zealand electric outlets are installed. Television, tea or coffee, telephone and broadband lines are available in rooms. Vic is a practising physician with an interest in astronomy. Liza is a quilter and cares for outdoor dogs. Please contact us for reservations and directions.

Collingwood Township *25 km S of Takaka*
Heron's Rest *Cottage with B&B + cooking facilities*

Maureen & Angus Scotland
23 Gibbs Road,
Collingwood , Golden Bay

Tel (03) 524 8987
Fax (03) 524 8987
be@herons-rest.co.nz
www.herons-rest.co.nz

Double/Twin $110 - $130
Single $70 - $90 (Special breakfast)
Children Negotiable
Visa MC accepted
Internet Available
1 Queen 1 Double 1 Twin
2 Single (3 bdrm)
Nicely appointed, with ensuites
Bathrooms: 2 Ensuite 1 Family share
Bath available and separate toilet

Travelling towards the tip of the South Island, your journey is rewarded by spectacular sea, mountain and estuary views, all visible from Heron's Rest. We're situated between the Abel Tasman and Heaphy Tracks and surrounded by superb sandy beaches, being a short bush-walk (or drive) away from Farewell Spit Tours and Collingwood eateries. Welcoming hosts offer relaxation, comfort and lasting memories served up with home-made and locally-produced foods plus complimentary drinks. Potter's studio, internet Wi-Fi, hairdryer, BBQ, laundry available. Directions: Website and Lewis Street signboard along estuary.

Pakawau *9 km N of Collingwood*
Twin Waters Lodge *Luxury Lodge*

Trish & Mike Boland
PO Box 33,
Collingwood

Tel (03) 524 8014
Fax (03) 524 8054
twin.waters@xtra.co.nz
www.twinwaters.co.nz

Double/Twin $200 - $250
Single $175 - $200
(Full breakfast)
Dinner by arrangement
Visa MC accepted
Not suitable for children
Internet available
1 King/Twin 3 Queen (4 bdrm)
Bathrooms: 4 Ensuite

Nestled harmoniously beside a tidal estuary and just fifty metres from a sandy beach, Twin Waters features curved timber ceilings, panoramic windows and multilevel decks. The elegant interior has ample space for guests to enjoy its charm and tranquility. Waking to tuis singing, breakfasting in the sun, sipping wine on the decks overlooking the estuary, or savouring a delicious dinner, there's sure to be a special moment to remember. Trish and Mike and their feline companions look forward to welcoming you at Twin Waters.

Nelson Lakes - St Arnaud *85 km S of Nelson*

Nelson Lakes Homestay *Homestay*
Gay & Merv Patch
RD 2,
State Highway 63,
Nelson 7072

Tel (03) 521 1191
Fax (03) 521 1191
Home@Tasman.net
www.nelsonlakesaccommodation.co.nz

Double/Twin $145
Single $110
(Full breakfast)
Visa MC accepted
Pet free home
Not suitable for children
2 King/Twin 1 Queen (2 bdrm)
Bathrooms: 2 Ensuite

Nestled on the sunny slopes of the St Arnaud Mountain Range, 4kms east of St Arnaud. Our spacious modern home is designed for the comfort and convenience of our guests. Spacious ensuite rooms, with doors opening on to our native garden, large comfortable lounge and terrace to relax on at the end of the day and admire the magnificent mountain views. Nelson Lakes National Park, is a beautiful region of picturesque lakes, forests mountains and rivers.

Murchison *0.1 km E of Murchison*

Murchison Lodge *B&B*
Shirley & Merve Bigden
15 Grey Street,
Murchison, 7007

Tel (03) 523 9196
or Freephone: 0800 523 9196
info@murchisonlodge.co.nz
www.murchisonlodge.co.nz

Double/Twin $150 - $210
Single $125 - $185
(Full breakfast)
Children over 12 welcome
Free wireless broadband,
use of bicycles and golf clubs
Visa MC accepted
1 King/Twin 2 Queen
1 Twin (4 bdrm)
Bathrooms: 3 Ensuite 1 Private

Warm and quiet timber Lodge with comfortable beds and hearty BBQ breakfasts, using our own eggs and fruit. Four acres support various animals (including a friendly dog) and access the Buller River and its fishing & swimming holes. Trees and mountains surround us, yet Murchison's cafes are within five minutes walk. A great base to explore three National Parks; fly-fish, raft or play golf. Return home to a cold beer or a wine in front of the log fire. Free WI-FI throughout

West Coast
Karamea
67
Carters Beach
Cape Foulwind
Westport
6
Charleston
69
Punakaiki
Reefton
Barrytown
7
Greymouth
Hokitika
Ruatapu
West Coast
Kilometres
0
60
Miles
0
36
6
Whataroa
Franz Josef
Fox Glacier
6
Castle Hill Village
Lake Coleridge
Darfield
Mt Hutt
Staveley
Methven
Mount Cook
Rakaia
Ashburton
Lake Tekapo
Kimbell
Ealing
Burkes Pass
Fairlie
Geraldine

Reefton *.1 km N of Reefton Central*
Quartz Lodge *B&B*

Paddy & Alan Rainey
78 Shiel Street,
Reefton, West Coast

Tel (03) 732 8383
or 0800 302 725
quartz-lodge@xtra.co.nz
www.quartzlodge.co.nz

Double/Twin $90 - $130
Single $70 - $95
(Full breakfast)
Children $25
Dinner $15-$30
Visa MC accepted
Children and pets welcome
1 King 1 Queen 1 Twin
1 Single (3 bdrm)
Bathrooms: 1 Ensuite
1 Private 1 Guest share

A friendly welcome awaits you when you arrive at Quartz Lodge superior accommodation in the heart of Reefton. Guests only entrance will take you upstairs to rooms with huge picture windows, luxurious beds, quality linen, robes and so much more. Complimentary coffee and a selection of teas are available in your spacious private lounge/dining area. Laundry service and Internet is also available upon request. We pride ourselves on making you feel at home. Quality and comfort says it all!

Karamea *84 km N of Westport*
Beachfront Farmstay B&B *B&B Farmstay*

Dianne & Russell Anderson
3578 Karamea Highway,
RD3, Karamea

Tel (03) 782 6762
or 027 249 8827
Fax (03) 782 6762
farmstay@xtra.co.nz
www.WestCoastBeachAccommodation.co.nz

Double/Twin $160 - $180
Single $140
(Special breakfast)
Children negotiable
Dinner $70
Visa MC accepted
Children welcome
1 King 1 Queen (2 bdrm)
Bathrooms: 2 Ensuite

Our 500 cow dairy farm has 2.5kms of coastline, a 2min walk and you will be on a sandy beach usually all to yourself. Relax in elegant rooms with your own private deck. Special farmhouse breakfasts, home preserving, tasty whitebait, bacon and egg dishes, espresso coffee. Join us for delicious country cuisine, farm grown meat, fresh fish, organic vegetables, homemade desserts served with NZ wine. Inquire about a BBQ and bonfire on the beach, a unique Kiwi tradition, (weather permitting) or a fishing experience with Russell and his Kentiki Torpedo.

Westport - Cape Foulwind *11 km S of Westport*
Steeples Cottage, Studio & B&B *B&B Homestay Separate Suite*
Cottage with Kitchen

Pauline & Bruce Cargill
48 Lighthouse Road,
Cape Foulwind, Westport

Tel (03) 789 7876
or 0800 670 708
thesteeples@xtra.co.nz
www.steeplescottage.co.nz

Double/Twin $100 - $120
Single $70 - $90
(Continental breakfast)
Children $20
Whitebait meal by arrangement
Cottage $120 plus $20 extra person
Children welcome Internet available
4 Queen 1 Single (4 bdrm)
1 in cottage 1 in studio 2 in house
Bathrooms: 2 Ensuite 1 Private 1 cottage ensuite studio ensuite, 1 private or guest share

Peaceful rural accommodation, lovely gardens, magnificent sea views, rugged coastline, beautiful beaches, tranquil sunsets. swimming, surfing, fishing, kayaking mountain biking. Walk the popular seal colony walkway, Great dining The Bay House Restaurant or friendly Star Tavern. Local attractions 18 golf course, Coaltown Museum, jet boating, horse riding, underworld & white water rafting, caving, bush walks, unimog trips, all year swimming centre, full gymnasium & Punakaiki National Park. We have a Jack Russell and cat. Laundry and off-street parking. Whitebait meals by arrangment. Internet available.

Westport *0.01 km N of Westport Central*
Havenlee Homestay *B&B Homestay*

Jan & Ian Stevenson
76 Queen Street, Westport

Tel (03) 789 8543
or 0800 673 619
mobile 027 627 2702
Fax (03) 789 8502
info@havenlee.co.nz
www.havenlee.co.nz

Double/Twin $120 - $170
Single $100 (Full breakfast)
Children negotiable
Visa MC accepted
Children welcome
Internet available
2 Queen (2 bdrm)
Two double rooms with a
queen sized bed in each
Bathrooms: 1 Private 1 Guest share

Peace in Paradise - this is Havenlee: a welcoming, relaxed, spacious, quality homestay where you will feel at home right away. Centrally located, an idyllic base from which to explore the environmental wonderland, share local knowledge or just to take time out. Check out the adventure experiences and local attractions. Soak up the nature, rest and restore body and soul in the peace and quiet of a garden oasis. Delicious full breakfast served. Laundry facilities available. Denniston Heritage site is a 'must see'

Westport - Carters Beach *3 km S of Westport*
Bellaville *B&B Separate Suite*

Marlene & Ross Burrow
No 10 State Highway 67 A,
Carters Beach
PO Box 157, Westport

Tel (03) 789 8457,
or cell 027 613 1689
or Free phone 0800 789 845
bellaville@xtra.co.nz

Double/Twin $100 - $120
Single $70 - $80 (Full breakfast)
Children $15 Adult $25
Pet free home
Children welcme
1 Queen 1 Single (1 bdrm)
Extra large room with
rollaway available
Bathrooms: 1 Ensuite 1 Private
Spa Bath with separate shower

Hear the sound of waves pounding our safe swimming beach. Ouiet sunny extra large, studio room, private entrance, parking at door. No steps, no traffic noise. Private ensuite, large bathroom spa bath, shower separate toilet. Ideal family unit. Electric blankets, TV, fridge, tea & coffee and home-baking. Laundry available. Close to all activities, coastal walks, seal colony. 3mins walk to licensed cafe/bar, golf course, playground. Have travelled extensively overseas & in NZ. Don't rush, stay a day or two, you will be glad you did.

Westport - Carters Beach *4 km S of Westport*
Carters Beach B&B *B&B*

Sue & John Bennett
Main Road Carters Beach,
On State Highway 67A,
Westport

Tel (03) 789 8056
or 0800 783 566
cartersbeachaccom@xtra.co.nz
www.bnb.co.nz/cartersbeachbb.html

Double/Twin $100 - $120
Single $70 - $80
(Continental breakfast)
Pet free home
Children welcome
2 Queen 1 Twin (3 bdrm)
Very spacious
Bathrooms: 1 Ensuite 1 Private

Carters Beach - a lovely relaxed atmosphere, Situated only 4km south of Westport. 3 minute walk to our beach, with fully licenced resturant/cafe and bar. Golf links, world famous seal colony and Bay House Cafe within a few minutes drive. Our rooms are very spacious with TV and tea/coffee making facilities. Own private entrance-ways with sun decks. Laundry facilities available by arrangement. Ideal accommodation for couples travelling togeather. We look forward to meeting and sharing our local knowledge with you. Cheers, Sue and John Bennett.

Punakaiki - Barrytown *27 km N of Greymouth*
Golden Sands Homestay *Homestay*

Sue & Tom Costelloe
4 Golden Sands Road,
Barrytown,
RD 1,
Runanga, 7873

Tel (03) 731 1115
goldensands@clear.net.nz

Double/Twin $115 - $125
Single $70
(Continental breakfast)
Dinner by arrangement
Visa MC accepted
2 Queen 1 Twin (3 bdrm)
Bathrooms: 1 Ensuite 2 Private

Nestled between the paparoa range and tasman sea on the corner of golden sands road Barrytown and Greymouth-Westport scenic highway, we offer a warm welcome with a cuppa, fresh baking,f riendly atmosphere and comfortable rooms. Handy to Punakaiki, Pancake Rocks and National Park 15 minutes north, with Greymouth 25 minutes south. Stunning views and wonderful sunsets, a cosy fire in the winter and Jasper the cat. We have local knowledge on walking tracks and activities. Enjoy breakfast with rural and sea views

---

Punakaiki - Barrytown *20 km N of Greymouth*
Kallyhouse *B&B Homestay Apartment with Kitchen*

Kathleen & Alister Schroeder
13 Cargill Road,
Runanga, RD 1, 7873,
Westland

Tel (03) 731 1006
Fax (03) 731 1106
kallyhouse@xtra.co.nz
www.kallyhouse.co.nz
www.bnb.co.nz/schroeder.html

Double/Twin $115 - $140
Single $75
(Continental breakfast)
Visa MC accepted
Pet free home
Children welcome
3 Queen 1 Twin (4 bdrm)
Bathrooms: 1 Ensuite 1 Guest share
1 Spa Bath

We have a new spacious home on a quiet rear section, a garden setting, native bush backdrop and sea views. We offer a self-contained flat downstairs, with queen room and twin beds in spacious living area. Kitchen, bathroom, washing machine, parking and separate entrance. Also 2 queen rooms upstairs. Breakfast with host. Punakaiki Pancake Rocks and adventure activities in Paparoa National Park, 10-minutes north. Greymouth 20 minutes south. Turn at Allnations Hotel, past 3 houses on left, up lane, house on left. Licensed Restaurant handy.

Greymouth *0.5 km N of Greymouth Central*
Ardwyn House *Homestay*

Mary Owen
48 Chapel Street,
Greymouth

Tel (03) 768 6107
ardwynhouse@hotmail.com

Double/Twin $85 - $95
Single $55 - $60
(Full breakfast)
Children half price
Visa MC accepted
Children welcome
2 Queen 3 Single (3 bdrm)
Bathrooms: 1 Guest share

Ardwyn House is 3 minutes walk from the town centre in a quiet garden setting offering sea, river and town views. The house was built in the 1920s and is a fine example of an imposing residence with fine woodwork and leadlight windows, whilst being a comfortable and friendly home. Greymouth's ideally situated for travellers touring the West Coast being central with good choice of restaurants. We offer a courtesy car service to and from local travel centres and also provide off-street parking.

Greymouth *6 km S of Greymouth*
Paroa Homestay (formerly Pam's Homestay) *Homestay*

Pam Sutherland
345 Main South Road,
Greymouth

Tel (03) 762 6769
or 027 323 3118
Fax (03) 762 6765
paroahomestay@xtra.co.nz
www.paroahomestay.co.nz

Double/Twin $110 - $140
Single $100 - $110
(Continental breakfast)
Children negotiable
Visa MC accepted
Children welcome
2 King 1 Double (3 bdrm)
Also 1 Super King Bed
Bathrooms: 1 Ensuite 1 Private
1 Guest share Off-suite bathroom (not guests share)

Relax on terraces overlooking the sea and watch incredible sunsets. 3 minutes walk to the beach. Towering trees, native bush surrounds spacious classic home with luxurious guest lounge. Excellent restaurants nearby. Experience superb continental breakfast as baking and cooking is Pam's forte (previously owning Greymouth's busiest cafe/bar). Pam has NZQA Food Hygiene qualifications. West Coast born, Pam's local knowledge is invaluable. Pam enjoys hospitality, antiques, organic gardening and bush walking. Pam has welcomed guests for 13 years. Guest comments 'Best breakfast in NZ' 'incredible hospitaliy'.

Greymouth *3.5 km S of Greymouth*
Maryglen Homestay *Homestay Bed and Breakfast*

Allison & Glen Palmer
20 Weenink Road,
Karoro, Greymouth

Tel 0800 627 945
or (03) 768 0706
mary@bandb.co.nz
www.bandb.co.nz

Double/Twin $125 - $150
Single $90 - $125
(Special breakfast)
Children negotiable
Snack $20
Full dinner (pre-notice) $45
Visa MC accepted Internet available
2 King/Twin 1 Queen 1 Single
(3 bdrm) 1 family room -
sleeps 3-4, 2 double rooms
Bathrooms: 3 Ensuite all private

Large Native ferns and bush surround our hillside home overlooking the sea. Our guests comment- amazing location. The sound of the surf will lull you to sleep. Off the main road, quiet location, 2 rooms have deck entrances. Amazing sunsets, Complimentary transport available from bus/train. Let us share our wonderful coast with you as we help you plan your days-scenic tours, bush walks, Misty, our cat will welcome you. Trans-scenic train (a must), Shantytown , Punakaiki Pancake Rocks. Your home away from home.

Greymouth *6 km S of Greymouth*
Sunsetview *B&B Homestay Apartment with Kitchen*

Russell & Jill Fairhall
335 Main South Road,
Greymouth, 7805

Tel (03) 762 6616
Fax (03) 762 6616
sunsetview@xtra.co.nz

Double/Twin $100 - $140
Single $90 - $120
(Full breakfast)
Children by arrangement
Dinner by arrangement
Lunch by arrangement
Visa MC accepted
Children and pets welcome
2 King/Twin 1 King
1 Queen (4 bdrm)
Bathrooms: 2 Ensuite 1 Private

Jill & Russell welcome you to our sunny home with amazing sea and mountain views. We offer well-appointed superior bedrooms. Sky TV in rooms. Home-cooked meals available on request. Outdoor areas, pool and barbecue. Short walk to beach, shop approx 5 to 10 minutes walk Courtesy car available to local resturants, travel centres. Off-street parking. Downstairs apartment has two bedrooms (either can be king double or single beds) bathroom with wardrobe/dressing room. Kitchen with dining/lounge area. Own entrance with undercover parking.

Greymouth *12 km S of Greymouth*
New River Bluegums B & B *B&B Farmstay Self-contained cottages*

Sharon, Michael & Harry Pugh
985 Main South Road,
New River,
Greymouth

Tel (03) 762 6678
Fax (03) 762 6678
mail@bluegumsnz.com
www.bluegumsnz.com

Double/Twin $135 - $195
Single $125 - $145
(Full breakfast)
Children $25
Dinner by arrangement
Visa MC accepted
Internet available
1 King 2 Queen 2 Double
2 Single (3 bdrm)
Bathrooms: 3 Ensuite

The Pugh family welcome you to the comfort of their log and stone home on a small farm. The homestead offers an ensuite king room (Tui room) and two superbly-appointed self-contained cottages. Tennis court. Laundry. Wireless Broadband. Feed the sheep and cattle or play with Coco (labrador). 15 min walk to beach & 5 min drive to Shantytown. 'Beautiful setting! Delightful home! Your relaxed and welcome manner made us feel like we were somewhere special and we certainly were, thank you!' G&K Guestbook.

Greymouth *35 km S of Greymouth*
Chapel Hill *B&B Homestay Farmstay*

Joy & John Ruesink
783 Rutherglen Road,
Paroa,
Greymouth

Tel (03) 762 6662
info@chapelhill.co.nz
www.chapelhill.co.nz

Double/Twin $110 - $140
Single $0 - $90
(Full breakfast)
Visa MC accepted
Children welcome
1 King/Twin 2 Queen
1 Single (3 bdrm)
Bathrooms: 1 Ensuite 2 Private

Touch the ferns out your window! Spectacular architect-designed country stay in a rainforest setting, ONLY 15 minutes south of Greymouth. Huge logfire for those cooler evenings, big comfy beds with electric blankets. Hearty country breakfasts included. Home-grown food. 1 hour north to Pancake Rocks & 1-1/2 hours to Arthurs Pass village. Non-smoking inside. Pets, farm animals and wildlife on the property. Unusual multi-level design is unsuitable for toddlers or disabled.

Greymouth *3 km NE of Greymouth*
Oak Lodge *B&B Cottage with Kitchen*

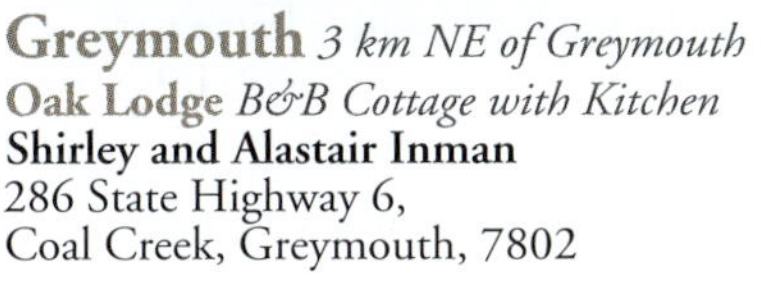

Shirley and Alastair Inman
286 State Highway 6,
Coal Creek, Greymouth, 7802

Tel (03) 768 6832
or 0800 625 563
Fax (03) 768 4362
relax@oaklodge.co.nz
www.oaklodge.co.nz

Double/Twin $150 - $245
Single $155 - $205
(Full breakfast)
Children 0-4yrs incl free,
5yrs-11yrs incl $20, 12yrs & over $40
Visa MC accepted
Pet free home Children welcome
3 King/Twin 2 Queen
2 Twin 4 Single (6 bdrm)
5 in Bed and Breakfast, 1 in cottage
Bathrooms: 5 Ensuite 1 Private

Oak Lodge is a quality B&B just 3 minutes north of Greymouth and has a rural outlook. There are 5 large comfortable bedrooms, all on the second floor, 4 have ensuites and one a private bathroom just across the hall. Each room has its own TV, chairs and bath robes. There is also a guest lounge with tea and coffee making facilities, TV, and leather lounge.

Oak Lodge has been designed with your relaxation in mind. A full breakfast is served, fresh muffins or pastries are cooked each morning for your enjoyment. Warm, friendly, relaxing atmosphere. Alastair and Shirley have been sheep and cattle farmers in the past and extend a warm welcome to you.

Also available is Oak Tree Cottage a one bedroom, self catering cottage, superking bed, full kitchen, washing machine and large deck area. Leisure activites are available at Oak Lodge, we have a tennis court, swimming pool, hot spa tub, sauna and billiards room. Feed the sheep and eels or just relax in the garden.

Greymouth *2 km S of Greymouth Post Office*
Jivana Retreat *Luxury B&B Private Chalet*
Sandie
8 Leith Crescent, Greymouth

Tel (03) 768 6102
Fax (03) 768 6108
sandie@jivanaretreat.co.nz
www.JivanaRetreat.co.nz

Double/Twin $140 - $168
Single $135
(Special breakfast)
Children negotiable
Dinner by prior arrangement
Private Chalet $168
Visa MC accepted
Internet available
1 King 2 Queen 1 Twin (3 bdrm)
Bathrooms: 1 Ensuite 1 Private
1 Guest share plus bush bath

Jivana Retreat is a serene, affordable, quality haven. Sandie spoils you with a homemade organic breakfast menu of your choice, served indoors in the sunny conservatory, or lush outdoors. Special diets catered for. Pamper yourself with an aromatherapy massage, reflexology, or relaxing therapeutic yoga session while you stay. Iridology,ayurveda health programs on request. Bikes, kayaks, & boogy boards, are available for guests. Fantastic outdoors activities. A stunning location & tranquil oasis in this mad world! Beautiful hospitality, which refreshes the soul B Jones.

Hokitika *2 km N of Hokitika*
Hokitika Heritage Lodge *Luxury B&B*
Homestay Cottage with Kitchen
Dianne & Chris Ward
46 Alpine View, Hokitika

Tel (03) 755 7357
or 0800 261 949
Fax (03) 755 7357
hokitikaheritage@xtra.co.nz
www.hokitikaheritagelodge.co.nz

Double/Twin $195 - $250
Single $195 - $210
(Full breakfast)
Children b/a   Dinner b/a
Visa MC accepted
1 King/Twin 1 King 3 Queen
1 Single (5 bdrm)
3 bedrooms in Bank House;
2 bedrooms in Gatehouse Cottage
Bathrooms: 3 Ensuites in Bank House; 1Private in Gatehouse Cottage

NZ hospitality at its best! Our Lodge overlooks Tasman Sea, Hokitika, Southern Alps. 'Bank House' provides full B&B. Three spacious ensuite bedrooms; guest lounge. Historic, stylish decor used throughout The Lodge to reflect NZ history. Gold, Jade and Heritage themed rooms. 'Gatehouse Cottage' is self-catering. Spacious. Includes 2 beautiful bedrooms, private bathroom, lounge, dining and full kitchen. Dianne, (Literacy Teacher) and Chris, (Property Consultant & Rotarian) enjoy chatting with guests over a welcoming drink and home-baking. Broadband Internet, wireless network, television and dinners are available.

Hokitika *2 km E of Hokitika*
Woodland Glen Lodge *Luxury B&B*
Janette & Laurie Anderson
96 Hau Hau Road,
Blue Spur,
Hokitika

Tel (03) 755 5063
or 0800 361 361 (NZ Only)
Fax (03) 755 5063
woodlandglen1@gmail.com
www.hokitika.net

Double/Twin $180 - $220
Single $150 - $180
(Full breakfast)
Visa MC Amex Eftpos accepted
Not suitable for children
Internet available
5 Queen 2 Twin 2 Single (5 bdrm)
Bathrooms: 3 Ensuite 1 Guest share

Our 6500 square foot lodge is located on 21 acres and is surrounded in native kahikatea trees providing quiet and privacy. A great place for a retreat or time out. Most guests base themselves in Hokitika for visits to the glaciers and Punakaiki, allow 2 nights. We welcome you to Woodland Glen Lodge, we are widely travelled and have many experiences to share with you. Laurie is a retired police officer and now commercial pilot, Janette is a health professional with a keen interest in quilting.

Hokitika *1 km NE of Hokitika*
Top View B&B *B&B*
Lin & Colin Jackson
24 Whitcombe Terrace, Hokitika

Tel (03) 755 7060
or 027 7381 7206
Fax (03) 755 7060
topview24@clear.net.nz
www.topview.co.nz

Double/Twin $120 - $140
Single $100
(Breakfast by arrangement)
Children price depending age
Reduced rates for longer stays
Visa MC accepted
Pet free home
Internet Available
2 Queen 2 Twin (3 bdrm)
Clean and comfortable, electric blankets,
Bathrooms: 2 Ensuite 1 Private

We offer you a place to relax with a superb view of mountains, sea and sunsets from the lounge/breakfast room. Colin and Lin are retired farmers with many interests including Lions, Diabetes Societies, outdoor activities. Can provide Whitebait nets, Fishing Rods. We look forward to your company. From the main road north, turn at the Airport sign on Tudor Street, take the next left into Bonar Drive to the top of the hill on to Whitcombe Terrace, turn left.

Hokitika Central *Post Office km N of*
Amberlea B & B *B&B*

Sharyn & Butch Symons
146 Gibson Quay,
Hokitika, 7810

Tel (03) 755 7346
or 027 697 1130
Fax (03) 755 7349
rpsmsymons@hotmail.com

Double/Twin $120 - $140
Single $100 - $120
(Full breakfast)
Children under 5 $10, under 12 $30
Children and pets welcome
3 Queen 1 Twin (4 bdrm)
All upstairs
Queen beds in ensuite rooms
Bathrooms: 2 Ensuite 1 Guest share
All bathrooms have showers

Sharyn and Butch along with their Bichons and cats invite you to their quiet friendly home situated beside the Hokitika River. Relax in the lovely gardens or watch the sunsets over the Tasman Sea and the Southern Alps. We are a five minute walk from the town centre and all of its tourist attractions, resturants and beach. Visit the Hokitika Gorge. Visit our great greenstone, paua, gold and ruby rock shops or relax at the beach or lakes enjoying the clean air.

Ruatapu *12 km S of Hokitika*
Berwick's Hill *B&B Homestay*

Eileen & Roger Berwick
106 Ruatapu-Ross Road,
State Highway 6,
RD 3, Hokitika

Tel (03) 755 7876
Fax (03) 755 7870
berwicks@xtra.co.nz
www.berwicks.co.nz

Double/Twin $100 - $130
Single $60 - $80
(Full breakfast)
Dinner $40 by arrangement
Visa MC accepted
2 King/Twin 1 Queen (2 bdrm)
Heater in bedrooms
Bathrooms: 1 Ensuite 1 Private
1 bath in ensuite

Welcome to Berwick's Hill. We offer you a friendly and relaxed stay in our comfortable home. Magnificent views of the Tasman Sea and the Southern Alps are seen from the main living areas. Experience the sunsets and sunrises. We are close to Lake Mahinapua, bush walks, Mananui Bush and Beach walk ,golf course. On our lifestyle farm we have sheep, Belted Galloway cattle and a farm dog also hens. We and our cat look forward to meeting you.

Franz Josef *5 km N of Franz Josef Glacier*
Ribbonwood Retreat *Luxury B&B Cottage with Kitchen*

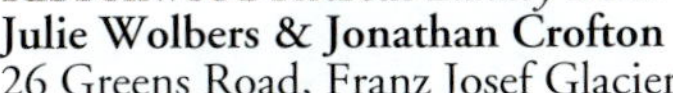

Julie Wolbers & Jonathan Crofton
26 Greens Road, Franz Josef Glacier

Tel (03) 752 0072
ribbon.wood@xtra.co.nz
www.ribbonwood.net.nz

Double/Twin $200 - $300
(Full breakfast)
A variety of restaurants
in Franz Josef village
Free Wifi and guest computer
Visa MC accepted
Pet free home   Children welcome
1 King 3 Queen 1 Single (3 bdrm)
3 rooms queen beds,
Cottage king plus single
Bathrooms: 2 Ensuite 1 Private
Luxurious tiled bathrooms,
Private bathroom next to room.

Welcome to our slice of paradise. Ribbonwood has stunning mountain, ice-field and forest views from our modern home and cottage. Hosts Julie is an international school teacher and Jonathan a wildlife ranger. Ribbonwood is five minutes drive from Franz Josef village and ten minutes drive from the glacier access. We offer comfortable new beds, low allergenic bedding and floors, high pressure showers, home cooked breakfast, free WIFI and a wealth of knowledge of local attractions and activities.

Fox Glacier *20 km S of Franz Josef*
Roaring Billy Homestay *B&B Homestay*

Kathy Kearney-Deans
PO Box 16, Fox Glacier
21 State Highway 6, Fox Glacier

Tel (03) 751 0815
Fax (03) 751 0815
billy@xtra.co.nz

Double/Twin $105 - $135
Single $105 - $135
(Special breakfast)
Visa MC accepted
Not suitable for children
1 King 1 Double 1 Twin (2 bdrm)
Bathrooms: 1 Private 1 Guest share

Welcome to the comfort, warmth and hospitality of our 2 storey home. Our livingroom, kitchen, diningroom and veranda are upstairs and lined with local timbers, with 360-degree views of glacier valley, mountains, farms and the township. We're the closest homestay to the glacier and 2 minutes walk to all eating and tourist facilities. We are happy to book your local activities. The bus goes past our home. We offer a special cooked vegetarian breakfast. We have 1 cat, 1 small dog.

Fox Glacier *0.5 km SW of Fox Glacier*

The Homestead *B&B Farmstay*

Noeleen & Kevin Williams
PO Box 25, Cook Flat Road, Fox Glacier

Tel (03) 751 0835
Fax (03) 751 0805
foxhomestead@slingshot.co.nz

Double/Twin $140 - $180
(Full breakfast)
Cooked breakfast $7pp
Pet free home
Not suitable for children
1 King/Twin 1 King 1 Queen (3 bdrm)
Bathrooms: 2 Ensuite 1 Private

Kevin and Noeleen, welcome you to our 2200 acre beef cattle and sheep farm. Beautiful native bush-clad mountains surround on 3 sides, and we enjoy a view of Mt Cook.

Our spacious 105 year old character home, built for Kevin's grandparents, has fine stained glass windows. The breakfast room overlooks peaceful pastures to the hills, and you are served home-made yoghurt, jams, marmalade, scones etc, with a cooked breakfast if desired.

We are very well travelled internationally and enjoy discussing and learning of other countries, trips, etc. Kevin has a wealth of knowledge of farming and local family history; a descendant of the two pioneering families. He loves talking to farmers from other countries.

The guest lounge, with its beautiful wooden panelled ceiling, has an open fire for cool autumn nights. A rural retreat within walking distance of village facilities, with Matheson (Mirror Lake) and glacier nearby. It is our pleasure to help you with helihikes, helicopter scenic flights and glacier walks.

Unsuitable for small children. Bookings recommended. Smoke-free. Directions: On Cook Flat Road, fifth house on right, 400 metres back off road before church.

Fox Glacier *.5 km SW of Fox Glacier*
Fox Glacier Homestay *Homestay*
Eunice & Michael Sullivan
58 Cook Flat Road,
Fox Glacier

Tel (03) 751 0817
Fax (03) 751 0817
euni@xtra.co.nz

Double/Twin $90 - $120
Single $80 - $90
(Continental breakfast)
Children welcome
1 Queen 1 Double 1 Twin
1 Single (4 bdrm)
Bathrooms: 1 Family share

Eunice and Michael are third generation farming and tourism family. We have 3 grown children and 3 cats (Bushy Tail, Sabrina & Tig). Our grandparents were founders of the Fox Glacier Hotel. We are a couple who enjoy meeting people and would like to share the joys of living in our little paradise (rain and all). Our home is surrounded by a large garden and has views of the mountains and Mt Cook. A 5 minute walk from township.

Fox Glacier *.2 km N of Fox Glacier*
The White Fox B&B *B&B Homestay*
Jane Wellard & Gary Scott
4 State Highway 6, Fox Glacier
PO Box 82, Fox Glacier

Tel (03) 751 0717
or 027 306 6759
Fax (03) 751 0717
thewhitefox@slingshot.co.nz
www.thewhitefoxbandb.co.nz

Double/Twin $140 - $170
Single $120 - $150
(Continental breakfast)
Children negotiable by age
Visa MC accepted
Children welcome
Internet available
1 Queen 1 Single rollaway (1 bdrm)
Bathrooms: 1 Ensuite

Relax & enjoy the warmth & hospitality of a genuine NZ family home. Gary is a 4th generation local & we have considerable knowledge to assist our guests. We offer an easy to find location. Your room has a super comfortable bed, quality linen, electric blanket, TV & modern ensuite. Wake to the aroma of freshly baked bread & enjoy a generous Continental breakfast. We share our home with 2 young daughters Meghan-7 & Isla-5, Jess the aging Border Collie & Irish the Tabby Cat.

Canterbury
Reefton
Kaikoura
Hanmer Springs
7
1
Inchbonnie
Culverden
Castle Hill Village
Hawarden
73
Okuku
Oxford
Rangiora
Ohoka
Kaiapoi
Christchurch,
see next page
Darfield
Mt Hutt
72
Westhaven
Okains Bay
Methven
Banks
Peninsula
Staveley
Akaroa
Rakaia
Akaroa
Harbour
Ashburton
1
0   Kilometres   40
0   Miles   24

Christchurch
City
1
Christchurch
International
Airport
1
Harewood
Burnside
Papanui
Burwood
Bryndwr
Yaldhurst
Fendalton
Avonhead
Merivale
Ilam
Templeton
Riccarton
Christchurch
Central
1
Sydnham
Opawa
St Martins
Redcliffs
Mt Pleasant
Cashmere
Sumner
Huntsbury
Murray Aynsley
75
Lyttelton
Lincoln
Lyttelton
Harbour
Tai Tapu
Teddington
0
Kilometres
5
0
Miles
3
Canterbury

Kaikoura *130 km SW of Blenheim*

Bay-View HomeStay *Homestay*
Grandma Margaret Woodill
296 Scarborough Street, Kaikoura

Tel (03) 319 5480
Fax (03) 319 7480
bayviewhomestay@xtra.co.nz
www.bayviewhomestay.wordpress.com

Double/Twin $120
Single $70 (Full breakfast)
Children under 14 $30
Children and pets welcome
1 Queen 1 Twin 1 Single (3 bdrm)
Bathrooms: 1 Ensuite 2 Private

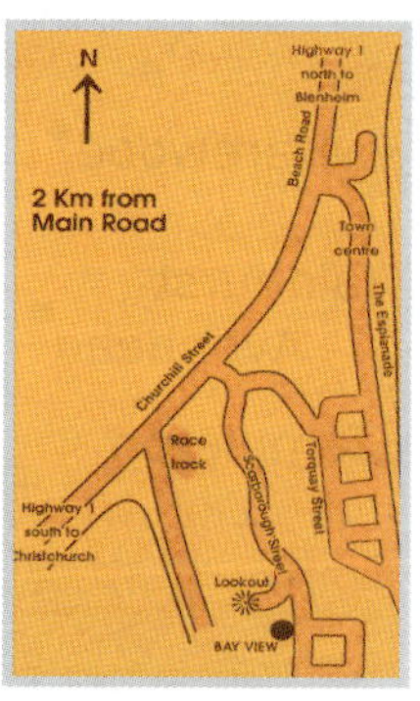

Margaret Woodill is the classic Kiwi grandmother and thinks nothing of getting up at 5.30am to cook a full breakfast including homemade bread before your whale-watching or dolphin swimming trip in Kaikoura, New Zealand. She's lived in her Kaikoura peninsula home with its sweeping views of sea and mountains since 1934.

She began taking in passing travellers over 20 years ago, just before the whales and dolphins turned the township into a tourist Mecca. When her four children left home, opening a bed and breakfast seemed a logical use for spare bedrooms and bathrooms. Since husband Bob's death in 1999, Margaret says guests are her family and that's why she calls it a HOMESTAY rather than a B&B.

In her one-acre garden she grows tomatoes to go with her home-laid eggs and the breakfast bacon. She bakes her own bread - without the aid of a bread-maker - and makes sure your dietary needs are met before your whale watching boat sails. This traditional kiwi cooked breakfast includes muesli & cereal, homemade preserves & jam and is available as early as required for whale/dolphin watching guests. Enjoy breakfast in the dining area or out on the sunny deck whilst taking in the magnificent mountain view.

This spacious family home is near the Kaikoura Lookout on Scarborough Street and is exceptionally quiet. It's only 5 minutes from the Kaikoura township, off the main highway south. The house rests on an acre of beautiful colourful garden and there is plenty of off-street parking. A guest lounge is available or you are more than welcome to socialise with Margaret.

Kaikoura - Oaro *22 km S of Kaikoura*
Waitane Homestay *B&B Homestay Cottage with Kitchen*

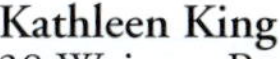

Kathleen King
38 Waitane Road,
Oaro,
RD 2,
Kaikoura

Tel (03) 319 5494
Fax (03) 319 5524
kathleen.king@xtra.co.nz

Double/Twin $85 - $95
Single $50
(Full breakfast)
Children $25
Dinner $25 by arrangement
Visa MC accepted
Children and pets welcome
1 Double 4 Single (3 bdrm)
1 in B&B, 2 in cottage
Bathrooms: 2 Private

Waitane is 48 acres, close to the sea and looking north to the Kaikoura Peninsula. Enjoy coastal walks to the Haumuri Bluff with bird watching, fossil hunting etc, or drive to Kaikoura along our beautiful rocky coast. This is a mild climate and we grow citrus and sub-tropical fruits, mainly feijoas. Guest room in house has 2 single beds. Self-contained unit has 2 bedrooms, sleeps 4. 1 friendly cat lives here. Join me for dinner - fresh vegies, home preserves and home-made ice cream.

Kaikoura *.2 km SE of Kaikoura Central*
Bendamere House *Luxury B&B*

Kerry and Julie Howden
37 Adelphi Terrace, Kaikoura

Tel (03) 319 5830
or 0800 107 770
Fax (03) 319 7337
bendamerehouse@xtra.co.nz
www.bendamere.co.nz

Double/Twin $160 - $220
Single $150 - $180
(Continental breakfast)
Children 14 years & over
Visa MC Diners Eftpos accepted
Not suitable for children
Internet available
3 King 2 Queen 2 Twin
3 Single (5 bdrm)
All ensuite rooms
Bathrooms: 5 Ensuite

Kaikoura's Bendamere House B&B offers you 5 quality ensuite rooms all with private balconies where you can enjoy the breathtaking ocean and mountain views. Relax in our expansive lawns and rose gardens or take a short stroll into the Kaikoura township .All rooms have sleepyhead beds, silent fridges,heat pumps, tea/coffee/bathrobes and more. Free wireless Internet and laundry facilities as well as secure offstreet parking.

Kaikoura *4 km NE of Kaikoura town centre*
The Point *B&B Homestay*
Peter & Gwenda Smith
85 Fyffe Quay,
Kaikoura

Tel (03) 319 5422
pointsmith@xtra.co.nz
www.pointbnb.co.nz

Double/Twin $110 - $140
Single $90 - $110
(Continental breakfast)
Visa MC accepted
2 Queen (2 bdrm)
Bathrooms: 2 Ensuite

Your hosts Peter and Gwenda welcome you to The Point, Kaikoura. Built in the late 1800's Enjoy the quiet and unique waterfront location of our 125 year old home, situated on a 90 acre Drysdale Sheep farm. Our daily Sheep Shearing Show provides a typical Kiwi Attraction for guests making this a popular stay. We have working dogs, one pet dog and a cat. While enjoying your continental breakfast - enjoy breathtaking views of the sea and the Kaikoura Seaward Mountain range. Facilities include wireless internet and off street parking. Ideally situated for Peninsula and Seal colony walks. Only a short walk to Kaikoura's top restaurants.

Kaikoura *1 km NW of Kaikoura Central*
Driftwood Villa B&B and cottage *B&B Cottage with Kitchen*
Deluxe B&B
Suzy & Chris Valkhoff
166A Beach Road, Kaikoura

Tel 027 476 7000
stayatdriftwoodvilla@xtra.co.nz
www.driftwoodvilla.co.nz

Double/Twin $140 - $180
Single $95 - $125
(Full breakfast)
Children 2 years and under free,
Up to 15 years $10
Full use of kitchen
Visa MC accepted
Children welcome
Internet Available
1 King 3 Queen 1 Twin
4 Single (6 bdrm)
4 bedrooms in B&B, 2 in cottage
Bathrooms: 4 Ensuite 1 Private bath in cottage only

Bed and Breakfast with a difference! Our Qualmark 4 star Villa enjoys access to the beach and good mountain views. It is set up specifically for Guests enjoyment. You have use of all the facilities in the Villa including a large kitchen, living areas, outdoor spa plus FREE internet when mentioning this book on booking. Many guests have commented how wonderful and relaxed a stay they have had having use of the entire house. Hosts: Chris and/or Suzy and daughters Annabelle, 5 and Sophie, 3.

Kaikoura *130 km S of Blenheim*

A Rest-n-Kai *B&B*

Carmel Tindall
5 Fyffe Ave,
Kaikoura

Tel (03) 319 7330
cartin@slingshot.co.nz
www.arestnkai.co.nz

Double/Twin $130 - $150
Single $50 - $70
(Full breakfast)
Children $20
Babies $10
Pet free home
Children welcome
Internet available
1 Queen 1 Single (2 bdrm)
1 Queen/ 1 Single
Bathrooms: 1 Ensuite 1 Family share

Welcome to my home where I offer a Rest-n-Kai. Kai meaning food in Maori. I am a retired nurse and still enjoy caring for people. The home is comfortable, with lovely mountain views from the main rooms and external access from the large bedroom. A short walk into the township, waterfront and other attractions including Whalewatch and Dolphin Encounter. I am happy to assist guests with directions and bookings. Many complimentary comments in visitors book indicate satisfaction with A Rest-n-Kai.

Kaikoura - Mangamaunu *15 km N of Kaikoura*

'Surfwatch' *B&B Separate Suite Cottage with Kitchen*

Lynn & David Robinson
1137 State Hwy One,
Mangamaunu, 7371

Tel (03) 319 6611
or 027 616 2903
Fax (03) 319 6658
bnb@ofu.co.nz
www.surfwatchbnb.com

Double/Twin $250 - $250
Single $250 - $250
(Continental breakfast)
Best for children over the age of 8
Visa MC accepted
Internet available
1 King 1 Queen 1 Single (2 bdrm)
1 Ensuite, 1 Cottage
Bathrooms: 1 Ensuite 1 Private

The views here say it all. Five acres of tranquil rural country setting with stunning views overlooking the Pacific Ocean. Quiet and relaxing, melt away the city hustle-bustle in our spacious lawn and gardens. From the OceanView Ensuite you can watch dolphins play while Sharkeys Cottage is nestled in the garden. Both have kitchenettes, private entrances, parking, and are uniquely decorated with local wood and stone. Enjoy breakfast at your leisure. Wireless broadband. Lynn, David, Jessica and dogface Layla look forward to meeting you.

Kaikoura *130 km SW of Blenheim*
Churchill Park Lodge *B&B Separate Suite*
Gordon & Priscilla Wright
34 Churchill Street, Kaikoura, Marlborough

Tel (03) 319 5526 or 0800 363 690
cplodge@ihug.co.nz
www.churchillparklodge.co.nz

Double/Twin $130
Single $100 (Continental breakfast)
Children by arrangement
Extra guests Add $30 per night
Visa MC accepted
1 Queen 1 Double 1 Twin (2 bdrm)
Self contained unit
Bathrooms: 2 Ensuite

Churchill park lodge is conveniently located in central Kaikoura on SHWY1 (Churchill street) on the hill capturing the magnificent Kaikoura mountain and sea views.

We welcome you to our purpose built, self contained upstair units with ensuite bathrooms (the double ensuite is compact but well appointed). We get many guests comment on how comfy the beds are. The units have T.V., fridge, lounge settee, dining suite, balcony table and chairs, heating and electric blankets with tea and coffee making facilities including plunger coffee. There is also off street parking and a private guest entrance with laundry facilities available. We serve a continental breakfast to your room for you to enjoy at your leisure. We believe the sea and mountain views from your room are unbeatable in Kaikoura.

Our B&B is only 5 minutes walk through Churchill park to the town centre. Where you will find shops, restaurants, cafes, the information centre and beach.

Cilla & Gordon are a down to earth 'Kiwi' couple who are keen fishermen. You are welcome to join us on any trips we have planned, checking the lobster pots, catching a fish by boat or surfcasting from the beach. Also the local stream has many brown trout which are very challenging to catch. We have two friendly dogs (who do not have access to the guest area) 'Miss Spanky' a fun Bichon/Tibetan terrier X and 'Xena' an aging pointer. We can book local activities or tours, and will happily meet you at the bus.

South Bay - Kaikoura *130 km S of Blenheim*
Ann's B & B *B&B*

Ann and Brent Fearnley
28 Moa Road,
Kaikoura, 7300

Tel (03) 319 5586
or 0274 521 075
Fax (03) 319 5584
brent.fearnley@xtra.co.nz

Double/Twin $120
Single $70
(Continental breakfast)
Pet free home
Children welcome
Internet available
1 Queen 1 Twin (2 bdrm)
Spacious and comfortable,
Queen and King Single Beds
Bathrooms: 1 Guest share

We have a great location very close to the beginning of the stunning Peninsula Walk Track and beach walks. Our lounge and dining areas offer excellent views of the mountains and the sea. We are a friendly couple with 4 grown children. Ann enjoys art and Brent's a keen hunter. We have spacious guest rooms, comfortable beds and a new guest bathroom. We offer a Continental Breakfast. We can offer local knowledge and are keen to help make your stay enjoyable.

Hanmer Springs *0.1 km E of in Hanmer village*
Cheltenham House *Boutique Heritage B&B Cottage Apartment*

Maree & Len Earl
13 Cheltenham Street,
Hanmer Springs

Tel (03) 315 7545
or 0274 547 205
Fax (03) 315 7645
enquiries@cheltenham.co.nz
www.cheltenham.co.nz

Double/Twin $220 - $280
Single $190 - $230
(Special breakfast)
Children by arrangement
B&B extra $50pp. Villa $20pp
Visa MC Diners Eftpos accepted
Children and pets welcome
Internet Aavailable
4 King/Twin 7 Queen 1 Single (10 bdrm)
4 in-house suites + 2 garden suites at B&B. 4 bedrooms in Villa
Bathrooms: 8 Ensuite 1 Private 5 ensuites + 1 private at B&B. 3 bathrooms in Villa

Situated 200 metres from the Thermal Pools, restaurants & forest walks, this gracious heritage B&B has four spacious, sunny suites in the house & two in the park like grounds. Central heating throughout. Enjoy a gourmet breakfast served in your own suite and complimentary wines in the billiard room in the evening. Star-gaze from the garden spa. Free wireless internet. Alternately enjoy our new 5 star self contained villa with its magnificent views. Together with our sociable Siamese & Labrador, we look forward to meeting you.

Hanmer Springs *1 km SW of Hanmer Springs*

Albergo Hanmer Lodge & Alpine Villas *Luxury B&B Separate Suite Apartment with Kitchen Cottage with Kitchen B&B & Self-contained Villas*

Lindsay and Johanne
88 Rippingale Road, Hanmer Springs

Tel 0800 342 313 or (03) 315 7428
Fax (03) 315 7428   albergo@paradise.net.nz
www.albergohanmer.com

Double/Twin $160 - $270
Single $120 (Special breakfast)
Villa $260-$525 Visa MC accepted
Children welcome Internet Available
3 King/Twin 1 King 1 Queen 2 Single (3 bdrm)
Bathrooms: 4 Ensuite

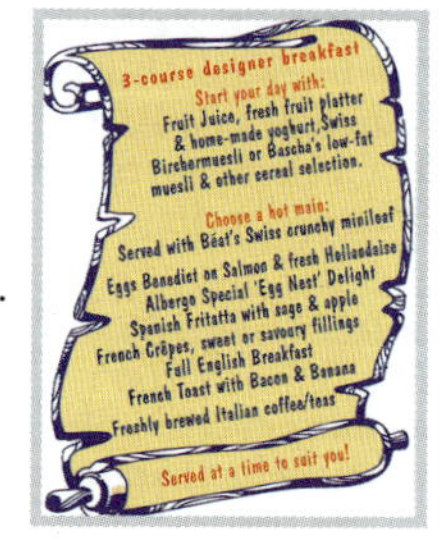

BREAKFAST - WELLNESS - CUISINE

Arrive at Albergo to blitz your senses in the fresh n' fun eclectic interiors with whimsical touches. **Dramatic alpine views** from all windows. **Stretch out on super king beds**, with TV/fridge/tea & coffee, and spacious ensuites (great water pressure) - choose the spa one for that bubble bath delight! European comforts for all seasons: u/floor heat, double glaze, aircon. Relax in cosy corners or wander out to the sunken Feng Shui courtyard, with soothing waterfall & fragrant lavenders galore. **Privacy & all day sun:** 2 minutes from Hot Pools, shops & cafes, or via new scenic walkway.

For privacy plus choose one of the stand alone Alpine Villas, with self-catering options. The awesome cinema & DVD library compliments the superb American king bedroom with large ensuite, boasting 'wow' views from the high panorama window, while you shower! Slip on a fluffy bathrobe, wander out to the split-level courtyard with private Jacuzzi and soak up Hanmer's starry night skies.

Go WOW over Albergo's renowned 3-course breakfast, served at a time to suit you, offering over 10 choices: Creative fruit platters or Swiss Birchermuesli, followed by the wafting smell of **homemade Swiss breads, & fine Italian coffee**. This perfect fusion of NZ & Swiss cuisine features: Salmon Eggs Benedict, French fluffy omelets, wafer-thin crepes, 'Albergo Egg Nests' or 'Full English', with crispy bacon. Fondue dinners by prior arrangement.
'Best breakfasts ever and Gold award for porridge' Sheila Bennett, NYC. *'Loved the milk jug containing cow - the decor and food was divine'* Charlotte, UK. *'Your quirky decors are a feast for the eyes, what an accommodation experience'* Gavin & Kerrie, Brisbane

DIRECTIONS: At junction before main village, 300m past Caltex Garage, take Argelins Rd (Centre branch), take 2nd road left Rippingale Rd.

Hanmer Springs *005 km N of village centre*
Hanmer View *Luxury B&B*

Margaux & Paul Delamain
8 Oregon Heights,
Hanmer Springs, 7334

Tel (03) 315 7947
or 027 431 9620
Fax (03) 315 7947
hanmerview@xtra.co.nz
www.hanmerview.co.nz

Double/Twin $180 - $260
Single $150 - $210
(Full breakfast)
Visa MC accepted
Not suitable for children
Internet available
1 King/Twin 1 King
1 Queen (3 bdrm)
Ensuited with views and balcony access

Hanmer View adjoining the forest and Conical Hill walkway enjoys stunning panoramic views of the village and Hanmer Basin. Enjoy a tranquil stay in air-conditioned ensuited rooms with views and balcony. Margaux and Paul with their cats and dog have pleasure in welcoming you and ensuring you have an enjoyable stay at Hanmer View. We are happy to help you choice and enjoyment of the activities Hanmer Springs and its environs offer. Stroll to the village centre and pools. Special packages and wireless internet available.

Hanmer Springs
Amuri House *Luxury Boutique B&B*

Barbara & Paul Faulkner
10 Amuri Avenue,
Hanmer Springs

Tel (03) 315 7985
Fax (03) 315 7986
paul.faulkner@xtra.co.nz
www.amurihousehanmersprings.co.nz

Double/Twin $165 - $195
Single $165 - $175
(Full breakfast)
Book Early for World Cup
Visa MC Eftpos accepted
Not suitable for children
Internet available
2 Queen (2 bdrm)
Guests have own entrance
Bathrooms: 2 Ensuite

Amuri House offers luxury boutique Bed & Breakfast accommodation, perfectly located just 3 minutes walk to the village centre, the renowned Hanmer Springs Thermal Pools & Spa and cafe's, restaurants & shopping. Whether you are a honeymooning couple or just wanting to get away for a weekend, Amuri House is the ideal place to base yourselves to enjoy the delightful alpine village of Hanmer and the surrounding area. Your hosts Barbara and Paul welcome you and take pride in offering friendly hospitality and first class service. Their dog, Miss Molly loves guests but does not go into any of the guest areas.

Culverden *3 km S of Culverden*
Ballindalloch *Farmstay*

Diane & Dougal Norrie
Longplantation Road,
Culverden,
RD 2,
North Canterbury, 7392

Tel (03) 315 8220
or 027 437 3184
Fax (03) 315 8220
norrie@amuri.net

Double/Twin $140
Single $100
(Full breakfast)
Children $40
Dinner $40 by arrangement
Children welcome
1 Queen 2 Single (2 bdrm)
Bathrooms: 1 Guest share

Welcome to 'Ballindalloch'a family farming enterprise with 3 family members farming on their own behalf on 4,000 acre irrigated farms, now milking 3,000 cows. We are just over 1 hour north of Christchurch, half an hour to Hanmer Springs, 1 1/2 hours to Kaikoura Whale Watch. Culverden is situated between 2 excellent fishing rivers. Having travelled extensively overseas we appreciate relaxing in a homely atmosphere - this we extend to our guests. We look forward to welcoming you to our home. A new addition to our family is Oscar, a spoodle pup.

Hawarden *2 km N of Hawarden*
The Dutch Station *Apartment with Kitchen Countrystay: Luxury B&B*

Rein Bakker & Gertruud Steltenpool
135 Bentleys Road, RD 1, 7385

Tel (03) 314 2200 or 021 261 3461
info@thedutchstation.co.nz
www.thedutchstation.co.nz

Double/Twin $100 - $170
Single $70 - $75 (Full breakfast)
Children $15; please contact us first
Dinner by arrangement
See our website www.thedutchstation.
co.nz for further information
and arrangements
Children and pets welcome
1 King 1 Queen 2 Single (4 bdrm)
B&B: Kingbed, separate bed for child
Self contained suite (2 bedrooms):
Queen/Kingsingle+Single
Bathrooms: 1 Ensuite 1 Private
Sliding showers; ensuite with shower over bath and bidet

Vision: being the most caring host in a carefree environment. Located on 17 ha with great views on the Southern Alps in rural peaceful surroundings. Luxury accommodation, friendly hosts and free Dutch Golf - on own course (unique in the Southern Hemisphere). What else do you want? Self-contained unit: 2 bedrooms, bathroom, fully equipped kitchen, living, satellite TV. B&B-room (en-suite): coffee/tea facilities, satellite TV, extra bed. We have a cat, a dog and 2 alpaca's, which you can handfeed.

Rangiora - Fernside *5 km SW of Rangiora*
Petes Farm Stay B&B *B&B Farmstay*

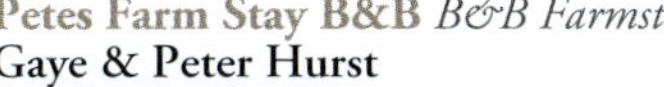

Gaye & Peter Hurst
45 Mairaki Road,
Rangiora RD 1, 7471

Tel (03) 313 5180
or 027 221 8989
Fax (03) 313 5182
petesfarm@xtra.co.nz
petesfarm.co.nz

Double/Twin $150 - $170
Single $100 - $120
(Continental breakfast)
Children half price
Dinner $40 per person
Included in price is sheep
shearing demo and farm tour
Visa MC accepted
Children welcome
1 King/Twin 1 King 1 Queen 1 Double 2 Single (4 bdrm)
Large spacious and great views
Bathrooms: 1 Ensuite 2 Private

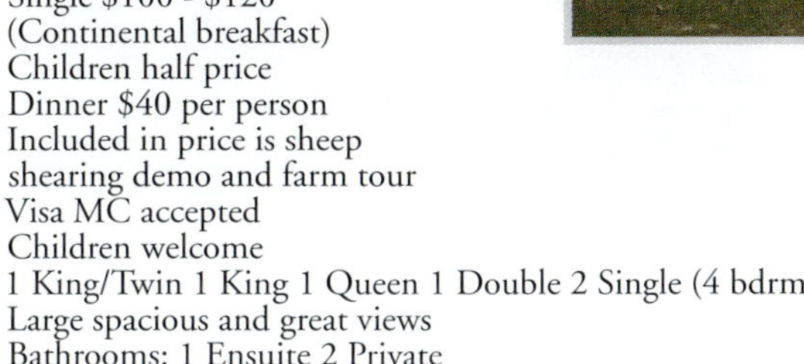

Welcome to Pete's Farm B&B. We are situated 25 minutes from Christchurch Airport & City. Also just seconds off Inland Scenic Route 72. See a sheep shearing and dog demo. Relax in our new home and experience first hand the quietness and great views we get from every room in the house.

Oxford *60 km SW of Christchurch*
Country Life *B&B Apartment with Kitchen*

Helen Dunn
137 High Street,
Oxford,
North Canterbury, 7430

Tel (03) 312 4167

Double/Twin $75 - $100
Single $45 - $60
(Full breakfast)
Dinner $20 by arrangement
Children and pets welcome
4 Twin (2 bdrm)
Self Contained Unit -
2 Twin beds, kitchen & ensuite,
2 Twin in house - bathroom handy
Bathrooms: 1 Ensuite 1 Family share

Country life has been operating since 1987, the house is 80 years old and has a spacious garden, warm and sunny. Helen enjoys meeting people from far and wide - whether overseas visitors or those wanting a peaceful break away from Christchurch - all are welcomed at Country Life. High Street is left off the Main Road. Sign outside the gate.

Oxford *54 km SW of Christchurch Airport*
Hielan' House *B&B Homestay Farmstay Countrystay*

Shirley & John Farrell
74 Bush Road, Oxford,
North Canterbury

Tel (03) 312 4382
or 0800 279 382 (freephone)
Fax (03) 312 4382
hielanhouse@ihug.co.nz
www.hielanhouse.co.nz

Double/Twin $150 - $175
Single $120 - $140
(Full breakfast)
Children price on application
Dinner by arrangement
Visa MC accepted
Children and pets welcome
Internet available
1 King/Twin 1 Queen (2 bdrm)
Bathrooms: 2 Ensuite

Quality upstairs guest rooms with relaxing areas, ensuites, separate entrance. TV/DVD, tea/coffee facilities, fridges, hairdryers, bathrobes, slippers. Complimentary laundry, internet, sauna, spa, outdoor swimming pool, golf clubs to use. Safe parking. Enjoy John's breakfasts, dinners with home-grown meat/vegetables. Relax, unwind on 6 acres in peaceful, rural Oxford or stay longer and make us your base for day trips to Arthurs Pass, Hamner, Akaroa. Situated 3 mins from Inland Scenic Route 72, via Bay/Bush Roads. We enjoy meeting people and look forward to spoiling you.

Oxford *5 km N of Oxford*
Pumula Country Stay *Farmstay*

Jaccy Creak
729 Depot Road,
RD 1, Oxford 7495

Tel (03) 312 3377
or 027 474 7655
Fax (03) 312 3377
jaccy@pumula.co.nz
www.pumula.co.nz

Double/Twin $105 - $130
Single $80 - $100
(Breakfast by arrangment,
included in tarriff)
Children $60
Dinner $30
Visa MC accepted
Children and pets welcome
1 Queen 1 Double 1 Twin 1 Single (4 bdrm)
Bathrooms: 1 Ensuite 1 Private

Pumula offers you a doorway and jump off point to the Alpine region of New Zealand. place to recharge your batteries and relax, experience the large range of recreational, leisure activities in the area or just stay around the farmstay and hear the wind rustle through the trees. We, with our menagerie of animals - 6 donkeys, 2 little dogs, 1 cat and Ruby the rabbit(no empty nest syndrome here), Donkey cart rides and Cheese making in the kitchen demos by arrangment.

Ohoka *6 km SW of Kaiapoi*
Oakhampton Lodge *B&B*

Angus & Jackie Watson
24 Keetly Place, Ohoka,
Kaiapoi, RD 2, 7692

Tel 03 3126413
or 021 502 313
Fax 03 3126314
info@oakhampton.co.nz
www.oakhampton.co.nz

Double/Twin $150 - $180
(Full breakfast)
Not suitable for young children
Dinner $35 dinner available on request
Visa MC accepted
1 King 1 Queen 1 Twin (2 bdrm)
All bedrooms have views or
access to large country garden
Bathrooms: 2 Ensuite

Set amongst 4 acres of lawns, mature trees and herbaceous borders, Oakhampton Lodge is the perfect place to unwind and experience a slice of country life. Ideal for weekend stays or as a stopover while travelling around New Zealand. Heading north from Christchurch on the Northern Motorway (SH1) take second Kaiapoi/Ohoka turnoff over Waimakariri River, follow signs to Ohoka. Keetly Place is 6 kms along Mill Rd, on right, just before Ohoka Hall and Service Station. No 24 is on your right.

Kaiapoi *15 km N of Christchurch*
Morichele *B&B*

Helen & Richard Moore
25 Hilton Street,
Kaiapoi

Tel (03) 327 5247
morichele@xtra.co.nz

Double/Twin $100
Single $70
(Full breakfast)
Children negotiable
Dinner by arrangement
1 Double 1 Twin (2 bdrm)
Comfortable
Bathrooms: 1 Guest share

Helen & Richard+ Sooky the cat provide comfortable accommodation in a beautiful garden setting, close to rivers, beaches, golf course and walks. With off-street parking, own entrance, sitting/dining area with fridge, tea and coffee making facilities, TV and video. Cafes and restaurants within walking distance alternatively, if you prefer, you are welcome to bring back takeaways or barbeque in the garden. Ski fields, Hanmer Springs themal reserve, Akaroa (home of the Hector's Dolphin) and Kaikoura (whale watching)are less than two hours away.

Kaiapoi *22 km N of Christchurch*
Copper Beech *Luxury B&B*

Anita & Greg Inwood
273 Woodend Beach Road,
RD 1, Kaiapoi 7691

Tel (03) 312 7999 or 027 712 7999
enquiries@copperbeechnz.com
www.copperbeechnz.com

Double/Twin $120 - $190
Single $90 - $120 (Full breakfast)
Children welcome by arrangement
Dinner by arrangement: Kiwi Roast
Lamb, Seafood our speciality
Tours: Guided Walks, Hunting,
Fishing, Classic car tours, Local
Vineyards and Thermal Pools
Visa MC accepted
Pets welcome   Internet Available
1 King 2 Queen 1 Twin 1 Single (4 bdrm) Modern & Warm
Bathrooms: 1 Ensuite 1 Private 1 Guest share 1 Family share
Ensuite with 2 person spa bath and twin shower with rain head

Copper Beech is ideally situated for visitors to Christchurch, only 1 km from SH1. 20mins to: Christchurch Airport, Christchurch 'The Garden City', Waipara Vineyard Trail. Our comfortable well appointed substaintial home is set on 8.5 acres with established English garden with picturesque lake. Relax in our peaceful private garden. We have 2 outside dogs & 2 house cats as well farm animals. Local Beach, Woodend Village, New Pegasus Town with beautiful feature lake including Wetland board walks & 18 hole International Golf Course all within 5 mins.

Kaiapoi - Mandeville *20 km N of Christchurch*
Ohoka Meadows B&B / Gatehouse Cottage *B&B Farmstay Cottage*

Mary and Graeme Chisnall
49 Ohoka Meadows Drive,
RD 2,
Kaiapoi, 7692

Tel (03) 3131781
or 0274 311979
ohokameadows@xtra.co.nz
www.ohokameadows.co.nz

Double/Twin $150 - $220
Single $120 - $150
(Full breakfast)
Children price on application
Dinner by arrangement
Children welcome
1 King 1 Queen 1 Twin (2 bdrm)
2 in B&B, 1 in cottage
Bathrooms: 3 Ensuite

Graeme and Mary welcome you into their home.Enjoy privacy and peace while staying in modern B&B rooms with your own facilities, our luxurious fully equipped Gatehouse Cottage with full kitchen. Chester and Devon, the alpacas are a treat to feed. Enjoy 4 acres of landscaped grounds and admire the mountains. Only 22 kms to Christchurch International Airport and Shopping Malls. Our interests include model engineers, jetboating, teaching and entertaining guests. Enquire about a package deal including all meals.

Christchurch - West Melton *22 km NW of*

Haven on Weedons *Luxury B&B Homestay Cottage No Kitchen*

Judy and Stephen Tucker
975 Weedons Ross Road, West Melton, 7675

Tel (03) 347 8149 or 021 223 372
Fax (03) 343 1498   haven.farm@xtra.co.nz

Double/Twin $165 - $365 Single $120 - $245 (Full breakfast)
Dinner Wide selection see menu for costs
Special on request available
Visa MC Eftpos accepted
Not suitable for children   Internet Available
3 King 2 Single (4 bdrm)
Each room has an ensuite, television
Bathrooms: 4 Ensuite
Deluxe room has corner spa and double head shower,
superior room has a bath and shower

This rural picturesque private setting is only 15 minutes from the airport and 20 minutes from the city centre (rugby Stadium). Judy and Stephens 400 square metre home was designed to cater for guests on a 35 acre farmlet . They have a bichon frise dog (Rosie) , 3 legged cat (Chelsa), alpacas , poultry , cattle , wild quail , feasants and rabbits . The home is surrounded by mature trees and offers privacy and peace with all the luxuries like outdoor spa pool , sauna and exercise equipment. Every bedroom has its own television with ensuite and external access .

Judy is experienced in business and catering having just retired recently while Stephen is ceo/director of a national franchise network . Stephen and Judy enjoy socialising having guests and have travelled extensivley . Add to this the home its idealy located to use as a base being only approx 10 minutes from a major fishing river all major hiways , local vinyards and race tracks and one hour 20 minutes from the picturesk village Hamner for natural (thermal pools) and the Akoroa French town port . Stephen and Judy can pick you up from the airport and will help arrange any trips or tranfers you wish to make.

Christchurch - Harewood *3 km E of Christchurch Int Airport*

AirportGuestHouse *Guest House*

Alan & Deb Jackson
283 Wooldridge Road,
Harewood,
Christchurch 8051

Tel (03) 359 6682
or 0800 359 622
Fax (03) 359 6692
enquiries@airportguesthouse.co.nz
www.airportguesthouse.co.nz

Double/Twin $100 - $120
Single $80 - $90
(Breakfast by arrangement)
Children under 5 free in same room
Dinner by negotiation
Visa MC accepted
Children and pets welcome
1 Double 1 Twin 1 Single (3 bdrm)
Bathrooms: 1 Guest share

Friendly family atmosphere. 10 mins from city centre. 3 mins from airport. Country setting within City living. Close to cafes, resturants, wineries, parks, shops & bus stops.

Christchurch - Harewood *7.5 km N of Christchurch Centre*

St James B&B *Luxury B&B*

Margaret Frankish
125 Waimakariri Road,
Harewood,
Christchurch 8005

Tel (03) 359 6259
or 027 455 3554
Fax (03) 359 6299
dj.frankish@xtra.co.nz
www.stjamesbnb.com

Double/Twin $120 - $180
Single $95 - $120
(Full breakfast)
Children $40
Visa MC accepted
Children welcome
1 King 1 Queen 1 Single (2 bdrm)
Bathrooms: 1 Ensuite 1 Private

Located 5 minutes from Christchurch Airport, 10 minutes from city. Begin/ end your South Island trip in our warm, modern home with its tranquil garden setting, and the horses who share our 3 acre property. Our lovely guest rooms include private lounges, ensuite bathroom and private spa/bathroom upstairs. Rooms have tea/coffee facilities and TV. Internet access is available. Our beautiful spoodle collects the daily newspaper. Close by are golf courses, excellent restaurants, shopping, Wildlife Reserve, McLeans Island Recreation Area and Antarctic Centre.

Christchurch - Avonhead *8 km SW of Christchurch Central*
Gladsome Lodge *B&B*

Stuart & Sue Barr
314 Yaldhurst Road,
Avonhead, Christchurch 8042

Tel (03) 342 7414 or 0800 222 617
Fax (03) 342 3414
sue@gladsomelodge.com
www.gladsomelodge.com

Double/Twin $110 - $140
Single $100 - $115 (Full breakfast)
Children 0-5 free, 5-12 $20
Dinner $25 by arrangement
Cooked breakfast available
Visa MC accepted
Children welcome
3 Queen 1 Double 1 Twin
2 Single (5 bdrm)
Bathrooms: 2 Ensuite 3 Guest share

Located close to airport with easy access to key attractions. Be assured of professional, attentive hosting in a friendly environment. Enjoy our tennis court, swimming pool or sauna. Guest wireless internet access available. We are able to accommodate family groups travelling together. Have knowledge of Maori history and culture. Our spacious home is centrally heated. On site parking. On bus route to city. On route to ski fields and West Coast Highway.Outside friendly dog. Hosts Sue and Stuart, New Zealanders who have travelled and have a wide variety of interests. Warmly welcome you.

Christchurch - Burnside *7 km SW of Christchurch*
Airport Stableford B&B *B&B*

Margaret & Tony Spowart
2 Stableford Green,
Burnside,
Christchurch, 8053

Tel (03) 358 3264
or 021 883 804
stableford@xtra.co.nz
www.stableford.co.nz

Double/Twin $140
Single $130
(Full breakfast)
Visa MC accepted
2 Queen 1 Twin (3 bdrm)
Bathrooms: 2 Ensuite 1 Private

Welcome to Stableford, the closest B&B to the Christchurch Airport, making it ideal for arriving or departing visitors. Airport transfers and city bus-stop at door. We are situated adjacent to the Russley Golf Club. Stableford is new, clean, warm and comfortable with a separate guest lounge. All bedrooms have their own ensuite or bathroom with a powerful shower. Secure off street parking available. Good restaurants nearby. Our interests are travel, sport, music, & antiques. Cat and small dog in residence. Ask about our winter rates. Come and enjoy our beautiful home.

Christchurch - Burnside *8 km NW of City Centre*
Blossom Tree Homestay *B&B Homestay*

Lorna Watson
29 O'Connor Place,
Burnside,
Christchurch 8053

Tel (03) 358 2635
Fax (03) 358 2665
blossomtree@xtra.co.nz

Double/Twin $100 - $120
Single $60 - $80
(Continental breakfast)
Children $20
Children welcome
1 Queen 1 Double 2 Single (3 bdrm)
Bathrooms: 2 Private 1 Guest share

Located 5 minutes from Christchurch Airport, free transfer to and from airport, car hire depots very close, 15 minutes from City Centre. Good bus services closeby. Russley Golf Course and a variety of excellent restaurants and cafes nearby. Modern 10 year old home, along with it's owners, Lorna & Lyndsay and lovely cat Emma, welcomes bed & breakfast guests. Enjoy lovely surroundings and a generous continental breakfast. Off-street parking and laundry facilities available. We look forward to welcoming you.

Christchurch - Ilam *7.5 km NW of Christchurch*
Anne & Tony Fogarty Homestay *B&B Homestay*

Anne & Tony Fogarty
7 Westmont Street,
Ilam,
Christchurch, 8041

Tel (03) 358 2762
Fax (03) 358 2766
tony.fogarty@xtra.co.nz

Double/Twin $100
Single $60
(Continental breakfast)
Dinner $30 by arrangement
Visa MC accepted
4 Single (2 bdrm)
Bathrooms: 1 Guest share
1 Family share

Our home is in the beautiful suburb of Ilam, only minutes from Canterbury University and Canterbury University College of Education. Close to Christchurch Airport (7 minutes by car) and the railway station (10 minutes). A bus stop to the central city, with its many attractions is 50 metres from our home. Willing to arrange transport from airport or train.Excellent local information. Guests are welcome to use our laundry. Complimentary tea and coffee at any time. Stay with us and get value for money.

Christchurch - Papanui *5 km E of Christchurch Airport*
Heatherston Boutiqe Bed and Breakfast *Luxury B&B*

Jan and Murray Binnie
46 Searells Road,
Christchurch, 8052

Tel (03) 355 3239
or 027 418 8961
Fax (03) 355 3259
enquiries@heatherston.co.nz
www.heatherston.co.nz

Double/Twin $130 - $180
Single $120
(Full breakfast)
Not suitable for children
2 King/Twin 1 Queen
1 Single (3 bdrm)
Bathrooms: 3 Ensuite

Comfortable, convenient and quiet. A superbly situated, purpose-built, modern house with every convenience, only ten minutes from the Airport, and ten minutes from Central Christchurch. Heatherston has a sunny guests' kitchenette/lounge, bedrooms with comfortable beds, refreshment facilities, and television. Ensuites have heated towel rails, hairdryers and toiletries. Heatherston is close to shops and restaurants, and is conveniently located for sight-seeing in the city, or travelling to wineries, walking tracks, golf courses, and skifields. Heatherston is the perfect tranquil retreat!

Christchurch - Fendalton *5.0 km NW of Christchurch city centre*
230 c Glenveagh B&B *B&B*

Alison & Ian Boyd
230C Clyde Road,
Fendalton, Christchurch

Tel (03) 351 4407
or 0800 000 107
Fax (03) 351 4406
boyd45@xtra.co.nz
www.glenveagh.co.nz

Double/Twin $130 - $190
Single $130 - $150
(Continental breakfast)
Children by arrangement
Visa MC Amex accepted
Internet Available
1 King/Twin 1 Queen
1 Twin 2 Single (3 bdrm)
King/twin/triple/ queen/twin/single
Bathrooms: 1 Ensuite 1 Private

Ian & Alison welcome you to our beautiful home in a quiet area of Fendalton, Christchurch. Just off airport,city road. We have three guest rooms, upstairs and downstairs a lounge, courtyard. Tralee: King/twin/triple with ensuite and TV. Erigal: Twin with private bathroom and TV. Galway: Queen with private bathroom and TV. Restaurants within walking distance. Off-street parking. Courtesy car from airport, bus, train. Five minutes by car to central city, bus at gate. Wireless internet. Continental breakfast. No smoking inside. Look forward to your company.

Christchurch - Riccarton *6 km SW of City centre*
Thistle Guest House *B&B Guest House*

John and Alison Goodfellow
21 Main South Road,
Church Corner,
Upper Riccarton,
Christchurch, 8042

Tel (03) 348 1499
or 0800 93 21 21
Fax (03) 348 1577
stay@thistleguesthouse.co.nz
www.thistleguesthouse.co.nz

Double/Twin $86 - $96
Single $58 - $78
(Continental breakfast)
Visa MC Amex Eftpos accepted
Children welcome
1 King 4 Queen 3 Twin
4 Single (10 bdrm)
Bathrooms: 1 Ensuite 3 Guest share

A small friendly guest house offering quality homestyle accommodation. 10 private bedrooms with fridge, tea/coffee facilities and wireless internet access for laptops. Fully equipped guest kitchen, lounge, off-street parking and attractive garden. Laundry facilities and guest telephone also available. Handy to Canterbury University and College of Education and two minutes walk to shops, restaurants and supermarket. On good bus route to city (15 mins) and 10 minutes drive from airport. Courtesy pick-up by arrangement. Weekly rates and tariffs excluding breakfast also available.

Christchurch - Bryndwr *5 km NW of Christchurch City centre*
Condell Gardens B & B *B&B*

Barbara and Murray Matthews
95 Condell Avenue,
Christchurch, 8053

Tel (03) 352 8127
or 0800 216 943
Fax (03) 352 8126
condellgardens@xtra.co.nz
www.condellgardens.co.nz

Double/Twin $130 - $150
Single $115 - $125
(Continental breakfast)
Children by arrangement
Dinner by arrangement
Visa MC accepted
Internet available
1 Queen (1 bdrm)
Bathrooms: 1 Ensuite

We look forward to welcoming you with everything you need for a relaxing visit. Private, peaceful garden setting, a few minutes drive from airport. Spacious, comfortably furnished, air-conditioned guestroom to relax in, with independent entrance and garden views. Own garden doorway. Lounge furniture, tea/coffee facilities, fridge, TV in room. Free wireless broadband. Phone/fax, computer, bicycles, barbeque, laundry facilities available. Generous continental breakfast. Meals, cooked breakfast and special requests by arrangement. Secure off-street parking. On bus route and near cycleway to city centre. Complimentary airport transfers.

Christchurch - Bryndwr *5 km NW of city centre*

Rowan House *B&B Homestay*

Patricia and Win Clancey
89A Aorangi Rd,
Bryndwr,
Christchurch, 8053

Tel (03) 351 6092
Fax 03 351 6092
wclancey@xtra.co.nz
www.rowanhousebedandbreakfast.com

Double/Twin $140 - $150
Single $100 - $110
(Full breakfast)
Children By arrangement
Visa MC accepted
Children welcome
Internet available
2 Queen (2 bdrm)
En suite with queen bed
Bathrooms: 2 Ensuite

We warmly welcome you to our spacious, quiet, comfortable home set in attractive gardens. Two large en suite rooms with queen beds, each with TV, heating and tea/coffee facilities. A sunroom is available as a private lounge. Generous breakfasts and home baking. Four excellent restaurants nearby. Close to airport, fast access to city centre with bus stop near gate. We are widely travelled, love meeting people and sharing experiences. Happy to help you plan your trip. Courtesy pick-up. Off street parking. Laundry facilities.

Christchurch - Merivale *2 km N of Christchurch*

Leinster B&B *B&B Homestay*

Kay and Brian Smith
34B Leinster Road,
Merivale,
Christchurch

Tel (03) 355 6176
or 027 433 0771
Fax (03) 355 6176
brian.kay@xtra.co.nz
www.leinsterbnb.co.nz

Double/Twin $150 - $180
Single $120
(Full breakfast)
Children negotiable
Visa MC accepted
Children welcome
1 Queen 1 Double 1 Single (2 bdrm)
Bathrooms: 1 Ensuite 1 Private

At Leinster Bed & Breakfast we pride ourselves on creating a relaxed friendly atmosphere in our modern sunny home. Only 5 minutes to city centre (art gallery, museum, botanical gardens, Cathedral Square, casino, town hall etc), 10 minutes from the airport. For evening dining convenience there are excellent restaurants just a leisurely stroll away at Merivale Village. Laundry, email, fax and off-street parking facilities makes us your home away from home. Bedrooms have TV, electric blankets, heaters, tea/coffee. Well behaved puss & pooch in residence.

Christchurch - Richmond *2 km E of CBD*
Avon Grove Villa Bed & Breakfast *B&B*

Janice and Ian Cundall
273 River Road,
Christchurch, 8013

Tel 03 381 7099
or 027 442 3076
enquiries@avongrovevilla.co.nz
www.avongrovevilla.co.nz

Double/Twin $140 - $160
Single $90 - $110
(Full breakfast)
Visa MC accepted
Children welcome
2 Queen 1 Single (3 bdrm)
Bathrooms: 2 Ensuite 1 Private

This 1900's Villa is situated beside the Avon River, in a quiet location, and is close to the CBD, being only 5 minutes by car or a 30 minute walk along the river. Two large, comfortably appointed double guest rooms, each with original fireplace and bay windows, are available. Each room has an ensuite, TV, and tea and coffee facilities. There is also a single room with a separate private bathroom. A full cooked breakfast is served in the dining room.

Christchurch - Burwood *4 km N of Christchurch City*
Finlay Banks B&B *B&B*

Fay & Lindsay Turner
7 Banks Avenue,
Burwood,
Christchurch

Tel (03) 385 1012
or 027 485 1015
Fax (03) 385 1014
finlaybanks@xtra.co.nz
www.finlaybanks.co.nz

Double/Twin $150 - $200
Single $110 - $150
(Full breakfast)
Child/extra adult POA
Dinner POA
Visa MC accepted
1 Superking/Twin Singles 1 Queen
Bathrooms: 2 Ensuite

Fay & Lindsay welcome you to 'Finlay Banks' - your home away from home. Being close to the international airport our family home is a convenient place to stay. Located in the heart of the picturesque garden city, it is the perfect location to discover the city and all it has to offer, yet peaceful and private in its rose garden surroundings. Restaurants, cafes, theatres, shopping mall and the Rugby World Cup stadium are close by for your convenience.

Christchurch City *.5 km NW of Christchurch CBD*

Windsor B&B Hotel *B&B Hotel*

Carol Healey & Don Evans
52 Armagh Street, Christchurch 1

Tel (03) 366 1503 or 0800 366 1503   Fax (03) 366 9796
reservations@windsorhotel.co.nz   www.windsorhotel.co.nz

Double/Twin $140 Single $98 (Full breakfast) Triple $180
Quad/Family $200 Visa MC Diners Amex Eftpos accepted
12 Double 18 Twin 10 Single (40 bdrm)
Bathrooms: 24 Guest share
Free internet/wifi available

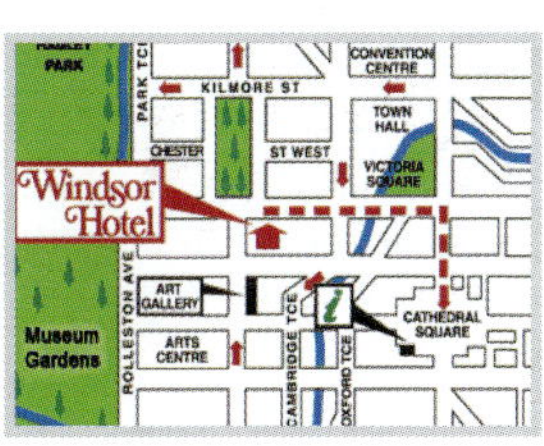

Looking for Bed & Breakfast in Christchurch, then try The Windsor. Built at the turn of the century this inner city residence is located on the Tourist Tram Route and is within 5-10 minutes walk of the city centre, restaurants, convention centre, casino, galleries, museum and botanical gardens. Guests are greeted on arrival by our pet dachshund, Miss Winnie and shown around our charming colonial style home. Often described as traditional, this family operated bed & breakfast hotel prides itself on the standard of accommodation that it offers. The warm and comfortable bedrooms are all decorated with a small posy of flowers and a watercolour by local artist Denise McCulloch. .

The shared bathroom facilities have been conveniently appointed with bathrobes provided, giving warmth and comfort in the bed & breakfast tradition. Such things as 'hotties' and 'brollies' add charm to the style of accommodation offered, as does our 1928 Studebaker sedan.

Our generous morning breakfast (included in the tariff) offers fruit juice, fresh fruits, yogurt and cereals followed by bacon and eggs, sausages, tomatoes, toast and marmalade, and is served in the dining room each morning between 6.30 and 9.00. The 24 hour complimentary tea & coffee making facilities allow guests to use them at their own convenience. 'Supper' (tea, coffee and biscuits) is served each evening in the lounge at 9.00.

As part of our service the hotel offers 'Free' broadband internet / wireless access, coin operated laundry, luggage lift, off-street parking for the motorist and bicycle and baggage storage.

QUOTE THIS BOOK FOR 10% DISCOUNT

Christchurch City *0.8 km N of Christchurch Cathedral Square*
Home Lea B&B *B&B*

Pauline & Gerald Oliver
195 Bealey Avenue,
Christchurch

Tel (03) 379 9977
or 0800 355 321
Fax (03) 379 4099
homelea@xtra.co.nz
www.homelea.co.nz

Double/Twin $145 - $190
Single $95 - $135
(Special breakfast)
Children negotiable
Dinner by arrangement
Extra adult $35
Visa MC Amex Eftpos accepted
Children welcome
Internet available
1 King 2 Queen 4 Single (4 bdrm)
Bathrooms: 2 Ensuite 2 Private

Home Lea offers the traveller a comfortable and enjoyable stay. Built in the early 1900s, Home Lea has the charm and character of a large New Zealand home of that era: rimu panelling, leadlight windows, and a large lounge with a log fire. Off-street parking. Complimentary Wireless/broadband internet available. Special diets catered for. Pauline and Gerald are happy to share their knowledge of local attractions and their special interests are travel, sailing and music.

Christchurch City *1.3 km N of Information Centre*
Eliza's Manor on Bealey *Luxury B&B*

Ann Zwimpfer & Harold Williams
82 Bealey Avenue,
City Central, 8013

Tel (03) 366 8584
or 0800 366 859
Fax (03) 366 4946
info@elizas.co.nz
www.elizas.co.nz

Double/Twin $210 - $315
Single $190 - $295
(Full breakfast)
Visa MC Diners Amex
Eftpos accepted
Pet free home
Not suitable for children
4 King 4 Queen 1 Single (8 bdrm)
All with ensuites - Heriatge and Classic Rooms
Bathrooms: 8 Ensuite Large tiled walk in showers

Eliza's is a beautifully restored Victorian mansion, built in 1861. The original architecture includes a magnificent staircase in the foyer, lead light windows and wood panelling. The tariff includes a full continental and cooked breakfast. It is a short drive from the airport and a 15 minute level walk to the arts centre, botanical gardens, art gallery, museum, city centre, golf course and restaurants. Free parking and internet access is available to guests. We are a day trip to Hanmer Springs, Akaroa, and Kaikoura.

Christchurch City *0.1 km NW of Christchurch CBD*
The Devon B&B *B&B*

Sandra & Benjamin Humphrey
69 Armagh Street,
Christchurch

Tel (03) 366 0398
or 0800 283 386
Fax (03) 366 0392
stay@thedevon.co.nz
www.thedevon.co.nz

Double/Twin $145 - $180
Single $125 - $145
(Full breakfast)
Children under 15 years $30
Extra adults $40
Visa MC Diners Amex
Eftpos accepted
Internet available
1 King 7 Queen 12 Single (11 bdrm)
Bathrooms: 9 Ensuite 1 Private

The Devon is a personal guest house located in the heart of beautiful Christchurch City, which offers elegance and comfort in the style of an olde worlde English manor. Just 2 minutes walk to Christchurch Cathedral, Town Hall, and Convention Centre, casino, museum, art gallery, hospital and botanical gardens in Hagley Park. TV lounge, tea & coffee making facilities. Off-street parking. Free broadband internet/wireless access and luggage storage.

Christchurch - City *.5 km N of Centre*
The Grange Guesthouse / Motel *B&B Apartment with Kitchen*

Des & Tracey Ramsay
56 Armagh,
Christchurch, 8013

Tel (03) 366 2850
or 0800 932 850
Fax (03) 374 2470
reservations@thegrange.co.nz
www.thegrange.co.nz

Double/Twin $145
Single $125
(Full breakfast)
Visa MC Diners Amex
Eftpos accepted
Children welcome
2 King/Twin 14 Queen (16 bdrm)
Bathrooms: 16 Ensuite

The Grange is a category II listed historic mansion built in 1874 now tastefully refurbished offering 8 bnb ensuite rooms full of character and original features , or 8 stylish studio and 1 bedroom motel rooms over looking our private courtyard.Being within the Cultural Precinct its just a short stroll to the Botanic Gardens Art Gallery and Cathedral Sq Free Parking , broadband internet / wireless.

Christchurch - Westhaven *10 km N of City central*
Granita B & B *Luxury B&B Homestay*
Juanita & Graeme Wilson
17 Lytham Green,
Christchurch, 8061

Tel 03 385 2343
or 027 205 5807
Fax 03 385 2343
wilson@granita.co.nz
www.granita.co.nz

Double/Twin $0 - $195
Single $0 - $165
(Full breakfast)
 Visa MC accepted
Not suitable for children
Internet available
2 Queen (2 bdrm)
Bathrooms: 2 Private
One shower room, one bath room

Granita B & B is located in a quiet suburb close to the airport, beaches, shops, golf courses and restaurants, yet only 10 minutes drive to the city centre. The accommodation has two queen rooms attractively decorated, each with private facilities and separate guest lounge and dining. A full breakfast is provided. We provide courtesy transfers, laundry facilities, internet access and garaging.

Christchurch -Airport/Templeton *3 km S of Hornby*
Cedarview Farm Homestay B&B *B&B Homestay Farmstay*
Carol & Terrance White
33 Barters Road, Templeton,
RD 8, Christchurch

Tel (03) 349 7491 or 0274 335 335
Fax (03) 3497 755
cedarviewfarm@xtra.co.nz
www.cedarviewhomestay.com

Double/Twin $135 - $175
Single $100 - $135 (Full breakfast)
Please provide childrens ages
when requesting a quote
High quality accomodation
in a very convenient location
Visa MC accepted
Pet free home   Children welcome
Internet available
1 King 1 Queen 2 Single (3 bdrm)
All 3 of our bedrooms are bright, modern & warm
Bathrooms: 1 Ensuite 1 Private

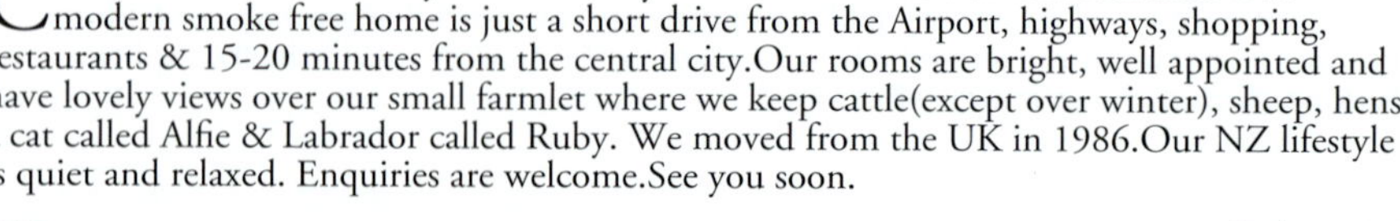

Cedarview Farm Homestay B+B is ideally situated for visitors to Christchurch. Our modern smoke free home is just a short drive from the Airport, highways, shopping, restaurants & 15-20 minutes from the central city.Our rooms are bright, well appointed and have lovely views over our small farmlet where we keep cattle(except over winter), sheep, hens, a cat called Alfie & Labrador called Ruby. We moved from the UK in 1986.Our NZ lifestyle is quiet and relaxed. Enquiries are welcome.See you soon.

Christchurch City - Sydenham *1.8 km S of Christchurch City Square*

Designer Cottage, Designer Retreat & Designer 55
B&B Cottage with Kitchen

Chet Wah

53 Hastings Street West, Sydenham, Christchurch City

Tel 0800 161 619 or (03) 377 8088
Fax (03) 377 8099
stay@designercottage.co.nz
www.designercottage.co.nz

Double/Twin $90 - $160
Single $60 - $120 (Continental breakfast)
Cottage House $140-$320 sleep 4-6 people
Visa MC accepted
Pet free home Internet Available
4 Queen 1 Double 1 Twin 1 Single (7 bdrm)
4 in B&B, 2 Cottages, 1 sleepout
Bathrooms: 3 Ensuite 1 Private 2 Guest share 1 Family share

Designer Cottage, Villa & Designer 55 is a charming place to stay. Just off Colombo Street situated in peaceful surroundings, and within 20 minutes walk to the city centre or 2 minute walk to shops and restaurants. We offer a variety of rooms, which are all tastefully decorated, including share facilities, private room with ensuite and a self-contained cottage. Seasonal, corporate & long stay rates apply. Wireless Broadband available. There is off-street parking and free pick up from city centre on arrival (by arrangement only).

Once settled in you will be welcomed with a 'mean' cup of coffee or tea by the friendly host. Check our youtube clip: http://www.youtube.com/watch?v=MfXPeXZ8t84 Your friendly host, Chet, has an honors degree in Landscape Architecture and is passionate about traditional buildings and his landscaping ideas. Designer Cottage is one of his finest collections of the charms of yesterday and all guests are welcome to view the concepts of Designer Village and hear his stories about these cottages.

Christchurch - St Martins *3 km S of Christchurch City Centre*

Kleynbos B&B *B&B Separate Suite Apartment with Kitchen*

Gerda De Kleyne & Hans van den Bos
59 Ngaio Street,
Christchurch

Tel (03) 332 2896
KLEYNBOS@xtra.co.nz
www.kleynbos.co.nz

Double/Twin $80 - $100
Single $70 - $80
(Continental breakfast)
Children are welcome, cot available
Apartment $100 - $130
Visa MC accepted
Children welcome
Internet available
2 Queen 2 Double 2 Single (4 bdrm)
Large Ensuite rooms
Bathrooms: 2 Ensuite
1 Private 1 Guest share

Quality accommodation with a personal touch, since 1991. We are 3km to city centre, in an easy to find, friendly, tree-lined street. Your large ensuite rooms are $100 with microwave, fridge and jug. A computer is available to keep in contact with friends and family. Self-catering options are available in the apartment, which sleeps 5 for $100-$130. The children are 21 and 18 years old. Directions; SH74 Barbadoes Street, Waltham Road, Wilsons Road, right into Gamblins Road, first left is Ngaio Street.

Opawa - Christchurch *4 km SW of Christchurch city*

Riverelm Lodge *B&B*

Peter & Rita Green
5 Locarno Street,
Opawa,
Christchurch, 8024

Tel (03) 981 3402
or 021 131 7177
riverelm_lodge@paradise.net.nz
www.riverelmlodge.com

Double/Twin $160 - $185
Single $120 - $140
(Continental breakfast)
Visa MC Eftpos accepted
Pet free home
Not suitable for children
2 Queen 1 Single (3 bdrm)
2 queens + 1 single,
bathrooms on suite
Bathrooms: 3 Ensuite

Let us welcome you to our riverside property along side the banks of the Heathcote River in this tree lined suburb. Your hosts Peter and Rita welcome you to stay in one of our rooms which comprise of 2 queen and 1 single all with thier own ensuite, central heating, TV & DVD, heated blankets, hairdryers and wireless internet. Your own lounge, microwave, fridge, tea/coffee making facilities and outside balcony area. Gorgeous fresh continental breakfast served in guest dining room. Close to all amenities.

Christchurch - Cashmere *0 km N of*
City Views *B&B*

Brenton and Martine Jackson
97 Longhurst Terrace,
Cashmere, 8022

Tel 03 3376411
brentandmartine@gmail.com

Double/Twin $130 - $170
(Continental breakfast)
Visa MC accepted
Pet free home
Children and pets welcome
Internet available
1 King 1 Queen (2 bdrm)
Bathrooms: 1 Ensuite 1 Private

You will enjoy the stunning views over the city; mountains and sea from our modern spacious house. Situated in beautiful Cashmere, each bedroom is huge and has ensuite or private bathroom. We are ideally suited for visitors to Christchurch. An easy 10 minute drive to central city and stadium. A few minutes walk to Victoria Park, with lovely hill walks. Free wireless broadband available. Enjoy your delicious breakfast in the privacy of your own room or on the veranda. Children welcome and cot available. Our well behaved children are five and two years old.

Christchurch - Huntsbury *4 km S of Christchurch Central*
Andaview B&B *Luxury B&B*

Anne & Keith Clark
18 Woodlau Rise,
Huntsbury,
Christchurch 8022

Tel (03) 332 5522
Fax (03) 332 5592
andaview@xtra.co.nz
www.andaview.co.nz

Double/Twin $200 - $240
Single $170 - $190
(Full breakfast)
Visa MC Eftpos accepted
Pet free home
Not suitable for children
Internet available
1 King/Twin 1 King (2 bdrm)
Bathrooms: 1 Ensuite 1 Private
Double Spabath

Experience genuine Kiwi hospitality only 10 minutes from the city centre. Suites are designed with executives and the discerning traveller in mind. Our guest rooms have spectacular views and amenities to satisfy your every need. Relax in our guest lounge with a New Zealand wine and watch the sun set behind the mountains. We offer free wireless internet access and complimentary airport/rail pick up or drop off by arrangement.

Christchurch - Murray Aynsley *4 km SE of City Centre Information*
Pool House *B&B Separate Suite*

Jill and Richard Entwistle
57 Aynsley Terrace,
Murray Aynsley,
Christchurch, 8022

Tel 03 337 0380 or 021 1316441
poolhouse@slingshot.co.nz

Double/Twin $135
Single $95
(Continental breakfast)
Children by arrangement
Please enquire about
prices during world cup
Visa MC accepted
Children welcome
1 King/Twin (1 bdrm)
1 king/twin bedroom
+ sofabed in lounge area
Bathrooms: 1 Ensuite

The Pool House offers quiet and comfortable, private self-contained accommodation with separate living and sleeping areas, bathroom en-suite. Ample self-serve continental breakfast provided. Wireless internet. Outdoor swimming pool. Only 20 minute walk to the Rugby World Cup in AMI stadium at Lancaster Park. Hansen Park and the Heathcote River offer gentle riverside walks and a children's playground. Central Christchurch and the Port of Lyttelton are 10 minutes by bus or by car. Local sandy beaches are 10-15 minutes by car.

Christchurch - Redcliffs *10 km SE of Cathedral Square*
Pegasus Bay View *B&B Separate Suite*

Denise & Bernie Lock
121A Moncks Spur Road,
Redcliffs,
Christchurch, 8081

Tel (03) 384 2923
or 021 254 2888
pegasusbay@slingshot.co.nz
www.pegasusbayview.co.nz

Double/Twin $140 - $160
Single $110 - $120
(Continental breakfast)
Visa MC accepted
2 Queen (2 bdrm)
1 bedroom and sofa bed in lounge
Bathrooms: 1 Private

Enjoy spectacular views over the South Pacific and across the city to the Southern Alps from our modern home. Your private guest suite has its own entrance and is tastefully furnished, with spacious bedroom, separate lounge (which can converted to a second double bedroom for additional family/friends) and private bathroom. Relax over a delicious breakfast, served outside on warm days, while enjoying the stunning panorama. Close to beach and restaurants and just 15 minutes drive from Christchurch City centre. We offer free wireless broadband access.

Christchurch - Mt Pleasant *8 km E of Christchurch*

Mt Pleasant Bed & Breakfast *B&B Separate Suite with self catering accommodation*

Nicola & Paul Kristiansen
14 Hobday Lane,
Mt Pleasant, Christchurch

Tel (03) 384 9220
or 021 070 3076
Fax (03) 384 9235
Kristiansen@xtra.co.nz
mtpleasantbandb.co.nz

Double/Twin $120
(Full breakfast provisions)
Private lounge, Private Kitchen
Visa MC accepted
Pet free home
 Not suitable for children
1 King (1 bdrm)
Bathrooms: 1 Ensuite
Private sauna holds six

This unique home offers a friendly and relaxed stay in your private suite. Enjoy your spacious and comfortable bedroom with king-size bed, and en suite bathroom with vintage cast-iron (such bliss our guests tell us!).

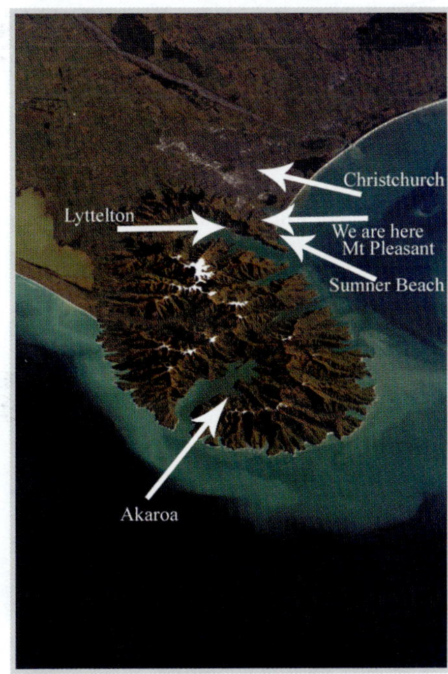

New LCD 32 inch TV. Sitting room with private entrance leading out on to the deck with a big view over the City to the Southern Alps. Own kitchen facilities, breakfast supplies included in the tariff - bacon, eggs, bread, cereals, milk, fresh fruits, selection of teas and coffee. Explore the huge rambling garden, fascinating with waterwheel, plentiful trees and abundant bird life.

Conveniently situated 15 minutes from City, 10 minutes to popular Sumner Beach, 5 minutes to windsurfing, gondola, walking and bike tracks. You'll love it!

Christchurch - Mt Pleasant *9 km E of Cathedral Square*
A Nest on Mount Pleasant *B&B Apartment with Kitchen*

Kathryn & Kai Tovgaard
24 Toledo Place,
Mount Pleasant,
Christchurch , 8081

Tel (03) 3849 485
or 027 203 0637
Fax (03) 3848 385
info@anestbnb.co.nz
www.anestbnb.co.nz

Double/Twin $100 - $125
Single $90 - $115 (Full breakfast)
Children discounted
Visa MC accepted
Pet free home
Children welcome
Internet available
2 Queen 2 Twin (3 bdrm)
Bathrooms: 1 Ensuite 1 Private

Unique fully self-contained home , yet with all the service and warm hospitality of a home-stay. This is the promise of The Nest. The Nest is situated in one of Christchurch's most loved hill suburbs with views of our estuary, sea and mountains beyond. Tranquil and secure, with garage parking, TV,DVD, stereo, internet & BBQ. Very close to Christchurch's best beaches with excellent cafes and restaurants, Ferrymead Historic Park, Lyttelton Harbour, Tamaki Heritage Village and hillside walks with breathtaking views to the Southern Alps.

Christchurch - Sumner *12 km E of Cathedral Square*
Villa Alexandra *B&B Separate Suite Self Contained Studio & 2 S/C Beach Front Apartments.*

Wendy & Bob Perry
1 Kinsey Terrace,
Clifton Hill, Sumner,
Christchurch 8081

Tel (03) 326 6291
Fax (03) 326 6096
villa_alexandra@xtra.co.nz
www.villaalexandra.co.nz

Double/Twin $120 - $140
Single $90 - $100
(Full breakfast)
Children under 12 $15
Apartments $150 - $295 P/N
Children welcome
1 Queen 1 Double 1 Twin
1 Single (3 bdrm)
Bathrooms: 2 Ensuite 1 Private

Enjoy the warmest hospitality in our spacious turn of the century villa overlooking Sumner Bay. Our home retains the graciousness of a bygone era while offering all modern comforts. In winter enjoy open fires, cosy farmhouse kitchen and on sunny days the verandah and turret. Spectacular sea views from Sumner to the Kaikouras. We enjoy food, wine, music, gardening, tramping, travel. 5 minutes walk to beach; off-street parking; laundry. Also self-contained beach front apartment, 2 double bedrooms, $150 per night, minimum 3 nights.

Christchurch - Sumner Beach *12 km SE of Cathedral Square*
Cave Rock Bed & Breakfast *B&B*

Gayle & Norm Eade
16 Esplanade, Sumner, Christchurch

Tel (03) 326 6844
or 027 436 0212
Fax (03) 326 5600
eade@chch.planet.org.nz
www.caverockguesthouse.co.nz

Double/Twin $135 - $145
Single $115 - $125
(Continental breakfast provisions)
Children $20
Corporate Rates available
Visa MC Amex Eftpos accepted
Children welcome
Internet available
3 Queen 1 Double (4 bdrm)
Bathrooms: 4 Ensuite
One with spa bath ensuite

The Cave Rock B&B - Sumner's ultimate Beachfront accommodation opposite Sumner's Cave Rock. Hosts Gayle & Norm Eade enjoy meeting people from overseas and within NZ. Large spacious double rooms with sea views, TV, heating and ensuite bathrooms, can sleep up to 4. Kitchen facilities. Sumner - the ideal holiday location, 15 minutes from Ch.Ch City, excellent bus service - cafe/bars, shops, cinema, within walking distance. Hill and cliff walks close by, safe sandy beach across the road. We have a friendly dalmatian dog and a very aloof cat. We have complimentary wireless internet.

Christchurch - Sumner *13 km E of Christchurch Cathedral Square*
Abbott House Sumner Bed & Breakfast *Self-contained suite with kitchen, & self-contained studio*

Janet & Chris Abbott
104 Nayland Street, Sumner,
Christchurch, 8081

Tel 0800 020 654
or +64 3 326 6111 from overseas
info@abbotthouse.co.nz
www.abbotthouse.co.nz

Double/Twin $120 - $140
Single $100 - $120
(Breakfast provisions first night)
Children $10 per extra child/night
(Max $30pw)
Weekly discounts (seasonal)
Visa MC accepted
Children welcome
3 King/Twin (3 bdrm)
Bathrooms: 1 Ensuite 1 Private

Your hosts, Chris and Janet Abbott welcome you to our historic restored 1870s villa in Christchurch's unique seaside village. Our home is one block from the beach, and an easy ten-minute walk along the beach to Sumner's many cafés, restaurants, boutique shops and cinema. Both suite and studio have king-sized beds, own kitchen areas, TV, DVD and internet access. Off-street parking. Laundry facilities (suite only). Home-baked bread. Wonderful base for many walks, swimming, surfing, mountain biking and road biking.

Christchurch - Sumner *15 km E of Cathedral Square*
Scarborough-Heights *Luxury B&B*
Barbara and Brian Hanlon
21 Godley Drive, Scarborough,
Christchurch 8081

Tel (03) 326 7060
or 027 229 7312
Fax (03) 326 7061
stay@scarborough-heights.co.nz
www.scarborough-heights.co.nz

Double/Twin $180
Single $120 (Full breakfast)
Children $50 (5-12years)
Dinner $50 by arrangement
Visa MC accepted
Children welcome
Internet available
1 King 1 Queen 3 Single (2 bdrm)
1 king or twin beds, 1 queen bed
Bathrooms: 1 Ensuite 1 Private
Private bathroom has bath and shower

Scarborough-Heights is a large, modern architecturally designed home set in an award winning garden, high on Scarborough Hill and offering luxurious bed & breakfast accommodation. All rooms offer spectacular views of the Southern Alps, Christchurch City and South Pacific Ocean. We provide friendly hospitality in peaceful, quiet surroundings yet are only 20 minutes from the city centre and 5 minutes from the trendy and popular seaside village of Sumner with its many cafes, specialty shops and cinema. We share our home with two cats.

Tai Tapu - Lincoln *20 km S of Christchurch*
Fantail Lodge on Greenpark *Country B&B*
Pamela & Doug Hueston
164 River Road,
Tai Tapu-Lincoln,
RD 2,
Christchurch, 7672

Tel (03) 325 7572
or 027 433 7706
hueston@netspeed.net.nz
www.phototours.co.nz

Double/Twin $100 - $130
Single $90 - $100
(Continental breakfast)
Visa MC accepted
1 King 1 Double (2 bdrm)
Bathrooms: 1 Ensuite 2 Family share

Located on River Road meandering along the Halswell River. Artist Pamela and Photographer Doug share the comfort of their elegant and spacious home, Set in extensive landscaped grounds, in tranquil country surroundings, views of the Alps, sunsets, nestled in our 10 acre farmlet, farming cattle and sheep. Native birds: Fantails and Pukekos often frequent our garden. Pick-up from Airport, (25km.) by arrangement.Near Lincoln University 5km & Local award winning winerys, restaurants within 5-12 km.We also guide Banks Peninsula Tours and Photography tours,One, Two,3-4 days or more. www.phototours.co.nz

Lyttelton *9 km E of Christchurch*
The Rookery *B&B Homestay*
Angus & Rene Macpherson
9 Ross Terrace,
Lyttelton, 8082
Tel (03) 328 8038
rooks@amma.co.nz
therookery.co.nz

Double/Twin $131 - $148
Single $84
(Full breakfast)
Internet available
2 Queen 1 Single (3 bdrm)
Bathrooms: 1 Ensuite 1 Private

The Rookery is one of Lyttelton's oldest cottages with delightful panoramic views over the harbour. To capture the character of the Victorian era we as designers have paid particular attention to the colours and finishes that ensure our visitors' enjoyment during their stay. Rooms are double glazed with underfloor heating and electric blankets. Only 15 minutes from the Garden City we are ideally located for exploring the Banks Peninsula. Angus, Rene and our cat Cleopatra offer you a warm and friendly welcome.

Akaroa *5 km N of Akaroa*
LeLievre Farmstay *Homestay Farmstay*
Hanne & Paul LeLievre
Box 4 Akaroa,
154 Takamatua Valley Road,
Banks Peninsula

Tel (03) 304 7255
Fax (03) 304 7255
Double.L@Xtra.co.nz
www.sealtours.co.nz

Double/Twin $140
Single $90
(Full breakfast)
Dinner $35
Children welcome
1 Queen 1 Double 1 Single (2 bdrm)
Two - Both with ensuites
Bathrooms: 2 Ensuite

Our home is situated 1.5km up Takamatua Valley and 5km from Akaroa. We farm sheep, cattle deer and usually have a menagerie of orphaned pets etc. Our interests include golf and bridge. We invite you to enjoy some good old fashioned country hospitality. A trip to the Akaroa Seal Colony, which featured on the TV programmes A Flying Visit, Totally Wild and The Great Outdoors, is a must do. Safari includes a scenic drive, through, a working farm, with the farmer.

Akaroa - Paua Bay *12 km E of Akaroa*

Paua Bay Farmstay *B&B Farmstay*

Murray & Sue Johns
Postal: C/- 113 Beach Road,
Akaroa, Banks Peninsula 7520

Tel (03) 304 8511 or 021 133 8194
pauabay@farmside.co.nz
www.pauabay.com

Double/Twin $120 - $150 (Full breakfast)
Children negotiable Dinner $40
Children welcome
1 Queen 1 Twin (2 bdrm)
1 Queen room one twin room
Bathrooms: 1 Ensuite 1 Guest share

Time spent at Paua Bay is a truely unique experience. Not only will you be able to enjoy the wonderful surroundings but also you will join a traditional NZ farming family sharing their daily endeavors. Set in a private bay our 900 acre sheep, cattle & deer farm is surrounded by spectacular coastline, native bush & streams. You are spoilt for choice, walk to the beach, enjoy seals and extensive birdlife, join in seasonal farm activities.

The farmhouse is surrounded by a wonderful garden and around each corner in the path is a new surprise, a secluded moonlight bath.....a hammock....a sculpture. The guest room has wooden floors, a clawfoot bath, fresh flowers and from the queensize bed you can watch the sun rise out of the South Pacific.

In the evening take the opportunity to enjoy the company of our 6th generation farming family. Share a generous meal of fresh farm produce with relaxed conversation around the large kitchen table. New Zealand wines & beers are included.

The nearby historic French settlement of Akaroa offers guests world renouned harbour cruises and its Hector dolphins. Quiet wanderings exploring this village allows guests time to reflect on days gone by.

Akaroa - Okains Bay *18 km N of Akaroa*
Kawatea *B&B Farmstay*

Judy & Kerry Thacker
1048 Okains Bay Road, Okains Bay, Banks Peninsula
Tel (03) 304 8621 Fax (03) 304 8621
kawatea@xtra.co.nz   www.kawateafarmstay.co.nz

Double/Twin $130 - $160
Single $90 - $160 (Full breakfast)
Children by arrangement   Dinner $40   Visa MC accepted
3 Queen 2 Single (3 bdrm)
1 Queen/Single with Ensuite, 1 Queen/Single, 1 Queen
Bathrooms: 1 Ensuite 1 Private 1 Guest share
Bath, Shower, Separate Toilet

Experience the grace and charm of yesteryear, while enjoying the fine food and wine of NZ today. Revel in the peace of countrylife, but still be close to sights and activities. Welcome to Kawatea, an historic homestead set in spacious gardens, and surrounded by land farmed by our Irish ancestors since the 1850s. Built in 1900 from native timber's, the carefully renovated house features stained glass windows and handcrafted furniture.

Linger over your choice of breakfast in the conservatory. Join us in the evening for creative country fare and seafood from the Bay whilst sharing experiences with fellow travellers.

Explore our 1400 acre farm and feed the pet sheep. Enjoy Okains Bay's unspoilt swimming beach, observe the birdlife on the estuary, or walk along the scenic coastline to secluded bays and a seal colony with excellent photographic opportunities. Learn about Maori culture and the life of early settlers at the acclaimed Okains Bay Museum.

Visit Akaroa with its French influence and galleries. Sample local wines and watch traditional cheese making. Golf, kayak, take a cruise or swim with the rare Hector Dolphins.

We have been hosting since 1988, and offer thoughtful personal attention and friendly hospitality in a relaxed atmosphere. Directions: Take Highway 75 from Christchurch through Duvauchelle. Turn left at signpost marked Okains Bay. Kawatea is 11km on right.

Akaroa *80 km S of Christchurch*
Wilderness House *Luxury B&B*

Approved

Jim & Liz Coubrough
42 Rue Grehan,
Akaroa

Tel (03) 304 7517
or 021 669 381
Fax (03) 304 7518
info@wildernesshouse.co.nz
www.wildernesshouse.co.nz

Double/Twin $295
Single $295
(Full breakfast)
Visa MC Eftpos accepted
Not suitable for children
Internet available
1 King/Twin 3 Queen (4 bdrm)
Bathrooms: 3 Ensuite 1 Private

Treat yourself to a memorable experience in one of Akaroa's gracious historic homes. Built in 1878 our home is set in a one acre garden including a petite vineyard. Rooms have free wireless internet, harbour/valley views and feature gorgeous linen, garden flowers, a selection of teas, coffee and home-baking. Linger over our special breakfasts. Secluded and private we are just a short stroll to the village. Join us for a glass of our wine each evening. Unwind, relax and enjoy! Resident cat George.

Akaroa Harbour - French Farm *70 km SE of Christchurch*
Bantry Lodge *B&B Cottage with Kitchen*

Approved

Dolina Barker
French Farm,
RD 2,
Akaroa

Tel (03) 304 5161
or 027 313 2406
Fax (03) 304 5162
barker.d@xtra.co.nz
www.bantrylodge.co.nz

Double/Twin $140 - $160
Single $90 - $100
(Full breakfast)
Dinner $40 by arrangement
Self-contained cottage sleeps 4
Visa MC Diners Amex accepted
Children and pets welcome
2 Queen 1 Double 1 Twin (4 bdrm)
3 in B&B, 1 in Cottage
Bathrooms: 2 Private 1 Guest share

This historic home has views across Akaroa Harbour 50 metres away. Groundfloor queen room has french doors to verandah and sea views, private bath. Upstairs queen room with balcony overlooks harbour , private bath. Coffee, tea facilities provided with home-baking. The comfortable sitting room is for relaxing or joining me for a drink. Full breakfast is served in the elegant dining room. Tranquillity and space. A self-contained cottage sleeps 4. Linen, breakfast ingredients supplied. 1 shy cat.

Akaroa *80 km SE of Christchurch*

Mulberry House *B&B Homestay Guest House Self contained spacious holdiay home*

Anne Craig & Jack Clark
9 William Street, Akaroa 8161,

Tel (03) 304 7778 or 021 610456
Fax (03) 304 7778
anneandjacknz@yahoo.com
www.mulberryhouse.co.nz

Double/Twin from $135 - $165
Single from $100 - $135 (Special breakfast)
$10 surcharge 1 night stay
Children welcome
3 King 1 Queen 1 Twin 4 Single (7 bdrm)
Bathrooms: 2 Ensuite 1 Private 2 Guest share

Experience the very best in homestyle accommodation and delight in the setting of Mulberry House, which accommodates up to thirteen guests. All rooms are beautifully decorated and feature quality beds and fine linen. There is a choice of double rooms, with or without ensuite, and a twin room which will delight children.

The romantic poolside summerhouse has its own kitchen, ensuite and garden to provide total privacy if desired. We also have a beautifully furnished,self contained cottage with full kitchen.

Breakfasts are a specialty and feature a choice of American, European, English, and New Zealand styles. Champagne breakfasts and other meals by arrangement. Meals can be served outside in the summer months overlooking the pool.

Your hosts: Well travelled and semi retired Anne Craig and Jack Clark offer unparalleled hospitality. Fussy about food, both Anne and Jack love to cook: Anne preserves and bakes, and Jack adds his American expertise to breakfasts of pancakes, waffles, omelettes, fresh fruits, and delicious coffee from the espresso machine.

Guest Comments - Desmond Balmer (LondonGuardian/Observer Travel) recommends Mulberry House as amongst New Zealand's Top Twenty. Featured on Sydney's channel 7 'Ernie Dingo's Getaway' as 'the place to stay 'in Akoroa. Featured in Autumn 2000 European "Wining and Dining.

Akaroa *80 km SE of Christchurch*
La Belle Villa *B&B*
Alice & Paul Hewitson
113 Rue Jolie,
Akaroa

Tel (03) 304 7084
or 021 045 9156
Fax (03) 304 7084
bookings@labellevilla.co.nz
www.labellevilla.co.nz

Double/Twin $140 - $170
Single $120 - $150
(Special breakfast)
Visa MC accepted
Children welcome
1 King/Twin 2 King
1 Queen (4 bdrm)
Bathrooms: 4 Ensuite

A warm welcome awaits you. Relax in the surroundings of a bygone era and appreciate the antiques in our much photographed historic villa. Built in the 1870's La Belle Villa is set in beautiful, mature grounds,with a trickling stream, it offers indoor/outdoor living including separate guest lounge. Our special alfresco breakfast which includes fresh local produce, homebaking and espresso coffee has won universal praise. Located in close proximity to restaurants, shops and cinema makes us the ideal place to stay in Akaroa.

Highcountry Canterbury - Castle Hill *33 km SW of Springfield*
The Burn Alpine B&B *B&B Homestay*
Bob Edge & Phil Stephenson
11 Torlesse Place,
Castle Hill Village,
Canterbury

Tel (03) 318 7559
Fax (03) 318 7558
theburn@xtra.co.nz
www.theburn.co.nz

Double/Twin $160 - $180
Single $90 - $100
(Continental breakfast)
Children under 13 half price
Home cooked dinner surcharge $40 pp
Cooked breakfast surcharge $15 pp
Visa MC accepted
Children welcome
3 Queen 1 Twin (4 bdrm)
Bathrooms: 2 Guest share
Two bathrooms with showering facilites and seperate toilets

One hour west of Christchurch, a carefree atmosphere prevails at The Burn. Nestled in the heart of the Southern Alps, it's arguably New Zealand's highest B&B. We designed and built our alpine lodge to maximise mountain vistas. Centered in the mystic Castlehill Basin, surrounded by native forest, this is a fantastic place to return after a days activity or just kick back and relax on the sunny deck. A host of outdoor sports include ski/snowboard-ing, hiking, mountain biking, and flyfishing. Professional flyfishing guiding available.

Darfield *4 km SW of Darfield*
The Oaks Historic Homestead *B&B Homestay*

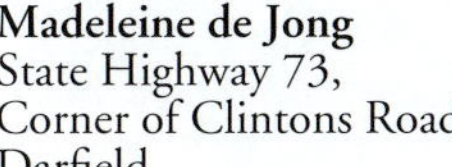

Madeleine de Jong
State Highway 73,
Corner of Clintons Road,
Darfield

Tel (03) 318 7232
or 027 241 3999
Fax (03) 318 7236
theoaks@quicksilver.net.nz
www.theoakshomestead.co.nz

Double/Twin $185 - $275
Single $160
(Full breakfast)
Dinner $75 pp on request
Visa MC Eftpos accepted
Children and pets welcome
3 Queen 1 Single (4 bdrm)
Bathrooms: 1 Ensuite 2 Private

One of Canterbury's oldest homesteads, restored to its former glory. Located amidst stunning scenery of the Southern Alps to the Westcoast, with ski fields, golf courses and tourist attractions on its doorstep. The Oaks features: guest rooms with ensuite/private bathrooms, a guest dining and living room featuring stunning open fires, a traditional large homestead kitchen, beautiful verandas for outdoor entertaining. Children welcome. Pets on request. Your Host Madeleine speaks 5 languages and is a keen cook. Wherever possible I try to use fresh organic produce.

Mt Hutt - Methven *6.4 km E of Methven*
Pagey's Farmstay *B&B Farmstay Kitchen - new*

Shirley & Gene Pagey
663 Methven-Chertsey Road,
Methven/Mt Hutt,
RD 12 Rakaia 7782

Tel (03) 302 1713
Fax (03) 302 1714
pageysfarmstay@clear.net.nz
www.tourism.net.nz

Double/Twin $120
Single $90 (Full breakfast)
Children under 12 half price
Dinner $30 pp   Spa pool
Pet free home   Children welcome
Internet available
1 King 1 Queen 4 Single (3 bdrm)
Large with quality beds
Bathrooms: 2 Private
New - large showers

Enjoy hospitality warmth and freedom in our lovely expansive home with new kitchen, bathrooms, large redorated bedrooms with luxurious beds, set amidst aged oak trees and large rose garden. Watch our 47' TV . Enjoy a pre-dinner drink, wine, crystal clear mountain water and home-grown cuisine. Star gaze in our luxurious massaging spa. Surrounding activities include breathtaking bush walks, 2 superior golf courses, ballooning and skiing. Short notice is our speciality. Directions from Methven town centre, turn down Methven Chertsey Road, 6km signposted.

Mt Hutt - Methven *11 km SW of Methven*

Glenview Farmstay *B&B Farmstay Cottage No Kitchen*

Helen & Mike Johnstone
142 Hart Road, Methven, 7782

Tel (03) 302 8620
Fax (03) 302 8620
helenmikejohnstone@yahoo.com

Double/Twin $120
Single $80 (Full breakfast)
Children $25
Dinner $30
Children welcome
2 Queen 2 Double 1 Twin 2 Single (5 bdrm)
Bathrooms: 1 Ensuite 1 Guest share
Ensuite in unit

Glenview Farmstay is situated at the base of Mt Hutt Ski Field, with the house designed to look at the mountains and down the Canterbury Plains to the Port Hills.

We farm cattle and sheep on our 1200 acre farm. We have several working farm dogs and a very friendly cat.

There is a peaceful unit in the garden which is suitable for a couple or a family. It has two bedrooms, one with 1 queen bed and the other with 1 double and 1 single bed, ensuite, TV, tea & coffee facilities and wonderful views. The rooms in the house have separate access, good heating and are non-smoking. Dinner by arrangement. Free farm tours on request.

Methven is only 10 minutes away and we are very close to good fishing, golf, ballooning, horse treking, para jumping, bush walks and jet boating. Free transfers to local walkways. One hour from Christchurch and we are on the way to Queenstown along Highway 72.

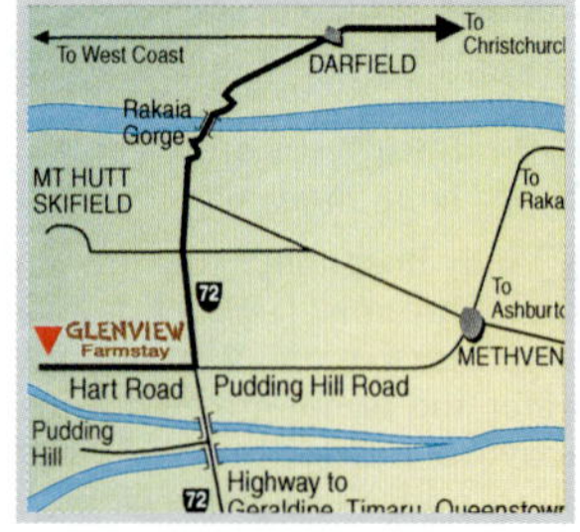

Mt Hutt - Methven *4 km NW of Methven - Mt Hutt Village*
Green Gables Deer Farm *B&B Farmstay*

Irene & Mike Harris
185 Waimarama Road, Methven-Mt Hutt Village

Tel (03) 302 8308
or New Zealand (0800 466 093)
Fax (03) 302 8309
greengables@xtra.co.nz
www.nzfarmstay.com

Double/Twin $140 - $180
Single $110 - $140 (Special breakfast)
Child $55   Dinner $55 pp by arrangement
Visa MC accepted Children welcome
2 King 2 Twin (3 bdrm)
Super King Beds
Bathrooms: 2 Ensuite 1 Private

Set in tranquil surroundings at the foot of Mt.Hutt, Green Gables Deer Farm is withing easy reach of Christchurch (1hr), Kaikoura for Whale Watching and Dolphins (3hrs), Mt.Cook (3.5hrs) and Queenstown (approx 5.5hrs).

Our stylish rooms have all the comforts you will require with your own private entrance opening out onto the garden with a backdrop of graceful deer wandering in the paddocks and the ever changing colours of the mountain views. There is plenty of room to stroll, maybe feed the pet deer and meet our friendly dogs or just relax and unwind.

Start your evening meal with a complimentary pre-dinner drink and enjoy the fresh local produce used in our home cooked meals and desserts.. ACTIVITIES:- Try out the many summer and winter activities close by - Golf courses at Methven and Terrace Downs (club & cart hire available), Fishing, Hot Air ballooning, Jet Boating, Skiing, 4WD Scenic Tours (available by arrangement), Horse Trekking, Scenic Flights, Ecotours and Alpine Rhododrendon Walks to name but a few. There are even trips to 'Eldoras' the Lord of the Rings film site at Mt.Sunday LOCATION:- Situated on S/H77 4kms N/W Methven. From Inland Scenic-Route 72 turn into S/H77 travel 5kms Green Gables Deer Farm is on the right.

Staveley - Mt. Somers *110 km SW of Christchurch*
Alpine Views Farmstay and B&B *Luxury B&B Homestay Farmstay*

Anna & Ken McNally
28 Symes Road,
RD 1, Ashburton

Tel (03) 303 0800
or 027 303 0700
anna@alpineviews.co.nz
alpineviews.co.nz

Double/Twin $120 - $150
Single $80 - $110
(Full breakfast)
Children welcome, pet animals to
feed!
Dinner available on request $50
Caravan sites available $20/night
Visa MC accepted
Children and pets welcome
2 Queen 1 Twin 1 Single (3 bdrm)
All with separate ensuitesBathrooms: 2 Ensuite 1 Family share

Located in the foothills of Canterbury with panoramic views of the Southern Alps, we are only 15 minutes from Mt Hutt Ski Area and Methven. Situated on the Inland Scenic Route 72, one hour from Christchurch Airport, and en route to Mt Cook and Queenstown destinations. Our homestead is amongst 3 acres of parklike gardens and beyond this we graze cattle and sheep. Feed pet deer and sheep and watch sheep dogs at work! Warm comfortable, quality accommodation and great food.

Rakaia *50 km S of Christchurch*
St Ita's Guesthouse *B&B Guest House*

Miriam & Ken Cutforth
11 Rakaia-Barrhill-Methven Road,
Rakaia Township, Canterbury

Tel (03) 302 7546
or 0274 888 673
Fax (03) 302 7564
stitas@xtra.co.nz
www.stitas.co.nz

Double/Twin $140
Single $90 (Full breakfast)
Children $40
Dinner $30 pp
Visa MC accepted
Children and pets welcome
Internet available
2 Queen 1 Double 4 Single (4 bdrm)
Large, warm rooms with garden views
Bathrooms: 3 Ensuite 1 Private with bath

Relax in our elegant and comfortable historic former convent, 600 metres from SH1 in small town New Zealand. Excellent base for exploring Ashburton District. Excellent first and last stop from Christchurch International Airport. Three bedrooms have ensuites and garden views. The fourth the Chapel has a private bathroom. Walking distance to local shops, great cafes, crafts and River Terrace Walkway. Close to golf and salmon fishing, 30 minutes to skiing, jet boating. Wireless available. Dinner by arrangement. Full breakfasts. Share the open fire with our moggie.

Ashburton *90 km S of Christchurch*
Weir Homestay *B&B Homestay*

Pat & Dave Weir
2A Sudbury Street,
Ashburton Central

Tel (03) 308 3534
pndweir@clear.net.nz

Double/Twin $100
Single $50
(Breakfast by arrangement)
Dinner $25
Visa MC accepted
1 Double 3 Single (2 bdrm)
Bathrooms: 1 Ensuite
1 Guest share 1 Family share

Our comfortable home is situated in a quiet street with the added pleasure of looking onto a rural scene. We are 10-15 minutes walk from town.Guest rooms have comfortable beds with electric blankets. We welcome the opportunity to meet and greet visitors and wish to make your stay a happy one. Your hosts are retired but active, hobbies general/varied from meeting people to walking etc. Request visitors no smoking inside home. Off-street parking.

Ashburton *7 km SE of Ashburton*
Lake Hood Homestay B&B *B&B*

Eric and Eleanor Weir
14 Witney Lane,
Lake Hood,
Ashburton

Tel (03) 302 6914
enquiries@lakehoodhomestay.co.nz
www.lakehoodhomestay.co.nz

Double/Twin $140 - $155
(Full breakfast)
Visa MC accepted
Pet free home
Not suitable for children
1 King/Twin 1 Queen (2 bdrm)
Bathrooms: 2 Ensuite

Lake Hood Homestay B&B is part of an exciting, modern development including the Lakehouse Restaurant. The area hosts water sports and is popular for jogging, walking, fishing or just relaxing. Lake Hood Homestay B&B, on the attractive, peaceful canal network adjoining Lake Hood, comprises two modern studio suites, each featuring: private en-suite, separate entrance, King or Queen bed (twin by arrangement), TV, tea/coffee making, opening to patio and canal-side garden. Delicious country-style cooked breakfast included. Complimentary use of kayaks and bicycles. See www.lakehoodhomestay.co.nz

Ashburton *1 km N of Ashburton Info Centre*
Carradale Manor *B&B Homestay*
Karen & Jim McIntyre
93 Pages Road, Allenton, Ashburton

Tel (03) 308 6577 Fax (03) 308 6548
jkmcintyre@xtra.co.nz
www.ashburton.co.nz/carradale

Double/Twin $120 - $150
Single $90 (Full breakfast)
Children under 12 half price
Visa MC accepted   Internet Available
2 King/Twin 1 Queen (3 bdrm)
Bathrooms: 1 Ensuite 1 Private

We are one hour from Christchurch International Airport. Our sunny spacious home, which is just off State Highway One in Ashburton, is situated in a beautiful, large and sheltered garden by a stream, where you can enjoy peace and tranquility. After offering hospitality for 16 years on Carradale Farm, we have now retired from Carradale Farm in the country to Carradale Manor in the town where we will continue to operate with those same high standards. .

We offer either a fully cooked breakfast, or continental breakfast, served with delicious home made jams and preserves. For your convenience tea/coffee making facilities, and electric blankets are for use in all rooms. Internet access available.

As we have both travelled extensively in New Zealand, Australia, United Kingdom, Europe, North America, Zimbabwe, South Africa, Vietnam and Singapore, we would like to offer hospitality to fellow travellers. Our hobbies include meeting people, travel, reading, photography, gardening, sewing, cake decorating, rugby, cricket, Jim belongs to the Masonic Lodge and Karen is involved in Community Affairs including Probus.

For young children we have a cot and highchair available. Our resident cat 'Lady Jane' is on hand to comfort you.

CARRADALE MANOR, 'WHERE PEOPLE COME AS STRANGERS AND LEAVE AS FRIENDS'

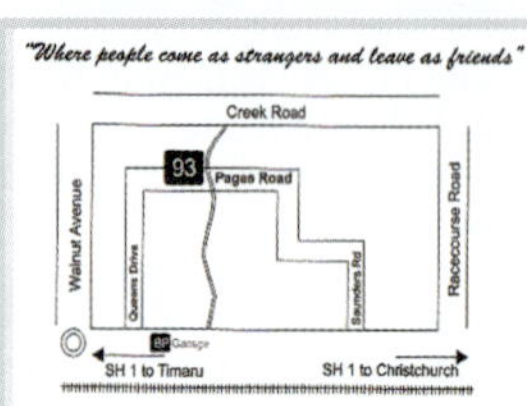

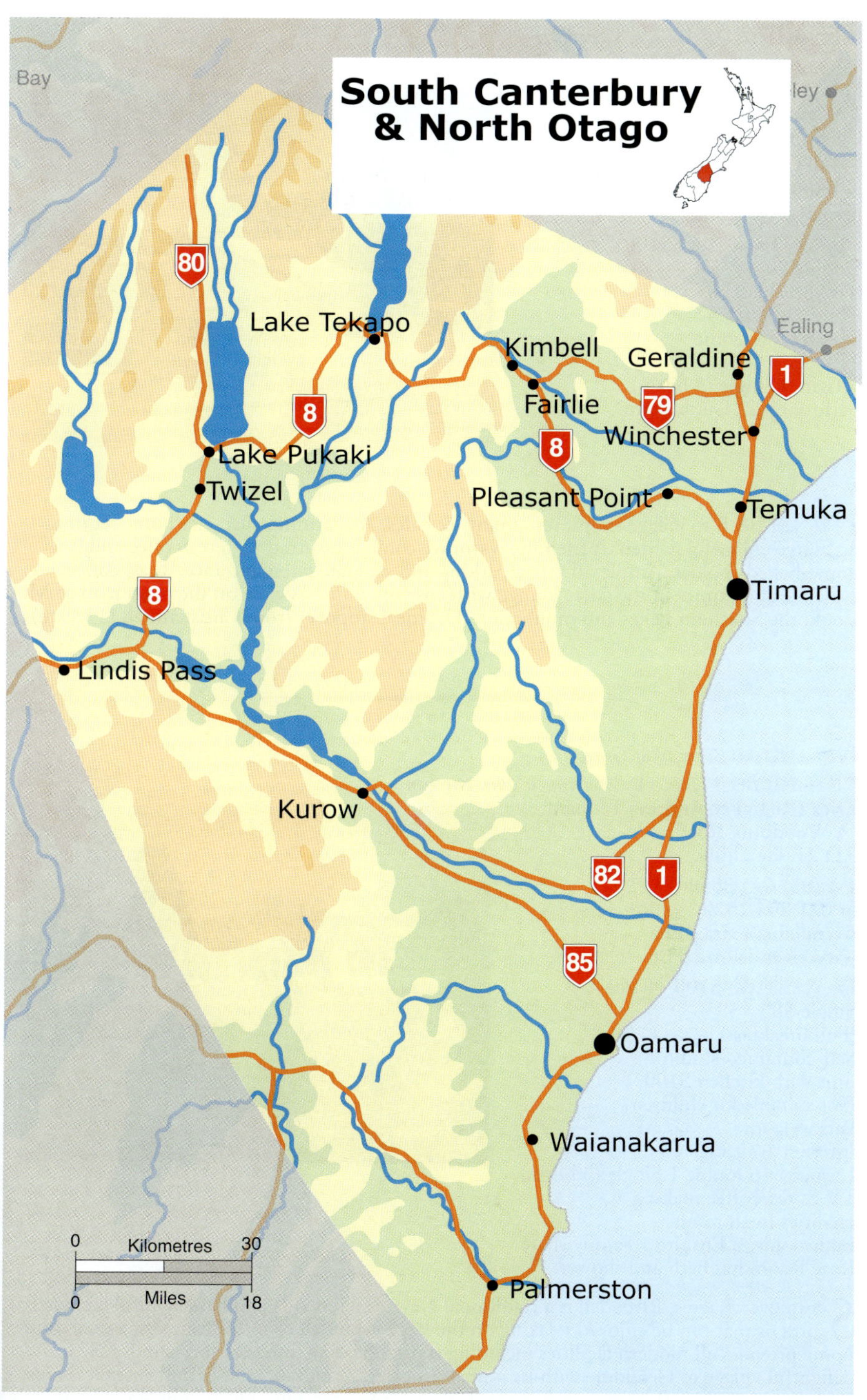
South Canterbury
& North Otago
Bay
80
Lake Tekapo
Kimbell
Geraldine
1
8
Fairlie
79
Lake Pukaki
Winchester
8
Twizel
Pleasant Point
Temuka
Ealing
8
Timaru
Lindis Pass
Kurow
82
1
85
Oamaru
Waianakarua
Kilometres
0
30
Miles
0
18
Palmerston

Geraldine *0.2 km S of Geraldine*
Lilymay *B&B*

Lois & Les Gillum
29 Cox Street,
Geraldine

Tel (03) 693 8838
or 0800 545 9629
lilymay@xtra.co.nz

Double/Twin $95 - $100
Single $70 - $75
(Full breakfast)
Children $20 - $25
Children welcome
2 Queen 1 Double
3 Twin 3 Single (3 bdrm)
Bathrooms: 2 Guest share

Closest B&B to village shops, restaurants & cafes. A charming character home set in a large colourful garden. A friendly, warm welcome is assured with tea/coffee and Lois' home-baked cookies. Ample off-street parking and separate guest entrance. Teas, coffee, etc. available at all times in the guest lounge with cosy open fire. We are on the main road to Mt Cook, the Southern Lakes and mountains. The ideal stopover from Christchurch (137 km).

Geraldine *3 km N of Geraldine*
Rivendell *B&B Homestay Apartment with Kitchen*

Erica (Ricky) & Andrew Tedham
74 Woodbury Road,
RD 21, Geraldine

Tel (03) 693 8559
or 021 264 1520
rivendellnz@xtra.co.nz
www.rivendellnz.co.nz

Double/Twin $100 - $140
Single $85 - $95
(Full breakfast)
Self-contained studio
unit with kitchen $100
Not suitable for children
Pets welcome
Internet available
1 Queen 1 Double 1 Single (3 bdrm)
TV & tea/coffee making
facilities in all rooms
Bathrooms: 2 Ensuite 1 Family share
Rose Room has bath and shower

Set in over 3 acres, Rivendell is a traditional New Zealand villa and has beautiful secluded gardens that can be enjoyed relaxing on the large verandah or in the heated spa pool. Our home provides all modern facilities including central heating, internet and laundry. The delightful village of Geraldine with its numerous cafes, restaurants, shops and cinema is only 5 minutes drive. We offer you a truly warm welcome together with our friendly dogs & animals.

Geraldine *0.5 km S of Geraldine*
Victoria Villa *B&B Cottage with Kitchen*

Jex and Dave Allison
55 Cox Street,
Geraldine 7930

Tel (03) 693 8605
or Free Phone 0800 537 533
leftofcentre2009@gmail.com
geraldineaccommodation.com

Double/Twin $140
(Full breakfast)
Children $10-$15
Dinner by arrangement
Detached studio unit
Visa MC accepted
Children and pets welcome
Internet available
3 Queen 2 Double 2 Single (4 bdrm)
Bathrooms: 3 Ensuite 1 Private

Included in the tariff is a delicious breakfast either cooked or continental, using high quality local ingredients. Other meals are available by arrangement, including picnic lunches. We are situated within easy walking distance of the centre of Geraldine, which has cafes, restaurants and boutique shops. There is also a wide range of outdoor pursuits available in the area.

Winchester *16 km N of Timaru*
Stonybanks *B&B*

Chris & Andrew Lush
32 Harrisons Rd,
Winchester,
South Canterbury

Tel (03) 615 8385
or 027 661 5888
thegrange@ihug.co.nz

Double/Twin $120
Single $80
(Full breakfast)
Pet free home
Children welcome
2 Queen 2 Single (4 bdrm)
Bathrooms: 1 Ensuite
1 Private 1 Guest share

Stonybanks is a comfortable, well appointed home set in 6 acres of beautiful grounds. We are just off Highway 1 in the village of Winchester, moments from Highway 79 to Mt Cook, Queenstown and Southern Lakes. The area is renowned for its world class salmon and trout fishing. We are within easy driving distance of restaurants, pubs and cafes, and are happy to share our knowledge of the south island with you. We are 200m north of the Winchester village on Harrison Road.

Temuka *15 km NE of Timaru*

Ashfield Manor House & Gardens *Luxury B&B*
and self-catering orchard cottage

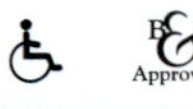

Mike and Bev Cotton
71 Cass Street,
Temuka, 7920

Tel (03) 615 6157
Fax (03) 615 6157
ashfield@paradise.net.nz
www.ashfield.co.nz

Double/Twin $150 - $195
Single $150 - $195
(Breakfast by arrangement)
Visa MC accepted
Not suitable for children
4 Queen (4 bdrm)
Spacious, all overlooking the gardens
Bathrooms: 2 Private 1 Guest share

Beautifully restored, Ashfield Manor House and gardens is one of Temuka's pominent old homesteads built in 1878. This gracious old lady is set in 4 acres of landscaped gardens. Use the homestead as a base or simply enjoy wondering through our gardens; enjoy a game of snooker on our full-sized table in the summer house, or relax in the spa pool or sauna. Only 15 minutes walk from shops and restaurants. Step back into a bygone era of luxury and comfort.

Timaru Central *1 km NW of timaru*

Jones Homestay *Homestay*
Margaret & Nevis Jones
16 Selwyn Street,
Timaru

Tel (03) 688 1400
Fax (03) 688 1400
nevisjones@xtra.co.nz

Double/Twin $120
Single $80
(Full breakfast)
Children half price
Visa MC accepted
Children welcome
2 Double 1 Twin (3 bdrm)
Bathrooms: 2 Ensuite 1 Guest share

Welcome to our spacious character brick home built in the 1920s and situated in a beautiful garden with a grass tennis court. A secluded property with off-street parking and views of the surrounding sea and mountains. Centrally situated, only 5 minutes from the beach and town with an excellent choice of cafes and restaurants. On arrival tea is served on our sunny verandah. Hosts have lived and worked extensively overseas, namely South Africa, UK and the Middle East, and enjoy music, theatre, tennis and golf.

Timaru - Seadown *4.8 km N of Timaru*
Country Homestay *Homestay*
Margaret & Ross Paterson
491 Seadown Road,
Seadown,
RD 3,
Timaru

Tel (03) 688 2468
or 021 213 7434
Fax (03) 688 2468 -

Double/Twin $90
Single $60
(Full breakfast)
Children half price
Dinner $25
Visa MC Diners Amex accepted
1 Double 2 Single (3 bdrm)
Electric blankets on all beds
Bathrooms: 1 Guest share

Our homestay is approximately 10 minutes north of Timaru, situated 4.8km on Seadown Road off State Highway 1 at Washdyke - third house on left past Pharlap Statue. We have hosted on our farm for 11 years - now retired and have a country farmlet with some farm animals, with views of farmland and mountains. Day trips to Mt Cook, Hydro Lakes and ski fields, fishing, golf course few minutes away. Laundry facilities available. Interests are farming, gardening, spinning, embroidery and overseas travel.

Timaru Central *0.1 km SW of Central Timaru*
Sefton Homestay Bed & Breakfast *B&B Homestay*
Trish & John Blunden
32 Sefton Street,
Seaview,
Timaru

Tel (03) 688 0017
or 027 473 7366
Fax (03) 688 0042
trish@seftonhomestay.co.nz
www.seftonhomestay.co.nz

Double/Twin $125
Single $110
(Full breakfast)
Children half price
Visa MC accepted
Children welcome
1 King/Twin 1 Queen
1 Double (3 bdrm)
Bathrooms: 1 Ensuite 1 Private

Relax in our superbly appointed and spacious 2 storey character brick home with sweeping views from the mountains to the sea. Refurbished with the feel of yesteryear, but with ambience and style you will love. All our children have left home with the exception of our labrador Ollie who enjoys meeting people as we do. A genuine 5 minute walk to the nearest restaurants

Pleasant Point - Timaru *17 km SW of Timaru*
Longview Bed & Breakfast *B&B Farmstay*

Anita & Alan Blakemore
86 Longview Road,
Pleasant Point,
Timaru 7983

Tel (03) 614 7766
or 027 308 5078
longview86@xtra.co.nz
www.longviewfarmstay.co.nz

Double/Twin $140
Single $80 - $100
(Full breakfast)
Children up to $40
Dinner by prior arrangement $40
Visa MC accepted
Children welcome
Internet available
2 Queen 1 Twin (3 bdrm)
Bathrooms: 1 Guest share

Nestled on 25 acres, Longview has stunning, 'must see to believe', panoramic views of the surrounding farmlands and mountains, just 2 hrs drive from Christchurch and Mt Cook. Two of our guest rooms and the private guest lounge have direct access to the terrace and gardens. Take a stroll through the olive grove (complimentary oil tastings available), meet Becky our Cocker Spaniel, visit our farm animals and soak up the tranquil country atmosphere. 5 minutes from local cafes.

Timaru *1 km S of Information centre*
Blueberry Cottage *B&B Homestay*

Barbara & Rodger Baird
72A High Street, Timaru

Tel (03) 684 3115
or 027 636 4301
Fax (03) 684 3172
relax@blueberrycottage.co.nz
www.blueberrycottage.co.nz

Double/Twin $115 - $120
Single $75 - $80
(Continental breakfast)
Children negotiable
Visa MC accepted
Pet free home
1 King/Twin 1 Queen (2 bdrm)
Tuscany Double and
Highland Twin/Superking
Bathrooms: 1 Private 1 Guest share
Bath and wet shower, separate toilet

Our delightfully upgraded 1950's brick home offers comfort and spectacular closeup views of the ocean and inland to Mt Cook. The tastefully furnished rooms have television, separate patios. Handy to hospital, gardens & beach. Walking distance to shops, cafe/bars, or eating place of your choice. Day trips to lakes, skiing in winter, Mt Cook, fishing rivers, bush walks and towns nearby. Our interests can be detected by our nautical theme, the vintage car in the garage and our choice of music. 'Relaxation at its best'.

Fairlie *3 km SW of Fairlie*

Fontmell *B&B Homestay Farmstay*

Anne & Norman McConnell
Nixons Road 169, Fairlie

Tel (03) 685 8379
Fax (03) 685 8379

Double/Twin $120 - $175
Single $65
(Full breakfast)
Children $35
2 King/Twin 1 Queen 1 Double 2 Twin 1 Single (4 bdrm)
Bathrooms: 1 Private 1 Guest share

Yes you have discovered us, the place where there is so much to do and see you'll want to stay another day at this property adjacent to the Christchurch-Queenstown tourist route. Tea or coffee and cookies on the terrace or in front of the open fired offered on arrival.

To quote past guests this is a house in a park not a garden. Other than birdsong the only sound is that of a murmuring creek at the bottom of the garden where walkways take you over bridges and past beds of flowers shaded by towering Ponderosa Pines and one hundred year old European trees.

First task for the day is feed pigs and gather eggs. On a short walk you can admire NZ's largest Radiata Pine, feed Annie the pet deer or Laddie the horse, photograph Highland cattle and red deer grazing then spot the wallabys in the woodlands. Take a 3km walk through the farm to the cottage from where there's a panoramic view over the Fairlie basin while enjoying tea or coffee on the sun deck, or drive up the Two Thumb Range (5500ft). After a short walk take a rest - enjoy a cut lunch - spot Mt Cook on the far side of the Mackenzie basin. A jeep chrokee is available for this venture. Looking forward to sharing these activities with you.

Fairlie - Kimbell *8 km SW of Fairlie*
Rivendell Lodge *B&B Homestay Countrystay*
Joan Gill
15 Stanton Road, Kimbell, 7987

Tel (03) 685 8833
or 027 4819 189
Fax (03) 685 8825
joan@rivendell-lodge.co.nz
www.rivendell-lodge.co.nz

Double/Twin $130 - $160
Single $85 - $100
(Full breakfast)
Children negotiable
Dinner $50 per person
Visa MC accepted
Pet free home
Children welcome
3 Queen 1 Double 2 Single (4 bdrm)
Bathrooms: 2 Ensuite 2 Private
Separate spa bath available

Quality country comfort and hospitality offered in a peaceful historic village on the Christchurch-Queenstown route. Joan is a well-travelled writer, passionate about mountains, literature and local history. I enjoy cooking and gardening and delight in sharing home grown produce. Take time out for fishing, skiing, walking, golf or water sports. Relax in the garden, complete with stream, or come with us to some of our favourite places. Complimentary refreshments on arrival. Laundry facilities available.

Lake Tekapo *40 km SW of Fairlie*
Freda Du Faur House *Luxury B&B Homestay*
Dawn & Barry Clark
1 Esther Hope Street,
Lake Tekapo

Tel (03) 680 6513
dawntek@xtra.co.nz
www.fredadufaur.co.nz

Double/Twin $170 - $190
Single $100 - $110
(Continental breakfast
or cooked on request)
Children $95
Visa MC accepted
Children welcome
1 Queen 1 Double 2 Single (3 bdrm)
Bathrooms: 2 Ensuite 1 Private

Experience tranquillity and a touch of mountain magic. A warm and friendly welcome. Comfortable home, mountain and lake views. Rimu panelling, heart timber furniture, attractive decor, blending with the McKenzie Country. Bedrooms in private wing overlooking garden, two opening onto balcony. Refreshments on patio surrounded by roses or view ever changing panorama from lounge. Walkways nearby. Mt Cook one hour away. Views of skifield. Five minutes to shops and restaurants. Call for Directions. Happy hr 6 7. Our new Persian kitten called Bella welcomes you.

Lake Pukaki - Mt Cook *7 km N of Twizel*
Rhoborough Downs, Pukaki *Homestay*

Roberta Preston
State Highway 8
Tekapo/Twizel

Tel (03) 435 0509
or 027 621 7941
ra.preston@xtra.co.nz

Double/Twin $130
Single $70
(Continental breakfast)
Children $50
Dinner not available
1 Double 1 Twin 1 Single (3 bdrm)
Bathrooms: 1 Guest share
Seperate toilets

A quiet place to stop, halfway between Christchurch and Queenstown or Christchurch and Dunedin via Waitaki Valley. 40 minutes to Mt Cook. The 10,000 acre property has been in the family 90 years. Merino sheep graze to 6000 feet, hereford cattle. Views of the southern sky. The homestead is set in tranquil gardens. Twizel has a bank, doctor, shops and several restaurants. we have a juvenile gold lab. Please phone for bookings and directions. Cot available.

Lake Pukaki *27 km SW of Lake Tekapo*
Tasman Downs Station *Farmstay*

Linda Hayman
Tasman Downs Station,
Lake Tekapo, 7945

Tel (03) 680 6841
Fax (03) 680 6851
samjane@xtra.co.nz
www.bnb.co.nz

Double/Twin $130 - $140
Single $85 - $100
(Full breakfast)
Dinner $45 pp by arrangement
1 Queen 1 Twin (2 bdrm)
Bathrooms: 1 Private 1 Guest share

We welcome you to a place of unsurpassed beauty located on the shores of Lake Pukaki, with magnificent views of the lake, Mount Cook and Southern Alps. Our local stone home blends in with the natural peaceful surroundings. This high country station has been in our family since 1914 and runs mainly Angus cattle. Linda and son Ian enjoy sharing their knowledge of farming with guests. An opportunity to experience farm life with friendly hosts. Or visit many nearby attractions. Dinner by arrangement.

Twizel - Mt Cook *2 km SW of Twizel Info Centre*
Artemis B&B *B&B Homestay*

Jan & Bob Wilson
33 North West Arch,
Twizel

Tel (03) 435 0388
Fax (03) 435 0377
artemistwizel@paradise.net.nz

Double/Twin $130
Single $110
(Special breakfast)
Visa MC Eftpos accepted
Pet free home
Not suitable for children
Internet available
2 Queen 1 Single (2 bdrm)
Bathrooms: 1 Ensuite 1 Private

Jan and Bob welcome you to the magnificent Mackenzie Basin and the Mount Cook National Park. Our modern home, which is situated on a hectare of land, has stunning mountain views along with space and tranquility. We are a short drive to Mount Cook National Park and a three minutes drive to restaurants. There is a guest sitting room with a balcony and tea/coffee making facilities. We look forward to sharing our home with you and are happy to discuss your New Zealand itineraries and sightseeing.

Twizel - Mt Cook *0.5 km S of Twizel*
Hunters House and Hunters Cottage Self Contained
B&B Cottage with Kitchen

Anne & Matt Hunter
58 Tekapo Drive,
Twizel

Tel (03) 435 0038
Fax (03) 435 0038
annehunter@xtra.co.nz

Double/Twin $180
Single $140
(Full breakfast)
Visa MC accepted
Not suitable for children
Internet available
2 King/Twin (2 bdrm)
Bathrooms: 2 Ensuite

Hunters House is architecturally designed for guests and features every comfort in a warm welcoming environment. It overlooks the native tussocks and trees of the Green Belt on the township boundary with the mountains as a backdrop. All rooms are tastefully decorated with all facilities and french doors opening to the peaceful outdoors sited for the sun and views. We also have a self contained cottage fully equiped with all home comforts and same views Situated in its own private setting. 'Cead Mile Failte'

Twizel - Mt Cook *1 km N of Twizel*
Pinegrove *B&B Cottage with Kitchen 2 Cottages with kitchens*

Al & Joh Ingram
29 North West Arch, Twizel, 7944
PO Box 88 Twizel

Tel 03 435 0430
or 021 464 726
aljohpinegrove@hotmail.com

Double/Twin $140 - $160
Single $100
(Special breakfast)
Children $10 - $20
Visa MC Eftpos accepted
Children welcome
2 Queen 1 Double
2 Single (2 bdrm)
2 bedrooms in each cottage
Bathrooms: 2 Private
Walk in showers

Rest a while in the beautiful Mackenzie District with its mountains and lakes. We are only 45 mins from Mt Cook and 2 mins drive to near by restaurants. We welcome you to our sunny cottages situated in an extensive garden with fishpond and tranquil areas to sit in. The cottages are fitted with modern conveniences with your comfort in mind. You can indulge in home baked goodies from the breakfast hamper. We look forward to meeting you and welcoming you to our haven.

Twizel *0.2 km S of Central Twizel*
Aoraki Lodge *B&B*

Ian & Sandy Darwin
32 Mackenzie Drive,
Twizel

Tel (03) 435 0300
Fax (03) 435 0305
ian.sandy@xtra.co.nz
www.aorakilodge.co.nz

Tariff $180 - $200
(Full breakfast)
Children not suitable under 12
Walking distance to restaurants
and other facilites
60 kilometres to Mt Cook
Visa MC Eftpos accepted
4 Queen (4 bdrm)
3 Double 1 Twin
Bathrooms: 4 Ensuite

Relax in the informal atmosphere of our Lodge set amongst a rambling country-style garden. Aoraki Lodge is located in the centre of Twizel at 32 Mackenzie Drive. Our Lodge is a short walk to local Restaurants, Clubs and other facilities, yet offers complete privacy. Ian & Sandy Darwin welcome you and will advise on what to see and do in this beautiful part of the world. Ian, a member of the NZPFG Association, is well known Fly-Fishing Guide in the local area.

Lindis Pass *17 km SW of Omarama*
Dunstan Downs *Farmstay*

Tim & Geva Innes
Dunstan Downs,
Omarama, 9448

Tel (03) 438 9862
Fax (03) 438 9517
tim.innes@xtra.co.nz
www.dunstandowns.co.nz

Double/Twin up to $260
Single up to $130
(Full breakfast provisions)
Children under 12 half price
Tarrif includes dinner, bed & breakfast
GST will be added to all tariffs
Visa MC accepted
Children and pets welcome
1 Queen 2 Twin 1 Single (3 bdrm)
Bathrooms: 1 Ensuite 1 Guest share
1 Family share

Dunstan Downs is a merino sheep station in the heart of the South Island high country. Our home is full of country warmth, you are welcome to join us for dinner (wine served) or bed and breakfast. The surrounding mountains and valleys are an adventure playground, tramping, mountain biking, fishing,farming activities or lazing around soaking up the peace and tranquillity. No pets inside.

Oamaru - Waianakarua *27 km S of Oamaru*

Glen Dendron *B&B Farmstay*

Anne & John Mackay
284 Breakneck Road, Waianakarua,
RD 90, Oamaru 9495

Tel (03) 439 5288 or 021 615 227
Fax (03) 439 5288
stay@glendendronfarmstay.co.nz
www.glendendronfarmstay.co.nz

Double/Twin $135 - $170
Single $110 - $135 (Full breakfast)
Children $50
Dinner $40 with wine
Visa MC accepted
Pet free home   Children welcome   Internet available
2 King/Twin 2 Queen (4 bdrm)
Ensuite rooms include TV and tea making facilities
Bathrooms: 2 Ensuite 1 Guest share Spa bath

Our Award Winning Homestay offers tranquility and beauty when you stay in our stylish modern home, spectacularly sited on a hilltop overlooking the picturesque Waianakarua River and surrounded by 5 acres of landscaped garden. After breakfast, feed the sheep and alpacas. Then take a stroll through the forest, native bush complete with waterfalls and birds or beside the river. Play a round on our private golf course. Later, watch the seals and penguins on a beach nearby. Then, complete a perfect day with our 3 course dinner with NZ wine before retiring in peace and comfort.

After a lifetime spent in farming and forestry we relish the opportunity to share our home and semi-retired lifestyle with guests. Our adult family lives overseas so we travel frequently and have a great interest in other countries and cultures. We are very keen gardeners, read widely and enjoy antiques. Anne is a floral designer and John a tree connoisseur.

An overnight stay is not enough to do justice to this lovely area - with so much to see, why not stay awhile! The area's many attractions include Oamaru's historic architecture. Garden, heritage and fossil trails. Beaches, fishing, seals, penguins and famous Moeraki Boulders. Use us as a base for day visits to Oamaru, Dunedin, Waitaki Valley and Mt Cook. We dont mind short notice.

Oamaru *1.3 km N of Oamaru Centre*
Highway House Boutique B&B *B&B*
Stephanie & Norman Slater
43 Lynn Street,
(Cnr Thames Highway & Lynn St),
Meadowbank, Oamaru

Tel (03) 437 1066
or 0800 003 319
Fax (03) 437 1066
breakfast@highwayhouse.co.nz
www.highwayhouse.co.nz

Double/Twin $150 - $175
Single $130 - $155 (Full breakfast)
Children negotiable
Visa MC Amex accepted
Pet free home Internet available
1 King/Twin 2 King (3 bdrm)
Thoroughly appointed
Bathrooms: 1 Ensuite 1 Guest share
1 Family share Large-size showers

Our character residence on Thames Highway, (1.3km north of town centre), has been entirely refurbished. We provide a wholesome light and a full cooked breakfast along with other refreshments as required. We can assist with tours of historic Oamaru or penguin visits. Our courtesy car can collect or take you to nearby dining establishments. Laundry available. If you appreciate a quality ambiance and particular assistance from Stephanie and Norman who have travelled widely overseas, Highway House will be ideal for you. French also spoken.

Oamaru *0.5 km SW of Oamaru centre*
Homestay Oamaru *B&B Homestay*
Doug Bell
14 Warren Street,
Oamaru

Tel (03) 434 1454
or 027 408 2860
homestayoamaru@paradise.net.nz
www.bellview.co.nz

Double/Twin $80 - $100
Single $55 - $70
(Full breakfast)
Dinner $25 by arrangement
Pet free home
Not suitable for children
Internet available
2 Queen 1 Double (3 bdrm)
Warm & relaxing decor,
quality beds & great showers
Bathrooms: 2 Ensuite 1 Family share

Sweeping views over the town and harbour. Warm, spacious and comfortable accommodation for the travelling enthusiast, with books, maps, atlases and guides for you perusal. Quiet, private site, close to town centre. (see map on website). Off-street parking. Southern scenic walkway access at property boundary. Some of the area's attractions include sea and river fishing, historic architecture, unique geological features and eco-tourism. Host has detailed local knowledge. Site unsuitable for young children or pets.

Oamaru *8 km S of Oamaru*
Ranui Retreat Bed and Breakfast/Homestay *B&B Homestay*
Sheryl Laraman and Family
27 Woolshed Road,
Totara,
Oamaru,
8D RD

Tel (03) 439 5241
ranui_retreat@actrix.gen.nz
www.ranui-retreat.co.nz

Double/Twin $140 - $160
Single $100
(Full breakfast)
Children negotiable
Dinner 25 pp
Visa MC accepted
Children and pets welcome
Internet available
2 Queen (2 bdrm)
Bathrooms: 1 Ensuite 1 Private

Welcome to Ranui Retreat. We are close to historic Oamaru and the main highway to Dunedin. Views of Otago rural landscape stretching to the Kakanui Mountains enhance the rural sense of this five acre property of mature oak, elm and ash trees. There is birdsong aplenty. Character rooms include rich, handmade quilts which add to the relaxed ambience. Join the family for the evening or you may like to retire to other spaces with music and a good book from our library selection.

Oamaru *0.5 km S of Oamaru*
Federation House Homestay Inn B&B *B&B Homestay*
Rodger McCaw
60 Tyne Street,
Oamaru, 9400

Tel (03) 434 9537
Fax (03) 434 9537
info@federationhouse.co.nz
www.federationhouse.co.nz

Double/Twin $100 - $150
Single $50 - $100
(Full breakfast)
Dinner by arrangement
Off Season Rates - special discount
from May until October
Visa MC accepted
Pet free home Children welcome
3 King/Twin 2 Twin (5 bdrm)
Bathrooms: 3 Ensuite
1 Guest share 1 Family share

A Welcome Inn - Sound night's sleep assured. An urban haven for discerning guests. This magnificent heritage house has panoramic views of the harbour, ocean and town; close to penguin colonies and restaurants. Refurbished to provide modern facilities, ensuing privacy with ensuite bathrooms and quality King/Twin beds. Tariff varies for guests breakfast requirements with choice of full cooked, continental, or lodging only. Relax and enjoy Shiner's Saloon. Wireless internet available.

Otago &
North Catlins
Mount Cook
Haast
6
Twizel
Kimb
Makarora
Omarama
Lindis Pass
Lake Hawea
Kurow
Wanaka
Albert Town
6
Glenorchy
Lowburn
Danseys Pass
Arrowtown
Cromwell
Queenstown
Clyde
Alexandra
85
Palmerston
Garston
Middlemarch
6
Waikouaiti
Roxburgh
1
Ettrick
Millers Flat
Otago
Wendonside
Peninsula
Balfour
Mosgiel
8
Waikaka
Dunedin
Lawrence
Winton
Gore
Mataura
Balclutha
Wyndham
Kilometres
0   40
rcargill
Kaka Point
The Catlins
Owaka
Mokotua
Miles
0   24
Nuggets
Tokanui

Makarora *65 km N of Wanaka*
Makarora Homestead *B&B Cottage with Kitchen*

Kenna Fraser & Rick McLachlan
53 Rata Road,
Makarora, 9346

Tel (03) 443 1532
Fax (03) 443 1525
info@makarora.com
www.makarora.com

Double/Twin $130 - $145
Single $100 - $120
(Continental breakfast provisions)
Restaurant in walking distance (500 m)
Visa MC accepted
Children and pets welcome
7 Queen 1 Double 7 Twin (8 bdrm)
3 Detached B&B rooms,
5 in Homestead
Bathrooms: 3 Ensuite 3 Guest share

Makarora Homestead offers a secluded retreat in the midst of the Southern Alps & is perfect for travellers looking for the peace & tranquility of the mountains. We offer a self-contained studio with kitchenette, ensuite & private balcony OR 2 detached bedrooms each with ensuite, tea/coffee making facilities & shared sundeck. Nestled at the edge of the native forest with panoramic views of the mountains & surrounding wapiti deer farm. Hand feed our tame deer Nigel & various friendly sheep.

Wanaka *1 km S of Wanaka*
Berryfarm Homestay *B&B Homestay Separate Suite Guest lounge*

Annette & Bob Menlove
83 Orchard Road,
Wanaka, Central
Otago

Tel (03) 443 4248
or CP 021 494 149
Fax (03) 443 4249
bobannette@menlove.net
www.berryfarmhomestay.co.nz

Double/Twin $150 - $180
Single $150
(Full breakfast)
Visa MC Eftpos accepted
Children welcome
Internet available
1 King/Twin 1 Double
1 Twin (3 bdrm)
Bathrooms: 2 Ensuite 1 Private
Spa and Bath

We are a Berryfarm growing raspberries, strawberries boysenberries and tomatoes, on the outskirts of Wanaka, just three minutes from town. We are very close to good restaurants, a golf course, ski fields and excellent lake and river fishing. We have two cats and a labrador dog and have just retired from a sheep, cattle and deer farm. Bob and I have been hosting for a number of years and both enjoy meeting people.

Wanaka *0.4 km SW of Centre Wanaka*
Lake Wanaka Homestay *B&B Homestay*

Gailie & Peter Cooke
85 Warren Street,
Wanaka, 9305

Tel (03) 443 7995
or 0800 443 799
Fax (03) 443 7945
wanakahomestay@xtra.co.nz
www.lakewanakahomestay.co.nz

Double/Twin $130 - $140
Single $100 (Full breakfast)
Center of Wanaka
Visa MC accepted
Not suitable for small children
2 Double (2 bdrm)
Double beds, Heaters, Electric
blankets, Dressers, Tables
Bathrooms: 1 Private 1 Guest share
Guest share, Our Private, Great shower

Welcome to Lake Wanaka Homestay ideally situated in centre of Wanaka just 5 minutes walk (470 metres) to shops, Restaurants & Lake. Relax with Peter & Gailie, enjoy breathtaking views of Lake & Mountains. Complimentary tea, coffee, homebaking anytime during stay. Full cooked breakfast no extra cost, off street parking, two warm comfortable double bedrooms. After many years farming we moved to Wankaka now enjoy hosting guests in our home. Interests; fishing, golf, skiing, gardening. Kate our Labrador is everyone's friend. Guests comments: 'Great hosts, wonderful breakfast'

Wanaka *3 km N of Wanaka Shops*
Beacon Point *B&B Homestay Apartment with Kitchen*

Diana & Dan Pinckney
302 Beacon Point Road,
PO Box 6, Lake Wanaka

Tel (03) 443 1253
or 0272 460 222
Fax (03) 443 1254
dan.di@lakewanaka.co.nz
www.beaconpoint.co.nz

Double/Twin $130
Single $100
(Continental breakfast)
Children $40
Dinner $45
Rolla Beds
Pet free home
Children welcome
1 Queen 1 Twin (2 bdrm)
Bathrooms: 1 Ensuite

Beacon Point B&B has an acre of lawn and garden for your enjoyment. Leads to a walking track to the village around the edge of the lake. Private spacious studio with ensuite, queen and single beds (2 rooms), kitchen, TV, DVD, sundeck and BBQ. Studio equipped with every need for perfect stay. We enjoy planning your days with you. Our intrests include farming, forestry, fly fishing, real estate, boating, gardening and grandchildren. Turn right at lake - Lakeside Road - then to Beacon Point Road 302.

Wanaka *1.3 km S of Wanaka*
Harpers *B&B Homestay*
Jo & Ian Harper
95 McDougall Street,
Wanaka

Tel (03) 443 8894
harpers@xtra.co.nz
www.harpers.co.nz

Double/Twin $140 - $1500
Single $110
(Continental breakfast)
Visa MC accepted
1 King/Twin 2 Single (2 bdrm)
2 in home
Bathrooms: 2 Ensuite

We take pride in offering a friendly, comfortable home. Share breakfast and awesome lake and mountain views with us. Also explore our extensive garden, which provides a tranquil environment for relaxing. We offer tea/coffee and muffins on your arrival. This is a smoke-free home. Recent guests' comments: 'Wonderful welcoming homestay.' 'Friendly hosts, excellent breakfasts. 'Wonderful hospitality, fantastic breakfast.' 'Excellent hosts, breakfasts to die for.' 'Very comfortable. Great hosts. Top spot.' 'Wonderful views. The muffins and pancakes do live up to expectations.' 'A home from home.'

Wanaka *4 km S of Wanaka*
Stonehaven *Homestay*
Deirdre & Dennis
217 Maxwell Road,
RD 2, Wanaka

Tel (03) 443 9516
or 027 310 9323
Fax (03) 443 9513
moghul@xtra.co.nz
www.stonehaven.co.nz

Double/Twin $145
Single $105 (Full breakfast)
Children $20 negotiable
Children under 4 free
Portacots and highchairs available
Visa MC accepted
Children and pets welcome
Internet Available
2 Queen 2 Single (2 bdrm)
Spacious with comfortable beds
Bathrooms: 1 Ensuite 1 Private

Our home is set in two acres about five minutes drive from Wanaka. All beds have electric blankets. Tea and coffee is freely available. We have extensive views of surrounding mountains. Families are welcome and child care available. Our nearby tree collection has an accent on autumn colour. Local walks a speciality. Organic fruit both in season and preserved. We have a small dog and a cat. Please phone for directions. Please arrive after 4 p.m. unless arranged.

Wanaka *0.2 km E of Wanaka Central*
Te Wanaka Lodge *B&B Guest House*
Ski Lodge/Chalet in Winter

Mandy & Wayne Enoka
23 Brownston Street, Wanaka

Tel (03) 443 9224
or FreeCall: 0800 WANAKA
(0800 926252)
Fax (03) 443 9246
tewanakalodge@xtra.co.nz
www.tewanaka.co.nz

Double/Twin $165 - $235
Single $150 - $195
(Full breakfast)
Garden cottage room $230
($250 for 3 persons)
Visa MC Eftpos accepted
Children welcome
9 Queen 4 Twin (13 bdrm)
Ensuite with private balcony
Bathrooms: 13 Ensuite

Owned & run by outdoor enthusiasts, the lodge is a place for active people who want to get out & explore our picturesque town and locale. Get good advice from your hosts about all the local walks and great things to do. Te Wanaka enjoys a reputation as a relaxed, fun and friendly place to stay. After an adventurous day exploring our mountains, lake & streams, guests can soak in the private garden hot tub/spa, sit back in one of our comfy lounges or enjoy the sun in our pretty courtyard garden. All bedrooms with ensuite and private balcony.

Wanaka *2.3 km NW of Wanaka Centre*
Peak-Sportchalet *B&B Apartment with Kitchen Chalet*

Alex & Christine Schafer
36 Hunter Crescent,
Wanaka 9305

Tel (03) 443 6990
stay@peak-sportchalet.co.nz
www.Peak-Sportchalet.co.nz

Double/Twin $130 - $170
Single $100 - $110
(Special breakfast)
Visa MC accepted
Children welcome
Internet available
1 King 1 Queen 1 Twin (3 bdrm)
High quality mattresses; luxury
duvets; private sundecks
Bathrooms: 2 Ensuite 1 Private
underfloor-heating; hairdryer;
high quality showers

Welcome at Peak-Sportchalet - your Qualmark 4 Star accommodation in Wanaka. Experience ambience and hospitality in our 3 guest suites and selfcontained Chalet. All are individually designed and appointed with fine furniture, ensuite or private bathrooms, TV, DVD, Freeview and Sound System. Sliding doors open onto private sundecks with great mountain views. Awake refreshed after a relaxing nights sleep on our prime quality mattresses and duvets. Start your day healthy with our memorable breakfast-buffet. We also cater for special diets. free Broadband/Wireless

Wanaka - Albert Town *6 km NE of Wanaka*
Riversong *B&B Homestay*

Ann & Ian Horrax
5 Wicklow Terrace,
Albert Town, Wanaka

Tel (03) 443 8567
or 021 113 6397
Fax (03) 443 8564
info@riversongwanaka.co.nz
www.riversongwanaka.co.nz

Double/Twin $160 - $180
Single $120
(Full breakfast)
Children $25
Dinner $55pp by arrangement
Visa MC accepted
Children welcome
Internet Available
1 King/Twin 1 Queen 1 Single (3 bdrm)
Bathrooms: 1 Ensuite 1 Private

Riversong is 5 minutes from Wanaka Township, at Albert Town, on the banks of the majestic Clutha River. At our secluded haven all rooms have river and mountain views, with immediate access to the river. Ann's background is healthcare and Ian's law. We invite you to share the comforts and privacy of our home and garden and Ian's knowledge of the region's fishing and guidance service. We aim to provide a memorable and comfortable stay. We have 1 outside lab dog. Wireless/broadband available.

Wanaka *2.4 km E of Wanaka*
The Cedars B&B *B&B*

Mary & Graham Dowdall
7 Riverbank Road,
RD 2, Wanaka, 9382

Tel Landline (03) 443 1544
or Mobile 021 1208 960
Fax (03) 443 1580
thecedarswanaka@xtra.co.nz
www.thecedars.co.nz

Double/Twin $195 - $230
Single $150 - $185 (Full breakfast)
Highchair and portacot available
Three course dinner or BBQ by
arrangement with 24 hours notice
Visa MC accepted
Children very welcome
Internet available
2 Queen 1 Single (2 bdrm)
Spacious, TV, fridge, fluffy bathrobes
Bathrooms: 1 Ensuite 1 Private with Spa Bath

Cead Mile Failte - One hundred thousand welcomes. A warm Irish/Kiwi welcome awaits you at The Cedars, by Mary, Graham, Rough Collie Nessa and cat Cara. Our stone home on 11 acres is close to all Wanaka's attractions and restaurants,has panoramic mountain views, expansive gardens,paddocks with alpacas and sheep, guest lounge with large open fire. We enjoy travelling, dining, music, literature and sports. Full breakfast is served with fresh and home-made produce. We offer evening meals or BBQ by prior arrangement.

Wanaka *0.5 km N of Wanaka*
Criffel Peak View *B&B Apartment with Kitchen*

Caroline Holland
98 Hedditch Street,
Wanaka

Tel (03) 443 5511
Fax (03) 443 5521
stay@criffelpeakview.co.nz
www.criffelpeakview.co.nz

Double/Twin $150 - $160
Single $120 (Full breakfast)
Apartment from $220 for 4 people
Visa MC accepted
Children welcome
Internet available
2 King/Twin 1 King
2 Queen (3 bdrm)
Plus 2 bedroom apartment
Bathrooms: 2 Ensuite 2 Private

A cosy modern cottage situated in a quiet cul-de-sac, just a short walk from the lake and town. Great mountain views, large sunny deck, friendly young hosts and a crazy cat called Splodge. Our 3 guest rooms look out towards the Criffel Range and are equipped with ensuite bathrooms and super king or queen sized beds. The guest lounge has Wireless Internet access, guest computer, tea/coffee making and variety of reading material. Our apartment is perfect for larger groups and families.

Wanaka *12 km E of Wanaka*
Kanuka Lodge *B&B*

Heather & Graeme Halliday
110 Shortcut Road,
SH 8A,
Luggate,
RD 2
Wanaka

Tel (03) 443 7448
hallday@es.co.nz

Double/Twin $125
Single $100 - $100
(Full breakfast)
Children $25
Visa MC accepted
Children and pets welcome
1 Queen 1 Double 1 Single (3 bdrm)
Bathrooms: 1 Guest share

O ur home is near the Clutha river, 10 minutes drive from Wanaka. It features NZ art and books. We welcome you with a glass of fine NZ wine. At breakfast you must try the Central Otago apricots and Heather's wildflower honey. You can admire the alpine landscape with geologist, photographer and fisherman Graeme, and plan your exploration of Wanaka. We have friendly cats and horses. Heather, originally from Bath in England, gives rides in her vintage buggies and grows the exotic spice saffron.

Lake Wanaka *1 km N of Post Office*
Black Peak Lodge *B&B Homestay Apartment with Kitchen*

Helen and David Rule
38 Kings Drive,
Wanaka

Tel (03) 443 4078
or Mobile 027 457 3539
Fax (03) 443 4038
hellbell@xtra.co.nz
www.blackpeaklodge.co.nz

Double/Twin $180 - $220
Single $180 - $200
(Full breakfast)
Visa MC accepted
Children gladly welcomed
Internet available
2 King/Twin 2 Queen (4 bdrm)
3 in B&B and 1 or 2 in apartment
Bathrooms: 1 Ensuite 3 Private

Welcome to Black Peak Lodge. Unwind in comfort.... in winter by the log fire, in summer on the open deck in awe of the spectacular view. Relax in the lounge, indulging in fine wines and mouthwatering appetizers. Recharge and recuperate in the spa amidst the tranquil ambiance that is ....Black Peak Lodge. Join us in our recreational activities: biking, fishing, boating, water skiing, walking or enjoying time with our gorgeous Golden Retriever, Rosa Bella.

Wanaka *0 km N of*
Aspiring Lofts *B&B Self Contained Unit*

Don & Lorraine Irvine
42 Manuka Cresent,
Wanaka

Tel (03) 443 7856
or 021 236 1518
info@aspiringlofts.co.nz
www.aspiringlofts.co.nz

Double/Twin $150 - $180
Single $150
(Full breakfast)
Visa MC accepted
1 King/Twin 1 Queen (2 bdrm)
Bathrooms: 2 Ensuite

Welcome to Aspiring Lofts - with stunning lake and mountain views. Relax in our new architecturally designed studio apartments. Enjoy luxurious rooms opening onto your own private balcony with outstanding views, an easy walk to lake and cafes and a private entrance. Relax in our contemporary garden. Wireless/broadband available. Don, a retired lawyer and Lorraine, a teacher have extensive local knowledge and can help you plan your day. Wanaka offers untold beauty, tranquility, inspiration and adventure. We invite you to share the experience with us.

Wanaka *0.5 km E of Centre Wanaka*
d'lavande Bed & Breakfast *B&B*
Helen & Wayne Blair
97 Warren Street,
Wanaka, 9305

Tel (03) 443 7670
or 027 245 4407
contact@dlavande.co.nz
www.dlavande.co.nz

Double/Twin $140 - $160
Single $110
(Full breakfast)
Visa MC accepted
Not suitable for children
1 King/Twin 2 King (3 bdrm)
1 King ensuite; 1 King &
1 King single private
(Single group booking only)
Bathrooms: 1 Ensuite 1 Private

Only a 5 minute stroll to town centre with an abundance of cafes and restaurants. A warm welcome awaits you. Purpose built in 2009 and decorated to a high standard with quality linen and toiletries plus private access. TV/DVD, T&C making facilities and complimentary home baking in all rooms. Enjoy a scrumptious breakfast with lake and mountain views. Our aim is to provide luxury accommodation at affordable prices and a calm, relaxing environment to recharge your batteries. Skye is our very shy cat.

Cromwell *1 km S of live in Cromwell*
Stuart's Homestay *B&B Homestay*
Elaine & Ian Stuart
5 Mansor Court,
Cromwell

Tel (03) 445 3636
Fax (03) 445 3617
ian.elaine@xtra.co.nz
www.stuartshomestayandb.co.nz

Double/Twin $110 - $130
Single $70 - $80
(Full breakfast)
Dinner $25 to $35 by arrangement
Visa MC accepted
Pet free home
Children welcome
2 Queen 2 Single (3 bdrm)
Bathrooms: 1 Ensuite 1 Guest share

Welcome to our home which is situated within walking distance to most of Cromwell's amenities. We are semi-retired Southland farmers who have been hosting for over 15 years. Cromwell is a quiet and relaxed town with historic gold diggings, vineyards, orchards, trout fishing, boating, walks, close to ski fields. 45 minutes to Wanaka or Queenstown. Share dinner with us or just bed & breakfast. Tea and coffee, home-made cookies available. We enjoy sharing our home and garden with visitors and a friendly stay is assured.

Cromwell *0.5 km N of Cromwell town centre*
Cottage Gardens *B&B Homestay detached twin studio*

Jill & Colin McColl
80 Neplusultra Street,
Cromwell,
Central Otago

Tel (03) 445 0628
Fax (03) 445 0628
cottage.gardens@ihug.co.nz
www.cromwellbedandbreakfast.co.nz

Double/Twin $100 - $110
Single $55 - $75
(Continental breakfast)
Children n/a
Visa MC accepted
Not suitable for children
Internet available
2 Twin 1 Single (3 bdrm)
Bathrooms: 1 Ensuite 2 Private

Welcome! Hospitality is our specialty. For 16 years we have welcomed travellers. Our home features local stone and timbers and overlooks an 18 hole Golf course. The Twin studio unit adjoins the garden. The upstairs Twin room has private bathroom, TV, and tea making. Cromwell is surrounded by vineyards, orchards and Lake. Meet retired seeing eye dog Tango and cat Bluebelle. Members of Lions International and Woolcrafters, Retired Orchardist and Teacher. Queenstown, Wanaka 45 minutes. Fiordland, 2.5 hours. Shops and Restaurants 10 minutes walk. Free laundry.

Cromwell *5 km N of Cromwell*
Lake Dunstan Lodge *Homestay*

Judy & Bill Thornbury
Northburn,
RD 3, Cromwell

Tel (03) 445 1107
or 027 431 1415
Fax (03) 445 3062
william.t@xtra.co.nz
www.lakedunstanlodge.co.nz

Double/Twin $120 - $140
Single $90
(Full breakfast)
Children negotiable
Dinner $30-40 by arrangement
Visa MC accepted
Children welcome
2 Queen 3 Single (3 bdrm)
Bathrooms: 2 Ensuite 1 Guest share

Friendly hospitality awaits you at our home privately situated beside Lake Dunstan. We are ex-Southland farmers and have a cat Ollie. Our interests include Lions, fishing, boating, gardening and crafts. Bedrooms have attached balconies, fridge, tea and coffee facilities. Guests share our living areas, spa pool and laundry. Local attractions: orchards, vineyards, gold diggings, fishing, boating, walks, 4 ski fields nearby. Enjoy dinner with us or just relax in the peaceful surroundings. No smoking indoors please. Directions: 5km north of Cromwell Bridge on SH8.

Cromwell - Lowburn *14 km N of Cromwell*

Smoothwater Haven *Luxury B&B*

Bonnie & Susie Perry
68 Gilmore Road,
(Luggate-Cromwell Hwy, SH6),
Mt Pisa, Cromwell, 9383

Tel (03) 445 3231
or 0210 242 3859
Fax (03) 445 3231
info@smoothwaterhaven.co.nz
www.smoothwaterhaven.co.nz

Double/Twin $140 - $190
Single $120 - $150 (Full breakfast)
Asian or European dinner by
arrangement $35 pp. inc. wine
Visa MC accepted
Children and pets welcome
1 Queen 2 Twin (2 bdrm)
Exclusive en suites for each bedroom
Bathrooms: 2 Ensuite

New, centrally heated, lakeside home, overlooking Bendigo Wildlife Reserve, Lake Dunstan. Enjoying uninterrupted panoramic views of wildlife, lake and mountains, we grow olives, truffles and many varieties of nuts. Two large self-contained bedrooms opening onto terraces with expansive views of garden, lake and mountains. We grow our own fresh fruit, berries, free-range eggs, vegetables and wholesome natural food. Breakfast often served on terrace overlooking the lake. Delightful dog and cat. Your hosts, Bonnie & Susie, have lived and travelled in many countries, and enjoy swapping experiences with our guests.

Arrowtown *0.5 km SW of Arrowtown*

Westrange *Luxury B&B Separate Suite*

Margaret & Ian Chamberlain
80 Cotter Avenue,
Arrowtown, 9302

Tel (03) 442 1280
or 0274 361 661
Fax (03) 442 1210
ijchamberlain@xtra.co.nz

Double/Twin $150
Single $100
(Continental breakfast provisions)
Pet free home
Not suitable for children
1 Queen (1 bdrm)
Pullout bed in Living room
Bathrooms: 1 Private

Our luxurious new fully self contained apartment, close to skifields, golfcourses and wineries has superb views over the Wakatipu Basin to the surrounding mountains. The centrally heated apartment has it's own entrance, bedroom, lounge with TV and DVD, kitchenette, and bathroom with hairdryer . Off street parking. Fifteen minutes easy walk to the town centre. 20 minutes drive to Queenstown.

Arrowtown *2 km SE of Arrowtown*
Arrowtown Heights B&B *Luxury B&B Apartment with Kitchen*

Rae & Winston Wallace
6 May Lane, Arrowtown

Tel Withdrawn
www.arrowtownheights.com

Double/Twin $150 - $195
Single $125 - $165
(Full breakfast)
Visa MC accepted
Pet free home
Internet available
2 King/Twin 2 Queen (4 bdrm)
private luxurious large and
sunnyBathrooms: 3 Ensuite 1 Private

You are always sure of a welcome at Arrowtown Heights. Our contemporary home provides spacious and luxurious accommodation in separate wings designed especially for guests. Step out of your bedroom to sit and relax in the garden, enjoy the panoramic views or the luxury of the outdoor spa. We are very central to all activities including the beautiful Gibston Valley of Wineries and 3 Golf Courses Join us for coffee and a chat. We are happy to assist or direct you to a wide range of local sights and activities. We look forward to your visit.

Arrowtown *4 km SW of Arrowtown*
Willowby Downs *B&B Homestay Farmstay*

Pam & David Mcnay
792 Malaghans Road,
RD 1,
Queenstown

Tel (03) 442 1714
or 027 222 0964
Fax (03) 442 1887
willowbydowns@xtra.co.nz
www.willowbydowns.co.nz

Double/Twin $150
Single $100
(Continental breakfast)
Children negotiable
Visa MC accepted
Children and pets welcome
2 Queen 1 Twin 2 Single (3 bdrm)
Double room has 1 Queen 1Single
Bathrooms: 2 Ensuite 1 Guest share

With Pam & David you are assured of a warm and friendly welcome, ex hoteliers they are passionate and practiced in the art of southern hospitality. With tea and coffee on your arrival you can relax in this warm and sunny home environment. 'Willowby Downs' has lovely well appointed guest rooms, electric blankets, T.V, laundry options available with guests welcome to the internet, fax and telephone facilities. Pam & David are able to arrange any extra tour or special events you may require.

Arrowtown *1 km N of Arrowtown*

Ella's B&B *B&B*

Joyce & Brian Egerton
119 Cotter Ave,
Arrowtown

Tel (03) 442 0266
or 021 0711313
bj.egerton@xtra.co.nz
www.ellasbandb.co.nz

Double/Twin $140
Single $100
(Continental breakfast)
Children $20
2 King/Twin (2 bdrm)
Bathrooms: 2 Ensuite

A warm and friendly welcome awaits, when you come to stay at Ella's B&B. Spacious rooms each with their own ensuites and doors onto a sunny balcony. A continental breakfast served either in the dining room or out on the deck. Enjoy the views over Tobins track, the hills above the Arrow River. Your hosts Joyce & Brian await your company at Ella's B&B in beautiful Arrowtown.

Arrowtown *0.5 km S of Central Arrowtown*

Bernsleigh *Luxury B&B Homestay*

David & Linda Peek
21 Bracken Street,
Arrowtown, 9302

Tel (03) 442 1550
or 021 969 610
Fax (03) 4421540
lindapeek@xtra.co.nz

Double/Twin $165 - $190
Single $130 - $150
(Continental breakfast)
Children price negotiable
Wireless internet
2 Queen 1 Twin 2 Single (3 bdrm)
Bathrooms: 1 Ensuite 1 Guest share

Welcome to our modern comfortable home situated in a peaceful location overlooking a world-class golf course and panoramic mountain and rural scenes. Private entry leads to your tastefully furnished rooms. Enjoy the sunny private courtyard or cosy indoor atmosphere. Facilities include: wireless internet, email, fax, laundry along with assistance in further activity planning. A short walk to a range of cafes and restaurants. Golf courses, ski fields, walking tracks nearby. Come and enjoy the warm hospitality of David & Linda.

Arrowtown - Queenstown *4 km SW of Arrowtown*
Willowbrook B&B Apartment with Kitchen Cottage with Kitchen

Approved

Trish & Tony White
Malaghans Road,
RD 1, Queenstown

Tel (03) 442 1773
or (027) 451 6739
Fax (03) 442 1780
info@willowbrook.net.nz
www.willowbrook.net.nz

Double/Twin $165 - $185
Single $135 - $145
(Continental breakfast)
Cottage $325 (4 persons)
Visa MC Diners Amex accepted
Children welcome
Internet available
2 King 2 Queen 3 Twin (7 bdrm)
3 in B&B, 2 in Cottage, 2 in Barn
Bathrooms: 5 Ensuite 1 Private

Willowbrook offers both B&B and self-catering accommodation in an idyllic rural setting below Coronet Peak. Only 15 minutes from Queenstown and 5 minutes from Millbrook Resort and historic Arrowtown, we are close to skifields and golf courses. Our accommodation comprises The Main House (B&B); The Cottage (self-catering) and The Barn (self-catering). All have Sky TV, wireless broadband and own barbeque. The large garden contains a tennis court, luxurious spa pool and some very friendly sheep. Trish & Tony look forward to welcoming you.

Arrowtown - Queenstown *12 km NE of Queenstown*
The Ferry Bed & Breakfast (circa 1872) B&B or Cottage

home
Approved

Glenys & Kevin Reynolds
92 Spence Road, Lower Shotover,
Queenstown, 9371

Tel (03) 442 2194 or 0800 111 804
Fax (03) 442 2190
info@ferry.co.nz
www.ferry.co.nz

Double/Twin $205 - $245
Single $205 - $245 (Full breakfast)
Children under 12 free
Whole House Deals
Contact for further information
Visa MC accepted
Children welcome
Internet available
1 King 1 Double 1 Twin (3 bdrm)
Two units, one with twin room
Bathrooms: 1 Ensuite 1 Private
Dbl with ensuite, or dbl/Family with private bathroom

Unique Historic B&B formerly a popular hotel for over 100 years. Kevin has traced the hotel's history back to 1868 - photos display this throughout. Glenys enjoys helping you to make the most of your stay in Queenstown offering advice & information. Kevin loves to talk Fly Fishing and Buckley our friendly English Springer likes to walk you along our beautiful track by the river. Situated in a delightful rural area, the perfect place to relax after a busy day. Free Wireless Broadband.

Queenstown *1.8 km NE of Queenstown Central*
Birchall House *B&B*

Joan & John Blomfield
118 Panorama Terrace,
Larchwood Heights,
Queenstown 9300

Tel (03) 442 9985
Fax (03) 442 9980
birchall.house@xtra.co.nz
www.zqn.co.nz/birchall

Double/Twin $160 - $180
Single $130 - $145
(Continental breakfast)
Children $50
Visa MC accepted
Pet free home Children welcome
Internet available
1 Queen 2 Twin (2 bdrm)
Double Room has smooth-top, fridge, microwave
Bathrooms: 2 Ensuite

Welcome to our Queenstown home, purpose built for guests in a beautiful setting. Birchall House enjoys a magnificent 200 degree view of lake and mountains within walking distance of town. Guest accommodation is spacious, private, separate entrances, centrally heated, electric blankets,tea/coffee making facilities, smoke-free. From Frankton Road, turn up Hensman Road, left into Sunset Lane. Or, Frankton Road, turn up Suburb Street, right into Panorama Terrace. Access via Hensman & Sunset Lane. Off-street parking. Visit our website: www.zqn.co.nz/birchall.

Queenstown *1 km N of Queenstown*
Monaghans *B&B Separate Suite*

Elsie & Pat Monaghan
4 Panorama Terrace,
Queenstown 9300

Tel (03) 442 8690
patmonaghan@xtra.co.nz
www.bandbclub.com/pages/
monaghan

Double/Twin $110
Single $100
(Continental breakfast)
Pet free home
1 Queen (1 bdrm)
Bathrooms: 1 Ensuite

Welcome to our home in a quiet location, walking distance to town. Enjoy this panoramic view while you breakfast. 1 couple - personal attention. Spacious comfortable room with separate entrance and garden patio. Queen bed, own bathroom, TV, fridge and tea/coffee biscuits. Interests - music, gardening, sport, travel. We will enjoy your company but respect your privacy. Off-street parking. Directions: turn right up Suburb Street off Frankton Road which is the main road into Queenstown then first right into Panorama Terrace.

Queenstown *0.8 km NW of Central Queenstown*

Coronet View Apartments & B&B *Luxury B&B Apartment with Kitchen Hotel Guest House Private B&B - Hotel*

Neil Dempsey
30 Huff Street, Queenstown

Tel (03) 442 6766 or 0800 89 6766
Fax (03) 442 6767 stay@coronetview.com
www.coronetview.com

Double/Twin $165 - $250
Single $150 - $230 (Continental breakfast)
Children $30
Dinner $35-$70
Apartments from $200-$700
Visa MC Eftpos accepted
Children welcome   Internet available
3 King/Twin 6 King 1 Queen (10 bdrm)
Bathrooms: 10 Ensuite

Centrally located just ten minutes walk from town, Coronet View enjoys superb views of Coronet Peak, The Remarkables and Lake Wakatipu.

Beautifully appointed rooms offer every comfort in either hosted accommodation or private apartments. Coronet View offers luxurious guest rooms either B&B or fully self-contained private apartments.

Guest common areas occasionally shared with gorgeous persian cat include elevated and spacious dining and living areas, outdoor decks, a sunny conservatory, outdoor barbeque, pool and jacuzzi area and computers with internet access.

Bed & Breakfast - A home away from home with true kiwi hospitality. Most rooms feature super king beds with lovely quilts, sheepskin electric blankets, tiled ensuites etc.

Your hosts are knowledgeable local people who can recommend and book your activities at no extra cost.

Apartments on site Queenstown. 1-6 bedroomed ensuited apartments. Most configurations feature ensuites, super king beds, generous living areas, fully equipped kitchens and laundries.

Queenstown *0.5 km NE of Town Centre*
Delfshaven *Homestay*

Irene Mertz
11 Salmond Place
(off Kent Street),
Queenstown

Tel (03) 441 1447
irenemertz@xtra.co.nz

Double/Twin $200
Single $150
(Special breakfast)
Visa MC accepted
Pet free home
Not suitable for children
Internet available
1 Queen (1 bdrm)
Bathrooms: 1 Private
Full Bathroom

Nestled on the lower slopes, close to town and in a quiet street, is my warm, modern 2-storied home offering great hospitality, magnificent views from all rooms over lake, mountains and township. The comfortable guest suite has bath and shower, TV and tea-making facilities and opens to the view and garden. It's a 5 minute downhill walk to the town. I am a retired teacher, widely travelled. I enjoy good food and wine, love art, music and meeting people. My piano waits to be played.

Queenstown *1.2 km N of Queenstown*
Campbells on Earnslaw *B&B*

Aderianne & Bevan Campbell
9 Earnslaw Terrace,
Queenstown

Tel (03) 442 7783
Fax (03) 442 7784
stay@campbellsonearnslaw.co.nz
www.campbellsonearnslaw.co.nz

Double/Twin $175
(Continental breakfast)
Extra person $50
Visa MC accepted
Children welcome
1 Queen 2 Single (2 bdrm)
Bathrooms: 1 Private

We look forward to welcoming you to our home, which has 180 degree spectacular panoramic views of lake, mountains and golf course. Guests own private living room with balcony, TV, fridge, toast, tea & coffee making facilities. Ideal for 2 couples or family, only 1 party at a time. Experienced hosts we can advise and arrange your sightseeing and activities. From Frankton Road turn up Suburb Street, right into Panorama Terrace, right into Earnslaw Terrace. We are only a 10 minute stroll into town centre.

Queenstown *3 km NE of Queenstown centre*

Larch Hill B&B/Homestay *B&B Homestay Apartment with Kitchen*

Lesley & Chris Marlow
16 Panners Way, Queenstown, 9300

Tel (03) 442 4811 or 027 339 6483
Fax (03) 441 8882   info@larchhill.com
www.larchhill.com

Double/Twin $150 - $220
Single $130 - $180 (Special breakfast)
Apartment (sleeps 4) $250-$320
Visa MC Amex Eftpos accepted
Children welcome   Internet available
2 King 1 Queen 1 Twin 2 Single (4 bdrm)
King; Queen; Twin; S/C Apartment
Bathrooms: 2 Ensuite 2 Private
All rooms have ensuite or private bathroom

Lesley and Chris offer you a warm welcome to Larch Hill in beautiful Queenstown, purpose built on an elevated site overlooking Lake Wakatipu.

As featured in 'National Geographic Traveler' and Cathay Pacific's 'Discovery' magazines, all rooms in our comfortable and relaxing homestay have spectacular lake views, with tea/coffee making facilities. Enjoy our warm, restful home with its panoramic views and sunny courtyard surrounded by cottage gardens.

We are just a 3 minute drive from the centre of Queenstown and within walking distance of the lake. Public transport passes our street regularly. Breakfasts are generous and include homemade bread, freshly baked croissants and pastries, fresh fruit salad, yoghurt, and freshly ground, percolated coffee. Our self-contained apartment is ideal for families or small groups. We can provide pre-arranged complimentary pickups from Queenstown airport. Feel free to use our local knowledge to help plan your itinerary. We are booking agents for Queenstown and Milford tours and activities. We have no pets and are non-smokers, but guests are welcome to smoke outdoors. FREE wireless internet available.

Directions: from Frankton drive 2.5 kms on State Highway 6A (Frankton Road) towards Queenstown. Turn right into Goldfield Heights at Sherwood Manor. Second left is Panners Way. Larch Hill B&B is No. 16 at the end of the accessway, 1/2 way down Panners Way on the left.

Queenstown *2 km SE of Queenstown*
Lake Vista Bed & Breakfast *Luxury B&B*
Ian & Bev McLenaghen
62 Hensman Road,
Queenstown, 9300

Tel (03) 441 8838
Fax (03) 441 8938
bookings@lakevista.co.nz
www.lakevista.co.nz

Double/Twin $175 - $245
Single $130 - $195 (Full breakfast)
Dinner by arrangement
Wireless internet available
Visa MC Eftpos accepted
Pet free home Children welcome
1 King/Twin 2 Queen
2 Twin 1 Single (3 bdrm)
1 full en-suite room
and 2 share facilities
Bathrooms: 1 Ensuite 1 Guest share
Large walk-in shower in new private guest share bathroom.

Set high on Queenstown hill, a major feature of Lake Vista is our encompassing views over Lake Wakatipu to the Remarkables mountain range. You can even enjoy the view lying in bed - imagine that! We offer wireless internet for your laptop or use our guest computer. All rooms have their own mini-bars, security boxes, TV, hair dryers, underfloor heating, electric blankets, heated towel-rails, radio/alarms and tea/coffee facilities. Gourmet breakfasts complete the package. Be pampered with the personal attention of your hosts, Bev & Ian.

Queenstown *1.40 km SE of Queenstown*
Kemnay *B&B*
Heather & Fraser Ronald
57 Panorama Tce,
Queenstown

Tel (03) 442 6270
hfronald@xtra.co.nz

Double/Twin $130 - $150
Single $100
(Full breakfast)
Children by arrangement
1 Queen 1 Twin (2 bdrm)
Bathrooms: 1 Private
Bath & Shower

Heather and Fraser warmly welcome you to their Queenstown Home. Wonderful views of lake and mountains, also overlooks golf course. Queen bed, plus twin, private bathroom. Small comfortable seating area with tea and coffee making facilities. One party at a time. Off street parking. 1.4km from town centre. Directions: Approaching Queenstown along Frankton Road, turn right into Hensman Road, then first turn left inot Panorama Tce.

Queenstown *8 km SW of Arrowtown*
Bearsden Bed and Breakfast *Luxury B&B*

Margie SlatterySmith & Ned Smith
333 Lower Shotover Road,
Queenstown, 9371

Tel 03 442 6656 or 021 222 1325
Fax 03 442 4813
bookings@bearsden.co.nz
www.bearsden.co.nz

Double/Twin $220 - $365
Single $190 - $325 (Full breakfast)
Visa MC accepted
Not suitable for children
Pets welcome   Internet Available
1 Queen (2 bdrm)
Each room has a queen size bed,
internal heating, TV/DVD, alarm
clock radio/IPOD dock and private
ensuite with shower, basin and toilet
including shampoo, conditioner and soap
Private entrance open to deck with mountain views
Bathrooms: 2 Ensuite

This luxury B & B is located in a rural setting, yet is only 7 minutes from Queenstown airport and 7 minutes from historic Arrowtown. A choice of 2 bedrooms with ensuites, views to Coronet Peak, private guest lounge, outdoor spa, free mountain bikes, hot breakfast choices, freshly made juices, espresso coffee, great hosts and friendly Black Lab. Smoke free inside and out.

Glenorchy *46 km N of Queenstown*
Precipice Creek Station B&B *Exclusive B&B in a separate unit*

Vladka Kennett
48 Nereus Way,
Glenorchy, 9350

Tel (03) 442 9948
or 027 680 4747
Fax (03) 409 0960
stay@precipicecreek.co.nz
www.precipicecreek.co.nz

Double/Twin $210 - $260
Single $190 - $230
(Special breakfast)
Not suitable for small children
Visa MC accepted
Pets welcome
1 King 1 Single (1 bdrm)
One bedroom with SuperKing bed
(or twin singles) and pull-out sofabed in lounge
Bathrooms: 1 Private

Located high on an ancient lake terrace nestled between high mountains and Lake Wakatipu, with spectacular views of the Humboldt Range, Mt Earnslaw and Rees Valley, Precipice Creek Station B&B provides a unique, very private and relaxing retreat. - recently opened high quality one-bedroom unit - fully separated with its own bathroom - sunny wooden deck with spectacular views - heat pump, wireless Internet access, SKY TV - homemade breakfast

Garston *50 km S of Queenstown*
Castle Hill Lodge Bed and Breakfast *B&B*
Mark and Sharon Ford
23 Mcmillan Road, Garston, 9750

Tel (03) 248 8816
or 021 064 7951
markandsharonford@hotmail.com
www.castlehilllodge.co.nz

Double/Twin $150 - $220 (Full breakfast)
Children very welcome and can help us feed our animals
Two course dinner by arrangement
Visa MC Amex accepted
Children and pets welcome
Internet available
4 Double 3 Twin (4 bdrm)
3 double en suite, 1 double with private bathroom
Bathrooms: 3 Ensuite 1 Private

Experience the Northern Southland countryside at its best.

Nestled within 9 acres of mature trees, gardens and stunning views is Castle Hill Lodge. This former Angler's Lodge is now home to our cat, sheep, 4 chickens, 2 goats and 2 Kune Kune pigs all of which will love your attention.

We are centrally located for trips to Te Anau, Milford Sound, Queenstown and Gore and we also offer packages for skiing, fishing and farm tours all detailed on our website. Our scrumptious home cooked breakfast will set you up for the day whether you decide to go and explore, fish the sparkling Upper Mataura river or just sit out on our decking and watch the world go by.

Welcome in the evening with a 2 course meal and complimentary wine (by prior arrangement) then unwind infront of an open fire. All the rooms have complimentary tea and coffee, electric blankets and the guest lounge has free internet access. Whatever you decide to do, Sharon and Mark look forward to meeting you.

Garston *50 km S of Queenstown*
Menlove Homestay *B&B Homestay Separate Suite*

Bev & Matt Menlove
17 Blackmore Road,
Garston
PO Box 39,
Garston 9750

Tel (03) 248 8516
mattmenlove@slingshot.co.nz

Double/Twin $90
Single $50
(Continental breakfast)
Dinner $25 by arrangement
1 Double 1 Single (1 bdrm)
Bathrooms: 1 Ensuite

We are organic gardeners and our other interests include lawn bowls, sailing, gliding and alternative energy. Garston is New Zealand's most inland village with the Mataura River (famous for its fly fishing) flowing through the valley, surrounded by the Hector Range and the Eyre Mountains. A fishing guide is available with advance notice. For day trips, Garston is central to Queenstown, Te Anau, Milford Sound or Invercargill. We look forward to meeting you.

Garston *50 km S of Queenstown*
Naylor House *Cottage with Kitchen*

John and Avis McIver
33 Naylor Road,
Garston,
Southland

Tel (03) 248 8809
or 027 6536110
Fax (03) 248 8809
naylorhouse@slingshot.co.nz
www.naylorhouse.co.nz

Double/Twin $160
(Breakfast by arrangement)
Dinner by arrangement
Visa MC accepted
Pet free home
Children welcome
1 King/Twin 1 Queen
2 Twin (3 bdrm)
Bathrooms: 1 Private

Welcome to Historic Naylor House situated in the heart of the beautiful and tranquil Garston Valley. Garston is Central to Queenstown, Te Anau, Milford Sound and Invercargill. The Mataura River which is famed for its fly fishing is on our doorstep. We look forward to sharing all our local knowledge and our beautiful location with you

Clyde *8 km SW of Alexandra*
Argyll Farmstay *B&B Homestay*
Trish & Alan May
1 Annan Street,
Clyde,
Central Otago

Tel (03) 449 3268
or 027 431 8241
Fax (03) 449 3268
argyllonclyde@yahoo.co.nz
www.argyllonclyde.co.nz

Double/Twin $130 - $160
Single $80 - $120
(Full breakfast)
Children negotiable
Dinner $35 by arrangement
Visa MC accepted
Children welcome
2 Queen 1 Twin (3 bdrm)
Comforable beds, Quality linen, Plush bath towels
Bathrooms: 1 Ensuite 1 Private 1 Guest share
Ensuite includes a bath

Alan and Trish welcome you to their near new modern home situated in historic gold-mining town of Clyde. They will make your stay a memorable one, pampering you with exquisite accommodation and cuisine. Relax in the spa, enjoy the comforable beds and the delicious cooked breakfast.

Clyde *0 km N of*
Hartley Homestead Boutique Bed and Breakfast *Luxury B&B*
Melanie & Rex Eade
23 Pyke Street,
Clyde, 9330

Tel (03) 449 3307
or 027 286 0438
info@hartleyhomestead.co.nz
www.hartleyhomestead.co.nz

Double/Twin $150 - $220
(Continental breakfast)
Visa MC Eftpos accepted
Pets welcome
Internet Available
2 King/Twin 1 King (3 bdrm)
Bathrooms: 1 Private
1 Guest share 1 Family share
Slipper Bath Hot tub outside

A grand 1900s mud brick homestead surrounded by almost an acre of lawns and mature gardens on the banks of the picturesque Clutha River. We are a few minutes stroll from restaurants, cafes and bars of the historic gold mining township of Clyde and within walking distance of the Otago Central Rail Trail. Two beautifully appointed bedrooms with guest lounge in the homestead and a very private super-king bed unit in the grounds. Resident cat Eme, and Mollie the Border Collie.

Roxburgh - Ettrick *17 km SW of Ettrick*
Wilden Station Homestead *B&B Homestay Farmstay*

Sarah & Peter Adam
Wilden School Road,
Wilden,
West Otago

Tel (03) 204 8115
Fax (03) 204 8116
wildenstation@farmside.co.nz

Double/Twin $190
Single $120
(Special breakfast)
Children $20
Dinner $55
Visa MC accepted
Children welcome
Internet available
2 Queen 2 Single (3 bdrm)
Bathrooms: 1 Ensuite 1 Private

Experience high-country farm life with us, our two boys and two cats. Watch our dogs work the sheep. Stroll through trees to a small lake, explore our historic farm buildings, fish the Pomahaka River, tour the property, or simply relax in our gracious homestead. Enjoy superb meals prepared by your internationally experienced chef/ hostess (all by prior arrangement). Unwind in our tranquil surroundings about 2 hours from Dunedin, Queenstown, Wanaka. Families most welcome. Please telephone for directions.

Roxburgh - Millers Flat *16 km S of Roxburgh*
Quince Cottage *B&B Cottage No Kitchen*

Wendy Gunn & Cally Johnstone
Rapid No 1581,
Teviot Road,
Millers Flat

Tel (03) 446 6889
thequince@clear.net.nz
www.quincecottage.co.nz

Double/Twin $220
Single $125
(Special breakfast)
Dinner $65pp
Visa MC accepted
1 Queen (1 bdrm)
Bathrooms: 1 Ensuite

Quince Cottage - half way between Dunedin and Queenstown/Wanaka or a destination in itself. The Cottage is set apart from the house surrounded by a big open garden dotted with trees, and lawn stretching into the distance. It is open plan with a dining table, TV, CD player, fridge, air-con and heating. Meals are served in the main house, however if you wish to dine in the cottage we are happy to deliver your meals. Dinner is $65 pp - 3 courses and complimentary Central Otago wine.

Middlemarch *4 km SW of Middlemarch*
The Farm *B&B Homestay Farmstay*

Lynley & Glynne Smith
154 Farm Road,
RD 2,
Middlemarch

Tel (03) 464 3610
or 027 436 2423
Fax (03) 464 3612
glynley@xtra.co.nz
www.thefarmhomestay.co.nz

Double/Twin $110
Single $90
(Full breakfast)
3 course meal including wine $45pp
Children and pets welcome
1 King 1 Twin (2 bdrm)
Can be altered to 4 singles
Bathrooms: 1 Guest share
Spa available outside

Our charming old stone house and gardens are set amongst mature oaks, with the spectacular Rock and Pillar Range as a backdrop. Lynley & Glynne welcome you to their peaceful relaxed haven which includes a 200 acre farm, sheep, cattle, horses, 1 family cat & a Border Terrier dog. From high country farming background, interested in horses, hunting and a tranquil lifestyle. On the Central Otago Rail Trail, 1 hour from Dunedin, this is a convenient and hospitable stop for exploring this picturesque area.

Please let your hosts know if you have to cancel.
They will have spent time preparing for you.

Palmerston - Waikouaiti *40 km NE of Dunedin*
Boutique Bed & Breakfast *Luxury B&B Farmstay Separate Suite*

Barbara & John Morgan
107 Jefferis Road,
Waikouaiti,
RD 2,
Palmerston South

Tel (03) 465 7239
or 027 224 8212
Fax (03) 465 7239
info@boutiquebedandbreakfast.co.nz
www.boutiquebedandbreakfast.co.nz

Double/Twin $160 - $190
Single $150
(Full breakfast)
Visa MC accepted
3 Queen 1 Double (3 bdrm)
3 Ensuite

Boutique Bed and Breakfast is a refurbished historic cottage in mature gardens on our homestead grounds. Three private self cotained rooms each with ensuite and double doors opening on to verandahs,are tastefully furnished for your comfort and privacy. Enjoy a delicious farm breakfast followed if you wish, by a deer farm tour by John and dogs George and Mildred. 5 minutes to Waikouaiti and Palmerston with their cafes,shops museums and historic buildings. Explore nature reserves, see yellow eyed penguins, seals at Tavora Reserve, white sanded beaches, golf courses. One hour from the rail Trail at Middlemarch/Hyde.

Dunedin *2 km SW of Dunedin*
Magnolia House *B&B*

Joan & George Sutherland
18 Grendon Street,
Maori Hill,
Dunedin 9010

Tel (03) 467 5999
mrsuth@xtra.co.nz

Double/Twin $140
Single $100
(Special breakfast)
Not suitable for children
1 Queen 1 Double 2 Single (3 bdrm)
Bathrooms: 1 Private 1 Family share

Our quiet turn-of-the-century villa sits in broad, flower-bordered lawns backed by native bush with beautiful, tuneful birds. All rooms have electric heating, comfortable beds with electric blanket, and antiques, while the queen room has an adjoining balcony. Close by is Moana Pool, the glorious Edwardian house Olveston, and Otago Golf Course. Our special breakfast will set you up for the day. We have a courtesy car, and two burmese cats. It is not suitable for children or smokers.

Dunedin *5.5 km E of Dunedin Centre*
Glenrowan Heights *B&B Homestay Separate Suite*

Sue & Dick Williman
60 Connell Street,
Waverley,
Dunedin

Tel (03) 455 4931
or 021 455 874
dick@williman.co.nz
www.bnbdunedin.co.nz

Double/Twin $140 - $180
Single $130 - $170
(Continental breakfast)
Visa MC accepted
Pet free home
Not suitable for children
Internet available
1 King 1 Queen 1 Twin (3 bdrm)
Bathrooms: 1 Ensuite 1 Guest share

Our new home offers all the modern conveniences and the most amazing panoramic views of Dunedin and the Otago Harbour, right out to the heads. We are conveniently located not far off the Highcliff road that runs down the Otago Peninsula to Larnach Castle and the Albatross centre. Sue and I have recently retired from operating a motel in the city. We enjoy advising guest on the many opportunities on offer. Our house is at the end of the top section of the private road.

Dunedin *7 km NE of Dunedin*
Harbourside B&B *B&B Homestay*

Shirley & Don Parsons
6 Kiwi Street,
St Leonards,
Dunedin

Tel (03) 471 0690
Fax (03) 471 0063
harboursidebb@xtra.co.nz

Double/Twin $100 - $120
Single $80 - $120
(Full breakfast)
Children $30 Dinner $30
Pet free home
Children welcome
1 King/Twin 2 Queen
3 Single (3 bdrm)
Bathrooms: 1 Ensuite 1 Guest share

We are situated in a quiet suburb overlooking Otago Harbour and surrounding hills. Within easy reach of all local attractions. Lovely garden or harbour views from all rooms. Children very welcome. Directions: drive into city on one-way system watch for Highway 88 sign follow Anzac Avenue onto Ravensbourne Road. Continue approx 5km to St Leonards turn left at Playcentre opposite Boatshed into Pukeko Street then left into Kaka Road, straight ahead to Kiwi Street turn left into Number 6.

Dunedin *1 km SW of Dunedin*

Highbrae Guesthouse *B&B Guest House wireless internet availability*

Fienie & Stephen Clark
376 High Street, Dunedin 9016

Tel (03) 479 2070
or 027 4328 470
Fax (03) 479 2100
 enquiries@highbrae.co.nz
www.highbrae.co.nz

Double/Twin $110 - $140
Single $80 - $110
(Continental breakfast)
Children $25 in room with parents
Cooked breakfast extra
Visa MC Amex accepted
Pet free home
Children welcome
Internet available
1 King 2 Queen 1 Twin 1 Single (4 bdrm)
Bathrooms: 1 Private 1 Guest share 1 Family share

Experience a taste of early Dunedin. This heritage home was built on the High Street in 1908 to provide first class accommodation to its residents. Today it is still an impressive home with spectacular views of the city and harbour. The upstairs guest rooms and self contained unit are carefully maintained to preserve their character for visitors, who delight in the many features in the home. Wireless internet is available and a courtesy vehicle can meet you at the bus or train if required.

Dunedin *8 km SW of Dunedin*

Grant's Farm *B&B Apartment with Kitchen*

Tom and Jeanette Grant
151 Old Brighton Road,
Fairfield
RD 1,
Dunedin, 9076

Tel (03) 488 0336
info@bnb-dunedin.co.nz
www.bnb-dunedin.co.nz

Double/Twin $110 - $190
Single $90 - $120
(Continental breakfast)
Children by arrangement
Dinner not supplied
Visa MC accepted
Pet free home
Internet available
1 Queen 1 Double 1 Single (2 bdrm)
Bathrooms: 1 Ensuite

Our typical NZ woolshed on 20ha is now a unique home with fully self contained guest accommodation with woodfire and wireless internet. Situated on the Kaikorai Estuary we have heaps of bird life sheep cattle and also an airstrip with biplanes. We are in a peaceful rural setting with wonderful views, only 15 minutes from Dunedin Airport and 8 minutes to either Dunedin or Mosgiel. Excellent restaurants and miles of beach walks are minutes away. 1 loving outdoor cat. Guests wish they could stay longer!

Dunedin *0.1 km N of Dunedin Central*

Albatross Inn *B&B*

Glynis Rees
770 George Street, Dunedin, 9016
Tel (03) 477 2727 or 0800 441 441
Fax (03) 477 2108   albatross.inn@xtra.co.nz
www.albatross.inn.co.nz

Double/Twin $120 - $170
Single $115 - $130 (Special breakfast)
Children $15   Visa MC Diners Amex Eftpos accepted
Children welcome   Internet Available
2 King/Twin 1 King 3 Queen 2 Double 5 Single (8 bdrm)
Bathrooms: 7 Ensuite 1 Private

Welcome to Dunedin and Albatross Inn! Our beautiful late Victorian house is ideally located on the main street close to the university, gardens, museum, shops and restaurants.

Our attractive rooms have ensuite/private bathrooms, telephone, TV, radio, central heating, tea/coffee, warm duvets and electric blankets on modern beds. Firm beds upon request. Quiet rooms at rear of house. Several rooms have kitchenette and fridge.

Enjoy our sumptious breakfast in our cosy breakfast room. We serve freshly baked bread and muffins, fresh fruit salad, yoghurt, juices, cereals, teas, freshly brewed coffee. We are happy to recommend and book tours for you. All wildlife tours pick up and drop off here. We can recommend many great places to eat, most just a short walk down George Street. Nearby laundry, non-smoking, cot and highchair.

Some comments from our visitors Book! The right balance of everything location, breakfast and lovely room. Delightfully different. Absolutely fantastic as always. Home away from Home. A touch of Class, lovely home beautifully presented. Perfecto!

Homepage: www.albatross.inn.co.nz. Winter special $90 Double - special conditions apply. Complimentary e-mail and wireless internet.

Hazelhurst - Dunedin *5 km SW of Octagon*
Hazel House Boutique Bed & Breakfast *B&B*
Sandy & Brent Ward
50 Hazel Avenue,
Hazelhurst,
Dunedin, 9012

Tel (03) 487 6550
or 021 163 4799
info@hazelhouse.co.nz
www.hazelhouse.co.nz

Double/Twin $125 - $165
(Full breakfast)
Visa MC Eftpos accepted
1 King 1 Queen (2 bdrm)
Bathrooms: 1 Ensuite 1 Private
King with private bathroom, queen with ensuite

A classic 1900's villa located only five minutes from Dunedin's City Centre. With the majestic rooms, ornate ceilings and lead light windows, it is an absolute delight to offer a peaceful and quiet location with warm inviting rooms, scrumptious breakfasts and southern hospitality.

A spectacular guests lounge, spacious king bedroom with private bathroom, or queen bedroom with ensuite, include top quality linen and facilities.

Sky TV, wireless internet, tea and coffee, central heating, courtyard, veranda, and warm welcome from hosts Sandy & Brent Ward.

Dunedin *0.5 km SW of Dunedin*
Deacons Court *B&B*
Kristin Peacock & Ashley Grey
342 High Street,
Dunedin, 9016

Tel (03) 477 9053
or 0800 268 252
Fax (03) 477 9058
info@deaconscourt.com
www.deaconscourt.com

Double/Twin $100 - $160
Single $80 - $130
(Full breakfast)
Children $20-$50
Visa MC Eftpos accepted
Children welcome
2 King/Twin 2 King
1 Queen 3 Single (4 bdrm)
Extra large and spacious
Bathrooms: 2 Ensuite 1 Private 1 Family share

Deacons Court is a charming superior spacious Victorian villa 1km walking distance from the city centre and is on the city's heritage building register. We are only 500m from cafes, bars and some of Dunedin's unique attractions and offer you friendly but unobtrusive hospitality in a quiet secure haven. Guests can relax in our delightful rose garden and spacious conservatory. Our extra large bedrooms , have ensuite or private bathrooms, TV and comfortable seating. Complimentary broadband, 24 hour tea or coffee, and free parking available.

Otago Peninsula - Broad Bay *16 km E of Dunedin*
Chy-an-Dowr *Self Contained B&B two luxury suites*
Susan & Herman van Velthoven
687 Portobello Road,
Broad Bay, Dunedin 9014

Tel (03) 478 0306
or 021 156 0715
Fax (03) 478 0306
hermanvv@xtra.co.nz
www.chy-an-dowr.co.nz

Double/Twin $195 - $295
Single $175 - $275
(Full breakfast provisions)
 Visa MC accepted
Pet free home
Not suitable for children
Internet available
1 King/Twin 1 King 1 Queen (3 bdrm)
1 King ensuite, 1 King/Twin or Queen with private bathroom
Bathrooms: 1 Ensuite 1 Private

Chy~an~Dowr, quality self contained boutique B&B accommodation located on scenic Otago Peninsula. Our character home with its harbourside location has panoramic views and is situated across the road from a small beach and enroute to the Albatross and Penguin colonies.The main house is for guest use with two guest suites and sunroom upstairs and guestlounge and kitchen downstairs. Breakfast provisions supplied or full served breakfast available on request. Originally from The Netherlands, we enjoy welcoming guests and sharing our wonderful location.

Otago Peninsula - Macandrew Bay *11 km E of Dunedin*
MacBay Retreat *B&B Cottage with Kitchen*

Jeff & Helen Hall
38 Bayne Terrace,
Macandrew Bay,
Dunedin 9014

Tel (03) 476 1475
Fax (03) 476 1975
jhall9@ihug.co.nz
www.macandrewbay.co.nz/
macbayretreat

Double/Twin $150
Single $135
(Continental breakfast)
$30pp extra
Visa MC accepted
Pet free home
1 King 1 Double (1 bdrm)
Bathrooms: 1 Ensuite

Mac Bay Retreat - Otago Peninsula. Welcome to your private self-contained smoke-free retreat, 15 minutes from Dunedin centre on the Otago Peninsula. Relax with the spectacular view overlooking the harbour from Dunedin City to Port Chalmers. Your cosy retreat is separate from the host's house and gives you a choice of either a super king or double bed plus an ensuite, modern kitchen and TV. Suitable for 1 couple, possibly 2 couples, travelling together. Only minutes from Dunedin's most popular attractions.

Otago Peninsula - Portobello *20 km SE of Dunedin*
Peninsula B&B *B&B*

Toni & Stephen Swabey
4 Allans Beach Road,
Portobello,
Dunedin, 9014

Tel 0800 478 090
or (03) 478 0909
Fax (03) 478 0909
toni@peninsula.co.nz
www.peninsula.co.nz

Double/Twin $145 - $195
Single $120 - $140
(Full breakfast)
Children POA
Free wireless broadband internet
Visa MC accepted
Children welcome
1 King/Twin 1 King
2 Queen 1 Single (4 bdrm)
Bathrooms: 2 Ensuite 1 Guest share

Come and relax in the elegant and romantic Victorian ambience of our beautiful 1880s villa. Situated in peaceful gardens, enjoy wonderful views of the harbour from your ensuite room. Relish your delicious cooked breakfast in the morning, with home baking. Catch up with our complimentary newspaper and make yourself at home with tea/coffee making facilities. Keep in touch with home with our free wireless broadband internet. We are ideally located for wildlife and scenic attractions and just a minute's walk from Portobello's two restaurants.

Otago Peninsula - Portobello *16 km NE of Dunedin*
Captain Eady's Lookout *B&B Homestay*

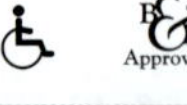

Richard & Ana Good
2 Moss Street,
Portobello, 9014

Tel (03) 478 0537
or 021 478 785
capteady@earthlight.co.nz
www.capteady.co.nz

Double/Twin $160 - $195
Single $150 - $185
(Special breakfast)
Children negotiable
Dinner $40 by prior arrangement
Twin Room: $100-120
(Rainbow Friendly)
Visa MC accepted
Children welcome Internet available
2 Queen 1 Twin (3 bdrm)
Bathrooms: 2 Ensuite 1 Family share

Captain Eady's Lookout is a delightful bed and breakfast on the water's edge. This character house, built early last century by Captain Eady, a ferry master, stands on a small bluff overlooking Otago Harbour. One bedroom opens onto a secluded garden, one overlooks the harbour. Breakfast in our conservatory whilst taking in the splendid harbour views. The house has many antiques and on the walls are paintings by local artists. You may sample the large jazz collection. Cats in residence. We are rainbow friendly.

Otago Peninsula - Broad Bay *15 km N of Dunedin*
Fantail Lodge *2 self-contained cottages with Kitchens*

Vic and Tessa Mills
682 Portobello Road,
Broad Bay, Dunedin

Tel (03) 478 0110
or 0274 156 222
fantail.lodge@xtra.co.nz

Double/Twin $150 - $150
Single $100 - $120
(Accommodation only)
Extra Adults or Children $20 each
Continental Provisions extra
Visa MC accepted
Pet free home
Children welcome
2 Queen 2 Single (3 bdrm)
Bellbird (Pictured) has Queen,
Fantail has queen/2 singles
One ensuite in each cottage

Peacefully situated on the beautiful Otago Peninsula, close to beaches, seals, penguins and albatrosses, our lush, harbourside garden contains two, delightfully rustic, self -contained cottages. Fantail Cottage has queen bed accommodation with two singles on a mezzanine. Bellbird offers a queen bed and an exclusive spa pool. Both are equipped for self catering or continental breakfast hampers by arrangement. Free use of kayaks. An ideal base for touring and a great location for a romantic getaway.

Mosgiel *2 km SW of Mosgiel*
The Trees *B&B*

Jenny Blackgrove & Rex Moore
70 Main South Road,
East Taieri,
Mosgiel 9024

Tel Landline (03) 489 4837
or Mobile 021 0244 2839
Fax (03) 477 1479
rex.moore@clear.net.nz

Double/Twin $125
Single $75
(Full breakfast)
Dinner $45 by prior arrangement
Visa MC accepted
Not suitable for children
Internet available
1 King 1 Twin (2 bdrm)
Large, sunny rooms, TV
Bathrooms: 1 Guest share S
hower and separate bath

Welcome to our quiet, semirural home set on an acre of lawns and trees. We are 15km SW of Dunedin, half-way between Dunedin and the airport. There are 3 golf courses in close proximity. Resident animals are 2 cats. Rex enjoys flying light aircraft and sailing, Jenny is a Cordon Bleu trained cook and besides cooking, Jenny's interests include gardening and reading. We both have travelled extensively. Facilities include off-street parking and make yourself tea, coffee & juice.Hair dryer. Robes.

Mosgiel *1 km N of Mosgiel*
Marg's Manor *Homestay*

Margaret
103 Main South Road,
East Taieri,
Mosgiel,
Dunedin

Tel (03) 489 2030
Fax (03) 489 2030
msscott@xtra.co.nz

Double/Twin $100
Single $80
(Continental breakfast)
Dinner $30 by arrangement
Full breakfast by arrangement
Not suitable for children
1 Queen (1 bdrm)
Bathrooms: 1 Ensuite

Haere Mai, welcome to my sunny cottage home, situated halfway between Dunedin Airport and Dunedin city. With rural views over the Taieri Plains. Enjoy your own entrance and outdoor table just beside your room, or relax up in the back garden spaces amongst the vegetables and herbs that I enjoy cooking with. Dinner and cooked breakfast by arrangement, off street parking available. Resident cat called Fluff.

Balclutha *4 km N of Balclutha/Catlins*
Lesmahagow *Luxury B&B Boutique*

Noel & Kate O'Malley
146 Benhar Road,
Benhar, RD 2,
Balclutha 9272

Tel (03) 418 2507
or 0800 301 224 (NZ only)
lesmahagow@xtra.co.nz
www.lesmahagow.co.nz

Double/Twin $160 - $190
(Full breakfast)
Dinner $40
Lunches on request
Visa MC Eftpos accepted
Children and pets welcome
Internet available
2 Queen 1 Double 1 Single (3 bdrm)
Bathrooms: 3 Private

Lesmahagow offers excellent accommodation in an historic homestead and garden setting. Centrally situated, discerning travellers can make Lesmahagow their base to explore the Catlins region, Dunedin and the Otago Penninsula or the historic goldfields of Lawrence. Centrally heated, with delightful bedrooms and gorgeous bathrooms, you can be sure of wonderful hospitality and a truly memorable stay. Evening meals are our speciality and our breakfasts will satisfy all taste buds! Come and discover this hidden paradise! You will love the experience.

Owaka - The Catlins *15 km SW of Owaka*
Greenwood Farmstay *Luxury B&B Farmstay*

Alan & Helen-May Burgess
739 Purakaunui Falls Road,
Owaka, The Catlins, South Otago

Tel (03) 415 8259
or 027 438 4538
Fax (03) 415 8259
greenwoodfarm@xtra.co.nz
www.greenwoodfarmstay.co.nz

Double/Twin $180 - $200
Single $160
(Full breakfast)
Children $100 under 10 (negotiable)
Dinner $50 per person (3 course)
Kitchenette is available for guests
Children welcome
2 Queen 2 Single (3 bdrm)
Bathrooms: 2 Ensuite 1 Private
Every guest room has their personal bathroom

Welcome ... Within walking distance to beautiful Purakaunui Falls. Alan who has a wealth of local history and farming knowledge enjoys taking people around our sheep, cattle and deer farm and you may stand on the cliffs that overlook Purakaunui Bay, where part of the movie 'Narnia' was filmed. We enjoy conversation and evening diner with our guests. We help you to explore the Catlins. Our home offers warm, very comfortable accommodation. All guest rooms have an ensuite or a private bathroom. Rooms open out to our large garden. Relax and enjoy our many indoor and outdoors areas for guests. Email/phone for directions.

Owaka - The Catlins *1 km N of Owaka*
J T's Catlins B&B *B&B Homestay*
John & Thelma Turnbull
Rapid No, 2885 Main Road,
Owaka 9586

Tel (03) 415 8127
or 027 649 7693
jtowaka@xtra.co.nz
www.jtscatlinsbnb.co.nz

Double/Twin $0 - $120
Single $0 - $80 (Full breakfast)
Dinner by arrangement
Children welcome
1 Queen 1 Twin (2 bdrm)
Bathrooms: 1 Guest share
Toilet, shower & bathroom,
3 seperate rooms

Welcome to our warm and comfortable home on the Southern Scenic Route, situated on a 25 acre farmlet, surrounded by colourful, peaceful gardens with splendid unspoilt views. Located in the heart of the Catlins, renowned for its wildlife and spectacular scenery, we are within walking distance of Owaka Township with its restaurants, museum and other amenities. Our guests are encouraged to dine with us for the evening meal when we enjoy quality local food and wine. We look forward to meeting you. Travel safely.

Owaka *25 km N of Balclutha*
Catlins Retreat *B&B*
Robbie Hodge
27 Main Road, Owaka, Balclutha

Tel (03) 415 8300
or 027 433 4146
Fax (03) 415 8300
enquiries@catlinsretreat.co.nz
www.catlinsretreat.co.nz

Double/Twin $125
Single $55 - $125
(Full breakfast)
Children $45
Dinner by arrangement
1 Double with shared B/R $90
Visa MC accepted
Pet free home
Children and pets welcome
2 Queen 1 Double 4 Single (4 bdrm)
One Queen also has one single
Bathrooms: 2 Ensuite 1 Guest share

Welcome to Catlins Retreat, your home away from home in the heart of the Catlins. You're centrally located for visiting the Catlins Heritage Trail and Southern Scenic route, the incredible Catlins coastline including fur seal and sea lion colonies and the walks of the Catlins, Parukanui Fall, Catlins River walk and Cathedral Caves. You'll receive a warm welcome from your host Robbie who is happy to provide you with local information and guidance on what to do and see in this unique and very special part of New Zealand.

Southland,
South Catlins &
Stewart Island
Queenstown
Gibbston
Cromwel
Earnscleugh
Kingston
Garston
Ettrick
R
Te Anau
Manapouri
94
Mossburn
99
Lumsden
Balfour
96
6
Gore
99
Waianiwa
1
Riverton
Invercargill
92
Progress Valley
Bluff
Stewart Island
0 Kilometres 30
0 Miles 18

Te Anau - Manapouri *20 km E of Manapouri*
Crown Lea *Farmstay*

Florence & John Pine
310 Gillespie Road,
RD 1,
Te Anau, 9679

Tel (03) 249 8598
or 021 1680 299
Fax (03) 249 8598
crownlea@farmside.co.nz
www.crown-lea.com

Double/Twin $180
Single $180
(Full breakfast)
Dinner $40
Pet free home
1 King/Twin 1 Queen
1 Twin (3 bdrm)
All with garden views
Bathrooms: 1 Ensuite 2 Private

Our 900 acre sheep, cattle and deer farm offers a farm tour after 6pm, and views of Lake Manapouri, Fiordland mountains, and Te Anau Basin. Day trips to Doubtful and Milford Sounds, visits to Te Anau, glowworm caves, or hikes on the walking tracks in Fiordland all within easy reach. Having travelled in South Africa, UK, Europe, USA, Canada, Australia, Hong Kong and Singapore, we look forward to welcoming you to and sharing our home with you.

Te Anau *1 km NE of Te Anau Centre*
Shakespeare House *B&B Separate Suite*

Marg, Jeff, Kylie & Ray
10 Dusky Street, Te Anau
PO Box 32, Te Anau

Tel (03) 249 7349
or 0800 249 349
Fax (03) 249 7629
shakespearebnb@xtra.co.nz
www.shakespearehouse.co.nz

Double/Twin $100 - $130
Single $90 - $110
(Full breakfast)
Children $5-$15
Self-contained, 2 bdrm - sleeps 5
Visa MC Eftpos accepted
Pet free home
Internet available
8 King 3 Twin 4 Single (8 bdrm)
Bathrooms: 8 Ensuite No Baths

Shakespeare House is a well established Bed & Breakfast, where we keep a home atmosphere with personal service. We are situated in a quiet residential area yet are within walking distance of shops, lake and restaurants. Our rooms are ground floor and have the choice of king, queen or twin beds. Each room has private facilities, TV, tea/coffee making. Tariff includes continental or delicious cooked breakfast. Guest laundry available, internet and payphone facilities on site. Winter rates May to September.

Te Anau *0.2 km SE of Te Anau Central*
Cosy Kiwi B&B Guesthouse *B&B Guest House*

Eleanor & Derek Cook
186 Milford Road, Te Anau, 9600

Tel 03 2497475
or 0800 249 700
Fax (03)249 8471
info@cosykiwi.com
www.cosykiwi.com

Double/Twin $165 - $175
Single $155 - $165
(Special breakfast)
Extra person $45
Visa MC Eftpos accepted
Children welcome
Internet available
4 King 3 Queen 4 Twin
5 Single (7 bdrm)
Studio Rooms
Bathrooms: 7 Ensuite

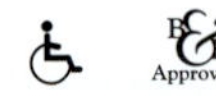

Eleanor Derek and Mia (our miniture schnauzer) welcome you to our Bed & Breakfast Guest House. Privacy with comfort, quiet spacious ensuited bedrooms, quality beds, individual heating and televison. Breakfast buffet of home-made breads, jams, fresh fruits, dessert fruits, yoghurt, brewed coffee, special teas,plus mouthwatering pancakes with maple syrup or ham and cheese. Two minute walk to shops and restaurants, bookings arranged for all tours, pick-up at gate. Guest lounge with internet access,wireless for laptops, laundry, off-street parking and luggage storage.

Te Anau *2 km E of Te Anau*
Rose 'n' Reel *B&B Farmstay Cottage with Kitchen*

Lyn & Lex Lawrence
89 Ben Loch Lane,
RD 2,
Te Anau

Tel (03) 249 7582
or 027 4545 723
Fax (03) 249 7582
rosenreel@xtra.co.nz
www.rosenreel.co.nz

Double/Twin $120 - $130
Single $75 - $100
(Continental breakfast)
Visa MC accepted
2 Queen 1 Double 1 Single (3 bdrm)
Bathrooms: 1 Private 1 Guest share

Genuine Kiwi hospitality in a magic setting 5 minutes from Te Anau. Hand feed tame fallow deer, meet our friendly cat Ben and dog Meg. Sit on the veranda of our fully self-contained cabin and enjoy watching deer with a lake and mountain view. The 2 room cabin has cooking facilities, fridge, microwave, TV, 1 queen, 1 double plus bathroom. Our 2 storey home is set in an extensive garden. 2 guest bedrooms. Lex is a fishing guide, I love to garden. Directions: please phone.

Te Anau *1 km NE of Town Te Anau*
Te Anau Lodge *Luxury B&B*

George Garden and Margaret Lamb
52 Howden Street,
Te Anau

Tel (03) 249 7477
Fax (03) 249 7487
info@teanaulodge.co.nz
www.teanaulodge.com

Double/Twin $200 - $350
Single $170 - $270
(Full breakfast)
Visa MC Eftpos accepted
Children welcome
3 King/Twin 3 King 4 Queen
3 Twin 7 Single (7 bdrm)
Bathrooms: 7 Ensuite 1 Private
7 Bathrooms in total, 2 with spa baths

Experience the genuine warmth of traditional hospitality in the relaxed and peaceful environment of our 1936 relocated former convent. Set on 2.7 hectares with breathtaking lake and mountain views, Te Anau Lodge has been lovingly restored maintaining its original and delightful charm, with modern facilities. Enjoy our famous cooked breakfasts in the Chapel, spend your evenings relaxing in our library or having a drink in our sunny courtyard. Complimentary laundry facilities, luggage storage and high speed wireless internet access. A unique and special accommodation experience.

Te Anau - Manapouri *8 km S of Manapouri*
'Connemara Cottages' *B&B Farmstay Cottage with Kitchen*

Bev & Murray Hagen
415 Weir Road,
Manapouri,
Te Anau

Tel (03) 249 9399
or 027 292 3651
hagen@farmside.co.nz
www.connemarafiordland.co.nz

Double/Twin $140 - $200
(Full breakfast provisions)
Children by arrangement
1 Queen 1 Double (1 bdrm)
Bathrooms: 1 Ensuite

Yours exclusively, two cosy self-contained cottages. 'Connemara Farm Cottage', situated on our Deer Farm 8mins from Manapouri - Gateway to Doubtful Sound. Lounge/Kitchenette, ensuite Queen bedroom, sofa/bed in lounge. Lovely mountain and farm views. Our farm bounds two excellent fishing rivers. Farm tour available by arrangement. 'Connemara Anglers Arms' situated in Manapouri, Two bedroom cottage with Queen beds finest furnishings, open plan living, overlooks the beautiful Waiau River with lovely views of the bush & mountains. Doubtful/Sound Boats only a 2min. Walk. Min stay 2nights. Not suitable for children.

Te Anau *0.4 km N of Te Anau Centre*
Antler Lodge *B&B Cottage with Kitchen*
Helen & Chris Whyte
44 Matai Street,
Te Anau

Tel (03) 249 8188
Fax (03) 249 8188
antler.lodge@xtra.co.nz
www.antlerlodgeteanau.co.nz

Double/Twin $140 - $155
(Continental breakfast provisions)
Visa MC Eftpos accepted
1 King 2 Queen (3 bdrm)
Bathrooms: 3 Ensuite

Helen and Chris invite you to enjoy their comfortable bed & breakfast accommodation. Situated in a quiet residential area close to shops, restaurants and within walking distance of the lake. We offer 3 spacious self contained units, each with a private ensuite. The 2 cottages each have kitchen facilities, tv, electric heating and comfortable furnishings. Our third unit is an upstairs suite with private entrance and sunroom dining area. Continental breakfast provisions are provided in this unit. This suite has beautiful mountain views.

Te Anau *1 km S of Central Te Anau*
Cat's Whiskers B&B *B&B*
Anne Marie & Lindsay Bernstone
2 Lakefront Drive,
Te Anau, 9600

Tel (03) 249 8112
Fax (03) 249 8112
bookings@catswhiskers.co.nz
www.catswhiskers.co.nz

Double/Twin $175 - $215
Single $140 - $165
(Full breakfast)
Children $40
Visa MC Eftpos accepted
Children welcome
Internet available
2 King 2 Queen 4 Single (4 bdrm)
Bathrooms: 4 Ensuite

Our peaceful lakefront home is a comfortable villa with 4 guest rooms all with ensuite bathrooms. Relax while you take in stunning views of Lake Te Anau. Meet fellow guests for a cooked or continental breakfast in our dining room. Opposite Department of Conservation Visitor Centre. Our cat Lucy lives with us. King, Queen or Twin beds. Wireless internet access and skype. 12 television channels, fridges, tea and coffee making facilities. Booking service for local trips. Off street parking. Guest laundry and short term luggage storage.

Te Anau *.2 km N of central Te Anau*
House of Wood *B&B Homestay*

Merle & Cliff Buchanan
44 Moana Crescent, Te Anau, 9600

Tel (03) 249 8404
or (021) 158 6686
Fax (03) 249 7676
houseofwood@xtra.co.nz
www.houseofwood.co.nz

Double/Twin $130 - $150
Single $110 - $135 (Full breakfast)
Children by arrangement
3 course dinner with drinks
usually served
Visa MC Eftpos accepted
Pet free home Children welcome
2 King/Twin 1 King 3 Queen (4 bdrm)
Bathrooms: 3 Ensuite 1 Private
1 room with private bath
Separate shower & toilet

A warm welcome is assured when you arrive at our home. We really enjoy meeting guests from overseas (and locals). Our house is a unique architecturally designed home of native and exotic timber. Sit at the outdoor tables and enjoy the beautiful views. Our interests are boating, golf, fishing, rowing, gardening. We can help you plan your activities and book trips, with pick up at door. Two minutes walk from town 5 minutes to Lake. Dinner by arrangement. Wireless internet available. Check-in after 2pm please.

Mossburn *25 km S of Mossburn*
Turner Farmstay *Farmstay*

Joyce & Murray Turner
RD 1,
Otautau,
Southland 9689

Tel (03) 225 7602
Fax (03) 225 7602
murray.joyce@farmside.co.nz
www.innz.co.nz/host/e/etalcreek.html

Double/Twin $120
Single $80
(Full breakfast)
Children under 12 $30
3 course dinner with NZ wine $40
Internet available
1 Queen 4 Single (3 bdrm)
Bathrooms: 1 Private 1 Guest share

Our modern home on 301 hectares, farming sheep, is situated half-way between Invercargill and Te Anau, which can be reached in 1 hour. We enjoy meeting people, will provide quality accommodation, farm-fresh food in a welcoming friendly atmosphere. You can have a farm tour or just relax with our pet bichons Holly & Katie. The Aparima River is adjacent to the property. Murray is a keen fly fisherman. Guiding & advice available. Evening meal on request. Directions please phone 24 hours notice to avoid disappointment.

Gore *3 km NW of Gore*
Hokonui Bed & Breakfast *Luxury B&B Rural Lifestyle*

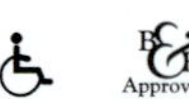

Brian & Shona McLennan
258 Reaby Road,
RD 4, Gore, 9774

Tel (03) 208 4890
or 0800 70 72 75
Fax (03) 208 4890
bssm@sld.quik.co.nz
www.bnb.co.nz/hokonuihomestay.html

Double/Twin $100 - $120
Single $80 - $90 (Full breakfast)
Children negotiable
Dinner by arrangement
Visa MC accepted
Children welcome Internet available
1 King 1 Queen 1 Twin (3 bdrm)
All bedrooms have great views
Bathrooms: 2 Ensuite 1 Private

Brian & Shona welcome you to their private, spacious, and modern new home on a 12 acre lifestyle property with uninterrupted panoramic views. Private upstairs unit, underfloor heating and full size snooker table. Close to the Mataura River which is world famous for Trout Fishing, 18 hole Golf Course and Native Bush Walks. A perfect base for sightseeing Southland and attending the Gold Guitar Awards, Waimumu Fieldays and Hokonui Fashion Awards Interests- golf,fishing,snooker,horse riding and dog trialing, gardening, music and wine tasting. We have Horses, Sheepdogs and Sheep. Please phone for directions.

Progress Valley - South Catlins *6 km N of Waikawa*
Catlins Farmstay B&B *B&B Farmstay*

June & Murray Stratford
174 Progress Valley Road,
South Catlins,
Southland

Tel (03) 246 8843
Fax (03) 246 8844
catlinsfarmstay@xtra.co.nz
www.catlinsfarmstay.co.nz

Double/Twin $185 - $260
Single $130 - $160
(Full breakfast)
Children negotiable
Visa MC Eftpos accepted
Children welcome
1 King 2 Queen 1 Twin (3 bdrm)
Bathrooms: 3 Ensuite

Ours is a great location close to fossil forest at Curio Bay. Spacious guest rooms plus king self-contained suite available with private entrances. We farm 1000 acres running, 2500 sheep, 500 deer, 150 cattle with 3 sheepdogs. Farm tours by arrangement. Directions: turn off at Niagara Falls into Manse Road, drive 2km. Ask about our new Waterside s/c cottage at Waikawa. Dinner available at Niagara Falls Cafe. Licensened Restaurant 2km drive from our house.

Invercargill *5 km N of Invercargill city*
Glenroy Park Homestay *B&B Homestay*

Margaret & Alan Thomson
23 Glenroy Park Drive,
Invercargill

Tel (03) 215 8464
or 027 376 2228
Fax (03) 215 8464
home_hosp@actrix.co.nz
www.bnb.co.nz/glenroypark.html

Double/Twin $120 - $130
Single $85 - $100
(Full breakfast)
Children up to 12 years $12
3 course dinner $35
Children welcome
1 Queen 1 Twin 1 Single (3 bdrm)
Bathrooms: 1 Private 1 Guest share
Heated tile floors

Exclusively yours, in a quiet retreat near restaurants and parks. Be our special guests and share an evening of relaxation and friendship. Our interests are golfing, meeting people, travel and cooking. We look forward to your visit. Invercargill is the gateway to Queenstown, Fiordland, Catlins and Stewart Island. Directions: from Queenstown turn left second lights (Bainfield Road), take first left, third house on left. From Dunedin turn right second set of lights (Queens Drive), travel to end, turn left, first street right, third house left.

Invercargill *5 km SW of Invercargill*
The Oak Door *B&B*

Lisa & Bill Stuart
22 Taiepa Road,
Otatara,
RD 9,
Invercargill 9879

Tel (03) 213 0633
Fax (03) 213 0633
blstuart@xtra.co.nz

Double/Twin $130
Single $90
(Full breakfast)
Children POA
Pet free home
2 Queen 2 Twin (3 bdrm)
Bathrooms: 1 Private 1 Guest share

Bill (Kiwi) & Lisa (Canadian) welcome you to their warm, self-built, unique home. Enjoy attractive gardens and native bush setting; minutes from: Invercargill CBD, Scenic route amenities, airport. Coffee/tea awaits you on arrival at The Oak Door. Guests comment on a warm comfortable visit, where beds, breakfast and hospitality are quality plus! A Warm Welcome! (Nonsmoking/no pets). Directions: Drive past the airport entrance. Take first left (Marama Avenue South). Turn right at Taiepa Road ,second drive on right (#22).

Invercargill *3 km N of Invercargill City Centre*
Gimblett Place *B&B*

Alex & Eileen Henderson
122 Gimblett Place,
Kildare,
Invercargill, 9810

Tel (03) 215 6888
Fax (03) 215 6888
the_grove@xtra.co.nz
www.bnb.co.nz/hosts/gimblettplace

Double/Twin $100
Single $70
(Full breakfast)
Children negotiable
Dinner by arrangement
Visa MC Eftpos accepted
Pet free home
Internet available
1 Queen 2 Single (2 bdrm)
Bathrooms: 1 Private

Eileen & Alex are experienced hosts who are ex-farmers and offer comfortable accommodation in a quiet cul-de-sac close to city amenities, golf, parks, restaurants. We are pleased to assist with local and tourist information and can guide if required (ie Catlins). Alex is a vintage car and machinery enthusiast and can arrange good viewing. Close to famous trout fishing rivers. Directions: find Queens Drive, Gimblett Street is first left north of Thomsons Bush, fourth right into Gimblett Place (cul-de-sac)

Invercargill *10 km E of Invercargill on Southern Scenic Rte*
Long Acres Farmstay *Farmstay Self-contained & B&B*

Helen & Graeme Spain
Waimatua, RD 11, Invercargill

Tel (03) 216 4470
or 027 228 1308
Fax (03) 216 4470
longacres@woosh.co.nz
www.longacres.co.nz

Double/Twin $160 - $170
Single $130 - $160 (Full breakfast)
Children negotiable Dinner $50
Self-contained $180 - $200
Visa MC accepted
Children welcome
2 Queen 1 Twin 1 Single (4 bdrm)
Self-Contained 1 Queen, 1 Twin
Homestead 1 Queen, 1 Single
Bathrooms: 1 Queen Ensuite
1 Queen Private 1 Single guests share

Long Acres Farmstay retreat offers quality warm accommodation, Superb Hospitality and a 1500 acre working farm with cows, calves, beef cattle, 1 dog, 1 cat and hens. A free farm tour with Graeme. Amazing native bush/bird walk. Ideal stopover for Stewart Island, Catlins, Te Anau, Queenstown and Dunedin. Hearty breakfasts provided and evening meals available from home grown produce. A peaceful relaxed farmstay for the length of time you choose. Directions. From Invercargill, east on Southern Scenic Route 10kms.Farmstay Sign on left.

Invercargill *4 km N of Invercargill Central*
Stoneleigh Homestay *B&B Homestay*

Joan & Neville Milne
15 Stoneleigh Lane,
Invercargill

Tel (03) 215 8921
joan@stoneleighhomestay.co.nz
www.stoneleighhomestay.co.nz

Double/Twin $110 - $125
Single $80 - $90
(Full breakfast)
Dinner $35
Visa MC accepted
Pet free home
1 Queen 3 Single (3 bdrm)
Bathrooms: 1 Private 1 Guest share

We welcome guests to share our modern home in a quiet lane 5 minutes from the main centre, and just off the main road to TeAnau and Queenstown. We have underfloor heating, electric blankets and guests have their own TV. We are keen golfers and members of the Invercargill club, a championship course rated in the top 10 in N.Z. Our interests are golf, travel, gardening, cooking, wine and meeting people. Enjoy our hospitality, share an evening meal with us. Pick ups can be arranged.

Invercargill *6 km SE of Invercargill*
The Manor *B&B Farmstay*

Pat & Frank Forde
9 Drysdale Road, Myross Bush,
Invercargill. 9872

Tel (03) 230 4788
or 027 667 0904
Fax (03) 230 4788
the.manor@xtra.co.nz
www.manorbb.co.nz

Double/Twin $120 - $160
Single $80 - $90 (Full breakfast)
Children negotiable
Dinner by arrangement
Visa MC accepted
Pet free home Children welcome
Free SKYPE available
Free wireless internet available
3 Queen 2 Single (3 bdrm) Very comfortable beds
Bathrooms: 1 Ensuite 1 Private 1 Guest share one

Relax, enjoy our warm, comfortable home, underfloor-heating, a sheltered garden setting, 10 acre farmlet (sheep, lambs, horses, hens). Private guest area, television,Free wireless internet,Free SKYPE available. refrigerator, tea/coffee making facilities. We are retired farmers, golfers, enjoy gardening, harness racing, travel, meeting people. Pleasant outdoor areas, meals of fresh home-grown produce, cooked/continental breakfasts. Courtesy pick up. A stop on your way to Stewart Island, Southern Scenic Route, Queenstown or Te Anau. We would enjoy having you stay with us. 5 minutes drive north east Invercargill along State Highway 1.

Southland South Catlins

Invercargill *0.01 km NW of Invercargill City Centre*
Victoria Railway Hotel *Hotel*

Trudy & Eian Read
3 Leven Street,
off Picadilly Lane,
Invercargill

Tel (03) 218 1281
Fax (03) 218 1283
vrhotel@xtra.co.nz
www.vrhotel.info

Double/Twin $145 - $195
Single $117 - $130
(Full breakfast $10.50 - $20 pp)
Children $15
Dinner Mains $28 - $32 pp
Visa MC Diners Amex
Eftpos accepted
Internet available
5 Queen 4 Double 2 Twin (11 bdrm)
Bathrooms: 11 Ensuite

Come and enjoy old world charm and southern hospitality in a boutique hotel in the heart of the city. This Invercargill Landmark built in 1896 is a Class 1 heritage building. Architecturally designed upgrade completed May 2004. City Council Environment Award recipient May 2007. Variety of accommodation options including Executive and VIP, plus two Ground floor Accessible units. Come relax in our lounge bar before dining in and enjoy traditional home cooked meals and a selection of fine NZ wines and local Invercargill Beers.

Bluff *25 km S of Invercargill*
The Lazy Fish *Separate Suite Cottage with Kitchen*

Robyn & Roy Horwell
35 Burrows Street,
Bluff, 9814

Tel (03) 212 7245
or 021 211 7424
Fax (03) 212 8868
horwell@thelazyfish.co.nz
www.thelazyfish.co.nz

Double/Twin $100 - $120
(Continental breakfast
by arrangement $10 pp)
Children welcome
Internet available
2 Double (2 bdrm)
Bathrooms: 2 Ensuite

Very homely fully self-contained unit attached to our home, in a peacefull garden setting. Sleeps 4, double bed in bedroom and sofa bed in lounge. Also double bedroom attached to house, tea & coffee making facilities and microwave. Sunny shelterd courtyard. Friendly labrador in residence. Gateway to Stewart Island and Southern Scenic Route. Take a break and absorb our Coastal and native bush walks, maritime museum, restaurants and supermarket all within walking distance. 5 minutes walk to Stewart Island ferry. Continental breakfast by arrangement.

Riverton *45 km SW of Invercargill*

Reo Moana *B&B*

Jean Broomfield
192 Rocks Highway,
Riverton, Southland

Tel (03) 234 9044
alanb@orcon.net.nz

Double/Twin $150
Single $100
(Full breakfast)
Children negotiable
Extra roll away bed and cot available
Pet free home
Children welcome
1 King 1 Twin (2 bdrm)
Well appointed spacious rooms
with sea views
Bathrooms: 2 Ensuite
Excellent Showers & heated tile floors

Reo Moana overlooks a beautiful secluded swimming and surfing beach with extended views to the open sea beyond, and northward to the mountains and hills of Southland. Tastefully decorated, the warm and spacious guest rooms each have ensuite bathrooms and sea views. A spacious lounge with lovely open fire and library is a comfortable space to sit and relax. Your host Jean has many years experience in the tourism industry. I welcome you to Riverton, 30 minutes from Invercargill on the Southern Scenic Route.

The difference between a B&B and a hotel
is that you don't hug the hotel staff when you leave.

Stewart Island *0.2 km SW of Oban township*
Sails Ashore Boutique B&B & Kowhai Lane Self Catering

Holiday Home and Apartment
Luxury B&B Holiday Home & Self-catering Flat
Iris and Peter Tait
11 View Street & 6 Kowhai Lane,
Stewart Island

Tel (03) 219 1151
or 0800 783 9278 (0800 Stewart)
tait@sailsashore.co.nz
www.sailsashore.co.nz

Double/Twin $195 - $435
(Breakfast by arrangement)
Restaurants nearby
Please Note Photos are of Sails Ashore
Visa MC Eftpos accepted
Pet free home Not suitable for children
Children welcome
5 King/Twin 1 Queen 2 Single (7 bdrm)
2 in Sails Ashore 5 at Kowhai LaneBathrooms: 7 Ensuite

Iris, Anne and Peter welcome you to Stewart Island, to Sails Ashore Boutique Hosted Accommodation and to Kowhai Lane Holiday Home. We are the only Qualmarked Guest & Hosted and Holiday Home accommodation available on Stewart Island and as well as being your hosts will also be your guides on your packaged Ulva Island walk. Both properties overlook Halfmoon Bay and are about five minutes easy stroll from the waterfront. As well as delightful sea views both have private gardens for you to enjoy.

Stewart Island *1 km S of Oban*
Glendaruel Bed & Breakfast *B&B*

Raylene Waddell
38 Golden Bay Road,
Oban, Stewart Island

Tel (03) 219 1092
or 027 519 092
Fax (03) 219 1092
glendaruel@xtra.co.nz
www.glendaruel.co.nz

Double/Twin $220
Single $110 - $160
(Full breakfast)
Children by arrangement
Dinner $50 by arrangement
Visa MC accepted
Internet available
1 King/Twin 1 Queen
1 Single (3 bdrm)
Bathrooms: 3 Ensuite

Peaceful bush setting, ten minutes' walk from village, three minutes from Golden Bay, base for water taxis to Ulva Island Bird Sanctuary in beautiful Paterson Inlet. Large guest lounge and extensive decks with bush and sea views. Colourful garden alive with birdsong. Central Heating. Tea/Coffee Facilities in each room. Courtesy Transfers. Advice and assistance with local activities. I speak French and a little German and enjoy hosting guests from around the world. My Cairn Terrier, Macpherson, and I assure you of a warm welcome.

Index

The New Zealand
Bed & Breakfast
Book

Please help us to keep our standards high

To help maintain the high reputation of **The New Zealand Bed & Breakfast Book** we ask for your comments about your stay.
You can simply stick a stamp on this form or save all your comment forms and return them in an envelope.

Alternatively, leave your comment at our website
www.bnb.co.nz

Name of Host or B&B_______________________________

Address _______________________________

____

Considering things such as breakfast, meals, beds, cleanliness, hospitality and value for money, what is your overall satisfaction rating, with 1 being the lowest and 10 being the highest rating?

1   2   3   4   5   6   7   8   9   10

Do you have any comments?

We may display your comments on our website. The rating will be confidential and will be kept for administration purposes.

Fill in your details to go into our regular prize draws!
Your details will not be passed on to anyone else. If you do not have email we suggest you use a friend's email address.

Your name   _______________________________

Your Town/city
and country   _______________________________

Email   _______________________________

Please Post this form to:
The New Zealand B&B Book,
PO Box 6843, Wellington, New Zealand

www.bnb.co.nz

Place stamp
here or send
forms in one
envelope

Moonshine Press
PO Box 6843
Wellington
New Zealand